ID0938740

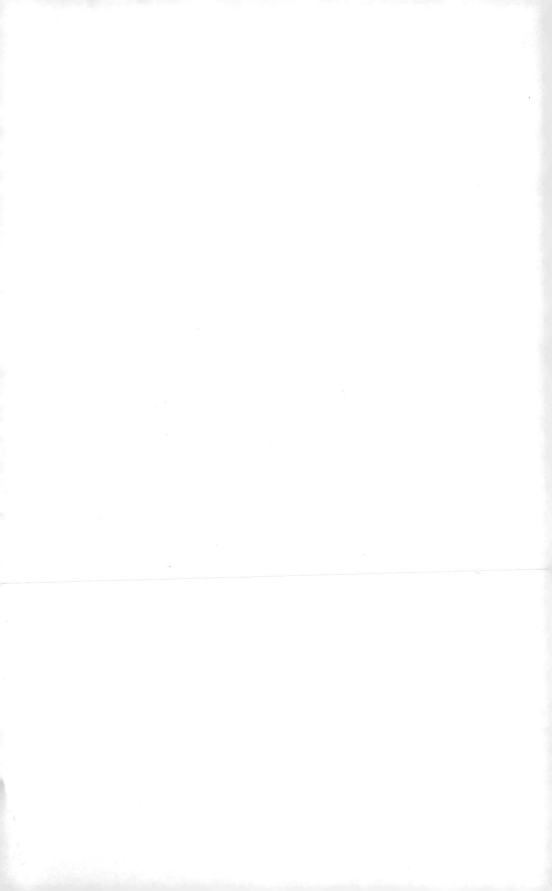

BOOKS AND READERS
IN THE EARLY CHURCH

BOOKS AND READERS IN THE EARLY CHURCH✝
A HISTORY OF EARLY CHRISTIAN TEXTS

Harry Y. Gamble

Yale University Press
New Haven and London

Published with assistance from the
Louis Stern Memorial Fund.

Designed by Sally Harris/Summer Hill
Books.
Set in Trump Medieval type by Keystone
Typesetting, Inc.
Printed in the United States of America by
BookCrafters, Inc., Chelsea, Michigan.

*Library of Congress Cataloging-in-
Publication Data*

Gamble, Harry Y., 1941–
  Books and readers in the early church : a
history of early Christian texts / Harry Y.
Gamble.
      p.   cm.
  Includes bibliographical references and
index.
  ISBN 0-300-06024-6 (cloth: alk. paper)
      0-300-06918-9 (pbk.: alk. paper)
  1. Christian literature, Early—
Publication and distribution—Rome.
2. Bible N.T.—Publication and
distribution—Rome.   3. Books—History—
To 400.   4. Books—History—400–
1400.   5. Christians—Rome—Books and
reading.   6. Literacy—Rome.   7. Church
libraries—Rome.   8. Christian libraries—
Rome.   9. Church history—Primitive and
early church, ca. 30-600.   I. Title.
BR67.2.G35   1995
002'.08'8211—dc20   94-24351
                                           CIP

The paper in this book meets the
guidelines for permanence and durability of
the Committee on Production Guidelines
for Book Longevity of the Council on
Library Resources.

10   9   8   7   6   5   4   3   2

CONTENTS

PREFACE AND ACKNOWLEDGMENTS

The idea of this book arose several years ago in the course of research on the history of the New Testament canon. In considering how and when the twenty-seven documents that belong to the New Testament came into circulation, gained wide use and authority, and were gradually shaped into an exclusive collection, scholars have explored a broad range of evidence: quotations from these documents in the writings of the fathers, statements by patristic writers about the use or authority of a particular document, the contents of ancient manuscripts, early canon lists, and so forth—all indispensable considerations. Yet there are prior questions, questions about the production, circulation, and use of books in the ancient church, that are almost never raised by historians of the canon even though the whole process of the formation of the canon depends upon them. What physical form(s) did early Christian writings take, for example? How and by whom were they transcribed? By what means was a text published and made known to a readership? Once published, how were these books duplicated and disseminated? How rapidly and extensively did they become available to Christian communities? Who were the sponsors and custodians of such texts? How were they transported, stored, collected, and used? Who, in fact, read them, and in what circumstances and to what purpose?

The importance of these questions clearly goes well beyond the history of the New Testament canon, for they pertain in principle to all early Christian literature, scriptural and nonscriptural. Nevertheless, in standard histories of early Christian literature these questions are neither asked nor answered. The customary issues of the history of early Christian literature—the date, provenance, authorship, integrity, historical situation, and content of individual documents—have their own importance and interest. Nonetheless, the actual *history* of early Christian literature, including the publication and dissemination of texts and their reception and *Wirkungsgeschichte*, can hardly be conceived of, much less written, without taking into account the concrete bibliographic dimensions of the process. What is needed is a supplement to the standard handbooks, a treatment of early Christian literature that prescinds as far as possible from issues of content and attends instead to what might be called the bibliographic substructure: the practical and technological factors that belonged to the production, circulation, and use of early Christian books and the social and institutional correlates of that process. My study is intended, then, as a contribution to the history of early Christian literature, although it largely ignores the normal agenda of that discipline. My interest lies less in the literature than in the texts—the books—that were its vehicles, and my aim is to think about these texts as concretely as I can. Because I recognize both the relation and the difference between my task and the history of early Christian literature, I call this study a history of early Christian texts. It offers a history of no one particular text but rather—insofar as it attends to issues entailed by texts as such—of all early Christian texts.

The details of the publication, circulation, and use of texts were taken for granted by early Christian writers. Although sometimes mentioned in passing, they are seldom discussed in the writings themselves. Consequently, it is no easy matter to summon the evidence or to elicit from it a reliable reconstruction of the bibliographic side of the history of early Christian literature. Yet the effort is not futile. Because early Christianity was a subculture of both Jewish and Greco-Roman culture, my working hypothesis has been that whatever ideological or social differences distinguished them from their larger cultural environments, Christian groups did not radically depart from established conventions when they produced, circulated, and employed books. Hence, we can draw upon evidence about the bibliographic practices in effect for Greek, Roman, and Jewish literature of the period to illumine Christian practice. This evidence, however, must be used with discretion and an awareness of the particular capacities, requirements, special interests, and attested practices of Christians and must not be too hastily generalized. We must also attend to the evidence Christian sources do provide, partly to those comments in Christian literature that bear directly on the production, circulation, and use of texts, and partly to the physical evidence offered by extant manuscripts of the period. Evidence of both types occurs infrequently and more or less fortuitously but nevertheless furnishes useful insights. I have sought to identify and canvass the relevant data and, fragmentary as it is, to tease from it an understanding of the bibliographic practices of the ancient church. Inevitably, some points remain obscure, and sometimes even when matters of fact are tolerably clear, there is room for more than one interpretation. Even so, the questions I raise are important and deserve to be studied more thoroughly and more widely than they have been by historians of the early church and its literature.

The topic is a broad one, involving a variety of disciplines that have become distinct and specialized: the history of classical literature and of early Christian literature; the social, theological, and institutional history of the early church; paleography; textual criticism; and codicology. The range of considerations is daunting, and the potentially relevant materials nearly beyond compass, but the subject cannot be adequately treated within the confines of a specialized discipline or by a single approach. This is true even within the sphere of Christian literature itself, for my questions do not respect even the traditional disciplinary distinctions between New Testament studies, patristics, and church history or, for that matter, between the still more particular pursuits of exegesis and textual criticism. Anyone who ranges across so wide a field will often feel a lack of personal expertise, but in those cases I am grateful to have been guided by the work of others.

The progressive specialization of scholarly disciplines, and within them still more technical subdisciplines, has promoted high levels of expertise in particular problems and bodies of evidence. It has also worked to insulate specialists in one area from those in another and to deprive them of findings that have a larger relevance. Unless the knowledge gained through disciplinary specialization is deployed across the boundaries of narrower subjects and applied to larger issues, it cannot bear its full fruit. If this study provokes a historian of early Christian thought to realize that something interesting might be learned from a paleographer, prompts a literary theorist to think she should look at an ancient manuscript, or causes a social historian to find relevance in textual criticism, then it will have served a good purpose. It is always a risk to cross disciplinary boundaries (there is a bewildering landscape on the other side), but it is often a risk worth taking.

I owe many debts to those who have encouraged and assisted me in this study, especially to the Alumni Board of Trustees and the department of religious studies of the University of Virginia for releasing me from teaching and administrative duties, and to the dean, canons, and students of Christ Church, Oxford, for the honor of being the inaugural holder of the Pilkington Fellowship in Biblical Studies in the academic year 1990–91, when much of my research was done. Among the many friends and colleagues who have taken an interest in this project and furnished wise advice and criticism, I especially thank my colleague Robert Wilken at the University of Virginia, Alan Bowman, Peter Parsons, and Maurice Wiles of Christ Church, Oxford, and Bart Ehrman of the University of North Carolina at Chapel Hill. For her steady encouragement, keen intelligence, and ruthless editorial eye, I thank my wife, Tamara.

BOOKS AND READERS
IN THE EARLY CHURCH

LITERACY AND LITERARY CULTURE IN EARLY CHRISTIANITY

*I*n *[the apostles] there was no power of speaking or of giving an ordered narrative by the standards of Greek dialectical or rhetorical arts which convinced their hearers. It seems to me that if Jesus had chosen men who were wise in the eyes of the multitude, and who were capable of thinking and speaking acceptably to crowds, and if he had used them as the means of propagating his teaching, he might on very good grounds have been suspected of making use of a method similar to that of philosophers who are leaders of some particular sect. The truth of the claim that his teaching is divine would no longer have been self-evident, in that the gospel and the preaching were in the persuasive words of the wisdom that consists in literary style and composition.*

So wrote the Christian scholar Origen of Alexandria in the third century in defending the Gospels against the pagan critic Celsus, who faulted them for their lack of literary distinction and characterized their authors as ignorant men who "had not even had a primary education."[1] Origen's statement shows that the level of education and literary culture in early Christianity were already the subjects of criticism in the late second century, when Celsus composed his attack on Christianity. To a cultivated person like Celsus, the failure of Christian writings to meet contemporary standards of literary style and formal argument bespoke the ignorance of their authors and made them unpersuasive. Origen, however, who was a well-educated Christian and equally acquainted with the standards of the higher literary culture of antiquity, could agree with Celsus in his assessment of Christian writings yet find their very artlessness a strength, not a weakness, since it exempted them from any suspicion of sophistry and so made them the more persuasive. Yet, because the level of Origen's own education and literary cultivation was higher than that reflected in the Gospels, we must be careful not to form too simple a conception of literacy and literary culture in early Christianity. They were not uniform over time, nor from place to place, or among individuals, and they do not lend themselves to easy generalization.

Nevertheless, a consideration of literacy and literary culture is essential to a study of books and readers in the early church. Students of early Christianity have reached no agreement about its disposition toward literature or the place of texts in its life, issues that need to be canvassed in order to find the points of orientation for initial questions. First, to what extent were the skills of literacy available within early Christianity, and what role did literacy play in Christian life? Second, how far did early Christianity depend upon texts, consider them important, and undertake to produce and use them? Third, how are Christian texts to be understood in relation to the literature of the larger society of which the early church was a part?

My purview includes the Christian movement in the first five centuries, a period when Christianity both began and underwent dramatic historical developments and when Christian communities were found in a wide variety of geographic locations, social circumstances, and literary and linguistic environments. It would be far easier to consider Christian literacy and literary culture only in a particular location, at an isolable stage of its development, or in terms of a few Christian writers, but to do so would not yield a sense of the relation of Christianity to the larger societies of which it was a part. My admittedly ambitious approach assumes enough continuity within Christianity and enough stability in the relation between Christianity and its larger contexts to permit judgments that are broadly valid yet recognize the differences and developments that characterized Christianity over time.

EARLY CHRISTIAN LITERACY   To what extent were early Christians actually capable of writing and reading? The question has rarely been raised and has never been explored by historians of early Christianity.[2] Biblical and patristic scholars have shared with classicists the sanguine assumption that literacy prevailed in antiquity on a scale roughly comparable to literacy in modern Western societies and so have imagined that early Christianity was broadly literate.[3] This view has been tacitly disputed only by the early form critics, who aimed to study the oral transmission of early Christian traditions, and only for primitive Christianity, which they regarded as an illiterate or, at best, semiliterate folk culture that relied on oral tradition. But neither the view that early Christianity was broadly literate nor the claim that in its earliest phases it was illiterate is more than a hypothesis, and neither view has been systematically argued.

So the question remains unanswered: To what extent could early Christians read and write? This is a difficult question for several reasons. First, working definitions of literacy vary, and its indices are relative to its definition. If, despite the aid of empirical studies and statistical methods, it is hard to determine the types and extent of literacy in modern societies, it is far more difficult to do so for earlier periods, especially ancient ones. Literacy can refer to anything from signature literacy, which is the minimal ability to write one's name, to the capacity both to write lengthy texts and to read them with understanding. The problem of definition corresponds to the fact that "in reality there are infinite gradations of literacy for any written language," so that a useful definition would be neither too narrow nor too broad but would embrace a range of literacy and acknowledge its various types.[4] Second, direct evidence about literacy is scarce for antiquity generally and scarcer still for early Christianity in particular. This problem may be remedied in part by attending to evidence about education and social class, for literacy has historically been a function of both. Comparative analysis is also useful. The diffusion of literacy in any society is known to depend on certain preconditions and stimuli, and we can infer the extent of literacy in ancient societies from data on the development and scope of literacy in early modern and modern societies by determining how far necessary conditions were satisfied.[5] Third, the question of literacy in early Christianity is complicated by the fact that Christianity developed and spread in multicultural and multilingual settings and thus incorporated from the start a diversity that forbids the generalizations that are possible for more culturally and linguistically homogeneous groups. A Christian in first-century Palestine might have been thoroughly literate in Aramaic, largely literate in Hebrew, semiliterate in Greek, and illiterate in Latin, while a Christian in Rome in the late second century might have been literate in Latin and semiliterate in Greek but ignorant of Aramaic and Hebrew. So when it is said of a Christian holding the office of reader in the Egyptian church in the early fourth century that he "does not know letters," we should not suppose that he was illiterate, but rather that he was literate only in Coptic, not in Greek.[6] Although the situation became progressively complex with the missionary expansion of Christianity into the provinces, the linguistic pluralism of Christianity was present from the outset insofar as Christianity originated in the Aramaic-speaking environment of Judaism while its earliest extant literature was in Greek.

The composition, circulation, and use of Christian writings in the early church are manifest proof of Christian literacy but say nothing in themselves about the extent of literacy within Christianity. The abundance of Christian literature from the first five centuries skews our perceptions and leads us to imagine that the production of so many books must betoken an extensive readership. Yet the literature that survives reflects the capacities and viewpoints of Christian literati, who cannot be taken to represent Christians generally. Even the wide use and high esteem for Christian writings among Christian communities do not indicate that the larger body of Christians could read, for in antiquity one could hear texts read even if one was unable to read, so that illiteracy was no bar to familiarity with Christian writings. Because neither the existence of Christian literature nor its broad circulation and use can reveal the extent or levels of literacy within Christianity, it is all the more important to have an idea of the nature and scope of literacy in ancient society generally, especially under the Roman empire.

In the most comprehensive study to date, William Harris has sought to discover the extent of literacy in the ancient world.[7] Using a broad definition of literacy as the ability to read or write at any level, Harris draws on wide and varied evidence—explicit, circumstantial, and comparative—and takes some account of the types and the uses of literacy. He reaches a largely negative conclusion for Western antiquity generally: granting regional and temporal variations, throughout the entire period of classical Greek, Hellenistic, and Roman imperial civilization, the extent of literacy was about 10 percent and never exceeded 15 to 20 percent of the population as a whole.[8] "The written culture of antiquity was in the main restricted to a privileged minority —though in some places it was a large minority—and it co-existed with elements of an oral culture."[9] Although I have some reservations about the way Harris has posed and addressed the problem of literacy in the ancient world,[10] his invaluable survey has made it clear that nothing remotely like mass literacy existed, nor could have existed, in Greco-Roman societies, because the forces and institutions required to foster it were absent. This recognition must stand as a firm check on the romantic and anachronistic tendencies that have too often guided scholarly assessments of literacy in antiquity.

If, as Harris recognizes, his conclusions "will be highly unpalatable to some classical scholars," they should be equally sobering to historians of early Christianity and its literature. There may be special factors in the Christian setting, but it cannot be supposed that the extent of literacy in the ancient church was any greater than that in the Greco-Roman society of which Christianity was a part. This is true in spite of the importance the early church accorded to religious texts, for acquaintance with the scriptures did not require that all or even most Christians be individually capable of reading them and does not imply that they were.[11] It is also true should scholars reject the traditional view that early Christianity was a movement among the illiterate proletariat of the Roman Empire. In one of the most interesting developments in recent biblical scholarship, this conventional social description has been subjected to thorough criticism and revision.[12] Studies of the social constituency of the early church have shown that, especially in its urban settings, Christianity attracted a socially diverse membership, representing a cross section of Roman society. Although it certainly included many from the lower socioeconomic levels, it was by no means a proletarian movement. Both the highest and the lowest strata of society were absent. The most typical members of the Christian groups were free craftspeople, artisans, and small traders, some of whom had attained a measure of affluence, owned houses and slaves, had the resources to travel, and were socially mobile.[13] In terms of social status, Christian communities had a pyramidal shape rather like that of society at large. But since members of the upper classes were less numerous, high levels of literacy—as a function of social status or education, or both—would have been unusual. Still, moderate levels, such as were common among craftspeople and small business persons, may have been proportionately better represented within the early church than outside it.[14] Yet these insights offer no reason to think that the extent of literacy of any kind among Christians was greater than in society at large. If anything, it was more limited. This means that not only the writing of Christian literature, but also the ability to read, criticize, and interpret it belonged to a small number of Christians in the first several centuries, ordinarily not more than about 10 percent in any given setting, and perhaps fewer in the many small and provincial congregations that were characteristic of early Christianity.

We must assume, then, that the large majority of Christians in the early centuries of the church were illiterate, not because they were unique but because they were in this respect typical. The ancient world had virtually no system of education. What structures there were did not suffice to cultivate general literacy at even a basic level; indeed, no such aim was ever envisioned. The opportunity for formal schooling even at the primary level was a luxury, although it occasionally existed for slaves and freedmen.[15] Thus, access to education was not closed to Christians but was limited by social class. Moreover, Greco-Roman education was predicated on pagan texts infused with moral and religious ideas of which Christians disapproved, and this discouraged some who might otherwise have taken advantage of it.

It was exceptional in the early centuries of the church to be born and brought up Christian: well-educated Christians usually received their education before conversion and were themselves unable to recommend pagan schooling to those who were already Christian.[16] The results of this situation were diverse. On the one hand, Christian academies arose here and there, usually around a notable Christian teacher, like the schools associated with Valentinus, Ptolemy, Justin, and Clement in the second century. These were for higher education in scriptural or theological studies, however, for students of inquiring minds who were already equipped with a basic education and thus with literacy.[17] On the other hand, many Christians were suspicious of "the wisdom of this world," and among them there was a tendency, if not to sanctify ignorance, to neglect education in the interest of fideism, otherworldliness, or acquiescent orthodoxy. Domestic instruction in reading and writing under the guidance of a tutor was common among wealthy households, and home study was possible in Christian households too when they were well-to-do or when there was a literate family member.[18] Yet the ancient church never undertook an alternative system of education for the faithful, and Christian writers of the first five centuries acknowledge a standing distinction between a small number of literate and intellectually active Christians and the majority of believers, whom Tertullian (adv. Prax. 3) described as "the simple, not to say unwise and unlearned" (simplices, ne dixerim idiotae et imprudentes). A little later, responding to Celsus's charge that Christianity succeeded only among the uneducated, Origen (Contra Celsum 1.27) allowed that "it was inevitable that among the great number of people overcome by the word, because there are many more vulgar and illiterate people than those who have been trained in rational thinking, the former class should far outnumber the more intelligent."[19] Thus, all indications are that the extent of literacy within the church did not exceed its extent in society at large, and during the first three centuries it probably did not attain even that level.

It could perhaps be argued that the extent of literacy within Christianity actually declined at an early time, with Christianity's missionary transition from a Jewish to a predominantly Gentile constituency. Instruction in reading Hebrew was more widely given among Jews than instruction in Greek or Latin was among Gentiles and with less regard to social status.[20] According to Josephus, in first-century Judaism it was a duty, indeed a religious commandment, that Jewish children be taught to read.[21] Such training may often have been given at home by parents, but rabbinic sources suggest that by the first century schools were common in towns and were heavily enrolled. Before its destruction in 70 c.e., Jerusalem is said to have had 480 synagogues, each with both a "house of reading" *(bet sefer)* and a "house of learning" *(bet midrash)* attached—the former providing young children with instruction in basic skills to read scripture, the latter offering older children instruction in the oral Torah.[22] Even if the figures are exaggerated, there is little question that by the first century c.e. Judaism had developed a strong interest in basic literacy and that even small communities had elementary schools.[23] The aim of education in those settings was not literacy as such but the ability to participate in Jewish life, so the capacity to read and understand scripture, especially the Torah, stood at the center of instruction. Writing remained a professional skill separately acquired, and so fewer Jews could write than could read.

It would be unwarranted to claim that first-century Judaism sponsored mass literacy or a highly organized system of public education, but the reason and opportunity to become literate in Jewish society did not exist, at least not to the same extent, in Greco-Roman society, and so there was a higher rate of literacy among Jews than among Gentiles.[24] Beyond literacy in Hebrew, Greek was spoken and read by some Jews in Palestine by the time of Christian beginnings, and Greek had already displaced Hebrew in Jewish communities of the western Diaspora, where the scriptures were read in Greek.[25] If basic instruction in Greek was available in Palestine, it would have been meager and limited to aristocratic, cosmopolitan circles. Yet careful instruction of Jewish children in Greek must have been the rule in the Diaspora, again for the reading of scripture. Jewish education probably exerted some early positive influence on the extent of literacy among Jewish-Christians (compare 2 Tim. 4:14–15) but did not have lasting consequences for Christianity once it moved decisively beyond the boundaries of Palestine and Judaism.

It may seem paradoxical to say both that Christianity placed a high value on texts and that most Christians were unable to read, but in the ancient world this was no contradiction. In Greco-Roman society the illiterate had access to literacy in a variety of public settings. Recitations of poetry and prose works, dramatic performances in theaters and at festivals, declamations in high rhetorical style, street-corner philosophical diatribes, commemorative inscriptions, the posting and reading of official decrees, the routine traffic of legal and commercial documents all brought the fruits of literacy before the general population, educating the public in its uses and popularizing its conventions.[26] Among the literate as well, it was as common to be read to as to read for oneself in the ancient world. Besides, the papyri show that many illiterates had recourse to professional scribes for the composition of letters and contracts, and many of the epitaphs surviving from Greek and Roman antiquity were commissioned on behalf of the illiterate.[27] They were not, then, barred from the practical benefits of literacy nor from an acquaintance with the substance of texts.

If most Christians were illiterate, it did not prevent them from participating in literacy or from becoming familiar with Christian texts. Those who had only a cursory contact with Christianity through missionary preaching or propaganda could hardly have failed to notice its reliance on texts and to hear them quoted.[28] Those who were drawn to Christianity were intensively schooled in its literature, especially scripture. The extended catechetical process by which converts came into the church concentrated, at least from the second century onward, upon doctrinal and moral instruction. It certainly did not include learning to read or write, but it did include close familiarization with Christian scripture. Further, an essential element of Christian liturgical gatherings was the reading of scripture. In the early centuries scripture was not read in snippets but in long segments. Near the middle of the second century Justin Martyr commented (*Apol.* 1.67) that in the weekly service of worship "the memoirs of the apostles or the writings of the prophets are read as long as time permits." With such regular and lengthy readings, followed by their homiletical exposition, Christians who could not read nevertheless became conversant with the substance of scriptural literature and also with other texts that were occasionally read in the setting of worship.[29] Thus, although the limited extent of individual literacy certainly had a bearing on the composition, transcription, private use, and authoritative interpretation of Christian texts, it had little adverse effect on the ability of

Christians generally to gain a close acquaintance with Christian literature. The illiterate Christian found in the public reading of Christian
texts at least as large and probably a more consistent opportunity than
his pagan counterpart to participate in literacy and become familiar
with texts.

Yet because of the importance of scripture to Christianity the
church could not be wholly indifferent to literacy. If literacy was never
a requirement of membership in the Christian community, it was
undoubtedly a primary desideratum of Christian leaders and teachers
from the earliest days. A much-cited text characterizes the apostles
Peter and John as "illiterate and uneducated" (agrammatoi kai idiotai,
Acts 4:13), but the meaning is probably only that they were illiterate
in Greek and had had no Greek schooling.[30] Already in the middle of
the first century Paul's literary and rhetorical skills were instrumental
to his missionary activity; the itinerant teacher Apollos was reputed
to be "skilled in the scriptures" (dunatos en tais graphais, Acts 18:24),
a talent that must have gone beyond reading to interpretation and
exposition; and the author of 1 Timothy emphasized "the public reading of scripture, preaching, and teaching" (3:13) as duties of a community leader. There were in the first and second centuries charismatic
teachers aplenty who staked their authority not on the skills of literacy but on spiritual endowment. It would be mistaken, however, to
assume antinomy between charismatic authority and the acquired
skills of reading and writing: Paul, for all his writing, scripture interpretation, and administrative concerns, claimed to operate under inspiration (1 Cor. 7:40; compare 2 Cor. 12:1–7); the visionary prophet of
Patmos composed an apocalypse; and even the "itinerant charismat-
ics" who came to Corinth employed letters of recommendation (2 Cor.
3:1). When early in the second century we begin to encounter individual Christian bishops and presbyters—Clement of Rome, Ignatius of
Antioch, Polycarp of Smyrna, and Papias of Hierapolis—it is precisely
through their writings that we know them. Thus, in the early period,
just as later on, it appears that those who exercised leadership usually
possessed the skills of literacy.

Little or no attention has been paid to literacy in considering who
rose to leadership in Christian congregations and why. Given that
texts were important to Christianity from the beginning, though only
the Jewish scriptures at first, it is difficult to imagine any Christian
community where either no one could read or no authority accrued to
those who could. In a community in which texts had a constitutive
importance and only a few persons were literate, it was inevitable that
those who were able to explicate texts would acquire authority for that

reason alone. In his satire of Peregrinus, Lucian of Samosata recounts how Peregrinus, though a recent convert to Christianity, quickly acquired status in the community for his ability to deal with Christian texts: "He interpreted and explained some of their books, and even composed many, and they revered him as a god" (*De morte Per.* 11). Of course, in the ancient world literacy rarely stood alone in a person; ordinarily it was accompanied by other attributes—social, economic, intellectual, or moral—that determined one's status within the community. Still, it is scarcely accidental that from the second century onward Christian bishops appear to have been among the best-educated Christians, that well-educated converts tended to be quickly enrolled in the clerical orders, or that the vast bulk of early Christian literature was written by clerics.

This is not to say that Christian leaders were invariably literate, for exceptions (or partial exceptions) are known.[31] Nor does it mean that literacy was confined to clerics. Yet throughout the early centuries of the church only a small minority of Christians who were not clerics were literate. When cenobitic monasticism developed in the early fourth century, monks were assisted toward literacy.[32] Here too the ability to read was linked with religious vocation, as the spiritual exercises prescribed for monks included reading and meditating on scripture (though eremitic monks might or might not be literate). There were certainly literate lay Christians, and from time to time we find them being encouraged to read the scriptures privately at home. This practice cannot have been widespread, however, since most lay Christians lacked the education, not to mention the leisure, that would make private devotional reading possible.[33]

In sum, the extent of literacy in the ancient church was limited. Only a small minority of Christians were able to read, surely no more than an average of 10–15 percent of the larger society and probably fewer. Thus only a small segment of the church was able to read Christian texts for themselves or to write them. Still, every Christian had the opportunity to become acquainted with Christian literature, especially the scriptures, through catechetical instruction and the reading and homiletical exposition of texts in the context of worship.

THE LITERARY CULTURE
OF EARLY CHRISTIANITY

The notion of literary culture is ambiguous: sometimes it designates the cultivation and use of literature in the high sense of belles lettres, an activity that belongs to a privileged class, and sometimes it is used in a neutral way to refer to whatever texts are produced and employed by a society or group, without regard to their extent, type, or quality.[34] I use the phrase in the latter sense: in speaking of the literary culture of the early church I refer only to the fact that texts were produced and used in early Christian circles, without judging their literary quality.

It has been customary since the beginning of the twentieth century to describe earliest Christianity as a nonliterary movement. This description does not rest on the fact that relatively few documents were produced by the first generations, although that observation has its own weight. Rather, it is a judgment about the nature of the earliest Christian writings and about the disposition of earliest Christianity toward literature and literary activity. In part it is the proposition that early Christianity had no literary culture in the high sense, that its documents had no aesthetic quality, that their authors had neither literary technique nor artistic intentions, and that their readers did not assess them by literary standards. More than this, it has often meant that Christianity, at least in its earliest period, relied on oral tradition and was fundamentally disposed against writing and texts. These generalizations must be specified and tested for their value, and it is useful to begin by tracing the development of such descriptions of the early church.

THE INFLUENCE OF FRANZ OVERBECK AND ADOLF DEISSMANN

The question of whether early Christian writings are literature in any but the crude sense that they are written was initially posed and answered by Franz Overbeck in his widely influential essay, "On the Beginnings of Patristic Literature," published in 1882.[35] Overbeck maintained that earliest Christianity— that is, Christianity from its origins to the mid–second century—did not produce literature in a formal sense, but only *Urliteratur* (preliterature), and that a great divide separates these writings both from the literature of Greco-Roman antiquity and from subsequent Christian (patristic) literature. To the category of Urliteratur he assigned the documents of the New Testament, the writings of the Apostolic Fathers, and the fragmentarily preserved works of Papias and Hegesippus. In Overbeck's view, these documents are characterized on the one hand by a complete coincidence of form and content, and on the other by the immediacy of the relation between author and reader.

The coherence of form and content signified for Overbeck an artless naïveté. He thought that an indifference to form revealed an immediate and mutual relation between writer and readers that rests on shared religious conviction and community. This relation allows the writer to assume many things without stating them and, not less important, to rely entirely on the *content* of what is written to elicit the readers' attention and assent. Literary artistry under these circumstances would be superfluous. Hence "form" is not independently conceived or contrived but is wholly a function of content. What is written is written entirely for the sake of communicating matters of interest closely shared by the writer and the reader. The act of writing is a mere expediency, and its documentary result wholly occasional. "Here the written word, without intending as such to signify anything, is nothing but a completely artless and accidental surrogate for the spoken word."[36] In contrast, in every work of literature proper the form, according to Overbeck, is essential to the content. Because a writer of literature does not know her reading public, she must depend on conventions of style and genre to reach them. It is precisely because the forms of early Christian writings were not contrived that they serve as the most telling indices of the relation of these writings to their generative circumstances. Hence Overbeck gave particular emphasis to the question of form: "A literature has its history in its forms, so that every real history of literature *(Literaturgeschichte)* will be a history of its forms *(Formengeschichte).*"[37] With this perspective Overbeck in some ways anticipated what later came to be known as form criticism, although his attention was directed to the forms of documents, that is, to *Gattungen,* or rather, to genres.[38]

Overbeck observed that from a literary point of view the forms of the earliest Christian writings—letters, Gospels, Acts, apocalypses—were idiosyncratic. He considered the letter a literary "nonform" *(Unform),* while the other forms were mere "historical forms."[39] Urliteratur therefore was "a literature that Christianity created, so to speak, by its own means, since it grew up on the basis of the particular internal interests of the Christian community prior to its accommodation to the larger environment."[40] Overbeck did not mean by this that in its forms Christian Urliteratur was absolutely unique, but that within it we are dealing with forms that were completely unliterary (for example, letters), peculiarly Christian (for example, the Gospels), or already available in religious use (such as an apocalypse). In no case, according to Overbeck, did the earliest Christians make use of any conventional, secular form that was properly literary.[41] This is the difference between Urliteratur and patristic literature, for patristic literature began with the adoption of Greco-Roman literary conventions by Justin and the other apologists of the second century.[42] At this same time (about

150 to 180), Overbeck maintained, the forms of Urliteratur passed out of use.

The disjunction that Overbeck perceived in the history of early Christian literature—or, in his terms, the "fact" that Christian literature cannot properly be said to have begun before the mid–second century—he explained by asserting that Urliteratur belongs to *Urgeschichte*. The "prehistory" of Christianity is not simply the oldest phase of Christianity in an extended and otherwise undifferentiated historical continuum but is the originative and constitutive past that as such lies outside the subsequent history of Christianity and furnishes its definitive ground and possibility.[43] With the abandonment of Christianity's original eschatological orientation, there arose an awareness of this past as absolute and closed, an awareness that found its expression in the formation of the New Testament canon and enabled, indeed required, Christianity to undertake its history in the world and become a literary movement for the first time. The change from Urgeschichte to *Geschichte* coincided with the transition from Urliteratur to *Literatur* proper. Thus Christianity became a literary movement only when, and only because, it became a historical movement.[44] Letter, Gospel, acts, and apocalypse, the genres characteristic of the most primitive Christian documents belonged to a particular period in the church's history; once that period had passed, they necessarily disappeared.[45]

This, in sum, was Overbeck's view. The earliest Christian literature is occasional and intramural: it arises within and is oriented to the interests of the Christian community alone. Urliteratur belongs to a situation far removed from that of literature proper, for literature is composed for a wide public, and it self-consciously exploits literary form to elicit the interest and understanding of readers unknown to the author. As the functional equivalent of oral communication, early Christian literature has no significance in its own right, that is, as literature. Overbeck's brilliant and influential appraisal of the literary culture of early Christianity is not without weaknesses.[46] My purpose, however, is not to evaluate his view but only to show how it has contributed to the tendency to minimize early Christianity's investment in literature.

The nonliterary character of early Christianity was suggested from a different angle by Adolf Deissmann in his major work, *Light from the Ancient East*, first published in 1908.[47] Deissmann brought the rich discoveries of ancient papyrus documents to bear on the New Testament, claiming that they enabled for the first time a proper philological and literary appraisal of early Christian writings.[48] Most of the newly discovered papyri were nonliterary letters, accounts, receipts, contracts, and similar products of the quotidian life of ordinary people. For this very reason Deissmann found them to have particular value for the student of the New Testament: they derived from the same demographic milieu to which the early Christians belonged. Deissmann observed that the language of the New Testament documents, which was recognizably different from the cultivated style of classical literature, was nevertheless not a special biblical idiom either. Rather, he claimed, it was "on the whole just the kind of Greek that simple, unlearned folk of the Roman Imperial period were in the habit of using."[49] What is true of the language is also true of the literature composed in it: "The earliest Christian literature is of a popular kind, not artistic literature for the cultured," and shows us that "Christianity in its earliest creative period was most closely bound up with the lower classes and had as yet no effective connexion with the small upper class possessed of power and culture."[50] Although Deissmann knew the work of Overbeck, his own appraisal of the literary culture of early Christianity had a different focus. Relying on philological evidence, he correlated what he called the popular and nonliterary aspect of early Christian literature with a social conception of the constituency of the early church, whereas Overbeck, attending to literary form, maintained that Urliteratur was a function of a unique historical epoch in the history of Christianity.

FORM CRITICISM'S ESTIMATE OF EARLY CHRISTIAN LITERATURE   Under the influence of both Overbeck and Deissmann, form criticism decisively promoted the claim that early Christianity was a nonliterary phenomenon. The judgment of the early form critics, however, was not principally about the relation of early Christian documents to the larger literary culture of Greco-Roman antiquity, as it was for Overbeck and Deissmann. It was instead an aspect of form criticism's view that earliest Christianity constituted a fundamentally oral culture that was not at all inclined to writing. Hence, for the form critics, early Christianity was not merely nonliterary, but unliterary: its original and habitual mode of transmitting tradition was oral, not written. According to Rudolf Bultmann, Christian tradition "primarily existed only orally, and gained its written form only gradually due to the necessities of life."[51] Analogues to early Christian literature were therefore sought, not in the field of literature at all, but in cycles of (oral) folk tradition, which do not come from or depend on an author but are sponsored anonymously and collectively and are transmitted within the boundaries and according to the internal concerns of folk culture. Literature that might ultimately be derived from oral tradition was characterized by form critics, following the usage of folklorists, as *Kleinliteratur* (popular literature) and was set in contrast to *Hochliteratur* (cultured literature, or belles lettres). Early Christian writings, the Gospels particularly, were taken to be Kleinliteratur—products of the community rather than compositions of individual authors.[52] As anonymous compilations of communal Christian tradition, the Gospels were looked upon as the natural outworkings of oral tradition, and their eventual conversion to the written medium was not thought to mark any real change in the nature of the material. Accordingly, the writers of the Gospels were regarded not as authors but only as collectors or compilers whose work stood in the closest continuity with the community interests that had sponsored and shaped the tradition in the first place.[53] Hence the emergence of written Gospels did not mark a transition to literary culture proper.

Strictly speaking, form criticism was not concerned with literature at all, but with oral tradition. Documents came onto its horizon merely as the deposits of oral tradition and thus as the point of departure for an analysis of the prior process of oral transmission.[54] This procedure is possible only because the tradition, even when finally written down, bears the marks of oral formation and transmission, specifically in its forms. These are not, of course, the forms Overbeck spoke of, or the genres, as we might prefer to say, but the forms of the small units (pericopes, or *Einzelstücke*) that are characteristic of oral tradition. Although these oral forms may indeed be identified and described in their present literary context in the Gospels, they are understood in form criticism not as literary creations but as sociological products. Form is conferred in accordance with the use of the tradition in the community and so is a function of *Sitz im Leben*, or "social setting."[55]

The social setting envisioned by form criticism is not the immediate relation of writer and readers postulated by Overbeck, nor "the simple unlearned folk of the Roman Imperial period" of whom Deissmann spoke. Rather, it is in the first place the folk community *(Volksgemeinde)* and its life as conceived in nineteenth-century folklore studies. The idea of the folk community taken up by form criticism was not, however, an analytical concept based on empirical ethnographic studies, but a constructive concept rooted in a romantic notion of history and culture, a view characterized by a nostalgic concept of primitive societies uncorrupted by civilization. The value of this idea for form criticism was above all its emphasis on the anonymous and collective nature of authorship, and thus on the nonliterary character of folk tradition.[56] But in adopting the romantic notion of the Volksgemeinde, the form critics also adopted its sociological correlative: the "folk," despite the idealization, were consistently conceived in early folklore studies as the lower stratum of society, the *vulgus*.[57] Accordingly, Martin Dibelius characterized the constituency of early Christianity as one "which gave no place to the artistic devices and tendencies of literary and polished writing. The products of Kleinliteratur found their readers in circles not touched by Hochliteratur."[58] This sociological aspect of the idea of the folk community permitted the form critics to argue that primitive Christianity constituted an oral culture without interest in the written word, one that for all practical purposes might as well have been illiterate.

Hardly less important than these sociological assumptions was the further claim by form critics that, literate or not, the early Christians were deterred from writing by their eschatological expectations, and that resort to writing could only be made once those expectations had begun to dissipate. Dibelius summed up the prevailing view by commenting that "the company of unlettered people which expected the end of the world any day *had neither the capacity nor the inclination* for the production of books, and we must not predicate a true literary activity in the Christian church of the first two or three decades."[59]

We are now in a position to see that the description of early Christianity as a nonliterary movement has not always meant the same thing. Overbeck and Deissmann based their judgments on literary observations, genres and philological evidence respectively, and for both the standard of the literary was cultivated Greco-Roman literature, by comparison with which early Christian writings were said to be preliterary, nonliterary, or popular. The form critics, however, in their concern with oral tradition, employed the concept of Kleinliteratur to the very different effect of emphasizing the collective, anonymous nature of the tradition and ruling out the idea of creative individual authorship. For them the notion of Kleinliteratur signified not so much a distinction of Christian literature from Greco-Roman literature as a differentiation of cultures: primitive Christian culture as oral, Greco-Roman culture as literary.

It will have become clear that the frequent description of early

Christianity as a nonliterary movement does not represent a consensus, neither about the sense in which it is true nor about the grounds upon which it rests. If the writings early Christianity produced can be distinguished in various ways from the artistic literature of Greco-Roman antiquity, this does not suffice to show that Christianity in its earliest stage was nonliterary. If some early Christian writings bear the traces of oral tradition, this does not prove that primitive Christianity constituted an oral, unliterary culture. Further, the correlative claims that early Christian writings were merely popular, or that Christianity was early confined to the lower, nonliterary, or illiterate strata of society, are no more than inferences from larger hypotheses and await testing against appropriate evidence.

THE PROBLEM OF CATEGORIES: Under the influence of Overbeck, HOCHLITERATUR AND Deissmann, and form criticism, it KLEINLITERATUR became customary for New Testament scholars to classify early Christian writings as Kleinliteratur, in contrast to Hochliteratur, and thus to minimize their literary dimensions and diminish the literary culture of the early church. If in an earlier period of scholarship this distinction had the value of drawing attention to important aspects of early Christian literature, it is a question whether it is any longer useful, for it obscures other equally important features that reveal the continuity of early Christian literature with the literary traditions of its larger cultural contexts.

It has always been difficult to gain a clear picture of the literary culture of the ancient church because most of the extant Greek and Roman literature was written and read by the well-educated aristocracy, while what else was written, whether broader and more popular or narrower and more technical, has survived much less fully. As a result, early Christian writings, which on the whole were aimed at a different readership than the literati of the Roman empire, have seemed almost in a class by themselves, lacking both a context and useful analogues in the history of Greco-Roman literature. We have seen that, given the nature of the comparative materials, the earliest Christian writings were almost inevitably regarded as nonliterary, and not comparable in language, form, content, or function to the artistic literature of the high culture of the ancient world. This perception has been only partially altered by the thousands of papyrus documents discovered over the past century. Given the enormous value of the papyri for lexicography and social history, in literary terms only a little can be gained from the sales contracts, inventories, private letters, receipts, and so forth among the papyri for understanding the documents of the early church.

Nevertheless, to posit two categories, Hochliteratur and Kleinliteratur, and to assign Christian writings to the latter, concedes too much to the fortuitous state of the evidence and oversimplifies what increasingly appears to have been a far more variegated literary situation in the Roman world. We would do better to think of a continuum of antique literature ranging from the most sophisticated and artistically self-conscious prose and poetry through professional expository and technical writing to practical prose for a broader readership and finally to mere documentary materials in the vernacular. Along this continuum were many differences of language, style, and form, reflecting the many purposes of literary activity and the diverse functions of literature in society at large and among discrete social groups. To collapse this variety into polar extremes would seriously misrepresent a complex picture. Furthermore, although Greco-Roman society was indeed stratified along socioeconomic lines, its various levels were not insulated from one another. There were many public settings and occasions in which people of the middle or lower classes, even the illiterate, were exposed to the broad range of the literary culture, including its most sophisticated expressions, so that high culture shaded into popular culture.

Another reason why early Christian literature has been difficult to situate within Greco-Roman literature would be almost too obvious to mention had its significance for my question not been so neglected. Among the many religious movements of antiquity, only Christianity and Judaism produced much literature at all. Greek and Roman religions appear to have been largely indifferent to the use of texts. Although particular items—an occasional ritual manual, votive inscription, aretalogy, hymn, written oracle, or magical text—have been found, they do not occur in connection with a particular cult or in a quantity that would justify speaking of a religious literature. Exception might be sought in Orphism or Hermeticism, whose fragmentary literary remains are relatively extensive, but if these are exceptions they prove the rule. No Greco-Roman religious group produced, used, or valued texts on a scale comparable to Judaism and Christianity, so that apart from Jewish literature, there is no appreciable body of religious writings with which early Christian literature can be fruitfully compared.

Not only are the categories Hochliteratur and Kleinliteratur inadequate to the range of Greco-Roman literature and ill-suited to specifically religious literature, they are also culture-specific, whereas early Christianity was a transcultural movement. Assessing early Christian documents in relation to Greco-Roman literature alone would yield a distorted view of the literary culture of early Christianity. Because Christianity originated in Judaism and was shaped by Jewish culture, it is also necessary to ask, especially for the earliest period, how far Christian literature and literary culture were conditioned by Judaism. Despite the well-documented reliance of Pharisaic-rabbinic Judaism upon oral tradition, at the time of Christian beginnings Judaism was in no sense a nonliterary or unliterary culture. It was one of the most broadly literate of ancient societies with a long and rich written tradition. Judaism valued its texts as the authoritative cultural heritage of the nation—at once religious, moral, social, and aesthetic. Although Jewish tradition was not wholly reduced to written form, it was the written form that was most revered. By the time Christianity emerged, the oral tradition of Judaism was essentially a secondary growth upon texts that held a classical and normative status.[60] The Torah and Prophets had a place in Jewish life that was never approximated by any literature in Greek or Roman society. The Jewish scriptures were meticulously preserved, transcribed, studied, and interpreted by scribes and sages. They were learned by children in schools, recited publicly in synagogue and temple, and privately read and contemplated. They set the standards to which later Jewish literature aspired—imitating and adapting the styles, forms, and genres established by the religious authority of the scriptures.[61] Hence, in Judaism the continuum between high and popular literature is manifest, and the categories of Hochliteratur and Kleinliteratur have no useful application.

Form criticism, as noted, typically regarded the Gospel writers only as collectors and conservators of tradition, not as authors.[62] It may be true that the small units that make up the gospel tradition are orally formed products of the community about which there can be no question of authorship, but this does not mean that the larger documents in which these small units have been identified are themselves nonliterary. The success of redaction criticism in identifying the theological aims of the Gospel writers and observing how they selected, arranged, and recast the tradition in the service of those aims requires that the genuinely literary character of the Gospels and the creative work of their individual authors be fully acknowledged, as indeed it now is.[63]

I have also noted that form criticism regarded the eschatological expectations of early Christianity as a powerful disincentive to writing and thus to the production of literature. In the face of what was already known about Jewish apocalyptic literature, it is astonishing that this claim could ever have been made, but after the discovery of the Qumran scrolls, it simply cannot be sustained. The discovery at Qumran brought to light a Jewish sectarian community contemporary with Christian origins that held eschatological expectations no less fervent than those of the early church yet invested heavily in the production and use of literature.[64] Thus the claim of form critics like Dibelius that apocalyptic eschatology and literary activity are fundamentally incompatible was finally rendered untenable, for in Judaism the two were hand in glove, and imminent eschatology could not itself have inhibited literary activity in early Christianity.[65]

We have seen that the romantic conception of the folk community adopted by form criticism does not comport with other evidence. Early Christianity had a diverse social makeup, representing a limited cross-section of Roman society. The scheme of Hochliteratur-Kleinliteratur correlates poorly with a movement that was neither aristocratic nor vulgar but something in between. Nevertheless, few efforts have yet been made to draw the consequences of the changed estimate of the social character of early Christianity for the question of the literary culture of the early church.[66] For example, what level(s) of education and literacy would characterize a group that occupied this intermediate social position? With what sorts of literature was it acquainted, and what uses did that literature serve? Were the literary tastes and practices of aristocrats the standards to which lower classes aspired, or was their literary orientation governed by their own station, interests, and activities? If literary culture stands in a strong correlation with social class, as despite exceptions it seems to, then a revised conception of the social constituency of early Christianity entails a reassessment of its literary character.

My discussion has aimed to clear the way and provide bearings for a fresh assessment of the literary culture of the ancient church. I have questioned the characterization of early Christianity as nonliterary and of its texts as Kleinliteratur without claiming that the early church participated in the high literary culture of the ancient world. I have also indicated what must be taken into account: the broad range of the types and uses of Greco-Roman literature, the relation of Christianity to the tradition of Jewish literature, the relation between oral tradition and literary texts, and the sociological correlatives of literary activity. Yet the primary data must always be early Christian texts themselves, and we now turn to them.

Any appraisal of the literary culture
of the ancient church must attend
to early Christian literature itself.
It is not necessary here to analyze and describe individual documents
in literary terms, for this has been done often and well in histories of
early Christian literature, in commentaries, and in specialized studies.[67] The results of these contribute to my concern with early Christian texts: their types, currency, and functions. Although the literary
culture of the ancient church is a dimension of the history of Christian
literature, it is also correlative with the social and institutional history of the church, so that the answers to my questions must attend to
the circumstances and developments of the church in the first five
centuries.

The Scope of the Earliest Christian Literature Judgments about
the earliest period of Christian history are crucial, for they have a
major influence on the way the evidence for the later periods is as-
sessed. Thus, although the seminal phase of Christian history is obscure, it is mainly about this period that discussion is needed.

We know relatively little about the beginnings of Christian literature, but it is useful to summarize what we do know. The earliest
extant Christian writings are the authentic letters of the apostle Paul,
most of which were written during the sixth decade of the first century. Their dating is more certain than that of any other Christian
documents of the first century. The Gospel of Mark, reckoned by most
to be the earliest Gospel, is usually dated 65 to 70, and the Gospels of
Matthew and Luke between 80 and 90. Apart from the Pastoral Epistles (1–2 Timothy, Titus) and 2 Peter, all of which may be assigned to
the early second century, the rest of the literature found in the New
Testament is variously dated between 60 and 100, although it is hard
to establish a relative chronology among these documents.[68] Beyond
these points, on which there is broad agreement, other observations
must be brought into play.

The twenty-seven early Christian writings that belong to the
collection that goes under the name of "the New Testament" by no
means exhaust the stock of the earliest Christian literature. Around
those early documents is a wide penumbra of other Christian writings,
some of which either clearly derive from the same period or well may
have. Of the so-called Apostolic Fathers, which comprise fifteen diverse documents written by nine different authors, the letter known
as 1 Clement certainly belongs to the first century, and two others may

be just as early: the Epistle of Barnabas and the Didache. These three are probably earlier than several of the later writings contained in the New Testament, and indeed later on, when the New Testament canon was taking shape, they were occasionally reckoned to belong to it. In addition, some of the documents among the so-called New Testament apocrypha may come from the first century, the Gospel of Thomas, the Gospel of Peter, and the so-called Unknown Gospel being the likeliest candidates.[69] But no documents outside the New Testament have a strong claim to be earlier than the earliest documents in the New Testament.

It is important to observe that some literature that belonged to the earliest period has failed to survive. We do not know how many of the letters that Paul may have written have been lost, but some were. An indisputable case is a letter from Paul to the Corinthians that is alluded to in 1 Cor. 5:9 but is not preserved in the collection of Paul's correspondence. A Pauline letter to the Laodiceans mentioned in Col. 4:16—if it is not a pseudonymous postulate or identical with Ephesians or Philemon—must have suffered the same fate. Much of 1 Corinthians appears to be a response to a letter Paul had received from the Corinthian church, or at least from a group within it (1 Cor. 7:1, 7:25, 8:1, 12:1). Perhaps there were other congregations that corresponded with him, though no such letters have survived.

Moreover, there are excellent reasons to conclude that the collection of sayings of Jesus ("Q"), which was employed in the Gospels of Matthew and Luke, was not merely a fund of oral tradition but a written source.[70] Yet the sayings source failed to survive after it was incorporated into larger documents of a different genre. There are strong indications too that, apart from Q, the Gospels draw on or incorporate other early collections of traditions about Jesus, at least some of which, even if their origin was oral, must have been put into written form at an early date. The author of the Gospel of Luke claims in his preface (1:1) that "many" had undertaken to set down a narrative on the matters about which he himself was about to write. He seems to be referring to written sources, yet we can identify only two that he certainly knew, Mark and Q. If his statement is not purely rhetorical, he may have been acquainted with other Gospel-type documents, now lost. The passion narrative, which has a density and detail unparalleled in other parts of the gospel tradition, is acknowledged even by form critics to have taken shape very early and was probably set down in writing well before it was taken over by the author of Mark's Gospel. The collection of parables found in Mark 4 appears to have been written down in Aramaic before it was translated into Greek and became available to the author of Mark's Gospel. It is likely, too, that there existed written collections of miracle stories on which the authors of Mark and John drew.[71] Good arguments have been made that the Sermon on the Mount was accessible to the author of Matthew as a written source and that the eschatological discourse (Mark 13 and parallels) was an early, independent document.[72] Furthermore, the extended genealogies of Jesus given in Matthew and Luke are not the sort of material to have been orally preserved; their documentary content suggests that they were in written form from the beginning, and they must have had an early and Jewish origin since they presuppose Jesus' human ancestry.[73] There are many indications, then, that many specifically Christian texts, apart from Paul's letters, were current well before the composition of the earliest Gospels that we have. Although we can only guess exactly when these documents may have been written, at least some of them were current by the middle of the first century, as early as or earlier than Paul's letters, in which case they were available within twenty years of Christian beginnings. The absence of these documents from the usual inventory of the earliest Christian literature puts the historian at a large disadvantage. Conjectural as some of these items may be, it is important to keep in mind that we do not fully possess the earliest Christian writings.

Apart from the very early documents that have not survived, any estimate of early Christian literary culture must also acknowledge that from the outset Christianity depended heavily on Jewish literature, and particularly on the scriptures of Judaism. One of the most urgent tasks of the Christian movement in its infancy was to support its convictions by showing their consistency with Jewish scriptures. Messianic Jews who sought to persuade fellow Jews to their faith necessarily developed scriptural arguments, and there is every reason to suppose that the primitive church turned immediately to the study and interpretation of scripture and began to adduce those texts that enabled Jesus and the events of Christian experience to be understood and presented as outworkings of the divine will revealed in the Torah and Prophets.

The force of Christian dependence on Jewish scripture for the question of the literary culture of early Christianity is not much appreciated, and its implications have been neglected under the influence of form criticism's preoccupation with oral tradition. Although it need not be denied that there was a period, possibly a long one, during which some Christian traditions were orally transmitted, during that same period Christians were deeply and continuously engaged with texts. Christians were from the beginning assiduous students of Jewish scriptures. This not only presumes the literacy of at least some of them, but also implies what may be called a scholastic concern and activity. Like some other groups in Judaism, they studied and interpreted scriptural texts, employed them in preaching, teaching, and debate, and did so in a more or less systematic way. That they did this for religious purposes does not make the enterprise any less literary.

The parallel with Qumran is especially suggestive. The similarity between the exegetical methods of the Qumran sectarians and the early Christians has often been noted, and it rests on the self-conceptions of the two groups. Like the Qumran sect, the earliest Christians thought they were in a unique position to comprehend scripture. Both groups believed that they stood near the climax of salvation history and were witnessing events that consummated the divine purpose for creation and humankind. On that conviction, the proper interpretation of scripture was not merely a possibility granted to them, but a task to be carried out, and its accomplishment was vital to their identity and agency as "the true Israel." Thus the Qumran sect arranged for at least some of its members to be continually devoted to the study of scripture, and the community concerned itself not only with the interpretation but also with the reproduction and preservation of the sacred texts.[74] We have no direct evidence of similar arrangements in the primitive church, but we do know something about Christianity's use of Jewish texts in its first generations.

It appears that there was never a time when the kerygma of the church was not accompanied by an appeal to Jewish scripture. The most primitive confessional and homiletical materials incorporated allusions to and quotations from it.[75] In the earliest Christian documents preserved, the apostle Paul frequently resorts to Jewish scripture in writing to Gentile Christian congregations.[76] Paul's heritage is Jewish, but he clearly expects that his Gentile readers will also be familiar with Jewish scripture and that scripture will carry the weight of authority with them. The same expectations are evident in most of the rest of the literature of early Christianity. Notable examples are found in the Gospel of Matthew, the Gospel of John, and the epistle to the Hebrews. Furthermore, the use of scripture in these and other documents of the New Testament was not devised spontaneously or anew by their authors, but was drawn from a tradition of the exegesis of Jewish texts that was rooted in the beginnings of Christianity and highly developed by the time it comes into our field of vision in early Christian literature.

The nature and development of this exegetical tradition has been illuminated by a number of modern studies, most especially those of C. H. Dodd, K. Stendahl, and B. Lindars.[77] Lindars's careful appraisal of the features of the quotations of Jewish scripture in the earliest Christian writings shows that many of the quotations had been worked over time and again under changing circumstances. The selection and configuration of the texts, the reworking of their forms, and the distinctive uses made of them reveal a close correlation with important theological and apologetical issues in the life of primitive Christian communities. By observing the shifting applications of a text and changes in their wording it is possible to reconstruct the early history of Christian exegetical work and to see that it was an active and ingenious enterprise.[78] Stendahl has argued that the so-called formula quotations (Reflexionszitate) of the Gospel of Matthew are not creations of its author but the products of Christian scribal activity, for they reflect an advanced and sophisticated approach to the text that is normally associated in ancient Judaism with systematic, scholarly study.[79] To judge from the commentaries found at Qumran, this sort of work went on there also. Of course, the existence of a particular school behind the Matthean exegetical tradition can only be inferred. Yet, as to the primitive Christian use of Jewish scripture in general, it can hardly be doubted that from the beginning there were Christians, probably groups of them, who devoted themselves to the close study and interpretation of Jewish scripture, constructing from it the textual warrants of Christian convictions and making those texts serviceable for Christian preaching, apologetics, and instruction.

In various early Christian writings there is a group of quotations from Jewish scripture that occur in textual forms that often do not agree with traditional readings of either the Masoretic text or the Septuagint, and they are given interpretations and applications uncommon or unknown in Judaism. The recurrence of these quotations has given rise to the hypothesis that in the early church there was a collection (or collections) of "testimonies," anthologies of texts that had been extracted from Jewish scriptures and compiled as proof texts for Christian claims and that early Christian writers were indebted to these testimony books for their quotations.[80] This theory enjoyed favor among English-speaking scholars in the first half of the twentieth century but thereafter fell on hard times. Its appeal was diminished in large part by the work of Dodd, who, observing that early Christian writers often quoted different texts from larger but discrete portions of Jewish scripture, rejected the idea of a single testimony book. Dodd proposed instead that the substructure of early Christian thought consisted mainly of certain large blocks of Jewish scripture from which particular verses were quoted as needed, but always with the purpose of evoking their larger contexts.[81] It was another objection to the testimony book hypothesis that no such documents were known from the early Christian period.

The theory that written collections of testimonia were produced and used in primitive Christianity was, however, prematurely dismissed. Dodd's idea that extensive portions of scripture were in view when particular verses were quoted is more symptomatic of a modern biblical scholar's conscientious regard for context than of the view of scripture in antiquity that found significance in brief statements and small details.[82] Despite the variety of quotations from Jewish scripture in early Christian writings, the frequency with which some texts are cited (for example, Ps. 2:7, 8:6, 110:1, Is. 8:14, and Jer. 31:31–34) and the remarkable similarities in the way they are juxtaposed, interpreted, and applied by different writers are not accounted for by Dodd's explanation. His supposition that it was Jesus himself who pointed out relevant blocks of scriptural text and set the church's exegetical agenda is no more satisfactory than the alternative, that an anonymous collective spontaneously struck upon the basic proof texts.[83] Considering the evidence of the quotations themselves and the circumstances of the primitive church, the project of mining the scriptures for specific texts to underpin the Christian proclamation was probably a specialized endeavor. Such texts were neither numerous nor self-evident: many that were traditionally regarded as messianic in Judaism were not useful for Christianity, and many that were messianically construed by the primitive church had carried no such sense in Judaism. Thus the early Christian appeal to Jewish scripture was not a simple matter of discovering texts, but a textual enterprise requiring close reading and constructive interpretation and thus literary sophistication.

In the meantime, the testimonia hypothesis has received new life from the discovery of several documents containing just such collections of testimonia as had been conjectured. Two have appeared among the Qumran literature: 4QTestimonia compiles five scriptural texts taken to have messianic reference, and 4QFlorilegium collects three texts concerning eschatological figures.[84] Another example of the type is furnished by a fragment of a Christian papyrus codex discovered in Egypt, paleographically dated to the fourth century, which compiles ten citations in Greek from the LXX.[85] These documents represent in their own settings a practice widespread in Greco-Roman antiquity of drawing up convenient collections of *excerpta*.[86] The discovery that compilations of scriptural testimonies were used by a Jewish sect contemporary with primitive Christianity does not of course prove that early Christianity produced and used similar collections, but it measurably strengthens the possibility. As J. Fitzmyer has commented, "While the collections of *testimonia* that are found in patristic writers might be regarded as the result of early Christian catechetical and missionary activity, 4QTestimonia shows that the stringing together of OT texts from various books was a pre-Christian literary procedure, which may well have been imitated in the early stage of the formation of the NT. It resembles so strongly the composite citations of the NT writers that it is difficult not to admit that testimonia influenced certain parts of the NT."[87] The availability of scriptural texts in this format would go a long way toward making sense of features that characterize the quotations of scripture in early Christian literature: peculiar readings, similar groupings of texts, composite citations, misattributions of sources, and changes of application. Indeed, it is hard to find a satisfactory explanation of these phenomena without assuming the existence of primitive Christian collections of testimonies.[88] Books of testimonies would have been useful in many aspects of early Christian life—preaching, teaching, apologetics, and debate—and especially in missionary situations, since copies of whole scriptural books were not easy to come by in antiquity and neither individual Christians nor Christian congregations are likely to have had copies of the full corpus of Jewish scripture to consult.[89] There is, then, at least a strong circumstantial probability that collections of testimonies were current in the early church and should be reckoned among the lost items of the earliest Christian literature.[90]

This discussion of the use of Jewish scripture in the literature of the New Testament points out the implications of what is known of early Christian exegesis for the question of early Christian literary culture. That the earliest Christian writings are indebted to an already well-developed tradition of Christian exegesis shows that from the beginning Christianity was deeply engaged in the interpretation and appropriation of texts. That activity presupposed not only a mature literacy but also sophisticated scribal and exegetical skills. Since it began with Hebrew and Aramaic texts (though its results are presented to us in Greek), we must imagine a complicated process of collating and reflecting on both Hebrew and Greek versions of scripture. Since the results of this exegetical work appear in Paul's letters, it must have been intensive in the earliest years of the church. Apart from the evidence of the quotations themselves, the many allusions in the earliest Christian writings to the study and comprehension of scripture suggest that it was among the major occupations of the primitive church.[91]

Oral Tradition and Literary Culture The recognition that Christianity was engaged from the beginning in the careful study and interpretation of texts does not comport well with the claim of form criticism that primitive Christianity was a fundamentally oral culture, although form criticism is concerned specifically with the oral transmission of Christian traditions and not with the Christian use of Jewish scripture. Other, more recent studies that emphasize the oral character of early Christianity nevertheless disagree sharply with form criticism about the relation between oral and written tradition. What is the significance of oral tradition in early Christianity for the literary culture of the early church? Did the currency of oral tradition inhibit literary activity? More fundamentally, were the oral and written modes so radically divergent as to be mutually exclusive?

Various modern communication theory studies have attempted to determine the nature, contexts, and consequences of orality and literacy and have developed elaborate typologies of them. In studies of oral poetry, M. Parry and A. B. Lord found that the modes of composition and transmission of oral and literate societies are highly distinctive and mutually exclusive.[92] Their observations have been developed by others who claim there are extensive differences in the social, linguistic, cognitive, and hermeneutical dynamics of oral and literate cultures and a fundamental incompatibility between the two. They employ a binary theory to elucidate larger questions of intellectual and cultural history in the transition from the oral to the written medium.[93]

The questions of whether there is a basic structural difference between oral and literate societies, and if so, what sort, have scarcely intruded upon form criticism or biblical studies generally, but recently the problem has been sharply posed in relation to early Christianity. In a vigorously argued book, W. Kelber, while agreeing with form criticism that early Christianity was deeply indebted to the oral medium and had only tenuous connections with literate culture, claims that it failed to consider the phenomenon of orality itself and so overlooked the deep opposition between orality and literacy. Form criticism assumes instead a more or less natural and linear evolution of oral tradition into written form. Thus Kelber represents the conversion of oral gospel traditions into written form—a step he supposes to have been taken by the author of the Gospel of Mark—as a radical innovation, involving nothing less than a revolution in the basic cognitive, hermeneutical, and theological perspectives of early Christianity.[94]

What shall be made of this claim? There are, certainly, important distinctions between the spoken and the written that none would minimize. Yet it is not clear that these differences are so distinct as to make the two media mutually exclusive in a given community.[95] How far they diverge, and especially whether they are incompatible in practice, can only be decided by observing the activities of particular societies. Empirical studies of orality and literacy quickly reveal the inadequacy of theories that sharply juxtapose the two, infer universal laws for each, and assert a technological determinism in cultural change.[96] Whatever general theories may be postulated by social anthropologists, linguists, literary critics, and students of media, there is compelling evidence that in the ancient societies about which we are best informed the oral and written were certainly not mutually exclusive. In early rabbinic Judaism, for example, although the rabbis transmitted halachic tradition orally, they were at the same time habitual readers of scripture, and the written Torah was their foundation.[97] Or, to take another case, oral and written modes were not mutually exclusive in classical Greece, where despite a certain tension they coexisted and interacted in a fruitful symbiosis.[98]

A theory that posits a deep chasm between the oral and written modes is questionable in itself, but in the historical context of early Christianity it is problematic on at least two main counts. First, it does not adequately accommodate the literary and historical data at hand.[99] Evidence for the production, use, and appreciation of texts in early Christianity, even before the composition of the Gospels, is too strong to allow oral tradition and literary activity to be set off against one another.[100] Whatever may be said about the oral dimensions of the Jesus tradition or about the composition of the Gospel of Mark in particular, Christianity before 70 C.E. cannot be accurately described as an exclusively oral culture. Arising within the matrix of a broadly literate Judaism, early Christianity was never without a literary dimension, even though it did not immediately generate a large literature of its own.[101] Consequently, the beginning of the production of specifically Christian texts cannot be taken to mark a sea change in Christian attitudes toward written materials but must be seen as a development within a tradition already well accustomed to the written word. Second, a strong distinction between the oral and the written modes is anachronistic to the extent that it presupposes both the modern notion of the fixity of a text and modern habits of reading. Texts reproduced by hand, as all texts were before the invention of the printing press, were far less stable than modern printed texts because they were subject to accidental or deliberate modification in every new transcription.[102] Moreover, in antiquity virtually all reading, public or private, was reading aloud: texts were routinely converted into the oral mode. Knowing this, ancient authors wrote their texts as much for the ear as for the eye.[103] Thus, although the oral and the written remained different modes, they were far closer and interactive in antiquity than today, and a too sharp theoretical differentiation misconceives the situation. The cultivation of oral tradition does not itself imply either an absence of or a prejudice against written material.

Nevertheless, a prejudice against texts has often been perceived in some sectors of Greco-Roman culture and in the early church in particular. Those who would highlight the importance of oral tradition and minimize the importance of texts in earliest Christianity frequently point to the statement quoted by Eusebius from Papias, bishop of Hierapolis. According to Eusebius (*H.E.* 3.39.3–4), Papias remarked in the preface to his work, "An Exposition of the Dominical Oracles":

> *And I shall not hesitate to append to the interpretations all that I ever learned well from the ancients* [presbuteron] *and remember well, for I am confident of their truth. For I did not rejoice like the many in those who say much, but in those who teach the truth, nor in those who recall the commandments of others, but in those who recall those things given to the faith by the Lord and derived from the truth itself. But if anyone ever came who had followed the ancients, I inquired about the words* [logous] *of the ancients—what Andrew or Peter or Philip or Thomas or James or John or Matthew or any other of the Lord's disciples said, and what Ariston and the presbyter John, the Lord's disciples, were saying. For I did not suppose that things from books* [ek ton biblion] *would benefit me so much as things from a living and abiding voice* [zoes phones kai menouses].

This statement is often taken not only to prove the longevity and authority of oral tradition in the early church but also to document a Christian suspicion or perhaps outright rejection of books as novel, unreliable, or otherwise deficient. Yet such broad inferences are unwarranted. In the first place, it is not oral tradition as such that Papias esteemed, but first-hand information. To the extent that he was able to get information directly, he did so and preferred to do so. This does not mean, however, that he thought he could not get it elsewhere too—from texts in particular. Papias was well acquainted with books, and the *logoi* he set about to interpret appear to have been derived chiefly from books. As to written information about Jesus, Papias knew at least the Gospels of Mark and Matthew. Although he was aware that the Gospel of Mark was criticized by some, he himself cited a statement of "the elder" in defense of its reliability, and he apparently held the Gospel of Matthew in high regard (Eusebius, *H.E.* 3.39.15–16). In addition, he knew 1 Peter and 1 John (*H.E.* 3.39.17), the Apocalypse (frag. 11), and possibly other pieces of early Christian literature as well as Jewish scripture.[104] Thus, when he contrasts oral and written testimony, Papias is not denigrating texts.[105] Second, Papias himself wrote books and must have expected that what he wrote, drawing in part on the tradition he had received, would be read and valued by others.

The sentiment Papias expressed in the concluding part of his statement—"I did not suppose that things from books would benefit me so much as things from a living and abiding voice"—is not peculiar to him but frequently appears in ancient literature and indeed constitutes a topos in certain contexts.[106] A similar statement is made by the learned physician Galen, a near contemporary of Papias, in *De compositione medicamentorum*, 6: "There may well be truth in the saying current among most craftspeople *[pleiston techniton]* that learning out of a book *[ek suggrammatos]* is not the same thing as nor comparable to learning from the living voice *[zoes phones]*." Galen's comment shows that the idea of the "living voice" was proverbial and current, at least in the social context of craftspeople.

Apprenticeship has always been the normal means of training in the crafts because craftspeople recognize that demonstration is more effective than written instruction in the acquisition of manual skills. Yet the sense of the importance of first-hand instruction was also expressed in two other contexts: in rhetoric, where the importance of ex tempore composition and live performance were emphasized,[107] and among the hellenistic philosophical schools, where the transmission of tradition was thought to be ideally accomplished through personal tutelage and where books were often represented as written compendia of oral instruction best employed under the personal guidance of a teacher.[108] In none of these contexts, however, were texts unavailable, unused, or not valued. There were manuals of instruction in the manual arts; notes were used by rhetoricians, who also wrote speeches and produced or used handbooks; and philosophical treatises were routinely produced within the various schools. In short, in the topos of the living voice we have to do not with a principled rejection of books in favor of oral tradition, but with an express preference for personal instruction or demonstration in contexts where it was particularly useful. Papias's interest in the living and abiding voice is best understood in connection with the similar interest among the Hellenistic philosophical schools.[109] Neither he nor students of philosophy repudiated writing or texts, which had their important uses and commanded appropriate respect.[110] Thus, Papias's testimony is not rightly understood as evidence of a deep rift between orality and literacy, both of which were important to him.[111]

Certainly an oral tradition was both current and influential in the first century of Christianity's existence, and nothing I have said should be construed to the contrary. The point is rather that we have no reason to think that oral tradition stood in opposition to the production of texts, nor that it inhibited the literary culture of the early church. Just as in its larger Jewish and Gentile environments, so too in early Christian circles, the two media coexisted and interacted.

The Character of Early Christian Literary Culture If Christianity even in its first generations was active in the written as well as the oral medium, what kind or level of literary culture should be attributed to it? The answer depends on an evaluation of the linguistic and literary features of the earliest Christian literature, its language, style, and genres.

First, take language.[112] The starting point for all modern discussion of New Testament Greek is the work of Deissmann. His comparative study of the language of the papyri and the language of the New Testament writings led him to deny the prevailing views that biblical Greek was a hybrid of Greek and Semitic elements and that it was a unique holy language. He concentrated on the lexical issue, and was especially opposed to the notion that there were specifically "biblical" words.[113] His conclusion that the Greek of the earliest Christian documents was popular Greek (street Greek, as it were) and that although it had varying grades, vernacular Greek was to be found not in literary works but in papyrus documents, inscriptions, and ostraca—the written material of daily life—changed critical consensus.[114]

This recognition does not solve every problem, nor is it adequate to the whole of the literature it would describe. One weak point is the frequency of Semitisms in New Testament texts. Deissmann tried to account for these simply as accidents of the translation of Hebrew and Aramaic materials into Greek, thus denying them any importance. This explanation will not do, however, for Semitic usages frequently occur where there is no reason at all to suppose a Hebrew or Aramaic source.[115] In fact, the Semitic features of New Testament Greek are so numerous and widespread that others have urged, contrary to Deissmann, that New Testament Greek and the Greek of the Septuagint represent not ordinary secular Greek but a strongly Semitized dialect of Greek used by Jews in Hellenistic and Roman times—a uniquely Jewish Greek.[116] Although this view has not won wide acceptance, it is generally recognized that the Semitisms of New Testament Greek require a fuller acknowledgment and a different explanation than Deissmann gave them. Today they are most commonly explained by appeal to the influence of the Septuagint on Christian writers rather than to a special, spoken Jewish Greek.[117] Except in such gross instances as the Apocalypse, where Semitic influence runs roughshod over Greek usages, Semitisms may not be represented as barbarisms. They may not be ordinary usage, but in general they fall within the parameters of possible Greek constructions.

On another front, too, Deissmann's views have been found oversimple and misleading. His correlation of the language of the New Testament with that of the papyri led him to identify both as the vulgar Greek of people without power, position, education, or literary capacity. Yet the Greek of the earliest Christian writings, though not literary in an artistic sense, has characteristics that set it apart it from the vernacular.[118] Lars Rydbeck has made an important contribution by carefully studying grammatical features of New Testament literature that also occur in the papyri but are not found in classical Greek and hence have usually been classified as vulgar or merely popular *(volkstümliche)*.[119] Rydbeck has shown that these features also occur in the documents of technical writers of the period, such as Dioscurides on pharmacology, Ptolemy on astronomy, Nichomachus on mathematics, and Theophrastus on botany. These were educated persons whose purpose in writing was scholastic: to set out essentially factual data, offer description and scientific observation, and argue for or against hypotheses. Unlike most historians and philosophers, they did not employ literary methods, nor were they stylistically self-conscious. Rather, they wrote a straightforward, factual prose *(Sachprosa, Fachprosa)* commonly used by scholars with scientific and humanistic interests, which came into wide use in many fields at the beginning of the imperial period.[120] Rydbeck describes this prose as *Zwischenprosa,* one between elevated literary language and popular language.[121] That features of Zwischenprosa also show up in many papyri does not signify that it was merely a popular form, for the papyri themselves can be differentiated: a minority were entirely popular, but most were actually written and their language normalized by people who were reasonably well trained in writing Greek.[122] The parallels that Rydbeck adduces between examples of Fachprosa and the documents of the New Testament show how misleading it is to say, with Deissmann, that the earliest Christian literature was written in a vulgar, nonliterary Greek.[123] It was not the classicizing Greek of arts and letters, nor was it popular Greek, but the professional prose of the day.

Rydbeck's observations have now been confirmed and extended by L. Alexander.[124] Whereas Rydbeck concentrated on individual elements of grammar, Alexander has made a detailed comparison between the preface of Luke-Acts and the prefaces found in a wide selection of just the sorts of scholastic texts that Rydbeck considered. She found that in form, length, vocabulary, style, and syntax, the Lucan prefaces are remarkably similar to the prefaces in Fachprosa literature, a more impressive similarity than has ever been shown between the Lucan prefaces and the prefaces of the customary comparative materials of Greek historiography. She thereby demonstrates that, so far as its literary character is concerned, Luke-Acts stands in close relation to the tradition of professional scholastic or technical prose writing.

Of course, the recognition that a number of the earliest Christian writings are not composed in a low vernacular is nothing new. Deissmann, for all his insistence on the merely popular character of New Testament Greek, readily conceded that such documents as Luke-Acts, 1 and 2 Peter, and Hebrews are in literary terms relatively sophisticated.[125] What is new is the awareness that the language of the earliest Christian documents cannot be accurately appraised as long as the only descriptive categories are low vernacular and high classical diction. As with the dichotomy between Hochliteratur and Kleinliteratur, polar extremes do not accommodate known intermediate forms of the language. Indeed, it is astonishing how often the language of Koine texts is characterized as the spoken language of the Hellenistic world. In fact, we have no knowledge of Koine in its spoken form, and it must be assumed that written forms of any language are to various degrees elevated from its spoken forms, so that few Koine *texts* can be truly described as vulgar.[126] This is not to grant a special status to the language of Christian texts—a tendency rightly criticized by Deissmann—but only to recognize that they belong to a large class of texts that although not literary were certainly not vulgar. Between the most elevated Greek and the lowest there were intermediate prose styles acceptable to the educated and accessible to the uneducated.[127] Especially in a cultural setting where few were literate, the occurrence of language in a text (written form) is itself an indication that the language stands at some remove from wholly popular use.

Beyond these linguistic points, early Christian literature is deeply indebted to the techniques, forms, and modes of ancient rhetoric. Most Christian writers of the second through the fifth centuries were practiced in the rhetorical arts: not a few, Tertullian, Cyprian, Lactantius, and Augustine, for example, were teachers of rhetoric before they entered the church. Other and earlier Christian writers, however, though they may have lacked formal training, also made use of ancient rhetorical methods. The rhetorical criticism of early Christian texts as it is practiced today aims to identify the units, techniques, style, and structures of large blocks of argumentative discourse, and indeed of entire documents, and to comprehend the presuppositions and functions of their use in the specific historical and social contexts in which they were deployed. Though closely related to literary criticism, rhetorical criticism is distinguished by its interest in both the modes of persuasive argumentation and the functions of rhetoric under social circumstances, the "rhetorical situation." The rhetorical criticism of early Christian texts has already yielded fruit.[128] It has shown that even the earliest Christian writings made use of established rhetorical conventions. The apostle Paul was well versed in the forms of rhetorical argument, and he used a variety of them in his letters the better to persuade.[129] The Gospels, too, are indebted to rhetorical strategies in their elaboration and use of traditions about Jesus.[130] But what does the presence of rhetoric in this literature say about the literary cultivation of the early church, whether of those who wrote or those who read? The use of rhetoric to persuade does not itself signal a higher education or warrant a reclassification of Christian literature in belles lettres. It does indicate that the earliest Christian writers participated in the rhetorical culture of antiquity and that the earliest Christian literature cannot be set outside the larger literary culture, but must rather be seen in continuity with more studied and self-consciously artful uses of rhetoric by non-Christian intellectuals and later patristic writers trained in classical rhetoric.

In addition to language and style, genre also indicates literary culture. For Overbeck and later for form criticism, there could be no real question of the genres of the earliest Christian writings. The idiosyncrasy of the Gospels, the ephemerality of personal letters, and the provincialism of apocalypses all were said to disqualify their writers from literary intention, and the documents themselves from literary status. These writings were pronounced no more than ad hoc adaptations of nonliterary forms in the service of practical religious needs. Although these documents were unquestionably composed for practical purposes, that does not preclude a serious appraisal of their literary features. Nor has it, for much attention has lately been given to the literary aspects of particular early Christian writings, not least to the matter of genre. Since my concern is not with individual texts but with the broader issue of literary culture, I may simply formulate here, from a wealth of particular studies, general observations about the genres of early Christian literature.[131]

Within the conventions of form criticism the Gospel genre has been regarded as without analogy in the literature of antiquity. This claim was based not so much on comparison of the Gospels with Jewish and Greco-Roman literature as on the presumed authorlessness of Gospels and, it must be added, on a theological interest in minimizing the biographical-historical value of the Gospels. Modern literary assessments have shown that the Gospels, though without exact analogues, nevertheless stand within the broad, varied, and developing genre of Greco-Roman biographical literature.[132] This does not mean that Gospels are exclusively or even chiefly historical, for they are unquestionably religious documents offering theological interpretations of their subject, as redaction criticism has amply shown. Yet all ancient biographical literature had broader aims and uses than historical reportage. Hence, at the level of genre as well as in respect of their constituent forms, the Gospels are best understood as Christian examples of traditional Greco-Roman biographical literature.

The earliest Christian documents are most frequently in the form of letters, a well-established genre of ancient texts.[133] Early Christian letters, however, have often been described as nonliterary, either by denying that letters were a form of literature proper (Overbeck) or by locating the analogues of Christian letters in the ordinary private letters of the papyri (Deissmann). It is true that ancient epistolary theorists regarded the letter as a surrogate for personal presence rather than a type of literature,[134] and that there are affinities between early Christian and papyrus letters. Nevertheless, the educated wrote letters, not only as a means of private communication, but also as a vehicle for philosophical exposition, moral exhortation, literary criticism, and the treatment of other intellectual subjects, as is evident, for example, in the letters of Cicero, Seneca, and Fronto. Moreover, early Christian letters depart from the private letters of the papyri in length, in some formal features, and of course in their religious content and orientation to communities. On the whole, early Christian letters combine the familiarity of the private letter, the authority and community address of the official letter, and the expository and didactic functions of the philosophical letter.[135] Here too, then, we see a Christian adaptation of a form that, though not an established genre of Greco-Roman belles lettres, was nevertheless in wide use and was capable of artistic, literary elaboration. Already in the earliest Christian letters, Paul employs a wealth of dialogical, argumentative, and expository techniques drawn from the rhetorical tradition.[136] The great variety in the types and functions of early Christian letters illustrates the flexibility of the epistolary genre. The letters found in the New Testament and among the Apostolic Fathers do not, as a group, closely resemble either the private letters among the papyri or the literary letters of the elite but fall between these extremes of epistolary practice. The letters of many later Christian writers, such as Basil, Gregory of Nyssa, Gregory Nazianzus, Jerome, and Augustine, approximate much more closely the letters of the well educated and those of second- and third-century Christian writers somewhat less so. The persistence of Christian epistolography through the first five centuries attests to the usefulness of this genre to the ancient church, for it was well suited to communication between widespread congregations and a valuable instrument for teaching.

Acts literature, by contrast, had a relatively brief career in the early church, though it was prominent during the first two centuries. The canonical Acts and the apocryphal Acts resist strict definition by genre, yet both are clearly related to known Greco-Roman genres.[137] The term *Acts* (Greek: *praxeis*) was not the original title of the *Acts of the Apostles* but was used to refer to it in the second century. The designation reveals how readers may have thought of it but does not necessarily specify the genre as the author understood it. In the ancient world praxeis denoted historical works focused on the careers of individual persons, and this is how the Acts of the Apostles was read in Christian circles.[138] Later, similar documents, though they usually dealt with the activity of only one apostle, were similarly titled. Since the *Acts of the Apostles* exhibits many conventions of Greek historiography, and the author characterizes the whole of his work, which included the Gospel of Luke, as a "narrative" (*diegesis*, Lk. 1:1), it need not be denied that the author of Luke-Acts construed his work along the lines of a history. Greco-Roman historians, however, did not prize scientific objectivity but interpreted and dramatized past events in order to edify and entertain as well as to inform.[139] Later Acts literature was influenced by the *Acts of the Apostles* and continued to focus on apostolic figures but had more in common with Greek novelistic writing than with historiography as such, and its chief aims were to edify and entertain.[140]

Apocalypses were also prominent in Christian use during the first two centuries. Of the several genres of early Christian literature, the apocalypse is the most identifiably Jewish.[141] In the period of the second temple Jewish apocalyptic thought fostered an elaborate literary tradition, of which many products remain. Although these Jewish apocalypses are obviously the immediate models for Christian documents of the type, it should not be supposed that apocalypses were a wholly provincial type of writing. Jewish and Christian apocalypses together constitute but one tradition within a much broader body of revelatory literature current in many areas and subcultures of the Greco-Roman era.[142] All this literature cannot be subsumed under a single genre, but it shares as common stock many smaller forms. Greco-Roman revelatory literature was principally oracular, while the Judaeo-Christian was mainly visionary. As Christianity increasingly distinguished itself from Judaism, its apocalypses changed in focus from corporate to individual destiny (as the Apocalypse of Peter) and became increasingly oracular (*The Shepherd* of Hermas, for instance) before Christians ceased composing books of this sort.

Some general observations will help relate the genres of early Christian writings to the larger issue of early Christian literary culture. The genre intended is rarely stated in the earliest Christian documents, and their traditional titles, being secondary, cannot be invoked for this purpose. Genre can only be inferred through literary analysis and comparison of the texts themselves, and even this rarely produces a clean definition. Nevertheless, genre is presupposed in the act of writing and in the act of reading, and though they may not correspond absolutely, the aims of writing and reading can meet only if recognizable generic signs are provided either in the text or in the situation where the text is received and read, or both.[143] A sense of the genre of any particular text is essential to its comprehension: the reader must be able to judge what sort of writing is being read. Since, however, the definition of a genre is a formal abstraction to which actual examples correspond only approximately and since some elements of the definition will sometimes belong to more than one genre, not all actual documents can be easily classified. That early Christian documents do not represent ideal types does not mean that they were idiosyncratic. All of them have positive correlations with one or another known genre of ancient literature. This would have to be assumed even if it could not be shown, for Christian writings were not composed and did not circulate in a vacuum. They could not have been utterly peculiar to a sociocultural setting, since complete novelty of form and content would have made them unintelligible to Christian and non-Christian alike.

If in language, style, and genre the earliest Christian writings did not belong to the higher reaches of the literary culture of Greco-Roman society, their authors could not for that reason be said to have lacked all awareness of or approximation toward literary standards. By the same token, these writings cannot be called popular or nonliterary if this means that they sprang from an oral culture or the lowest eschelons of Greco-Roman society. These authors had the benefit of education, for otherwise they could not have written at all. They were not only literate but also literary to a degree. For axiomatic as it may be that Christians wrote for practical rather than aesthetic purposes, there is in writing that intends to teach and persuade both the opportunity and the need for literary skill, skill that must have been available to Christianity virtually from its birth.

Finally, in what sense may we speak of there having been a popular literature in the Roman empire, either Christian or non-Christian? If the restricted scope of literacy is emphasized, then it can be claimed that "there was no such thing as 'popular literature' in the Roman Empire, if that means literature which became known to tens or hundreds of thousands of people by means of personal reading."[144] Certainly, the capacity to read, the interest and leisure to do so, and the financial means to procure texts, belonged to few, and this circumstance must limit the idea of a popular literature. The ancient works that by virtue of style and theme are usually called popular (principally ancient novels) are therefore often understood as light reading for the small minority who could read and those who also read the more serious literature available to them.[145] Remember, however, that all ancient reading was reading aloud and that much of it occurred in public, quasi-public, and domestic settings where those listening might include the semiliterate and illiterate as well as the literate. Those contexts, as distinct from strictly private reading, lent themselves more readily to works of a novelistic sort, and their writers may well have had such a broader audience in view.[146] This is the sense in which early Christian literature too can be called popular. Most early Christian texts were meant to speak to the whole body of the faithful *to* whom they were read. These writings envisioned not individual readers but gathered communities, and through public, liturgical reading they were *heard* by the whole membership of the churches.[147]

THE LATER DEVELOPMENT OF CHRISTIAN LITERATURE AND LITERARY CULTURE

The sharp disjunction that Overbeck posited between the earliest Christian writings and patristic literature is a theoretical construct that is difficult to sustain in evaluating actual texts. As we have seen, the genres of the earliest Christian literature are broadly continuous with the various kinds of non-Christian literature, so that a sharp division cannot be made between primitive Christian and patristic writings. Gospels, acts, letters, and apocalypses—Urliteratur to Overbeck—continued to be written well into the second century and into the third, with letters persisting much longer still. If Overbeck identified the beginnings of Christian literature in the works of Justin and other apologists on the basis of their having taken up the forms and conventions of Greco-Roman literature, that same recognition must now be granted to earlier Christian literature.[148] Christians, whatever else they may have been, were also Jews, Greeks, and Romans, and in its composition and use of texts Christianity was never insulated from the literary dimensions of the cultures in which it found itself.

It is true that during the second and subsequent centuries Christian literature demonstrated an increasing diversity of forms and a more elevated style, but these factors did not signify a new literary ambition. Later Christian writings continued to be governed by practical concerns: apologies, theological treatises, church-orders, scriptural commentaries, and the like, works continuous with the earliest Christian writings but which in the context of Greco-Roman literature were more closely parallel to scholastic writings than to literature proper. Moreover, this literature continued to be directed principally to the Christian community, not to the general public. The differences between these and earlier Christian writings are neither of the type nor the magnitude Overbeck claimed and do not require the explanation he proposed. A sufficient explanation is rather the social one, namely that the success of the Christian mission brought Christian communities into routine contact with the social and cultural life of the empire so that from the second century onward the church was able to count among its converts ever larger numbers of people who were well educated and conversant with Greco-Roman literary and philosophical traditions. Such persons, though they constituted only a small minority within the Christian movement, loom large in early Christian history. It was from their ranks that there emerged the Christian literati who produced the greater part of the literature of the ancient church. A fair number of them appeared well before the time of Justin, though only a few are still known by name—Papias, Quadratus, Aristides, Valentinus, Ptolemy, and Heracleon. Like their successors—Clement of Alexandria, Irenaeus, Tertullian, Hippolytus, and the later Fathers—they did not disavow their intellectual and literary capacities when they converted to Christianity. They turned their talents to the Christian cause. This undeniably produced a more elevated literary style and a more direct engagement with the literary and philosophical interests of Greco-Roman antiquity, but it did not require a radical change in Christian self-consciousness, as Overbeck claimed. It owed itself instead to the changing circumstances, the new tasks, and the resources that emerged with the missionary expansion of the church in the Gentile environment and its presence as a social, religious, and intellectual movement in Greco-Roman civic and cultural life.

In a necessarily general way I have explained how far the Christian movement was indebted to texts, especially in its formative years, and located early Christian literature on the broad literary topography of the early Roman empire. I turn now to the transmission and use of Christian writings, considering first the outward, tangible form of those writings—the early Christian book.

II

THE EARLY
CHRISTIAN BOOK

Discussions of early Christian literature are usually concerned with the contents of documents, their generative historical circumstances, their chronological and theological matrices, and similar questions. Rarely is the question raised: in what physical form(s) was this literature known and used by the early church? The failure to consider the extent to which the physical medium of the written word contributes to its meaning—how its outward aspects inform the way a text is approached and read—perpetuates a largely abstract, often unhistorical, and even anachronistic conception of early Christian literature and its transmission. To be sure, every text has literary and historical dimensions, but no less important are its bibliographic aspects, for it is the physical presentation of the text that is most immediately evident and effective for its readers. There are, of course, good reasons why historians of early Christian literature have tended to neglect its purely bibliographic dimensions. In the first place, early Christian writers intimate little or nothing about how Christian documents were written or in what tangible form(s) they were available. Inferences from the larger context are difficult, since non-Christian writers of the period allude only occasionally to the subject of book production. Such matters were taken for granted by Christian and non-Christian alike. Second, no early Christian text is extant in its original form. The copies we possess are, at best, several stages removed from the originals. As recently as the beginning of the twentieth century there were no known copies of a Christian book older than the two famous biblical codices, Sinaiticus and Vaticanus, both from the fourth century. Modern archaeological discoveries, however, have dramatically altered the situation. Copies of Christian scriptural and nonscriptural documents from the second and third centuries have been recovered, the oldest dating to the early second century. Of course, these earlier texts are copies, not originals, and most are only fragmentarily preserved. Yet because we now possess manuscripts from the earliest period of Christian literature, we are in a far better position than ever before to describe the physical form of early Christian books. It is unfortunate that the close study of these manuscripts has remained almost exclusively the preserve of paleographers and textual critics, historians of early Christian literature having taken little interest in exploiting them for the history of Christianity and its literature.[1]

There is, however, much to be learned from these ancient manuscripts, not only about the form of the early Christian book but also about the circulation and use of literature within the ancient church. Indeed, the materials invite something like a sociology of early Christian literature, or at least of early Christian texts. Whatever else a text may be or may signify, it is a physical object, and as such it can be described, deciphered, and bibliographically located. Yet the physical object is also a social artifact. Its content was composed, its vehicle selected, and the words transcribed in a particular way. The book was made accessible to an audience or readership, and the text was subsequently reproduced to enable its further transmission and reading in varying circumstances. All aspects of the production, distribution, and use of texts presuppose social functions and forces—functions and forces that are given representation, or inscribed, in the design of the text as a concrete, physical object. Hence the careful physical evaluation of a manuscript. By observing precisely how the text was laid out, how it was written, and what it was written on or in one has access not only to the technical means of its production but also, since these are the signs of intended and actual uses, to the social attitudes, motives, and contexts that sustained its life and shaped its meaning. From this perspective a clean distinction between textual history and the history of literature is neither possible nor desirable.[2]

THE GRECO-ROMAN BOOK The modern book and its reader are removed from antiquity not only in time and culture but also by two major developments in the history of books: the change from the roll book (scroll) to the leaf book (codex), which transpired between the second and the fourth centuries, and the change from the handwritten to the printed book, which occurred in the fifteenth century. Ancient books, then, were fundamentally different from modern ones. Yet we can appreciate the nature and significance of early Christian books only if we first examine the nature of books in the larger environment of the ancient church. I begin by considering the books of the Greco-Roman world.[3]

The standard form of the book in Greco-Roman antiquity was the roll book or scroll, designated in Greek as a *biblos* or *biblion* and in Latin as a *volumen*.[4] Book rolls might be made either of papyrus or parchment. In the Hellenistic and Roman periods they were usually made of papyrus, but in the later Roman period parchment came increasingly into use.

Papyrus was produced from a plant of the same name (Latin: *Cyperus papyrus*). In antiquity, the plant was widely found in the shallow lakes and marshes of the near East but was especially abundant in the Nile valley, where it was systematically cultivated under close government regulation. Thus Egypt became the center of manufacture and trade in papyrus products. A great deal is known today about the diverse uses of papyrus in antiquity, but my concern is with its primary use as a writing material.[5]

In *Natural History* Pliny the Elder gives a valuable though not altogether lucid account of the manufacture of papyrus for writing. Careful studies of one passage (13.74–82), together with modern experiments, have cleared up long-standing obscurities and misconceptions and yielded a good understanding of the process. The papyrus plant, a reed that grows to 2¼ to 5 meters, has a long, jointless, three-sided stalk approximately the thickness of the human wrist. The stalk was cut into sections, the husk removed, and the pith peeled into thin, tapelike strips. It has traditionally been supposed that sections of the stalk were peeled or sliced along the length of the stem. In this view, these strips were then laid side by side on a hard, smooth surface, and another layer of strips was placed over them at right angles. The two layers were then fused by using a press to break down the cellular structure of the fibers and release the juice of the pith, which served as an effective adhesive.[6] Recent experiments have led to the alternative suggestion that the pith was peeled in a wide strip around the section and "unrolled" with a needle. The two wide strips thus obtained were laid one on top of the other at right angles and compressed to form the sheet.[7] Although this explanation cannot be ruled out, the first explanation envisions a less delicate and time-consuming procedure, which was probably more feasible for mass production. Whichever the actual method, the papyrus sheet was then dried and trimmed and the surface smoothed with pumice and polished with shell. Single sheets of papyrus might range from ten to twenty-nine centimeters in breadth and from twenty to thirty centimeters in height, but ordinarily a sheet was twenty-five centimeters high and eighteen to twenty centimeters wide.[8]

The next step of the manufacturing process was to paste the individual sheets together to form a longer strip, which was then rolled up. Each sheet had fibers running horizontally on one side and vertically on the other. These sides are commonly designated by papyrologists as recto and verso, respectively.[9] To form the roll, the sheets were arranged with the recto side facing up and joined together by gluing a small overlap (one or two centimeters wide) of the right edge of each sheet onto the left edge of the next in the series. The join thus formed is called a *kollesis,* and the individual sheet thus joined a *kollema.* Instead of the natural juice of the plant, a flour paste was used at this stage. The joins were smoothly made and scarcely noticeable, so that when the roll was inscribed the pen encountered no obstacle in moving across them. A roll of papyrus manufactured in this way could theoretically be of any length, but it appears that the standard manufactured length comprised twenty sheets and ran to about 3½ meters.[10] The strip of glued papyrus sheets was then rolled up with the recto, the intended writing surface, on the inside of the roll for protection. It was in the form of such a manufactured roll, known as a *chartes* (Latin: *charta* or *volumen*), that papyrus was shipped, stored, and marketed for retail sale. Rolls of any length might then be fashioned by cutting or joining the manufactured units.[11]

The result of this process was a serviceable writing material—smooth, light-colored, flexible, strong, and not much inferior to modern paper.[12] In explaining the eventual replacement of papyrus by parchment for the making of books it has often been said that papyrus was a fragile material liable to early discoloration and disintegration. This impression, however, drawn from papyrus documents nearly two thousand years old, is certainly mistaken. It is true that papyrus, when exposed for long periods to dampness, becomes friable. Yet all the evidence suggests that in its original condition papyrus was a high-quality product, which, when preserved and used under normal circumstances, was remarkably durable.[13]

Papyrus was by far the prevalent writing material during the Hellenistic and early Roman imperial periods, but parchment was also used. In some areas and for some purposes parchment was clearly preferred to papyrus, and later, in the medieval period, it altogether superseded papyrus. Animal skins, from which parchment is made, had been used from great antiquity for writing. Rolls made of skin were occasionally used by the Egyptians, and Persians and Jews appear to have had a clear preference for skin.[14] The term *parchment* is often used to include leather and vellum as well as parchment proper, but though all these are made from animal skins, there are important differences between them. Because it is not tanned, parchment is thinner, softer, and whiter than leather and was produced so as to allow the hair side as well as the flesh side to be used for writing. Vellum is a finer parchment made from the skin of calf or kid. The manufacture of parchment seems to have begun about the third century B.C.E. Legend falsely traced its invention to the city of Pergamum in western Asia Minor.[15] Owing perhaps to a refinement of the process or to the city's role as a major producer, Pergamum furnished one of the ancient names for parchment, the Greeks calling it *pergamene*, the Romans *pergamena*. Yet these terms are relatively late; before the fourth century C.E. the Greeks called parchment *diphthera*, the Romans *membrana*, "skin."

The manufacture of parchment was more complex than the making of papyrus.[16] The flayed skin of the animal, ordinarily a calf, goat, or sheep, was soaked in a solution of lime. The epidermis was then carefully scraped off the outer side, and the flesh was scraped from the inner side. After the skin was washed and set to dry on a stretcher, its thickness was further reduced by shaving the outside and smoothing the inside by rubbing with stone or bone. To produce high-quality parchment, these operations had to be carried out quickly and efficiently. The sheet, stretched and dried, was then smoothed, whitened with chalk, and trimmed to the desired size. Like papyrus, the two sides of a sheet of parchment differed: the flesh side was lighter and smoother and thus the better side for writing (and so constitutes the recto), though the rougher, more absorbent hair side held ink better. Parchment could be fashioned into rolls by stitching sheets together, usually with animal or vegetable fibers, but the joins were never as smoothe as those in a papyrus roll and could not be written on.

Efforts to account for the eventual replacement of papyrus by parchment as the preferred material for books have often led to comparisons of the merits of the two materials. The superior quality of parchment is clear, even when misconceptions about the strength and durability of papyrus are dispelled. Still, for mass production and general use, papyrus was preferable because it was more plentiful than animal skins and easier to manufacture. For the same reasons papyrus may have been less expensive than parchment, but there is not enough evidence to judge the relative costs of the two.[17] However that may be, among the Greeks and Romans papyrus was for many centuries the preferred material for the book roll, and parchment did not begin to displace it until the fourth century C.E.

The length of a papyrus book roll (as distinct from the standard unit of manufacture) was to some extent variable, with a mean of seven to ten meters. Short works took less space, but the upper limit was rarely transgressed. The maximum length was a function not of manufacture, since rolls of any length could be constructed, but of convenience to the reader. A roll of more than ten or eleven meters was too cumbersome for the reader to handle.[18] The reader grasped the roll in both hands, the left hand progressively rolling up what had been read, the right unrolling what was yet to be read. The procedure is shown in many ancient artistic depictions of readers with roll books.[19] The ordinary length came to be closely prescribed by custom. In the Hellenistic period and later, the subdivision of extensive works of literature into books *(tomoi, libri)* was determined as much by the conventional length of the book roll as by considerations of content. Older long works (such as those of Herodotus, Thucydides, and Homer) had divisions imposed on them, and authors of long new works made their own divisions by taking the customary length of rolls into account. Thus the physical unit of the roll tended to function also as a literary unit.[20]

The papyrus roll was inscribed on one side only, the side where the fibers ran horizontally, offering less resistance to the scribe's pen.[21] The book was rolled up so that the text was on the inside, protected. The first sheet of a roll (the *protokollon*) was not ordinarily inscribed. Both it and the last sheet *(eschatokollion)* were commonly affixed— probably by the writer or user of the book rather than by the manufacturer of the roll—with fibers running at a right angle to the rest of the roll. This too was for protection, since the beginning or end of a roll, being on the outside when the roll was closed, was especially liable to damage.[22] The text was written left to right in columns six to nine centimeters wide and fifteen to twenty-four centimeters high. In prose works the columns were usually tall and narrow, sometimes with only eight to ten letters on a line. Poetic works were inscribed to the length of one line of hexameter verse (sixteen syllables, thirty-four to thirty-eight characters). Like the length of a roll, the width of the columns also served the convenience of the reader: they were relatively narrow, since the roll was more easily handled if it needed to be opened only a little at a time. In Greek the column of a roll was called a *selis*, and the line of a column a *stichos* (the corresponding Latin terms were *pagina* and *versus*). Columns were not ordinarily numbered in literary texts, although they often were in documentary texts. The margins between columns and at the top and bottom of the roll were usually ample.[23] Greek texts were written in *scriptio continua*, that is, without divisions between words, without punctuation or accents, and without paragraphing, so that each column presented a monolith of characters. It is uncertain whether this practice was owing to the persistence of antique (inscriptional?) practice or was devised by scribes for ease of writing or uniformity of appearance. The Romans, who were accustomed to dividing words in writing Latin, gave up that habit in literary texts in order to conform to the Greek custom. Punctuation marks, accents, and other lectional aids, when they did occur, are normally found only in texts used by scholars and students.[24]

In roll books the title and the name of the author typically appeared not at the beginning but at the end, beneath or to the right of the last column of the text.[25] This convention may have developed because the end of a book was the best-protected, innermost part of a closed roll, or it may have arisen as a concession to the bad habit of not rerolling books after reading, so that on picking up a book the end was often the immediately accessible part. These are only guesses, however. Some rolls were also supplied with a papyrus or parchment tag (Greek: *syllabos* or *sittubos*; Latin: *titulus* or *index*) that was glued to the outside of the roll at a right-angle to the top margin and carried a short title. When the roll was stored on a shelf this tag would hang down and face outward, identifying the book.[26] Such tags could easily become detached. Sometimes the title was written on the outside of the roll.[27]

Book rolls could also be furnished with accessories. Often the ends of the roll were attached to wooden dowels that served as rollers, called navels (Greek: *omphaloi*, Latin: *umbilici*), and these were often tipped with decorative knobs or "horns" *(cornua).*[28] Sometimes rolls had protective parchment wrappers *(membrana, capsa)*, which might be colorfully dyed.[29] Such refinements were probably not standard but depended on the value of the book and the taste of its owner.

The book roll is well attested in Judaism. It was the standard form of the book in biblical times and is mentioned in many connections in Jewish scripture. Although it is unclear whether in the preexilic period such rolls were constructed principally of skin, papyrus, or both, by the time of Christian beginnings Judaism had developed a strong preference for skins. Skins were prescribed for copies of the Torah and seem to have been more commonly used than papyrus for other books as well.[30]

THE TRANSITION FROM THE
ROLL TO THE CODEX Given the ubiquity of the roll book in the Greco-Roman and Jewish traditions, one would expect early Christian books to have taken the same form. Remarkably, they did not. Almost without exception, the earliest Christian books known have the form not of the papyrus roll but of the papyrus codex, or leaf book, which is the model of the modern book. The evidence of this fact has been furnished by archaeological discoveries of the twentieth century. Time and again both systematic excavations and lucky finds in Egypt have yielded papyrus texts ranging in date from the third century B.C.E. to about the eighth century C.E. Some of these appear to have been stored away, but most have been retrieved from ancient rubbish heaps. It is not surprising that the vast majority are only fragmentarily preserved or represent highly diverse materials. Most are documentary texts—accounts, receipts, inventories, school exercises, and the like—but there are many private letters, magical texts, copies of Greek and Latin literary works, and Jewish and Christian texts. The earliest of the Christian texts belong to the second century.[31] Privilege of age belongs to P 52, a small fragment of the Gospel of John, paleographically dated to the first half of the second century. A number of other Christian papyrus fragments are not much later: P Egerton 2 (=Ap 14) from a codex of an apocryphal Gospel; P 4 + P 64 + P 67 from a codex of Matthew and Luke; P 77 from a codex of Matthew; P 66 and P 90 from codices of John; and P 32 from a codex of Pauline epistles. All these, not to mention some Christian copies of Jewish scripture, may be placed in the second century.

The comparative evidence is instructive. Of the remains of Greek books that can be dated before the third century C.E., more than 98 percent are rolls, whereas in the same period the surviving Christian books are almost all codices. Among Greek books the codex does not show up significantly until the third century (when less than 20 percent are codices), and only near the beginning of the fourth century does the codex come to be used almost as often (48 percent) as the roll.[32] Christian texts from the earliest examples of the second century, however, occur almost always as codices. Together the relevant evidence indicates that early Christianity had an almost exclusive preference for the codex as the medium of its own writings and thus departed early and widely from the established bibliographic conventions of its environment.[33]

To appreciate how peculiar this step was one must realize that a codex or leaf book was not recognized in antiquity as a proper book. It was regarded as a mere notebook, and its associations were strictly private and utilitarian. The humble origin of the codex is enshrined in its name: the Latin *caudex* means "a block of wood" and referred to a wooden tablet used for writing (among the Greeks such a tablet was called a *deltos* or *pinax*). From an early time it was customary to link two or more of these together by passing a string or thongs through holes along one edge, thus constructing a series of loose leaves of wood. The proper Latin name for such a collection of wooden tablets was *codex*.[34] The thinly cut wood, its surfaces smoothed and whitened, could be written on with pen and ink. More often the surface of the wood was slightly hollowed and filled with wax, which was often colored, and could be written upon with a metal stylus.[35] The size and weight of the tablets limited the number that could be conveniently assembled and used in this way. A codex of two leaves forming a *diptych* was fairly standard. Though more leaves were often used, no known example exceeds ten leaves. The Romans distinguished between large tablets *(tabellae)* and smaller ones that could be held in one hand *(pugillares)* and used in larger aggregates (see fig. 1). Tablets could be reused after they were washed or smoothed and were handy for recording ephemera of all sorts—school exercises, accounts, notes, first-drafts, and so forth.[36] Among the Romans they also had archival uses, being inscribed with birth certificates, wills, edicts, and other matter of legal consequence. Nevertheless, in format and use the codex was a long way from anything that might be regarded as a book.

This remained true when wooden tablets were replaced by sheets of parchment or papyrus folded and fastened together. The parchment or papyrus codex was lighter and easier to handle. It could contain many more leaves, and it remained reusable although writing on parchment and papyrus required ink, because the leaves could be washed or rubbed down to give a clean surface.[37] The earliest certain reference to a parchment notebook was made near the end of the first century C.E. by Quintilian *(Inst. Or.* 10.3.31–2), who refers to it as *membranae*.[38] How much earlier than that the parchment notebook had appeared cannot be determined, but it was certainly a Roman innovation. This is shown by a Christian text. The author of 2 Timothy requests (4:13) that Timothy, when he comes, should "bring the cloak that I left with Carpus at Troas, also the books *(ta biblia)*, and above all the parchments *(tas membranas)*" (RSV). The Greek term *membranai*, translated by the RSV as "parchments," is the Latin word *membranae* transliterated into Greek. There was no Greek name for the intended object. If parchment rolls had been meant, the standard Greek designation, *diphtherai*, would surely have been used. The

1. A fresco from Pompeii depicting a Roman woman holding a set of wax tablets *(pugillares)* and a stylus. Courtesy of the Museo Archeologico Nazionale, Naples.

Latinism, *membranai*, has the specific sense of "parchment codex," and its use in this Greek-Christian document indicates that the object, like the word, had a Roman origin.

The substitution of parchment or papyrus sheets for wooden tablets did not in itself alter the status or the use of the codex: it remained a notebook, nothing else. Eventually, however, it occurred to someone to use it in another way, namely, as a medium of literature, and thus as a substitute for the roll. Who took this important step, why, or to what immediate result, is not known. The first evidence of the development is found in the *Epigrams* of the Roman poet Martial in 84 to 86 C.E.[39] Martial recommends that readers who wish to carry his poems on journeys should purchase "those that parchment confines in small pages" (*Epigr.* I.2: *quos artat brevibus membrana tabellis*) so that they can be held in one hand. He gives the name and location of the bookseller from whom they can be obtained. In enumerating gift ideas for the Saturnalia, Martial mentions various well-known authors whose works were available *in membranis* or *in pugillaribus membranis*.[40] These works must have been in parchment codices. Though Martial does not use the word *codex*, he emphasizes both the capacity and the convenience of these editions, presumably in contrast to the conventional roll. Martial's comments imply that editions of literature in the codex format were novel to Roman readers, but we have no indication whether this innovation was actually made in Rome or how much it caught on there.

Some evidence is at hand from Egypt about the early use there of the codex for literature. There are remains of eighteen non-Christian manuscripts, datable to the second century, that both are in codex form and contain literary works.[41] The number is very small in comparison with literary rolls of the same period (less than 2 percent of the total) and shows the limited use of the codex. One of these codices, however, is particularly interesting: P. Oxy. 30 contains an otherwise unknown historical work, now usually called *De bellis Macedonicis*. It is the only Latin text in the group of eighteen and one of only four on parchment. Its chief interest lies in these facts, together with its early date near the beginning of the second century.[42] Although this is the earliest known codex and although it carries a literary text, E. G. Turner remarked that "this codex does not seem to be an experimental type of book, and its mere existence is evidence that this book form had a prehistory."[43] The prehistory of the parchment codex is not much illuminated by this manuscript, but an early Latin text on parchment in Greek-speaking, papyrus-rich Egypt is arresting and tends to support the earlier evidence from Martial that the parchment codex is connected with Rome.[44]

Another intriguing piece of Egyptian evidence is provided by P. Petaus 30, a fragment of a private letter dating to the second century.[45] It is brief enough to quote entirely: "Julius Placidus to his father Herclanus, greeting. Dius came to us and showed us six parchment codices *(tas membranas hex)*. We selected none of those, but we collated eight, for which I paid on account 100 drachmas. You will be on the lookout in any case. . . . I hope you are well . . . by Julius Placidus." We get a glimpse here of the ancient counterpart of the door-to-door bookseller. Among his offerings are parchment codices. These were apparently inscribed with texts but were perhaps not well inscribed, since six were not bought. It is not clear whether the eight others that were collated and purchased were rolls or codices (they seem to be differentiated from the codices by being outside the total of six).[46] However that may be, the mere mention of parchment codices may imply that Julius and his father had a special interest in acquiring codices. Here the name of the letter writer, Julius, may be a further indication of a Roman connection for the codex.

There is evidence, then, that by the late first and early second centuries the parchment codex was beginning to be used not merely as a notebook but as an alternative to the traditional roll, though its literary use was limited and would remain at best sporadic and tentative until the fourth century, when it finally came into its own. Yet there is considerably more physical evidence in the earlier period for papyrus rather than parchment codices. This may be owing to the Egyptian provenance of the evidence—papyrus being the favored and more abundant material there—but the question remains whether it was parchment or papyrus that was first employed for the codex. This question is sharpened by the fact that the codex takes distinctive formats depending on which material is used: the parchment codex consistently tends toward square dimensions (breadth = height), whereas the papyrus codex is more typically rectangular ($2 \times$ breadth = height).[47] No definite answer can be given, however, and it is possible that neither papyrus nor parchment was originally or exclusively associated with the codex form. Both may have been used, with papyrus gaining an early dominance among those who made the most use of the codex.

Given the evidence of surviving manuscripts and the dates paleographically assigned to them, Roberts and Skeat have maintained that those who made the earliest and most extensive use of the codex for literature were Christians and that in this practice Christianity swam against the strong tide of the bibliographic tradition of antiquity. This claim has not gone unchallenged. Joseph van Haelst has countered that the second-century dates assigned by Roberts and Skeat to a number of early Christian manuscripts—some of which they place in the early second century—are too early and that virtually all the earliest Christian codices belong rather to the second half of the second century or to the beginning of the third.[48] The later dates he assigns to some manuscripts enables van Haelst to suggest that, since we also encounter non-Christian codices at this time, the phenomenon of the transition from roll to codex is not *itself* uniquely Christian and that what distinguishes Christian usage is only the *rapidity* of the changeover.[49] Paleographic dating is, to be sure, an inexact business, and the judgments of paleographers commonly differ, though usually not widely. In the cases that are immediately relevant to the problem of the origin of the (literary) codex there remain—even for van Haelst's revised dating—a good number of Christian manuscripts that may be firmly placed in the second century and a few in the early second century. Apart from the problem of determining the absolute number of manuscripts that can be dated to the first half of the second century, it cannot be gainsaid that the *proportion* of codices among the earliest Christian manuscripts remains extremely high, while among non-Christian manuscripts it remains extremely low. This suffices to show that Christians had a stronger and more effective preference for the codex at an earlier time than did non-Christians, which is all that Roberts and Skeat wished to claim. Thus, the Christian use of the codex is a genuine anomaly that needs an explanation. Why did the codex come so early to be the favored format for Christian literature but take much longer to gain a similar status among non-Christians?

The answer has often been sought in particular features of the codex that are supposed to have been specially advantageous to Christians.[50] It has been claimed, for example, that the codex commended itself to Christianity for reasons of economy. Because the leaves of a codex were inscribed on both sides, whereas the roll was written on only one side, a codex could accommodate almost twice as much text on the same amount of writing material. Certainly, there were savings to be achieved in using the codex form, so far as the writing material itself was concerned, but the cost was not halved. The codex required more space for margins than a roll did, and whereas a roll came virtually ready-made, there were costs associated with the construction of a codex—cutting the sheets from a roll and then stacking and binding them. A careful estimate of the relative costs suggests that a codex may have been about 25 percent less expensive than a roll.[51] The appeal to economy as a peculiarly Christian motive entails the larger assumption that Christians belonged to the lower classes of Greco-Roman society, and that the codex, as a humbler type of book, was more familiar to them and more affordable than the roll.[52] Yet a preference for the codex over the roll as a matter of social class cannot be shown. For one thing, as we have seen, the assumption that Christianity was a thoroughly proletarian movement is much less plausible than it once was.[53] Further, it does not appear from early Christian books themselves that their makers were unusually parsimonious. Although no really early Christian texts were produced in de luxe copies, we do not find among them such patently economical measures as cramped hands, unusually narrow margins, or a frequency of opisthographs or palimpsests.

Alternatively, it has been suggested that convenience of use was the primary advantage of the codex, and under this head various facets of the codex have been highlighted as especially appealing to Christians. The codex was easier to use: unlike the roll, it could be held in one hand, and it was not reversed in the reading so as to require rerolling. The modern reader accustomed to the leaf book may think this an obvious convenience, but it is not clear that the ancient reader experienced any great frustration with the roll book.[54] Besides, any inconvenience would surely have been experienced generally, no more by Christians than others. Yet there are still other aspects of the convenience of the codex that are thought to have had special value for Christians. For one, the codex was compact, less bulky than a roll of the same text because the writing material was reduced by almost half. Martial emphasized the value of this to people who traveled with books, as early Christian missionaries probably did.[55] Another convenience was the comprehensiveness of the codex: it could compass in one physical entity a single text long enough to have required several rolls or several shorter texts that might normally be found in separate rolls. This advantage, however, seems not to have been exploited at an early time even by Christians, as all the really early Christian codices are of modest size. Besides, the early technology of codex manufacture placed limits on size.[56] Third, it has often been stressed that the convenience of the codex to Christians consisted above all in its ease of reference. Christians from the beginning engaged in discussions and debates in which points were scored by citing texts from Jewish and Christian writings. Arguments from scripture would supposedly have been easier to make from codices, in which it was possible to turn quickly to individual passages and perhaps to mark pages. Yet this view overlooks the fact that, with the exception of the possibility of placing bookmarks between the leaves of a codex, features that might have provided ease of reference were as rare in the codex as in the roll. Neither had divisions of chapters or verses, and pagination was not common in ancient codices, but when it was present it was of limited help since in books written by hand pagination varied from copy to copy of the same text.[57] Furthermore, the appeal to convenience of reference perhaps depends too much on modern scruples about exact quotation that did not obtain in antiquity, as quotations by Christian writers themselves show well enough.

In sum, although the codex had some small actual and some larger potential advantages over the roll, these cannot explain why the codex became the dominant form of the Christian book early on, yet required much longer to gain currency as the medium of non-Christian literature. Consequently, it has been thought that there must have been a material cause beyond practical considerations. In the words of C. H. Roberts, "So striking an effect must have had a cause of comparable weight."[58] In particular, it has been supposed that some early Christian document of high authority was originally issued in a codex and that the authority of its content carried over to the kind of book in which it was transcribed, and thus the codex was powerfully promoted as the standard form of the Christian book.

Roberts himself initially suggested that it was the Gospel of Mark that had this far-reaching result.[59] Relying on the tradition (Papias, in Eusebius, *H.E.* 3.39.15–16) that Mark had written down the reminiscences of Peter, Roberts supposed that Mark's Gospel was written in a parchment codex, the usual instrument for note taking. In support of this idea, Roberts pointed out that the parchment codex may have had a Roman origin (compare Quintillian and Martial) and that Mark's Gospel has often been associated with Rome. To explain why the earliest surviving Christian manuscripts are papyrus codices in Egypt he appealed to the tradition (Eusebius, *H.E.* 2.24) that associates Mark the evangelist with the founding of the Alexandrian church. Thus, according to Roberts, if the Gospel of Mark reached Egypt as a parchment codex, it would have been copied there onto papyrus, while the codex format would have been preserved because it had "a sentimental and symbolic value as well as a practical one" and because it usefully distinguished Christian from Jewish and pagan books.[60]

For all its ingenuity, this theory is liable to many objections. The proposition that Mark's Gospel consists of Peter's recollections, that it has an original connection with Rome, and that Mark the evangelist had a real link with Alexandria, are all tenuous notions with little or no support in modern scholarship. So also, then, is the assumption that the Gospel of Mark was issued in a parchment codex. Besides, the fact that the Gospel of Mark is poorly represented among the Egyptian papyri in comparison with other Gospels confounds the claim of its early and authoritative use there.[61]

Acknowledging the weaknesses of his original hypothesis, Roberts, together with T. C. Skeat, has more recently proposed a different theory to account for the early and unusual prevalence of the codex in Christian circles.[62] Setting the Gospel of Mark aside, Roberts and Skeat begin by observing that in Judaism, in spite of a proscription against committing the oral Torah to writing, there is evidence that individual halachic decisions were occasionally noted for private study on wax tablets and possibly in papyrus codices.[63] Given this precedent, they suppose that primitive Christians may have used wax tablets to transcribe "the Oral Law as pronounced by Jesus, and that these tablets might have developed into a primitive form of codex."[64] They further suggest that when and as a collection of dominical sayings evolved into a full-blown narrative Gospel, that Gospel may well have been transcribed in a codex, thus perpetuating the format of earlier materials. Since such a Gospel would have had substantial authority, the argument goes, it could have served to establish in Christian usage the codex form in which it was known. In this revised view, the Christian use of the papyrus codex need not be related to the parchment codex or to Rome but could have arisen independently in a Christian setting with a strong Jewish heritage and constituency. Antioch, they venture, is the likely location of that Christian community.[65]

This revised theory is less objectionable than the first only because it is less specific, but its general conjectures are still not plausible. To prove the use of papyrus codices in Judaism, Roberts and Skeat simply misinterpret some late and sketchy notices.[66] Further, to draw an analogy between the sayings of Jesus and oral Torah disregards the great difference between them in content, form, setting, and aim. Moreover, the idea that Jesus' teachings were originally inscribed on tablets, let alone papyrus codices, is completely speculative. Roberts and Skeat acknowledge that the use of tablets for writing elements of oral Torah did not result in any use of the codex in Judaism but counter that whereas in Judaism the use of rolls was "rooted in tradition and prescribed by the Law," Christians felt no such scruples.[67] Surely this underestimates the Jewish self-consciousness of first-century Jewish-Christians in Palestine and Syria. In any case, it would be deeply incongruous if Christians had felt bound by informal conventions governing the writing of oral Torah but not by the far stronger, formal Jewish convention of the roll book. Since the theory appeals to no particular document, Roberts' and Skeat's claims about the literary history or theological valuation of the sayings of Jesus simply hang in the air. In short, this explanation does not work. This does not mean, however, that a good hypothesis is not available.[68]

Though the theories of Roberts and Skeat are unconvincing, the basic assumption behind them is sound: there must have been a decisive, precedent-setting development in the publication and circulation of early Christian literature that rapidly established the codex in Christian use, and it is likely that this development had to do with the religious authority accorded to whatever Christian document(s) first came to be known in codex form. There are good reasons to think that this distinction belonged to an early edition of the letters of Paul.[69]

Roberts and Skeat tacitly assumed that nothing short of a Gospel-type document that evoked dominical authority could have predisposed Christians to the codex. Yet this is neither self-evident nor plausible. No known Gospel can be said to have attained by the early second century a fixed and general esteem over either oral tradition or other Gospel documents.[70] The situation is completely different with the letters of Paul. From the period of Paul's own activity and in accordance with his own aims, his letters were the documentary instruments of his apostolic teaching and authority throughout the Pauline mission field. Not only were Paul's letters, so far as we know, the earliest Christian writings, they were also the earliest to be valued, imitated, to circulate beyond their original recipients, and to be collected. Clement of Rome, Ignatius of Antioch, and Polycarp of Smyrna all attest that Paul's letters were known and used over a broad geographic area by the end of the first and the beginning of the second centuries.[71] Paul's letters were also the earliest Christian writings to be considered apostolic in origin and authority and the only ones with a clear prima facie claim to that distinction. It is not surprising, therefore, to find that they were the first Christian writings to receive the epithet of "scripture" (2 Pet. 3.15–16). Hence, if it is a question what early Christian document(s) had the religious authority and breadth of circulation to establish the codex as the form of the Christian book by the early second century, the letters of Paul must be considered first. Indeed, in the relevant period they have no rivals. If, however, these observations are suggestive, of themselves they prove nothing, and more particular points must be adduced.

The origins of the collected Pauline letters are obscure. Though theories about the agents, motives, shape, and provenance of the collection are diverse, there is broad agreement that a more or less full collection had come into existence by the late years of the first century.[72] There is no direct evidence about the content and order of the earliest collection, but important conclusions can be reached through a careful evaluation of later evidence.

During the second century there were two distinct editions of the collected letters of Paul. One was the edition used by Marcion, which consisted of ten letters of Paul arranged in the order Galatians, 1–2 Corinthians, Romans, 1–2 Thessalonians, Loadiceans (=Ephesians), Colossians, Philippians, and Philemon.[73] The other edition lies behind most early Greek manuscripts, including the earliest extant manuscript of Paul's collected letters, P 46, which is dated about 200 C.E. This edition offered the letters in a different order: Romans, Corinthians (1–2), Ephesians, Galatians, Philippians, Colossians, and Thessalonians (1–2). Manuscripts with this arrangement normally also include, after the letters to churches, the "personal letters," given in the order Timothy (1–2), Titus, and Philemon, although the letters to individuals probably did not originally belong to this edition, with the probable exception of Philemon.[74] The order of the letters in this edition (with or without the personal letters) is one of decreasing length, Romans being the longest and standing at the head, 1 Corinthians being the next longest and standing second, and so on. Both of these editions were already current by the middle of the second century. This is obvious for the edition of Marcion and hardly less so for the edition attested by P 46, which certainly did not originate in Egypt and which must have undergone development in order to include Hebrews.

There is also evidence, though less direct, of yet a third early edition of the letters of Paul. There is an old theory, mentioned in a number of ancient Christian sources, that the apostle had written to seven churches and that therefore, because the number seven symbolized totality or universality, Paul had addressed the church at large.[75] This idea almost certainly rests on an actual early edition of the letters that presented them as "letters to seven churches." Although no seven-churches edition has been preserved, we find its traces whenever the letters are enumerated by decreasing length, with letters to the same community reckoned as one unit: Corinthians, Romans, Ephesians,

Thessalonians, Galatians, Philippians, and Colossians (Philemon?).[76] This is an order of decreasing length because the two Corinthian letters are taken together as one length unit, and so also are the two Thessalonian letters. If Philemon were included, it would have been taken together with Colossians. Reckoning length in this way places the emphasis not upon the number of *letters* Paul wrote, but on the number of *churches* to which he wrote. This enumeration firmly indicates that there was once an edition of Paul's letters that contained ten letters presented as they are addressed: to exactly seven churches. This edition must go back to a very early time and indeed has the best claim to have been the most ancient edition of the Pauline letter collection.[77] Several observations serve to substantiate this.

First, an edition of Paul's correspondence as "letters to seven churches" is closely related to a problem that the ancient church had with Paul's letters, namely, their narrow particularity.[78] Paul wrote to individual Christian congregations about matters that were of immediate and local interest to them. This made it difficult for other congregations to appreciate the value and authority of the letters for them. How could such letters be relevant and useful to other churches even though they were written by an apostle? The textual tradition of Paul's letters preserves indications of an early, certainly first-century, effort to overcome the problem by deleting or generalizing the addresses of some of the letters and sometimes by omitting other locally specific matter as well, thus mechanically conferring on Paul's particular letters the appearance of general letters.[79] This was not, however, a really satisfactory solution, for the particularity of most of Paul's letters was too extensive to be obscured through textual emendation. An edition that presented the letters as written to seven churches solved the problem in another way: it demonstrated the universal value of Paul's letters in the form of the collection itself. Thus the problem of particularity was at once embraced and overcome. An edition of this type, then, is closely linked to a problem that arose in the first century, when the letters first began to circulate among churches to which they had not been addressed. This fact argues for its early date.

Second, although it is beyond my immediate purpose to argue for a genetic relation between all three editions of the collection attested for the second century, there is persuasive evidence of such a relation between two of them, namely, the edition used by Marcion and the seven-churches edition.[80] In the edition used by Marcion the letters are not arranged by decreasing length, for Galatians stands at the beginning, and Laodiceans (=Ephesians) follows the Thessalonian letters. Nevertheless, with these exceptions, the order of Marcion's corpus *is* governed by decreasing length if the two Corinthian letters are taken together as one length-unit and the two Thessalonian letters as another.[81] Since the principle of decreasing length is not consistently followed and has no constitutive significance for the edition used by Marcion, the presence of its clear vestiges reveals the indebtedness of Marcion's edition to an earlier one that did adhere to this principle. And, since the two Corinthian letters were taken to form one length-unit and the two Thessalonian letters to form another, the earlier edition must have given special emphasis to the *number of communities* addressed by Paul and hence must have been an edition of Paul's letters to seven churches.[82] The edition used by Marcion did not contain the pastoral Epistles (1–2 Timothy, Titus). With the exception of Philemon, it consisted of community letters only, and Philemon, strictly speaking, is not a private letter because it too is addressed to a community. It is not only possible but probable that in Marcion's collection Philemon did not stand at the end as a private letter but followed Colossians and preceded Philippians, so that Colossians and Philemon were construed as companion letters addressed to the same community, like the Corinthian and the Thessalonian letters.[83] Thus the edition used by Marcion has every appearance of being a modified form of an older edition, an edition shaped by the idea that Paul wrote to precisely seven churches and in which the letters were arranged in a sequence of decreasing length.[84] If this edition was older than Marcion's time, it was early indeed and must go back to the beginning of the second century at the latest.

Third, it is intriguing that at the end of the first century and the beginning of the next there appeared in Christian circles two other groups of letters addressed to seven churches: the letters at the beginning of the Apocalypse (2:1–3:22) and the letters of Ignatius of Antioch. The group of seven letters in the Apocalypse is a literary creation of its author, while the group of seven letters of Ignatius is an editorial creation of Polycarp. Neither is an imitation of the other, but if their appearance in the same general area and period is not a mighty coincidence, each may well reflect an early edition of the Pauline letters presented as a collection of letters to seven churches.[85]

There is therefore substantial evidence that in the early second century (and probably earlier), there was a collection of ten Pauline letters arranged on the principle of decreasing length and counting together letters addressed to the same community, thus emphasizing that Paul had written to seven churches. Because of its interest in demonstrating Paul's catholicity and because it seems to be presupposed by the edition Marcion used, this collection may be taken as the most primitive edition of the letters of the apostle.[86]

Now I can raise the question of immediate interest: in what kind of book was this edition of the Pauline letters published? The two outstanding features of the primitive edition of Paul's letters were, first, its emphasis on the number of churches addressed by Paul, and second, its arrangement of the letters by decreasing length. Neither feature could have been established or sustained unless the letters were contained in a *single* book. If the edition had consisted of a group of codices or rolls, even so small a group as two, it could not have signified Paul's catholic relevance, for nothing would prevent the individual codices or rolls from being taken separately and the sevenfold disposition of the letters thus being obscured or lost. Likewise, the order of the letters from longest to shortest would have been equally insecure, since the individual codices or rolls could have been reordered. The very nature of this edition therefore required its presentation as a physical unit, a single book. Yet was this book a codex or a roll?

Theoretically it could have been a roll, since a papyrus roll of any length could be constructed. As we have seen, however, a roll longer than eleven meters was cumbersome, and most were somewhat shorter. If the ten Pauline letters had been inscribed in a roll, what length roll would have been required? This question is not easy to answer because of transcriptional variables: the size of script, the height of the upper and lower margins, the width of intercolumniations, and the height of the roll itself would all have a bearing. Even so, it is possible to make a reasonable estimate. Theodore C. Skeat, in trying to determine the cost differential between a roll and a codex has derived figures that are useful for my purpose.[87] Taking the oldest extensive manuscript of the Pauline letters, P 46, as a basis, assuming the same size script, the same number of letters to the line, and the same number of lines to a column, he calculated an average column width of 1½ centimeters. Multiplying this by the number of columns (208), and adding 207 intercolumniations estimated at two centimeters each, Skeat arrived at the figure of 2,806 centimeters as the length of a papyrus roll required for the transcription of the text of P 46. If we deduct the space required by the text of Hebrews, which is found in P 46 but did not belong to the primitive edition, then the seven-churches edition of Paul's letters would have required a roll approximately twenty-four meters (eighty feet) long, which would have been more than double the maximum length of Greek rolls and roughly three times what may be regarded as a normal length. Because the length of rolls was determined by custom and convenience, a roll of such extent is extremely unlikely. For a book intended to be read and studied and thus regularly handled, as an edition of Paul's letters assuredly was, a roll of such length is plainly inconceivable.[88] If Paul's letters were transcribed in a single book, as the features of the earliest recoverable edition required, that book must have been a codex, not a roll.[89]

It is only in connection with a seven-churches edition of the Pauline letters that we can find in the early history of Christian literature both the materials and a motive that might have conspired to suggest the use of a codex rather than a roll. It is also only in connection with the letters of Paul that we can see by the early second century an esteem for the authority of any Christian documents sufficient to have promoted the codex into prominence as the appropriate medium of Christian literature. This coming together of transcriptional need and religious authority in the Pauline letter collection and nowhere else makes it nearly certain that the codex was introduced into Christian usage as the vehicle of a primitive edition of the *corpus Paulinum*.

On this hypothesis the adoption of the codex by early Christianity was neither circumstantial nor arbitrary, but a careful decision based upon the advantages of the codex for the text at hand. One advantage was its comprehensiveness, which permitted, as a roll would not, the transcription of all the letters in a single book so that both the number and the order of the letters could be firmly established. Another was what is commonly called ease of reference but might better be termed the capacity of the codex for *random access,* as distinct from the *sequential access* offered by the roll.[90] It is not easy to suppose that a narrative like a Gospel should have first been published in a codex. A Gospel was brief enough to be easily contained in a roll of normal length, and as a narrative it was meant to be read from beginning to end. For this, the codex offered no advantage over the roll. It is unlikely, however, that a sequential reading was ever envisioned for the Pauline letters, save individually in their original settings. As a group they have no necessary sequence but could be and certainly were read and studied selectively. Their availability in a codex permitted easy access to any part of the collection. On no other hypothesis would the unique features of the codex be so clearly an advantage as they are in the case of an edition of Paul's letters.[91]

In arguing that it was the Gospel of Mark that was first given out as a codex, C. H. Roberts commented that "the circle in which [Mark] moved in Rome—Jewish and Gentile traders, small businessmen, freedmen or slaves—would use wax-tablets or parchment notebooks for their accounts, their correspondence, their legal and official business, and it would be natural that St. Mark should use the same format for a work intended to be copied but not to be published as the ancient world understood publication."[92] Of course, we do not in fact know this about the author of the Gospel of Mark, whose identity and circle are completely obscure. We do, however, know it about Paul, thanks to recent investigations of his social circumstances and the social composition of the Pauline congregations.[93] The codex, whether of parchment or papyrus, would have been familiar to a small businessman like Paul and to the circles in which he moved. We cannot know in what medium his letters left his hand (or the hand of his amanuensis), but it is conceivable that they were written in small codices.[94]

However that may be, it is striking that the first mention of parchment codices in a Greek writing occurs in a letter belonging to the Pauline tradition: in 2 Tim. 4:13, Timothy is requested to "bring the cloak that I left with Carpus at Troas, also the books, and above all the parchments *(kai ta biblia, malista tas membranas)*" [RSV translation]. *Membranai* means "parchment codex." There are two problems in the interpretation of the last phrase in this statement, however. First, it is not clear whether the sense is: (a) "The books, especially the parchments *[tas membranas],*" or (b) "the books, that is, the parchments *[tas membranas].*" The former is the standard sense of the Greek and ought to be preferred.[95] Yet more important is the question of precisely how the term *membranai* should be taken: Does it mean parchment notebooks (in codex form) or codices (of texts)? The difference is not of form but of use: are the membranai regarded, according to their traditional Roman use, as mere notebooks of memorandums, or are they regarded, in accordance with the use of the term by Martial, as codices containing actual texts? Here the latter is certainly to be preferred, since, no matter how the first problem is resolved, the membranai are classified as *ta biblia,* that is, as actual books. Since 2 Timothy is undoubtedly a pseudonymous composition, we must regard this particular notice either as contrived for verisimilitude by the author, or as an element of an authentic Pauline fragment that was incorporated into the letter for the same purpose.[96] In either case the statement reveals that within the Pauline literary and theological tradition there was an established association between the apostle and the codex. Whoever wrote 2 Timothy "felt that mentioning the membranai which the author claims to have left in Troas would strike his fellow Christians as a genuinely Pauline detail."[97]

To claim that the most primitive edition of the Pauline letter collection was put out in a codex and that it was the religious authority of Paul's collected letters that set the standard for the transcription of subsequent Christian literature in codices is not to claim that this marked the first use of the codex in Christian circles. It is possible, perhaps likely, that the codex was first employed in primitive Christianity for collections of texts (testimonia) from Jewish scripture. Judging from the predominantly atomistic citation of Jewish scripture in earliest Christianity, this would not have been a matter of producing continuous transcriptions of Jewish scriptural books, but rather of compiling excerpta, that is, selective proof-texts or testimonia.[98] To record such compilations in a codex would have been in keeping with the ordinary use of the codex as a notebook. But even if this were done, it would not have marked a decisive step toward the use of the codex for a (continuous) literary text. Rather, that step appears to have been taken, as I have argued, in connection with the letters of Paul.

It cannot be persuasively argued that early Christianity "invented" the codex, nor that Christians were the first to use it for something more than notes. The evidence shows only that Christians adopted the codex in preference to the roll as a medium for literature sooner and more decisively than their contemporaries and so promoted its popularity.[99] That they did so says something important about the uses and functions of early Christian writings.

As I have noted, among the non-Christian manuscripts that can be dated to the second century the codex is poorly represented in comparison with the roll. It is worth seeing, nevertheless, what these early non-Christian codices can tell us.[100] Of the seventeen Greek codices that come into consideration, eleven are literary texts, while six are what may appropriately be called professional manuals—grammatical, lexical, and medical handbooks. It may well be that several of the literary texts in this group were working copies for educational use and so also fall into the category of professional manuals.[101] Thus, the early non-Christian evidence suggests an essentially utilitarian attitude toward the codex even when it is employed as the medium for a text, that is, as an actual book and not merely as a notebook. This ought not surprise us, since the original function of the codex as an instrument for recording ephemera was altogether practical, but it does indicate an intermediate stage in the developing use of the codex. We should not imagine that the codex moved directly and immediately from the status of a notebook to that of a book. Rather, what began as a utilitarian notebook came to serve as a utilitarian book, which eventually gained regard as a book proper and a genuine peer of the roll.

It is to this intermediate phase in the evolving status of the codex—in the late first and early second centuries—that the earliest Christian books belong. It is misleading to suppose that the Christian step was to employ the codex for the transcription of literature. The Christians who made them and made use of them did not regard them either as notebooks or as books of fine literature. Neither did they intend a bibliographic innovation nor aim to distinguish Christian books from pagan or Jewish books. These were, to be sure, consequences of the early use Christians made of the codex, and as consequences they are clear enough in retrospect. Still, the historian must guard against the temptation to identify results with reasons, a temptation to which students of the problem have been especially vulnerable. It is more probable that the early Christians adapted a familiar, practical medium for a new but still practical purpose. Christian texts came to be inscribed in codices not because they enjoyed a special status as aesthetic or cult objects, but because they were practical books for everyday use: the handbooks, as it were, of the Christian community.

THE CONSTRUCTION AND INSCRIPTION OF EARLY CHRISTIAN BOOKS

The practical nature of early Christian books is indicated not only by the choice of the codex but by features of their construction and inscription as well. Judging from the extant examples, they were books of relatively small size. Although there is some variation, they range between twenty and twenty-five centimeters in height and ten and fifteen centimeters in breadth. These dimensions were typical of codices made of papyrus. They took a rectangular shape, the height being about twice the breadth. Parchment codices, however, tended to be square.[102] The height of a papyrus codex was limited by the height of the roll from which the sheets were cut, while the height of a parchment codex was not. Though a papyrus codex could be made as broad as one wished by cutting a longer sheet from a roll, the tendency was clearly to cut the sheets more or less to the square.

Most early papyrus codices are constructed on the single-quire method; that is, one set of sheets is stacked, folded vertically at the center, and stitched along (rather than immediately in) the fold to form one large gathering. The multiple-quire method, by which smaller sets of sheets (as many as twelve but usually four) were stacked and folded and the smaller gatherings then stacked and stitched together, is also known in some early codices but is less common. Generally, it would appear that the single-quire method, being simpler and within certain limits perfectly functional, was the earliest method of constructing a papyrus codex.[103] A single-quire codex has deficiencies. It is limited in scope: no more than about fifty sheets (yielding a hundred leaves and two hundred pages) could be conveniently used in this way. The more sheets used, the greater the stress at the stitching along the fold, the more the closed codex tended to spring open, and the more the central leaves protruded at the fore edge when the codex was closed. With fewer sheets these problems were manageable.

The earliest Christian books, then, were not capacious. The largest of the Christian single-quire papyrus codices are the Chester Beatty codex of the Pauline epistles (P 46), which originally ran to 208 pages; and the Chester Beatty codices (IX–X) of Ezekiel, Daniel, Susanna, and Esther, which had 236 pages; of Numbers and Deuteronomy (VI), which had 216; and of Isaiah (VII), which had 224. Single-quire Christian codices, however, were usually smaller than these: P 47 contained the Apocalypse in 46 pages, P 52 contained the Gospel of John in 130 pages, and P 5 had the Gospel of John in 100 pages. The multiple-quire papyrus codex was not unknown for Christian books at an early time: P 66 (the Gospel of John), and P 4 + 64 + 67 (the Gospels of Matthew and Luke) both come from the second century. Up to a point, there appears to be no correlation between the manner of construction (single versus multiple quire) and the intended scope of content: P 75 had the Gospels of John and Luke in a single quire of 144 pages, whereas P 66 used multiple quires to contain the Gospel of John in 156 pages. Only when a book of much more than two hundred pages was wanted did it become necessary to consider the advantages of multiple-quire construction. Though it is not the earliest Christian codex to be made up in multiple quires, P 45, containing the four Gospels and Acts in about 440 pages, is the earliest (third-century) one whose content could not have been accommodated in a single quire.

The large majority of Christian codices in the earliest period contain the text of only a single document. With the exception of the letters of Paul, the practice of collecting discrete texts within a single codex was limited. Normally, each document was physically a book unto itself and not a very long one. Therefore, though multiple quires might be used, the single quire sufficed and was the norm for the

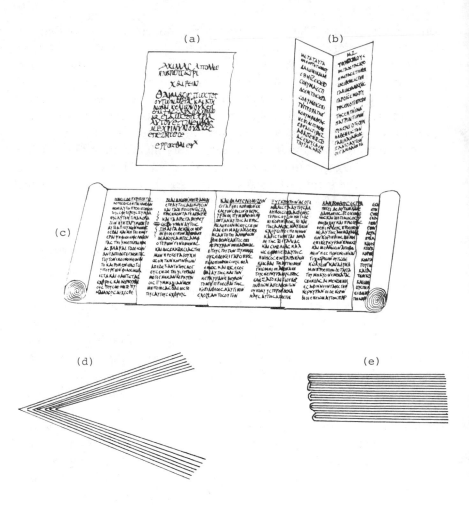

2.

A. A single sheet of papyrus used to write a letter.

B. A single sheet of papyrus folded vertically at its center (used to make a papyrus codex).

C. An open papyrus roll inscribed in columns, with the vertical lines indicating the joins *(kolleseis)* of single sheets of papyrus.

D. End-on view of a single-quire codex.

E. End-on view of a multiple-quire codex.

Drawings A, B, and C, by W. E. H. Cockle, are from E. G. Turner, *The Typology of the Early Codex* (Philadelphia: University of Pennsylvania Press, 1977), 45.

earliest Christian books. Hence, when we envision these books we must think of them as pamphlets, not as tomes (see fig. 2).

I have said that the papyrus roll was sometimes furnished with a parchment sheath for protection. The codex could also be given a cover, though of a different sort. No codex of the first three centuries has been preserved with its cover.[104] A dearth of evidence on this point has now been richly remedied by the discovery of the Nag Hammadi codices, generally dated to the mid–fourth century, of which eleven survived with their covers intact. These covers are usually made of leather, mainly sheepskin, each cut in a single sheet of slightly larger dimensions than the sheets of papyrus used for the codex, with the hair side on the exterior. The leading edge of the front of the cover extends to form a flap (triangular or rectangular) that overlaps the edge of the back when the codex is closed, and to this extension is attached a thong to be wrapped around the closed codex. Shorter thongs at the top and bottom were tied for further security. The skin was stiffened by gluing layers of discarded papyrus on the inside, folding the edges of the skin over it, and pasting a fresh piece of papyrus over the stiffener and folded edges. The cover was further strengthened by gluing an additional strip of leather along the length of the spine on the inside. Cordlike thongs extending from the spine were passed through the papyrus sheets to secure the codex within the cover.[105] These covers, which look more like leather envelopes than modern book bindings, may not be taken as representative of codex covers in general. Other and less well-worked covers, sometimes consisting of wooden boards linked at the spine with the codex glued in, were also used.[106] Like covers for rolls, covers were probably not always provided for codices, and when they were, the type of cover probably depended on the preferences of the owner and the value of the text.

Equally interesting for my purposes are the inscriptional features of early Christian books. Christian or not, papyrus codices were usually inscribed in one broad column for each page. This contrasts with the tall narrow columns in which rolls were traditionally written, and the reason is obvious: the relatively narrow page of the papyrus codex did not readily accommodate two columns of writing.[107] Parchment codices, however, with their more nearly square pages, were usually inscribed with two columns a page. The difference in the relative dimensions of the page between the papyrus and the parchment codex is a necessary condition of these different methods of inscription. The actual cause of the narrower double columns typical of parchment codices would seem rather to lie in the conservatism of scribes, who whenever possible followed the conventions developed in connection with the roll, even when they were writing in a codex. To the extent that tall, narrow columns were regarded by scribes as the proper format of the literary roll, it is plausible that "scribes who copied on a codex of papyrus in a single column were aware that they were writing a second-class book."[108] Here we may see a correlative of the evolutionary development of the codex from notebook to book. For Greek and Latin literature the codex achieved parity with the roll only in the fourth century, and when it did so it was principally the codex made of parchment, which was inscribed much as rolls had been. Earlier, however, when the roll persisted as the vehicle of literature and papyrus appears to have been the ordinary material of the codex, the method of inscription reflected the lower status of the codex: though not a notebook, neither was its format literary.

Inscription has to do not only with format but also with the character of the script. Roberts commented that the varieties of ancient scribal hands are "easier to recognize than to define,"[109] and paleography is truly an art as much as a science. Yet the paleographer is less concerned with the hands of individual scribes than with types of script, and since scribes were trained professionals, the scripts they used were largely standardized within certain periods. Only occasionally is it possible to discriminate individual hands within a given type. Within my period of study there are two fundamental types of writing, the bookhand and the documentary hand. In extreme examples the differences between these scripts are easily recognized, but manuscripts show an enormous range of gradations between the two, and an absolute dividing line cannot be drawn. The bookhand was normally employed, as the name indicates, for well-produced books of literary content. It is a careful script, characterized by well-formed, separated, and upright letters evenly maintained along the line and rarely extended above or below it. Its clarity, regularity, and impersonality render it both beautiful and highly legible. The documentary hand, by comparison, was for everyday purposes. More rapidly written than the bookhand, this cursive script is characterized by simplified and less careful letter formation, the frequent use of ligatures (strokes connecting or combining letters without lifting the pen between them), and the extension of certain letters well above or below the writing line. Lacking the stately elegance of literary script, the documentary hand is merely legible, neither well adapted to reading nor artistic in its appearance. It is natural to assume that a book written in a formal bookhand was more expensive than one written in a documentary hand, for the bookhand required more time and greater skill. And indeed there is evidence that scribes were paid not merely according to the unit of writing but also according to the quality of the script.[110]

Although early Christian manuscripts display considerable differences in the quality of their inscription, a fine bookhand is rarely found in Christian texts before the fourth century. In earlier Christian manuscripts we find instead a script of the "informal round" type that has sometimes been called reformed documentary.[111] As the name suggests, this type of hand finds its closest affinity not in literary texts but in the documentary papyri. It is a work-a-day rather than artistic script, yet it is "reformed" in that it shows some aspiration toward a bookhand, particularly in its more careful letter formation and somewhat more limited use of ligatures than the ordinary documentary hand. Other "documentary" features of early Christian manuscripts may be seen in the habit of using letters for numerical values instead of writing out numbers in full, as was the rule in literary works,[112] and in the tendency to enlarge slightly the initial letters of a page or section or occasionally to extend them into the margin.[113] Because it aims less at beauty than at higher legibility, this hand suggests an interest in the content of the text that is more or less indifferent to its appearance. Here too, perhaps, the status of the codex in Christian use is revealed in the use of a script that is practical and legible, that by no means approaches a calligraphic bookhand, and yet restricts the tendencies toward documentary scrawl (see figs. 3 and 4).

Apart from the type of hand characteristic of early Christian manuscripts, there is the question of the quality of their transcription, that is, the level of accuracy with which the scribes accomplished their work. Errors of transcription are inevitable in any hand-copied text, given the various psychological and mechanical operations involved.[114] A scribe's inadvertent departures from his exemplar tend to be typical: almost all scribes make the same kinds of mistakes for the same kinds of reasons. Even in the most carefully transcribed manuscript there will be instances of omission, addition, transposition, and, of course, misspelling. Sometimes scribes made intentional changes in the text as they copied, undertaking to improve the language or to clarify the sense, assuming that they were rectifying the error of a previous scribe. Scribal mistakes occur as often in Christian as in other hand-copied books, and indeed in the early period they were frequent. In addition to the general liability of scribes to error, early Christian texts held some particular inducements, especially to intentional changes. For example, the often closely parallel accounts among

3. A page of Codex Vaticanus (fourth century) showing the conclusion of 2 Thess. and the beginning of Hebrews. This parchment codex is written in three tall, narrow columns to the page, with forty-two lines to the column, and illustrates the regular and well-formed letters of a professional bookhand. From B. M. Metzger, *Manuscripts of the Greek Bible* (Oxford: Oxford University Press, 1981), 75.

4. A page of P 75, a Christian papyrus codex of the early third century, giving the text of Luke 16:9–21. The text is written in an "informal round" script in one broad column to the page. From B. M. Metzger, *Manuscripts of the Greek Bible* (Oxford: Oxford University Press, 1981), 69.

the Gospels led many a scribe to harmonize the text of one with the text of another. Inexact quotations of Jewish scripture in Christian texts were often conformed to the Septuagint. Some alterations were made for theological reasons, the scribe revising elements of the text that were doctrinally problematic.[115]

The study of scribal habits is important for textual criticism in its effort to determine the original text of documents.[116] It also sheds light on the nature of early Christian book production in which the scribe was an important agent and, in the earliest period, usually the only one. There is among early Christian manuscripts an enormous variety in the quality of transcription, and in part this reflects the diverse capacities and habits of individual scribes. It is one question how well-trained a scribe was, but another how he applied himself to his task. Some scribes of Christian manuscripts were scrupulous and copied their models faithfully. Others, though they may have been capable of good work, indulged a carelessness that suggests they were not professionally engaged or else did not consider themselves to be writing a high-quality book.[117] The number of corruptions in the earliest manuscripts indicates that during the first several centuries these texts were widely circulated and frequently copied and that Christian books were not reproduced under highly controlled conditions. This conclusion is borne out by the fact that the great majority of textual variants in those documents that were ultimately included in the New Testament appear to have arisen by about 200 C.E. The relatively free transmission of early Christian texts, which resulted in a proliferation of individual variants and diverse textual traditions, may indicate a greater interest in making these texts available than in the strict accuracy of their transcription.

There are, however, some interesting and important inscriptional peculiarities that belong to Christian manuscripts. In his meticulous examination of early codices, both Christian and non-Christian, E. G. Turner discerned a tendency in early Christian manuscripts for the scribe to write fewer lines to the page and fewer letters to the line than was usual. Turner thought this was not accidental, but aimed to facilitate the *public* reading of Christian texts before the development of large format codices in the fourth century.[118] The relative frequency with which accents, punctuation, and breathing marks occur in Christian manuscripts, compared with the larger run of ancient literary texts, corroborates a special interest in public reading.[119]

A more noticeable and extremely widespread peculiarity in the inscription of early Christian books is the phenomenon of the *nomina sacra*, the scribal convention of contracting the written form of a number of words, most but not all of them names, which have particular religious significance.[120] The terms were contracted in various ways: by writing only the first and last letters, or the first two and the last, or the first and last two, or the first and last syllables. A horizontal line was always drawn over these letters to indicate that a contraction had been made and that the word could not be pronounced as written. Fifteen terms were commonly subject to this practice in early Christian manuscripts, and these can be subdivided into three groups according to the frequency of their contraction: God, Jesus, Christ, Lord; Spirit, Man, Cross; Father, Son, Savior, Mother, Heaven, Israel, David, Jerusalem. Only the four in the first group were consistently contracted. The remaining terms were less frequently treated as nomina sacra, but those of the second group were nevertheless common.

No early Christian writer alludes to this transcriptional practice, and we can only conjecture its origin and purpose. It is found in the majority of manuscripts and appears fully developed in the earliest manuscripts available.[121] The earliest evidence of it, however, is not paleographic. The author of the Epistle of Barnabas, writing near the beginning of the second century, was acquainted with the system of nomina sacra. He discovers (9.8) in the number of Abraham's companions, 318 (Gen. 14:14), a prefiguration both of the cross and of Jesus. This may well presuppose that in his Greek manuscript of Genesis the number 318 was not written out in full *(triakosious deka kai okto)* but was represented by Greek letters used as numbers: tau, iota and eta. The tau (=300), he took as a symbol of the cross, and the iota + eta (=18) as a suspended (rather than contracted) form of the name Jesus. Hence the author knew at least the convention of treating the name Jesus as a *nomen sacrum*.

No theory of the origin and significance of the system of nomina sacra has yet commanded general assent. There is broad agreement that it has something to do with Jewish reverence for the Tetragram, the name of God, but it has proved difficult to say exactly what. Among Jews the piety that forbade pronunciation of the divine name did not necessarily extend to the way the name was written, but it did in some cases. In writing Hebrew biblical texts, Jewish scribes usually wrote the name in the normal way, though it was the custom when reading the texts to pronounce a surrogate, ordinarily *adoni*, "the Lord," instead of the Tetragram. This eventually gave rise to the practice in vocalized Masoretic manuscripts of the eighth century C.E. and later of attaching the vowels of adoni to the consonants of the Tetragram.[122] In the earlier tradition of the strictly consonantal transcription of Hebrew, however, there are numerous manuscripts in which the name is transcribed in diverse but conspicuous ways, clearly showing that reverence for the divine name had consequences in scribal usages as well as in pronunciation.[123]

Most directly relevant to the issue of the Christian nomina sacra is the way the divine name was treated in Greek manuscripts of Jewish scripture. Judging from the few identifiably Jewish manuscripts of the Septuagint that survive, it appears to have been customary to write the divine name in Hebrew or Aramaic characters, even in the midst of the Greek text (or, infrequently, to transliterate it with the Greek letters IAO).[124] Here, then, the sanctity of the name had transcriptional consequences. It was, of course, the Greek version of the Jewish scriptures that was the Bible of the early church. Within the increasingly and soon almost exclusively Gentile, Greek-speaking constituency of Christianity, texts rendering the divine name in Hebrew characters were anomalous at best and meaningless at worst. So it is not surprising that early Christian copies of Jewish scripture did not follow the Jewish transcriptional practice but rendered the Tetragram with the Greek words *theos* and *kyrios*, yet in the contracted forms *ths* and *ks*. This is peculiar, if only because neither Jews nor Christians would have attached to the Greek words *theos* or *kyrios* the special reverence belonging to the Tetragram, and much less would they have had scruples about pronouncing these words. Hence, the special way of writing these terms is perplexing.

An elaborate explanation of the nomina sacra has been offered by Roberts. To account for its early and widespread occurrence, he suggested that it must have originated early in the apostolic period (before 70 C.E.) and was probably devised by the primitive Jewish Christian community in Jerusalem. This community, he argued, embraced a mystical "theology of the Name," a theology, he claimed, that lay behind and was implicit in the scribal convention of transcribing certain terms in contracted form.[125] For all its ingenuity, this explanation is unconvincing. We know little about the theology of primitive Jerusalemite Christianity, and the evidence that it took a strong interest in the divine name is extremely slim. Moreover, by reaching so far back to find a sufficiently authoritative source for the nomina sacra, Roberts put himself in the awkward position of claiming that a scribal convention known only in Greek manuscripts was established in and by an Aramaic-speaking community, and this in a period before the composition of any known Christian literature.

Simpler explanations are available. Schuyler Brown has argued that it is a mistake to correlate the Christian nomina sacra and the Jewish reverence for the divine name too closely and that the Christian phenomenon is strictly scribal and has nothing to do with pronunciation. He thinks that when Christian scribes copying manuscripts of the Greek version of Jewish scriptures came across the divine name in Hebrew, they substituted the Greek equivalent, *kyrios,* but retained the function of the Hebrew term to distinguish the sacred name from the rest of the text. They did so by writing *kyrios* in a contracted form and drawing a line above it. In doing so, Brown urges, they were merely calling into service a documentary technique of secular scribes who sometimes contracted names and titles.[126] Subsequently, because in early Christianity *kyrios* was used of both God and Jesus, the practice of contraction was extended in both directions, to *theos* on the one hand and to *Iesous* and *Christos* on the other. The problem with this explanation is that the evidence is poor for contractions (as distinct from abbreviations) in secular documents, and there is none for the use of a superscriptive stroke. Yet there is no reason why the Christian method of writing divine names should have had an exact religious or secular analogue. The ability to set off the divine name in Christian manuscripts of Septuagintal texts, not by continuing to write it in Hebrew as Jews did but in some other way, must have occurred early to Greek-speaking Christian scribes copying Jewish manuscripts. The contracted forms of *theos* and *kyrios* probably derive, as G. Howard supposes, from Gentile Christians who, lacking the support of the Jewish tradition for retaining the Tetragram in (Greek) Christian copies of Jewish texts, adopted instead clearly designated contractions of Greek equivalents "out of deference to the Jewish Christians, to mark the sacredness of the divine name which stood behind these surrogates."[127] The principle, used at first with respect to texts of Jewish scripture, would have been extended under christological warrants to the further names, Jesus and Christ, in Christian documents. The still broader application of the practice to various other terms may have followed once the original significance of the first contractions had been lost.

Although the origin and meaning of the nomina sacra may never be fully explained, the mere fact of them is instructive for my purpose. Abbreviations (as distinct from contractions) were common in secular documentary texts but rare in well-written literary texts. In literary texts they occur only in working copies, objects of study. The use of nomina sacra may therefore be another pointer to the practical character of Christian texts. Further, the occurrence of this convention in Christian manuscripts is a clear indication that the transcription of early Christian books was not farmed out to the professional book trade but was done in-house by Christians themselves.[128] Again, early Christian books were not written to a high professional standard. Christian communities, except perhaps the smallest and most provincial, included persons who were competent to transcribe books, and only a few Christian manuscripts before the fourth century show a hand that approaches the professional bookhand. In addition to the relatively few educated members of a congregation, there may also have been some slaves trained for scribal tasks or professional scribes experienced especially in documentary work.[129] But even small-business-persons accustomed to dealing with records would have been able to write a clear, practical hand. The system of nomina sacra, though not an esoteric code, stands out as an in-group convention that expressed a community consciousness and presumed a particular readership.

In all, the inscription of early Christian books reflects the setting in which they were prepared and the purposes for which they were intended. They were neither private texts nor products of the trade, but books produced by and for the use of small Christian communities. Just as there is little to indicate that Christians had an aesthetic regard for their literature, neither do they seem to have had a cultic attitude toward their books, and in this the contrast with Judaism is noteworthy. Judging from rabbinic literature, Judaism followed strict procedures in the reproduction of the text of Torah. It was not permitted to transcribe Torah from dictation, but only by visual copying. Before the destruction of the Temple in 70 C.E. official copies had to be derived if not directly, then at least ultimately from an exemplar preserved in the Temple, and a high standard of scribal accuracy was required. There were detailed rules governing the type of material and the type of script that could be used.[130] Although there may be in such prescriptions an admixture of idealism, it cannot be doubted that in Judaism the construction and inscription of scriptural books were closely regulated enterprises rooted in deep reverence for the texts. In the case of early Christian books the situation is much different. There is a level of contingency in the transcription of scriptural texts that cannot be reconciled with the rigorous stipulations governing the production of Jewish scriptural books. Too much should not be made of this, however, because the regulations governing the transcription of the Hebrew text did not apply to the production of Septuagintal texts, and it was with these texts, used in hellenistic synagogues, that Christians were acquainted. Comparing Greek texts with Greek texts, the differences between Jewish and Christian copies of scripture are less apparent but still noticeable. When one compares copies of Septuagintal texts it is not always easy to distinguish the Jewish from the Christian, but on the whole Jewish manuscripts are better written. The transcription is more accurate, and the script is superior: Jewish manuscripts usually display an even, formal script with tendencies not only toward a bookhand but toward a somewhat decorated style with footed and serifed letters.[131]

It was not until the fourth century that Christian books began to be produced to a professional and literary bibliographic standard. This was in part because of the increasing popularity of the codex for non-Christian literary texts, which reduced the disparity of format, but more significantly it was the result of the establishment of Christianity as the religion of the empire. Obviously, this conferred a higher status and value on Christian texts than they had ever enjoyed before. It did not constitute them as literary, but it brought them fully into the public domain and put professional resources within easier reach. The new situation is illustrated in a letter that the emperor Constantine wrote to Eusebius, bishop of Caesarea, in 332, commissioning the production of new manuscripts of scripture:

> *Victor Constantius Maximus Augustus, to Eusebius: In that city which bears my name, by the assistance of God our Savior's providence, a vast multitude of men have joined themselves to the most holy Church. Whereas, then, all things there receive a very great increase, it seems quite necessary that there should be more churches erected in that city. Therefore do you most willingly accept what I have determined to do. For it seemed fit to signify to your prudence that you should order fifty copies of the divine scriptures, the provision and use of which you know to be chiefly necessary for the instruction of the Church, to be written on well-prepared parchment by copyists most skillful in the art of accurate and beautiful writing, which [copies] must be very legible and easily portable in order that they may be used. Moreover, letters have been dispatched to the chief financial officer of the diocese giving instructions that he should take care to provide everything necessary in order that the said copies might be completed. This, then, shall be your responsibility, to see that the written copies be provided forthwith.[132]*

Constantine obviously wanted books of first quality, professionally produced, and in no way inferior to the finest volumes of non-Christian literature, and he knew and furnished the resources of money and talent to get them.

It has sometimes been thought that the great biblical codices of the fourth century, Sinaiticus and Vaticanus, are surviving products of Constantine's requisition.[133] This is unlikely for several reasons. Constantine wanted the books to be produced quickly and to be easily portable, but neither could be expected if the books in question were whole Bibles. In any case, whole Bibles (pandects), including both the Christian Old Testament and the New Testament, were rare in the early centuries of the church. Indeed, there are no examples from the pre-Constantinian period of manuscripts containing even a complete New Testament, whose scope was still indeterminate. It is far more probable that the codices produced in the Caesarean scriptorium contained only the four Gospels rather than the whole New Testament or the entire Christian Bible.[134] Nevertheless, in the quality of their construction and inscription, if not in their scope, the codices Sinaiticus and Vaticanus at least suggest the kinds of books that Christianity began to produce and use in the fourth century: large codices inscribed on high-grade parchment in careful literary hands by accomplished scribes, laid out in three (Vaticanus) or four (Sinaiticus) narrow columns to the page, reminiscent of the manner in which literary rolls had been written. Never before had Christian books been so fine. A barrier was broken, though subsequent Christian manuscripts, even of the scriptures, did not usually measure up to this high standard.

Although the codex was early and strongly favored as the format of Christian literature, there are indications that not all early Christian texts were inscribed in codices. The author of the Apocalypse, who often speaks of books, describes in his first vision a heavenly book held in the right hand of the one who sits on the throne. The book is "written on the inside and sealed on the outside with seven seals" (5:1, *gegrammenon esothen kai opisthen katesphragismenon sphragisin hepta*) and thus is undoubtedly a roll book, though of a particular sort called a *diploma*.[135] A heavenly book in roll form is, of course, a conventional element of apocalyptic visions and as such need not be taken to reflect actual early Christian practice.[136] Certainly a specialized roll of this sort is not evidence of general Christian use. There are, to be sure, some extant pre-Constantinian Christian manuscripts that are rolls, but they are a small minority among Christian manuscripts of the period.[137] The existence of a late second-century roll of Irenaeus's *Against Heresies* (P. Oxy. 405) could suggest that works of scholarship, as distinct from scriptural texts, persisted for a while in roll form in Christian scholastic circles. In the *Acts of Peter*, composed in the late second century, there is an allusion (20) to Peter's rolling up a Gospel book. If this is not just an idiomatic reflex, it may imply that at least sometimes a scriptural book was in roll form. In the same period the *Acts of the Scillitan Martyrs* mentions a Christian who had "books and epistles of Paul" (12) in a capsa, which was normally a container for rolls.[138] Also, in some early Christian art we see figures depicted with rolls rather than codices,[139] but little can be made of this since ancient artists kept closely to traditional conventions. But if not every early Christian text was written in a codex, it would not contravene the evidence of the papyri that the codex was the heavily preferred form of the early Christian book well in advance of its broad adoption outside Christianity.

When in the late third and early fourth centuries the codex gained parity with the roll as the vehicle of Greek and Latin literature, eventually to displace the roll altogether, it was no doubt because the practical advantages of the codex had become widely recognized. The basis of this recognition must have been Christian use. Although the strong Christian preference for the codex was by then long-standing, it was only in the late third century, and still more powerfully in the fourth, that Christianity began to exert its influence within the mainstream of public life. Not least was this influence felt by well-educated users of books, a minority among whom Christians were increasingly numerous.[140] Such influence presupposes the wide currency of Christian books. The question of how Christian books attained their currency will be my concern in the following chapter.

THE PUBLICATION AND CIRCULATION OF EARLY CHRISTIAN LITERATURE

Among the papyri discovered in Egypt in the twentieth century are fragments from a manuscript of the treatise *Against Heresies*, which was composed about 180 C.E. by Irenaeus, bishop of Lugdunum (Lyons) in Gaul. The fragments are paleographically dated to the late years of the second century. Thus, within twenty years of its composition, this work had traversed the Mediterranean world to be read in provincial Egypt.[1] This is a striking example of the speed with which an early Christian text could be disseminated across the ancient world, but by no means the only one. *The Shepherd* of Hermas, composed in Rome near the mid–second century, was available in a late second-century manuscript in Egypt.[2] Still more surprising was the discovery in Egypt of a papyrus fragment of the Gospel of John datable to the early second century. Wherever this Gospel was written, it was certainly not in Egypt, and it was not composed until late in the first century; so again the discovery attests to the remarkably rapid and wide circulation of the text.[3] The appearance of these texts in the provincial regions of Middle and Upper Egypt, soon after they were composed though far-removed from their origins, poses interesting questions about the publication, circulation, and transmission of early Christian books.[4] Are they representative of early Christian literature in general? If so, what were the circumstances, means, agents, and purposes by which Christian writings were so quickly and widely dispersed?

Any item of early Christian literature available to us is available only in consequence of a long process of transmission. Given our indebtedness to that process, it is easy to forget that the transmission of a text over time is but an accidental function of its currency in its own time—of the extent to which it was duplicated, distributed, and used soon after it was composed. Yet before any text can be reproduced and begin to circulate it must first be produced—it must be published. By studying ancient manuscripts and reconstructing extended textual traditions we may draw any number of conclusions about the transmission of early Christian literature. It is far more difficult, however, to discover how the texts first entered into circulation and to determine the factors at work in their early reproduction and dissemination. Since early Christian sources shed little direct light on these issues, we must again attend to the larger context and ask first how non-Christian Greek and Latin literature was published and circulated during the early centuries of the church.

THE PUBLICATION AND CIRCULATION OF GRECO-ROMAN LITERATURE

In these matters modern conceptions of publication, edition, and book trade are irrelevant and misleading. Very different practices prevailed in antiquity: all books were handwritten, few people were literate, and since financial incentives were missing, the production and use of literature were largely private and depended on the motives and interests of individuals and small groups.

No author in antiquity had a significant financial interest in the sale of what he or she wrote, for there was no arrangement whereby profits accrued to an author through the enterprise of publishers and booksellers. The ancient world knew nothing resembling the modern copyright, whereby an author or an author's agent holds claim to the work, exercises control over its reproduction and use, and is in principle capable of realizing a profit from the disposition of the text as a piece of authorial property.[5] Ancient authors might hope to gain a reputation as a literary figure and to benefit from the patronage of wealthy or influential persons, but they could not expect to make money from the sale of the work itself, no matter how popular it proved to be. The relation between the author and the work was in fact highly tenuous in financial and other terms.[6]

Apart from works intended for public performance (such as dramas, poetic works to be recited at competitions, or addresses written for civic occasions), publication in the ancient world was a great deal more private than the modern phrase *private publication*, suggests. Authors who wished to make their work public had several ways to do so. They might make or have made at their own expense, several copies of an initial draft, which they would then distribute to friends. This alone did not amount to publication but constituted what we might think of as a referee procedure: the author expected a private reading and response from the recipients, with a view to revising and improving the work. Alternatively, they might invite a small group of friends to a reading *(recitatio)*, at which the work, or parts of it, would be read by the author and discussed by the gathered company. In these ways an author made his work known, but only to a small and sympathetic circle of acquaintances. The work remained essentially private, under the author's direct control, and was still subject to revision.

Only after the author had tentatively proffered a composition and then revised it would he or she make it available to a larger audience. Literature (as distinct from technical, scholarly work), and above all poetry, was traditionally made public not by multiplying and distributing copies of the text, but in oral performance, a practice that continued into the first century.[7] The tradition of public performance was rooted in the belief that literature yields its full sense only through the interpretive rendering of the writer. Gradually, in the first century C.E., although oral performance was by no means abandoned, the publication of the text itself gained increasing importance for writers who wanted to reach a larger public and for readers who sought freer access to literature.

Even an author who planned to make his text generally available had reason to read it in public first: during the first century and into the second the most efficient means of giving a literary work immediate and wide publicity was to hold a recitatio or public reading.[8] With or without a public reading, publication in the sense of putting the text into the hands of others occurred when the author made, or had made for him, one or more fair copies and distributed them to friends as gifts. Never numerous, these were careful and accurate copies prepared under the author's immediate supervision. It often happened that the work was dedicated to someone, usually a person of stature whom the author hoped would take interest and sponsor its wider distribution. The dedicatee would receive a gift copy of the text from the author. The provision of fair copies of one's work to friends and patrons was designated by the term *ekdosis* (Latin, *editio*), literally a "giving out." This was the act of the author himself and no one else.[9] Although the verb *ekdidonai* (Latin, *edere*) is commonly translated "to publish," it is distinct from what we now think of as publication. Neither should we confuse the ancient *ekdosis/editio* with our notion of an edition: the action was the author's own, not that of an editor working on the author's text, and it did not entail placing a large number of identical copies before the public at once.

In providing copies of a work to friends an author effectively surrendered further personal control over the text. A recipient might make her copy available to another, who could then make a copy in turn. No expense was involved other than the cost of materials and, if need be, the services of a scribe. In this way copies multiplied and spread seriatim, one at a time, at the initiative of individuals who lay beyond the author's acquaintance. Since every copy was made by hand, each was unique, and every owner of such a copy was free to do with it as he or she chose. In this way a text quickly slipped beyond the author's reach. There were no means of making authoritative revisions, of preventing others from transcribing or revising it as they wished, of controlling the number of copies made, or even of assuring that it would be properly attributed to its author. In principle the work became public property: copies were disseminated without regulation through an informal network composed of people who learned of the work, were interested enough to have a copy made, and knew someone who possessed the text and would permit it to be duplicated. Thus a text made its way into general circulation gradually and for the most part haphazardly, in a pattern of tangents radiating from the points, ever more numerous, where the text was available for copying.

Traditionally, then, publication took place in the context of social relations between persons interested in literature, and subsequent copies of the work circulated along paths of friendship or personal acquaintance. For the most part, these networks existed before and apart from literary interests, arising partly on the basis of those factors that defined the upper class, providing it the leisure to read, partly through the complex relations of patrons and clients, and partly through the natural affinity of persons of talent and cultivated interests. Financial interests had little bearing on the production or circulation of texts. Nevertheless, under the early empire there began to grow up a commercial book trade that operated more or less independently of social relations and, of course, from different motives. It provided an author with the means to put a work before the general public by depositing a copy with a bookseller who made copies for sale.

It is difficult to reconstruct the development of the book trade in antiquity and the modes of its operation.[10] Ancient sources offer only fragmentary and incidental information about commercial book dealing, and the necessarily conjectural descriptions of it are usually both overdrawn and misleading, especially because they so often depend on modern practices. A book trade of some sort had already developed in Greece as early as the fourth century B.C.E., but its extent was modest.[11] Evidence for a book trade in the Hellenistic East is almost wholly lacking, and there is no evidence of a book trade in Rome and the West before the first century B.C.E. In the late republican period we find Cicero mentioning a bookshop (*taberna libraria, Phil.* 2.21, the only such reference in the whole Ciceronian corpus) and Catullus referring to the availability of the works of fellow poets on the "shelves of book-dealers" (*librariorum scrinia; carm.* 14.17–20). Yet the book trade seems to have been poorly developed at the time; Cicero, at least, considered the stocks of bookshops to be so limited in quantity and poor in quality that he followed the custom of acquiring books either from friends or through their assistance.[12]

We begin to hear more about the book trade in the early imperial period. Commercial book dealers *(librarii, bibliopolae)* are occasionally mentioned in the literature of the first two centuries C.E.,, and some are known by name. The Sosii brothers produced and sold the works of Horace *(Ep.* 1.20.2, *Ars poet.* 345); Tryphon was a commercial agent for Quintilian *(Inst. orat.,* ep. praem.) as well as for Martial (4.72.2, 13.3.4), who also mentions Atrectus (1.117.13–7), Secundus (1.2.7–8), and Pollio Valerianus (1.113.5); and Seneca indicates that works by Cicero and Livy were sold by Dorus *(Ben.* 7.6). All these establishments seem to have been based in Rome, no doubt the center of commercial book dealing in the West, but there is also mention of booksellers in the provinces (Pliny, *Ep.* 9.11.2). Those engaged in the book trade were enterprising freedmen and thus lacked social distinction or natural ties with a literary elite.[13] Still we learn little from these scattered allusions about the organization or operation of the book trade.

In the absence of better evidence, scholars have often been tempted to see in T. Pomponius Atticus, the close friend of Cicero, a model of the commercial publisher in antiquity and to regard his activities as typical of the book trade.[14] It is evident from Cicero's correspondence with him that Atticus was instrumental both in supplying books to Cicero and in distributing Cicero's own works. Atticus was a wealthy and cultivated man with a large personal library and well-trained slaves he used to copy texts. Yet nothing suggests that Atticus was commercially engaged in the production and distribution of books. Rather, as a literary person with many good books of his own and reliable people to reproduce them, Atticus generously assisted his literary friends. In no sense can he be regarded as a commercial publisher, much less a book dealer.[15] Although he illustrates in a notably active and expert way the private production and circulation of texts customary in aristocratic literary circles, the example of Atticus sheds no light on the commercial book trade.

It remains, then, unclear just what arrangements existed among the authors, copyists, and book dealers engaged in the trade. Commerce in books, then as now, was prompted by financial interests, but by and large ancient authors were not dependent on the commercial book trade and had little to expect from it by way of profit. Some authors were more closely associated with it than others. Martial, Quintilian, and Pliny certainly put at least some of their works into the hands of booksellers.[16] In such cases, the author probably received a flat fee, and the dealer obtained the right to make and sell copies of the work. When ancient authors speak of profits, they appear to assume that these will accrue only to the dealer and that the benefit to them will be in the coinage of fame.[17] If an author anticipated a financial benefit from his work, it was from patronage rather than sales, and literary patronage had nothing to do with the commercial book trade.[18] Though he had no significant financial stake in the marketing of his work, an author might nevertheless have found it an advantage to work with a dealer: the work might come more quickly to the notice of the public than if it were transmitted strictly in the narrow channels of interested friends; the accuracy of the text might be better preserved if at the outset a number of copies are made directly from a dealer's authorial exemplar rather than allowing copies to be multiplied privately one from another; and it might be useful for an author to refer inquiries and requests to a dealer rather than handling them himself.

These suppositions are uncertain, however, since so little is known about the operations of booksellers themselves. The term *librarius* denoted both a professional copyist and a book dealer, and it is likely that in the early imperial period copyists themselves sensed a market opportunity and began making copies to sell to the public. Although it was only later that the term *bibliopola*, borrowed from Greek, came to designate a retailer of books as distinct from a copyist, copying and retailing must always have been carried on together in a commercial establishment. If trade expanded, it would have been natural for an enterprising copyist or merchandising entrepreneur to distinguish the tasks of production and marketing and to employ others. All the evidence, however, suggests that dealers in the book market were small operators. The hole-in-the-wall bookshops alluded to by Martial (1.2; 1.117; 13.3) are in keeping with the modest premises usually maintained by small business people and artisans in the ancient world. There is no reason to think that copies of texts were produced on any large scale either by a particular dealer or by the book trade as a whole. Though it is conceivable that a bookseller might, in the case of a well-known and popular author, produce several copies at once in order to have them on hand for sale, it is unlikely that capital would regularly have been risked by producing and stocking large numbers of copies in anticipation of demand.[19] The standard practice was probably for the dealer to produce single copies for individual customers at a price that would cover his costs and yield a little profit. The commercial market for any book must have been extremely limited: the number of prospective buyers could have been only a fraction of the small minority who were both literate and had the money to buy books. Further, although a work may have been initially available only through a particular book dealer, the copies he sold could be freely copied by anyone else, a situation not unlike that faced by modern publishers in the era of unregulated private photocopying. As a consequence, the dealer would have had only modest prospects for continuing sales. In any event, the bookshop did not displace the traditional practice among persons with literary interests of lending each other texts to copy. One would presumably have resorted to a bookseller only if the accustomed means failed. On the whole, a bookseller would have found his best opportunities in a reading public that lay beyond aristocratic and scholarly literary circles and in provincial areas where books were otherwise hard to come by (see fig. 5).[20]

How many copies of a text a dealer would produce for sale depended on the market and the method of copying. In modern discussions of the book trade in antiquity one sometimes meets with the idea of the "mass-production scriptoria of the big publishers of the ancient world."[21] If it is assumed that many copies were produced in a relatively short time, it must also be supposed that many copyists were simultaneously engaged in the task since each copy required a person to write it. This supposition entails the further assumption that, since there would normally have been only a single exemplar from which copies were taken and since a certain speed of production was desired, the method of copying was by dictation. Accordingly, one conjures a scene wherein a reader (*anagnostes*, Latin: *lector*) holds the exemplar and reads the text aloud to a number of copyists gathered around him, each of whom transcribes what is read, so that many copies are produced at once. Although the theory is attractive and commends itself to modern notions of efficiency, the evidence that such a scene actually took place before the early medieval period is poor.

There being no direct evidence that texts were replicated by dictation in the ancient world—at least on a scale that would benefit

5. A fresco from Pompeii showing, in the top panel, an open waxed tablet and stylus, and in the bottom panel (from left) a closed diptych of wooden tablets *(tabellae)*, a whitened and inscribed wooden tablet, a container *(capsa)* of roll books (note the title tags at the tops of the rolls), and a bag of coins. Courtesy of the Museo Archeologico Nazionale, Naples.

commercial copying—proof has been sought in ancient manuscripts themselves. Transcription errors may have had an auditory rather than a visual cause since they pertain to words that sound alike more than they look alike. Such so-called phonetic mistakes might seem conclusive evidence were it not for the fact that virtually all reading in antiquity, including private reading, was done aloud.[22] A copyist who was visually copying a text did so by reading it aloud to himself, so his copy would have been as vulnerable to phonetic errors as one written at the dictation of another.[23] Other arguments of a circumstantial kind favor the use of dictation in particular situations. One is the posture of the copyist. Apparently writing desks were not used: the copyist rested the manuscript on his lower thigh and knee, a position not conducive to visual copying since there is no convenient way to position or consult the exemplar.[24] Although this practice might indicate copying by dictation, we do not know that it *required* dictation. Finally, although the total number of hours required for copying would be nearly the same whether done visually or by dictation, more copies could be produced in a short time by dictation to a group of scribes.[25] Since we do not know whether or how often the book trade sought to produce many copies in a short time, the argument for dictation becomes circular and yields no result. Doubtless transcription by dictation was sometimes practiced in antiquity.[26] What remains uncertain is how often speed of reproduction required it and whether enough copyists were normally available for it to be used to its singular advantage. Though it probably was used under some circumstances, it cannot be shown that dictation was the regular method of duplication in commercial book production. On the whole it appears to have been the rare exception rather than the rule.[27]

To the extent that the two can be differentiated, exactly what relations existed between book dealers and copyists? Professional scribes were trained craftsmen, but within the craft there were levels and types of expertise. Some were calligraphers capable of writing a fine bookhand, others were notaries engaged mainly in documentary work, yet others were skilled at shorthand (tachygraphy). Many were educated slaves *(servi litterati)* whose masters, like Atticus, had good use for them in literary or documentary work. Those who were free made their living by their trade, but it was not a large living, and in the Greco-Roman world the profession did not carry the social prestige that traditionally accrued to scribes in the near East.[28] A skilled copyist did not necessarily find employment in the commercial book trade but might work for an author or a library or in a government post; or he might be self-employed, independently contracting his services to individual customers. Although book dealers required copyists, it is no more probable that they normally retained a number of copyists than that they normally produced copies in large numbers for general sale. Much would have depended on a dealer's venue and the habits and interests of his clientele. The idea that large scriptoria were a necessary corollary of the book trade has little footing in the evidence of the Roman empire. Copyists seem to have been paid at a piece rate, that is, by the actual amount of copying they did, calculated according to fixed units of measurement (stichoi), although the quality of the hand made a difference in the rate of pay.[29] A good copyist was not able to earn more through the trade than through contacts with private literary circles, since in the latter case any profit was entirely his. There is no reason to think that commercially produced books were of a higher quality than privately made copies. Indeed, frequent complaints suggest that they were often worse.[30]

Though little is certain about the emergence of the book trade, by the end of the first century C.E. it had secured a role in the circulation of literature. There were reasons for this. One of the social consequences of the transition from the republican to the imperial order was a shift in the composition of the literary public.[31] The weakening of the senatorial aristocracy and the rise of imperial power were attended by greater social differentiation and increased opportunity for upward social mobility. In this social change the book trade found its opportunity. Since literary interest was traditionally a mark of high social standing, the development of commerce in books indicated "a weakening of the hold of the traditional aristocracy on the control of access to social status."[32] Thus, under the empire, books were often used as status symbols. The avid acquisition of books and the formation of large, prettily displayed personal libraries by the upwardly mobile and nouveaux riches furnished first- and second-century writers with a frequent subject of satire.[33] Under the circumstances it was perhaps inevitable that authors would soon see the advantage of a more diverse and widespread reading public and regard book dealers as agents who could reach this market and promote an author's reputation. The prospect of commercial publication would have been especially attractive to writers like Martial and Statius, who may have seen in literary activity a point of entry into social circles otherwise closed to them.[34] Not all types of literature, however, would have had sufficient popular appeal to be of interest to booksellers. Poetry, biography, satire, history, oratory, and perhaps popular philosophy were doubtless more marketable than scientific treatises, scholarly monographs, and technical manuals.

If the book trade had come to stay, then the commercial copying and selling of texts did not replace their private reproduction and circulation, in Rome or elsewhere. I have already mentioned an Egyptian papyrus letter (P. Petaus 30) that speaks of a traveling book dealer in Egypt.[35] Still another interesting papyrus letter (P. Oxy. 2192) alludes to private efforts to obtain texts in Egypt in the late second century.[36] That letter carries a postscript in the hand of the sender that reads: "Make and send to me copies of books 6 and 7 of Hypsicrates' *Characters in Comedy*. For Harpocration says that they are among Polion's books. But it is likely that others, too, have got them. He also has prose epitomes of Thersagorus' work on the myths of tragedy." Here the writer asks his correspondent to make copies of books that he wants and suggests an individual who owns them who might permit them to be copied. Following this postscript is a note written in a different hand. It reads: "According to Harpocration, Demetrius the bookseller has got them. I have instructed Apollonides to send me certain of my own books, which you will hear of in good time from Seleucus himself. If you find any, apart from those I possess, make copies and send them to me. Diodorus and his friends also have some which I haven't got." It is not certain who appended this note; it was probably added by a member of the letter writer's circle as a supplement to the preceding postscript. The letter reveals a group of friends who acquired books by making copies from exemplars owned by friends who lived elsewhere (Harpocration, Polion, Diodorus, and their circle). Yet there is mention of the bookseller Demetrius, who could serve as a fall-back source. Here, then, in provincial Egypt we see the independent coexistence of private and commercial means of obtaining books.

We know that some of the individuals named in this letter—Harpocration, Polion (Pollio), and Diodorus—were professional scholars, known for their lexicographical work.[37] The books requested are scholarly, not books that have popular appeal, so it is surprising that the bookseller Demetrius might have them. One would expect a bookseller to deal in popular literature, as apparently was the case with the Roman booksellers we know by name. In a setting where a scholarly community was active, an astute dealer probably did not disdain service to that clientele. Yet, as a rule, classical texts and especially scholarly tools and studies circulated principally if not exclusively through private channels. The practices of Cicero in late republican

Rome, of the scholarly circle in Oxyrhynchus in the late second century, and of Libanius and his fellow scholars in fourth-century Syrian Antioch, widespread as these were in time and place, all attest that private copying and circulation formed the persistent norm for professional scholars.[38]

The reason for this was not only the limited market for scholarly works. The quality of commercial copying was not particularly high, whereas scholars were fastidious, at least about their books. The complaints voiced by many ancient writers about the quality of commercial copies were consistent and continuous. The employment of mediocre copyists and the failure to collate copies and exemplars—practices that Strabo (13.1.54) encountered in Alexandria as well as Rome—resulted in books that did not meet the scholarly standard. Strabo's comment shows that what constituted the quality of a book from a scholar's point of view was accuracy of transcription.[39] The private copyists, slave or free, whether attached to wealthy households or retained by scholars, were as a rule more skilled and careful than those employed by booksellers. It was in these households and among scholars that the pertinent texts were usually held and in copies of high quality. Cicero's heavy reliance on his secretary, Tiro, and his praise of Atticus's copyists, like Libanius's high esteem for his own secretary, express the conviction among men of letters that well-written and accurate texts were essential to their work.

THE PUBLICATION AND CIRCULATION OF EARLY CHRISTIAN LITERATURE It is within this broad Greco-Roman context that the publication and circulation of early Christian literature must be considered. To be sure, there are particular features that come into play in the Christian setting: texts were circulated less among individuals than among widespread congregations in which few were literate, and these congregations employed texts not for aesthetic or intellectual ends, but as practical instruments of a variety of religious purposes. The swift dispersion of Christian congregations across the Mediterranean world presented a larger challenge, but also a larger opportunity for the dissemination of texts. The situation was further complicated because among Christian groups there were both Greek- and Latin-speaking constituencies and others in which provincial languages like Syriac and Coptic prevailed. Yet no differentiating features of early Christianity require us to think that the publication and circulation of early Christian texts proceeded along unique or idiosyncratic lines. Without evidence to the contrary, it ought to be supposed that Christian writings were produced and disseminated in much the same way as other literature within the larger environment. For example, I have already noted that inscriptional features of early Christian manuscripts show that this literature was not commercially produced but was transcribed privately, that is, by Christians themselves. It can now be seen that this is no anomaly of early Christian texts: most ancient books were privately copied and circulated.

How were the works of Christian writers put into circulation, progressively copied, and disseminated? Obviously, we cannot put this question to every piece of early Christian literature. Even if we could, only certain documents would yield an answer. Few Christian writings of the first several centuries carry indications of how they entered the domain of the Christian public. Nevertheless, we can sometimes infer the answer from the intentions or expectations of Christian writers for the availability and use of their work by prospective readers. Whether or not these expectations were fulfilled, they indicate the circumstances the author envisioned for the reception and use of his work. Conclusions can also sometimes be reached from evidence that an author was acquainted with or used certain other writings near the time of their composition. Further, the evidence provided by the provenance, dates, and features of surviving ancient manuscripts is especially valuable, though not abundant. Although what can be determined on this basis and from the larger environment cannot be immediately generalized to all early Christian literature, consistent patterns can be discovered.

The bibliographic history of early Christian literature offers no clear dividing lines by which my inquiry might be organized. Indeed, as I hope to show, there is remarkable continuity and consistency within the literature of the early church in matters of book production and the publication and circulation of texts. There is no justification in bibliographic terms, for example, for an a priori discrimination between scriptural and nonscriptural texts, not only because the scriptural canon had not yet been determined, but also because the methods of producing and circulating texts were the same for all texts. It is largely for convenience, then, that I take up first the earliest Christian literature, then the literature of the second and third centuries, and finally the literature of the fourth and fifth centuries. These divisions correspond roughly to the successive periods of the origins, expansion, and establishment of the ancient church. It is, of course, impossible to attend to all the Christian literature produced over the first five centuries, and therefore I limit my discussion to that literature which sheds light on the means of publication and circulation.

THE EARLIEST CHRISTIAN LITERATURE A special interest attaches to the earliest Christian writings, most of which later came to constitute the New Testament. I begin with the letters of Paul because, as the earliest extant Christian literature, they represent the practices of a very early time and because they give insight into the history of their own early circulation.

It may be objected that because we have to do in this case with correspondence addressed by Paul to individual churches, we should not seek here general practices for the dissemination of literature. This objection arises from a misconception of Paul's letters and too narrow a definition of literature. Certainly Paul did not fancy himself as an author or think of his letters as having an especially literary value. Nevertheless, his letters cannot be construed with Deissmann as personal letters directly analogous to the private letters found among the papyri.[40] Paul's letters have an official character that distinguishes them from private letters. He writes as an authoritative person: in the prescripts of his letters he invariably calls attention to his apostolic status and assumes his apostolic authority throughout. He addresses not individuals but communities, whom he undertakes to instruct, admonish, and advise on important matters of their corporate life. Furthermore, in their length, their argumentative and expository development, and their rhetorical features, these letters more closely resemble the literary and philosophical letters of antiquity than any merely private correspondence.[41] These features of Paul's letters were recognized by his sophisticated opponents in Corinth, who considered them "weighty and strong" (2 Cor. 10:10): texts to be reckoned with. Paul's letters may have been occasional, but they were not in the least casual. They were composed and deployed as important instruments of his apostolic authority, teaching, and administration among the churches of his mission field.

My concern is not with the composition of the Pauline letters but with what I call their "publication" and circulation, yet I also attend to their initial transcription. The letters themselves indicate that Paul typically dictated his correspondence to a secretary.[42] Beyond the oral style of Paul's diction and the occasional instances of broken syntax, several letters conclude with a reference to Paul's own hand (Gal. 5:11; 1 Cor. 16:21; Col. 4:18; 2 Thess. 3:17; Phlm. 19), a convention showing

PUBLICATION AND CIRCULATION 95

that the preceding text of the letter was transcribed by an amanuensis. The addition of autographic greetings or other comments is so frequent that even where this is not explicitly noted we can assume that in the original manuscript the change of hands could be seen.[43] In one letter, Paul's secretary identifies himself and appends his own greetings to the recipients (Rom. 16:22). Thus there are good reasons to think that Paul's letters were normally transcribed from dictation to a secretary.[44] This would have been consistent with general practice.[45] Extant papyrus letters written by scribes often show a change of hand at their conclusions. A dictated text, whether or not taken down by a stenographer, would normally be reviewed for corrections or revisions and then rewritten to obtain a fair copy before being dispatched to its recipients.[46]

The mobility of Christians around the Mediterranean world was already a factor in the earliest phases of the dissemination of Christian writings. In the absence of a public postal service, Paul's letters, like any other private correspondence, were entrusted to associates or friends for delivery, and these couriers are sometimes mentioned in the letters themselves (Rom. 16:1; 1 Cor. 16:10; Eph. 6:21; Col. 4:7; compare 2 Cor. 8:16–7). Letter carriers are mentioned in many other early Christian letters (such as 1 Pet. 5:12; 1 Clem. 65.1; Ignatius Phil. 11.2, Smyr. 12.1, compare Polyc. 8.1; Polycarp Phil. 14.1). Correspondence was carried not only by persons specifically commissioned for the purpose, but also by Christians who were traveling for other reasons.[47]

In accordance with the meaning of *publication (ekdosis)* in antiquity, Paul's letters were published when they were received and read, and this took place in situations that Paul clearly envisioned though seldom alluded to. In 1 Thess. 5:27 Paul adjures "that this letter be read to all the brethren." Publication in this case occurred when Paul's letter was read aloud to the gathered community, presumably in the context of the service of worship. It was also in this context that the mutual greetings with the "holy kiss" would have been exchanged, as requested by Paul in the conclusions of several letters (Rom. 16:16; 1 Cor. 16:20; 2 Cor. 13:12; 1 Thess. 5:26). The liturgical settings in which the apostle's letters were first read were in some ways comparable to the recitatio in vogue in literary circles of that era: the letter was read aloud to a gathering of the writer's acquaintances, following which it may have been the subject of comment or discussion. In any event, the text, once placed in the hands of the recipients, was no longer under Paul's control and might be used as the community or its members saw fit.

Paul also envisioned the circulation of some of his letters, at least on a limited scale. Galatians is addressed "to the churches of Galatia" (1:2), that is, to several communities in a discrete region. How Paul arranged for the letter to reach these various Galatian congregations is not known, but he must have given thought to the matter and chosen the means. The possibilities were several. He might have had the letter carrier proceed from one congregation to the next, reading the letter or having it read to each in turn, or Paul might have had enough copies made for one to be carried to each of the communities he had in view and left there. If the letter was neither merely read to each in turn nor distributed in multiple copies, Paul may have expected the carrier to take the letter to the several Galatian communities and to have each of them make and retain a copy. We do not know which method was used, only that one of them must have been used. Similarly, the letter to the Romans, addressed to "all God's beloved in Rome" (1:7), was directed to different house churches in the city (compare 16:5, 10, 11, 14, 15). Since it is unlikely that all these would ever be gathered in one place, it may have rested with the courier (Phoebe, 16:1) to see that the letter circulated among them, either by ensuring that it was read to each group or that a copy was available to each. In the cases of Galatians and Romans it was a matter of circulating a single letter among different groups that together constituted the addressees. It is likely that this was achieved not merely by a series of public readings but by making copies: the first recipients of a Pauline letter were probably no better able than we to digest it at one reading and would have wished to retain it for subsequent consideration. Paul himself may well have hoped or expected that his letters would not only be heard but also studied.

The letter to the Colossians anticipates a different situation. The writer admonishes: "When this letter has been read among you, have it read also in the church of the Laodiceans, and see that you read also the letter from Laodicea" (4:16). Since Colossians is widely thought not to be an authentic Pauline letter, it cannot be assumed on the basis of this notice that Paul himself envisioned or encouraged the exchange of different letters between two communities. Nevertheless, the notice does show that the author either knew that letters of Paul were circulating among Pauline churches or wanted to encourage their circulation by offering a Pauline warrant.[48] An exchange of letters between the neighboring churches of Colossae and Laodicea would be only a short step beyond the circumstances that obtained for the Roman letter and the Galatian letter. The author of Colossians obviously did not think that such an exchange would be considered extraordinary.[49]

There is compelling evidence that some authentic letters of Paul did in fact circulate from an early time in communities other than those to which they were originally addressed. The textual traditions of Romans and 1 Corinthians preserve clear indications that these letters circulated at one time in generalized or catholicized forms from which their local addresses (Rom. 1:7, 15; 1 Cor. 1:2), and perhaps other particulars (Rom. 16), had been eliminated in favor of broad designations of their recipients ("Those who are beloved by God" [Rom. 1:7]; and "those who are sanctified in Christ Jesus" [1 Cor. 1:2b]). These editorial revisions were made very early and must have had as their aim the adaptation of these letters for use in communities other than those addressed by Paul. The letters, then, must have circulated individually, before any collection of Paul's letters, among various Christian communities.[50] Ephesians is a related case, for the oldest and best manuscripts do not have the address "in Ephesus" in 1:1, but only the general and grammatically peculiar address: "to the saints who are also faithful." Ephesians is by common consent a pseudonymous letter. It is addressed to a concrete historical situation, but not a purely local one. The textual variants in 1:1 make sense only if originally there was no single address but different addresses inserted in different copies.[51] If this is so, Ephesians was intended for broad dissemination from the outset and, like Colossians, offers indirect early evidence that other (authentic) letters of Paul were circulating outside the communities to which they were first addressed.

These observations show that the early copying and circulation of Paul's letters was not mere happenstance, and that, at least in the cases of Galatians and Romans, it was already taking place in Paul's lifetime. Later, after Paul's time, it took place on a larger scale and by additional means through the agency of his disciples. Not only did they promote the circulation of Paul's correspondence, they also editorially reworked parts of it and went on to compose pseudonymous Pauline letters—Colossians, Ephesians, 2 Thessalonians, 1–2 Timothy, and Titus—and ultimately, it may be supposed, to produce an edition of the collected letters of Paul.[52] Thus, the authority of Paul was perpetuated, the scope of his influence extended, and the substance of his teaching elaborated in new circumstances through these specifically literary means.

The intense literary activity that characterized the Pauline theological tradition in the late first century was not a complete departure from Paul's own working methods. Deissmann's appraisal of Paul's letters as purely private and occasional entailed a devaluation of the literary features of the letters and a deemphasizing of the role of literature in Paul's missionary activity. It is clear, however, that Paul relied heavily on letters to stay in touch with and to supervise his congregations. There was, in fact, much traffic in letters: Paul's letters to the churches (more than the few that have been preserved), the churches' letters to him (compare 1 Cor. 7:1), and letters used by other teachers on their own behalf in the communities (compare 2 Cor. 3:1, 2 Thess. 2:2).[53] Paul's associates, who served as his personal emissaries and liaison to the congregations, often had a hand in his correspondence, not only as letter carriers. It was Paul's custom to name others together with himself as cosenders of his letters.[54] This was probably not a formality but a reflection of the involvement of his associates in the conception, if not in the composition, of many of the letters. The evidence strongly suggests that Paul's missionary enterprise had a corporate structure and a school dimension and that Paul and his associates thought it important to formulate the apostle's teaching in writing and to employ those writings in the furtherance of Paul's missionary aims.[55] The literary activity of Pauline circles in the period following his death was not, then, a new development but a continuation and elaboration of the literary dimensions of Paul's own career. Paul's letters stand so much in the foreground for us that we must guard against overestimating their significance in early Christianity. The opposite danger of minimizing their significance in Paul's own time is just as real. The Pauline mission, both before and after Paul's death, was substantially invested in texts carrying the apostle's teaching.

Several points related to the formation of the Pauline letter-collection call for emphasis here.[56] To share a letter or to exchange letters with another community normally meant making copies. We have seen that the initial reception of Romans and Galatians must have required some copying and circulation in Paul's day. Later, the availability of authentic letters deprived of their locally specific addresses (Romans, 1 Corinthians) and of a pseudonymous letter of variable address (Ephesians), obviously entailed copying and distribution. From an early time, then, the letters of Paul began to be known and read outside the churches to which they were originally sent.[57] The very production of pseudonymous letters of Paul in the period after his death but before the emergence of the full-blown collection that included them, presupposes that (authentic) letters of Paul were in circulation among Christian communities other than those to which they had been sent by the apostle, that they were valued as authoritative instruction, and that therefore a previously unknown "Pauline" letter could find a receptive readership. Only under such circumstances could a pseudonymous writer anticipate that his own "Pauline" letter would not be an anomaly in the situation and liable to repudiation.[58] It was by means of such circulation that small collections of Pauline letters probably began to emerge in some Pauline communities not long after Paul's death.

The larger collections of Paul's letters that come into view in the second century, consisting variously of ten, thirteen, and fourteen letters, were outgrowths of these earlier small and perhaps regional collections. The methodical features of the second-century collections, however, prevent their being understood as merely the natural result of a progressive accretion of smaller collections. Rather, these second-century collections derive from early editions of the *corpus Paulinum* that were shaped by ideas about the number of letters or addressees and about the order of the letters and that had distinctive textual complexions. These editions, or at least the earliest of them, were produced within the historic Pauline mission field by persons who sponsored the Pauline theological heritage.

Christian writers standing near the juncture of the first and second centuries were familiar with collections of Paul's letters: Clement of Rome and Ignatius of Antioch were both acquainted with numerous letters of the apostle. Though it is impossible to tell how many letters each knew, that Rome and Antioch were the extreme poles of the Pauline mission field proves the breadth of their circulation. Somewhat later, both the pseudonymous author of 2 Peter and Polycarp of Smyrna show a knowledge and esteem for many of Paul's letters. The former, referring to "all his letters" (3:15), seems to presume a comprehensive collection.[59] Nevertheless, it is first with Marcion, near the middle of the second century, that there comes clearly into view a definite edition of the collected letters of Paul. The edition attested by Marcion is derived, as we have seen, from an older edition that was probably in existence by the beginning of the second century, and possibly earlier still.[60]

It is generally assumed that Paul had no part in the collecting of his own letters and that those who drew up the earliest edition of the collection did so by gathering copies or partial collections of copies from wherever they were preserved among Pauline churches. This is certainly possible, but it would correspond better with the circumstances and methods of the Pauline mission if the earliest edition of Paul's collected letters had been based on copies retained by Paul and preserved after his death by his associates. It seems unlikely that Paul would have written the kinds of letters he wrote without retaining copies. Ancient writers often kept copies of their private letters even when no particular literary merit or topical importance attached to them; and copies of instructional, administrative letters were all the more likely to be kept. In antiquity, collected editions of letters were nearly always produced by their author or at their author's behest, often from copies belonging to the author.[61] A dossier of Paul's letters would surely have been useful to Paul and his coworkers: it can hardly be supposed that each letter immediately had its intended effect, required no further clarification, and generated no new issues. The letters themselves are proof to the contrary. The tangled correspondence of Paul with the Corinthians, if not typical, certainly indicates that Paul needed to and did keep track of what he had written. Paul's copies would have been a valuable resource to his associates, who eventually collated and revised them. Ultimately, they would have transcribed them, together with some pseudonymous letters, in a comprehensive format. From a bibliographic point of view the production of such an edition was no small undertaking, though it should not be imagined that it was issued in any large number of copies. Hypothetical though it must be, this explanation of the origin of the Pauline corpus is coherent with ancient practice, with the known history of Pauline Christianity, and with what can be discerned about the actual history of the Pauline letter collection.

If we turn now to another type of the earliest Christian literature, we find no clear statements from which to construe the expectations of their authors for the publication and circulation of the Gospels. Yet much that is known about the Gospels themselves is relevant to the question. It can be seen more clearly today than in the heyday of form criticism that the Gospels were written in a literary context with literary skills and a literary view to a readership. Whatever the sources of the Gospel of Mark were, at least some of them were written. The authors of Matthew and Luke certainly used predominantly written sources, and this seems likely also of the Gospel of John. Each of these authors was self-consciously engaged in literary composition and therefore sensible not only of his own compositional techniques and theological aims, but also of the prospects for the valuation, circulation, and use of his work.

Of the Gospels that became canonical, the literary sensibility of the author is most obvious in Luke(-Acts). On the one hand, the prologue (Luke 1:1–4; compare Acts 1:1–2) addresses the reader, Theophilus, with a statement of literary intention: to compile a narrative that so orders events that the reader might know the truth of the things of which the reader is informed. It is likely that here, as often elsewhere, the dedicatee (Theophilus—whether a real or fictive figure) is implicitly made responsible for the diffusion of the work.[62] Indeed, the construction of the narrative so as to take full literary and theological advantage of its bibliographic division into two volumes, between which he deftly maintains both careful distinction and close coherence, reveals that the writer considered the bibliographic form in which his readers would receive the text. Such concerns were not less pressing in other Gospels. Each Gospel reveals something of the viewpoint from which it was written and thus indirectly the circumstances that served as the occasion of its composition. The careful literary crafting of each, however, and the small size of individual Christian congregations in the first century make it unlikely that any of the Gospels was composed for the strictly local and intramural use of a single community. Broader dissemination in Christian circles, if not beyond, must have been intended from the outset.[63] This would comport with the close relations between early Christian communities, with the largely kerygmatic nature of the traditions taken up in the Gospels, and also with what can be gleaned about the actual history of Gospel texts in the early period.

Mark's Gospel, wherever it was composed, must have circulated widely within ten to twenty years of its origin. How else might it have come independently into the hands of the author of Matthew and the author of Luke, whose different concerns suggest that they were as distant from each other geographically as culturally? Further, the Gospel of Mark was not displaced by the Gospels of Matthew and Luke, though they essentially replicated its substance while revising and enriching it. This shows that it had enjoyed an early and wide use sufficient to secure its own place.[64] Early in the second century, probably around 110, Papias, bishop of Hierapolis, knew both the Gospel of Mark and the Gospel of Matthew, though in western Asia Minor he was far-removed from the likely origins of either.[65] At least these two Gospels are thereby shown to have circulated widely at an early time.

The history of the composition of the Fourth Gospel appears to be long and complicated, and many points are still debated, but there can be no doubt that chapter 21 is an editorial addition to a work that once ended at 20:30–1. This epilogue, and probably some other matter of the Fourth Gospel, was added with a view toward the publication of the Gospel, that is, its initial release for duplication and circulation outside the Johannine community proper. If the earlier form of the text (ending at 20:30–1) had been confined to the community of its origin, it would explain why the manuscript tradition of the Fourth Gospel presents no evidence that the Gospel ever circulated without chapter 21. The concluding statements of the epilogue (21:24–5), like the prologue to the Gospel of Luke, are book conscious. Both have a readership in view and touch on the same motifs: the reliability of the author and his traditions (21:24; compare Lk. 1:2–3), the multiplicity of available traditions (21:24; compare Lk. 1:1–2), and the explicit awareness of producing one book among many others (21:25; compare Lk. 1:1, 3).[66] These observations intersect but are not identical with the many other questions about the larger compositional history of the Fourth Gospel, which must be distinguished from its literary history as a "published" document.[67]

Even in the field of literature, supply mirrors demand. The rich proliferation of Gospel documents in the late first and early second centuries, in all their canonical and apocryphal variety, reflects a lively interest in written accounts about Jesus. Though form criticism assumed that many elements of the oral tradition behind the Gospels served missionary and apologetic functions, modern scholars have usually supposed that written Gospels were intended only for intramural Christian use. Without denying that Gospel literature did have important functions within Christian communities, there is nevertheless a growing recognition that missionary and propagandistic aspects also belong to written Gospels. This implies, however, some circulation of Gospel-type documents outside the confines of Christian communities in the interest of gaining converts.[68] We have evidence from the early second century on that the Gospels did in fact have some non-Christian readers. Various apologists of the second century suggested that non-Christians were reading Christian scriptural books.[69] The pagan critic Celsus had certainly done so. In his attack on Christianity, *The True Doctrine*, issued about 180, Celsus shows himself remarkably familiar with its literature, not only Gospels, but epistles and apologies as well.[70] In the *Dialogue with Trypho* Justin suggests that Trypho had gained his acquaintance with Christian teaching in part by reading "the so-called Gospel" (10.2, compare 18.1), which assumes, even if the *Dialogue* is fictive, that the Gospels were accessible to non-Christians. The criticism often aimed by educated non-Christians at what they considered the inferior literary quality of Christian writings indicates that early Christian literature was often read, if not always appreciated, beyond the boundaries of Christian communities.[71]

Among the earliest Christian writings, the Apocalypse of John, composed in Asia Minor near the end of the first century, is especially interesting for the light it sheds on the publication and circulation of early Christian literature. The Apocalypse has a prominent epistolary dimension: the document as a whole is framed as a letter (1:4–5; 22:21), and it incorporates a set of letters to seven churches (2:1–3:22). Although the epistolary form had occasionally been employed among the *Gattungen* of Jewish apocalyptic literature, no other apocalypse is presented *as* a letter. The prominence of the epistolary element in the Apocalypse indicates the author's awareness that he stands in a specifically Christian literary tradition as well as in a broader apocalyptic one and attests that by the end of the first century the letter had become the format de rigueur of written Christian teaching. The letters of Paul certainly had a decisive role in this development, for nowhere were they better known than in the region of Asia Minor where the churches addressed in the Apocalypse were found.[72]

It is not too much to say that the author of the Apocalypse, despite his idiosyncratic grammar and style, may be the most textually self-conscious Christian writer of the early period. In no other early Christian text do the notions of books, writing, and reading occur so prominently.[73] Of course, the apocalyptic tradition in which the author stood was a self-consciously literary, indeed bookish, movement.[74] The literary consciousness of the author, however, in some measure must also reflect the significance of texts in the Christian communities of his time and place. The textual orientation of the Apocalypse is manifest at the beginning. To the title that announces the work and stresses its importance (1:1–2), the author adds a reference to its audience: "Blessed is the one who reads and those who hear the words of the prophecy and who keep the things that are written in it" (1:3). The text is to be read aloud to the gathered community, and the text that is read aloud is identical with the prophecy that is heard. A blessing is pronounced on those who both "hear the words of the prophecy" and "keep the things that are written in it." The phrase, "the things that are written in it" (*en aute*, that is, in the prophecy) asserts that the prophecy and the book are one and the same. This explains why the command, "Write what you see in a book, and send it to the seven churches" (1:9) is given *before* anything has been "seen," that is, in advance of the visions. Thus the prophecy is not a visual apprehension or an oral message subsequently preserved in writing: the text is what was originally intended.

If this is so, a question arises about the blessing pronounced in 1:3

on "the one who keeps what is written in it." The common interpretation of this statement defines *keeps* as "observe" or "obey," and the object ("the things written") as those admonitions or commandments found in the book. If the prophecy subsists in the text itself, however, the meaning of "keeping what is written" may instead be "preserving the text as it is written." In that case, the blessing concerns the use of the text as a text—not only its reading and hearing, but also its copying and transmission. A blessing in similar form occurs near the end of the book in 22:7: "Blessed is the one who keeps the words of the prophecy of this book" (compare 22:9, "Who keep the words of this book"). Here the emphasis on the preservation of the text is clearer than in 1:3, for what is to be kept is specifically "the words of the prophecy of this book." The author's concern for the text itself ("the words"), that it be preserved in its integrity, is finally unmistakable in 22:18–19: "I warn every one who hears the words of the prophecy of this book: if any one adds to them, God will add to him the plagues described in this book; if any one takes away from the words of the book of this prophecy, God will take away his share in the tree of life and in the holy city which are described in this book." It is misguided to regard this statement as a "formula of canonization."[75] It has to do, instead, with the fate of a handwritten text once it has been released into circulation by the author. The odds were heavy that once it was available for copying any ancient text would suffer additions or subtractions or both, if not by intention then by carelessness of transcription. The most that any ancient author could do to prevent adulteration was to issue a warning to prospective copyists or annotators against tampering with the text, and that is exactly what is done here. Similar warnings, though not usually in the form of a sacral curse, may be seen elsewhere.[76] The copying that the author of the Apocalypse has in view would not have been the copying necessary to supply the text to each of the seven churches addressed in 2:1–3:22, for the production of those copies would have occurred under the direct supervision of the author or his immediate agents. Rather, the author looks toward the free circulation of the text beyond his own control, to its general dissemination within the wider Christian community.

In this connection there is the old question of why the author addresses precisely the seven churches that he does, to the neglect of Christian communities in some more important cities of the same region. It is difficult to find a more plausible answer than the one proposed by W. M. Ramsay: the distribution of the work to these seven churches, each located in a natural center of communication, best promoted the further circulation of the work among all the churches of the Asian province and beyond.[77] In any event, the author well understands that he is publishing his text, and he both anticipates and guards against the hazards of releasing it for copying and circulation. This is the real burden of the "instruction" received by the author at 22:10: "Do not seal up the words of the prophecy of this book." The intention of disseminating the work could hardly be clearer. In the Apocalypse, then, we see an intention to publish and an expectation of a wide readership. The author's ambition is in this sense quite self-consciously literary.

Among the earliest Christian literature there are a number of letters that have come to be called the catholic or general epistles because they are addressed to no particular Christian community, as Paul's letters normally were, but to Christendom at large.[78] Among the catholic epistles that found a place in the New Testament we encounter general designations of intended recipients: "The twelve tribes in the dispersion" (Jas. 1:1); "the exiles of the dispersion in Pontus, Galatia, Cappodocia, Asia, and Bythinia" (1 Pet. 1:1); "those who have obtained faith" (2 Pet. 1:1); and "those who are called, beloved in God and kept for Jesus Christ" (Jude 1:1). For my purposes the documents known as the Epistle of Barnabas and 2 Clement may be added to these, though they are somewhat later, dating perhaps from the middle of the second century. From a literary standpoint all these documents are less pieces of occasional correspondence than they are theological essays in letter form. The epistolary aspect is prominent in some (1–2 Peter, 2–3 John), limited in others (James, Jude), and minimal in still others (1 John, 2 Clement, Barnabas). They typically treat issues of general interest and are not closely tailored to the particular circumstances of the addressees. Whether or not any of these documents ever had a nonepistolary form, it is a mistake to conclude from their general character that they were not actually dispatched as letters.[79] Even those that make only the slightest pretense to the letter form nevertheless reveal that they were written with a view to publication—copying, circulation, and reading. So, for example, although it lacks any recognizable epistolary prescript or conclusion, 1 John is punctuated by the phrase, "I am writing" (1:4; 2:1, 7, 12, 21, 26; 5:13). There are no conventional epistolary elements in the Epistle of Barnabas, yet the author clearly considers that what he writes is to be sent on and read elsewhere (1:5; 4:9; 6:5; 9:9; 17:1–2; 21). It has often been argued that in at least some of these cases the epistolary form is purely conventional. Yet in the context of the church at that time, an author who cast a homily or theological essay in the form of a letter, especially a general or catholic letter, must have anticipated, indeed intended, its broad, general circulation.[80]

It is useful to reflect in passing on the force of the practice of pseudonymous authorship for the question of the publication and circulation of early Christian documents and of catholic epistles in particular. Many of these earliest writings are pseudonymous, and even those that are anonymous acquired from a very early time an association with the name of an apostle or a disciple of an apostle. It was, to be sure, the broad concern of early Christianity to secure the authority of its traditions and teachings by rooting them in the testimony of the apostles. This fully theological aim need not be denied if we say also that the pseudonymous presentation of apostolic teaching in written form assumes that at least some apostolic literature was already current. The choice of letters as the favorite form of pseudonymously apostolic literature sprang from Paul's example, and it was the broad currency of Paul's letters that in the late first century produced the conjunction of apostle, written teaching, and letter. Ultimately, the whole phenomenon of pseudonymously apostolic writing found its root in Paul's actual practice. Of course, Paul's letters were not themselves catholic, but as we have seen, they early came to be thought of and used as such.

In the late second century the anti-Montanist writer Apollonius accused the Montanist Themiso of having written a catholic letter "in imitation of the apostle" (H.E. 5.18.5).[81] The charge indicates that the catholic epistle was recognized as an established literary genre in early Christianity. Though Themiso apparently wrote in his own name, Apollonius's criticism shows how indissolubly linked apostolic authorship and catholic address had become in Christian thinking. To write as an apostle meant to address the church at large, and the intention to address the church at large meant to write as an apostle. In this sense the adoption of an apostolic pseudonym was correlative with the intention of broad circulation. At the same time, the author of a pseudonymously apostolic document must have known that the means were available to achieve extensive circulation. In the usual case this probably meant the production at the outset of multiple copies to be simultaneously distributed over a broad area, potentially to any Christian community, but more likely to a limited number of churches well situated to promote yet further, secondary distribution.[82] In short, a catholic epistle, unlike a letter to a specific community, aimed from the start to reach a wide readership and was thus composed for publication.

CHRISTIAN LITERATURE OF THE
SECOND AND THIRD CENTURIES

The Christian literature of the second and third centuries must be appraised in both its continuities and discontinuities with the earliest Christian literature, not only in respect of its genres and content but also with regard to its publication and circulation. On these latter questions it furnishes a good measure of helpful data.

Like the Apocalypse of John, another document of early Christian prophecy, *The Shepherd* of Hermas, exemplifies the bookish aspect of apocalyptic literature. *The Shepherd* was written in stages during the first half of the second century, as we know from the variations of its constituent forms and from explicit comments in the text. Hermas is represented as making a copy of the "little book" *(biblaridion)* containing divine revelation, from which the elderly lady (a personification of the church) has read to him. He copies it, moreover, "letter by letter" *(metagraphein pros gramma,* Vis. 2.1.3–4). Unable to distinguish the syllables, Hermas copies mechanically, without actually reading the text, and so it is only later that Hermas receives a "revelation" of its content (Vis. 2.2.1). To the contents of that little book Hermas is instructed to add further revelations and then to make the whole known "to all the elect." The elderly lady gives Hermas these specific instructions: "You shall therefore write two little books and send one to Clement and one to Grapte. Clement then shall send it to the cities abroad, for that is his duty, and Grapte shall exhort the widows and orphans; but in this city you shall read it yourself with the elders who are in charge of the church" (Vis. 2.4.3).

This is one of the few early Christian texts that offer an explicit notice about the dissemination of a piece of Christian writing. Though the account is imaginative, it undoubtedly reflects what it would have taken to publish a document and place it in circulation. Hermas is to make two copies of the original composition and to deposit them with two different individuals so as to reach two constituencies. One copy is to be provided to a certain Clement, who is understood as the corresponding secretary, so to speak, of the Roman church: his regular function *(ekeino epitetraptai)* is to make and dispatch to churches in other cities *(eis tas exo poleis)* copies of documents that are intended for distribution. It is likely that the Clement who is intended here is the putative author of the letter of the Roman church to the Corinthian church that we know as 1 Clement, customarily dated to the end of the first century.[83] Depending on the date of *The Shepherd*, the reference to Clement may be only a literary device: in its present form *The Shepherd* was certainly not composed as early as the late first century. Yet the earliest parts may belong to the early second century and so perhaps to Clement's lifetime. Should the mention of Clement be a deliberate anachronism, however, the role assigned to him—to make and dispatch to churches elsewhere copies of Christian texts— must have been comprehensible and was probably actually familiar to Hermas's readers.[84] In addition to the copy that will serve as Clement's archetype, another copy is to go to Grapte. We are not told Grapte's position; perhaps she was a deaconess. She apparently looked after widows and orphans and would disseminate the work to those groups. Finally, Hermas, together "with the presbyters," is to read the text he retains to the church in Rome. Here, then, not only the intention but also the concrete means of the publication of the work are explicit.

We glimpse in Hermas's description of Clement's function what might almost be called an ecclesiastical publisher, a standing provision in the Roman church for duplicating and distributing texts to Christian communities elsewhere. The regular activity this implies would not be particularly surprising, even at so early a time, especially in a large and influential Christian center such as Rome. The churches in Rome, Antioch, Caesarea, and Alexandria (to name only the most obvious) were probably centers almost from the beginning for the composition of Christian writings and also for the confluence of Christian writings composed elsewhere. By virtue of possessing both texts and regional influence, these communities would have been instrumental in the further circulation of Christian literature. In fact, copies of Hermas's *Shepherd* spread quickly: the work was in circulation in Egypt, both in Alexandria and in provincial regions, well before the end of the second century and was known at the same time in Gaul and North Africa.[85] That *The Shepherd* became so widely known at such an early time seems more consistent with the systematic dissemination portrayed in the text than with merely random circulation.

An unusually well documented and instructive instance of the publication and circulation of Christian texts is furnished by another collection of letters, namely, those of Ignatius, bishop of Antioch. These letters were written as the Syrian bishop was being transported to Rome and martyrdom during the reign of Trajan (98–117 C.E.) and were dispatched to churches along the way that had offered him aid and comfort. Most important for my interest, however, is a letter from Polycarp, bishop of Smyrna, to the Christian community in Philippi, for it sheds much light on the early history of Ignatius's letters. It is not certain whether what we know as Polycarp's letter to the Philippians is a single letter; it may be a conflation of two letters written at different times.[86] If there were originally two letters (chapters 1–12 and 13–14), the earlier one (chapters 13–14) would be of concern here. Chapter 13 of Polycarp's letter reads:

> Both you and Ignatius write to me that if anyone is going to Syria he should also take along your letter. I shall do this if I have a convenient opportunity—either I myself or someone I send as a representative for you and me. We are sending to you, as you requested, the letters of Ignatius which were sent to us by him and such others as we have at hand. They are attached to this letter. You will be able to benefit greatly from them. For they deal with faith, endurance, and all the edification which pertains to our Lord. And let us know anything further which you learn about Ignatius and those with him.

Polycarp is plainly responding to a letter from the Philippians in which, among other things, they asked that he send them copies of letters of Ignatius. Presumably they had learned from Ignatius himself that he had written a letter to the church of Smyrna, a letter to Polycarp, and perhaps other letters to other churches. The letter from the Philippians requesting Ignatius's letters must have been sent soon after Ignatius had left Philippi, for in his response Polycarp does not yet know whether Ignatius has been put to death. Therefore, the events of Ignatius's departure from Philippi, the sending of the Philippians' letter to Polycarp, and Polycarp's reply probably took place within a period of a few weeks at most.

Polycarp obliged the Philippians by sending them copies of letters from Ignatius. But which letters? The letters "sent to us by him" must mean Ignatius's letter to the Smyrneans and his letter to Polycarp. Along with those, Polycarp included copies of letters Ignatius had sent to other congregations in Asia Minor, but we do not know which or how many of these he had. Whichever they were, it is not necessary to suppose that they were duplicated by the churches to which they had been addressed and the copies distributed to other churches of the area, like Smyrna. Considering how little time had elapsed, that seems unlikely. Rather, since Ignatius had written from Smyrna to the Ephesians, Magnesians, Trallians, and Romans, it is far more plausible that the church at Smyrna had retained copies of the letters written from there. In that case, the only extant Ignatian letter that might not have been immediately available in Smyrna was the one to the Philadelphian church, which Ignatius had dispatched from Troas, as he had the letters to Smyrna and to Polycarp. Yet Philadelphia was not too distant from Smyrna, and the letter to Philadelphia, if not sent to Smyrna in a copy by Ignatius, could have been readily obtained by the Smyrnean church. Thus soon after the composition of the Ignatian letters Polycarp had a collection of them, possibly a complete collection, and was able to furnish it to the Philippians on request. This he would have done by transcribing copies from the manuscripts in Smyrna, and thus the textual history of the Ignatian letters began. The dispatch to Philippi of the text of the collected letters would have constituted a de facto publication of the collection as such, for although the individual letters could be said to have been previously published when they reached their original addressees, it was as a corpus that the Ignatian letters came to be widely known and valued in the ancient church, and copies of individual letters, being less valuable, would have quickly become obsolete.[87]

The letters of Ignatius, then, give us a clear instance of the collection and dissemination of a group of Christian writings within a short period. It is tempting to see here a positive analogue to the collection and publication of Paul's letters. Other things being equal, Paul's letters were far more likely to have been valued, collected, published, and distributed in a shorter time than those of Ignatius. What is not equal would strengthen that possibility: Paul was a church-founding apostle, had well-established and close ties with a number of churches in diverse but contiguous regions, and was survived by a cadre of associates who had been intimately involved in his literary activity. If the less substantial letters of a bishop and prospective martyr were quickly brought together and disseminated as a group, it is all the more probable that similar measures were taken with the apostle's letters several decades previously.

There is more to be said on the basis of Polycarp's letter to the Philippians. Not only do we find Polycarp collecting and making copies of Ignatius's letters, he was engaged at the same time in drawing up yet another collection of letters. Ignatius had routinely asked the churches to which he wrote to pray for the church in Antioch. When word came to him that the Antiochene church had regained its peace, Ignatius desired that other churches should send delegates to Antioch to congratulate them (Philad. 10.1–2; Smyr. 11.2–3; Polyc. 7.2, 8.1), and he hoped that letters from the churches would be sent with those delegates (Smyr. 11.3).[88] Hence we find Polycarp (Phil. 13.1) receiving a letter from the Philippians addressed to Antioch, which he is asked to transmit to Antioch by a messenger. Ignatius's idea was apparently not that every church should send a messenger to Antioch, but only those nearby, and that more distant churches should send a messenger with a letter to Smyrna, whence the letters, once gathered, would be dispatched by a single messenger to Antioch.[89] At least this is how Polycarp and the Philippians understood the matter (Phil. 13.1). Thus, while Polycarp was making and sending off copies of the collected letters of Ignatius, he was also collecting letters from various churches in Asia Minor and arranging to send them to Antioch. In all this we glimpse a busy, almost hectic traffic of messengers and letters between the churches of the region. This intense activity shows that the church at Smyrna in particular had both the interest and capacity to reproduce and distribute texts, and this, moreover, during the first two decades of the second century, a period often regarded as still heavily committed to oral tradition and little interested in the written word.

In addition to letters, Gospels, and apocalypses, much of the earliest Christian literature consisted of apologies, the primary purpose of which was to defend Christianity against pagan criticism. Many were composed in the second century, "the age of the apologists." Modern scholars have doubted that the early apologies that are addressed to the Roman emperor were actually presented or dispatched to the emperors named. They regard the address as a literary fiction and think these tracts were intended only for intramural Christian use.[90] Apologies had an obvious value for Christians in their dealings with educated non-Christians, and the fact that these works were preserved within the church does indicate that many Christians read them. But this is no reason to deny that the apologists hoped their tracts might actually be read and considered by the emperor or within his secretariat. Neither the form nor content of the apologies makes this unlikely, and emperors did regularly receive and respond to petitions from various constituencies in the empire.[91] Perhaps the most plausible assumption is that they were open letters to the emperor, that is, sent to the emperor and at the same time circulated among Christians and, so far as possible, among the general public—or at least its more educated elements.[92] The apology of Justin, written about 150, gives every appearance of having been presented to Antoninus and was read by the pagan critic Celsus as well, and it was not the only apology Celsus knew.[93] In his so-called Second Apology

(15.1–3), Justin pleads for official permission to disseminate his work, arguing that Christian teachings are not harmful like various philosophical and poetic teachings, "which all are allowed to acquaint themselves with, both as spoken and as written" *(hois entugchanein pasi, kai legomenois kai gegrammenois)*. Despite Tertullian's claim that Christian literature was read only by those who were already Christian *(De test. an.* 1.4) (a circumstance he surely regretted), it is scarcely conceivable that even apologies that were not directed to the emperor, such as Theophilus's *Ad Autolycum*, Minucius Felix's *Octavius*, or Tertullian's own *Apologeticum*, had only a Christian readership in view and did not aim to reach a wider pagan audience. There is little exposition of Christian belief and practice in them except what was necessary to counter pagan calumnies.[94]

That the apologies were written not merely for Christian but also for pagan consumption has consequences for my conception of their publication and circulation. If pagans could be induced to read such works, they could hardly be expected to go to the trouble or expense of obtaining the copies they read. It has to be supposed that Christians produced the copies and insinuated them among non-Christian readers. Propaganda, more than other types of literature, requires a greater effort of distribution. We can only guess how widely Christian apologies circulated among pagans, but we know that they were rapidly disseminated in Christian circles. Irenaeus, writing in Gaul in the 180s, appears to have been acquainted with the apologies of Justin, Tatian, and Theophilus, and so was Tertullian near the end of the second century in North Africa.[95] It is especially notable that Theophilus's *Ad Autolycum*, composed in Antioch soon after 180, could be read by Irenaeus at the other end of the empire soon after. When we recall that Irenaeus's *Against Heresies* was available in Egypt by the late second century, it demonstrates the impressive speed and scope of the movement of Christian writings in the late second century.

Another second century text that illumines the peregrinations of early Christian literature is the *Martyrdom of Polycarp*, which is a letter from the church at Smyrna to the church in Philomelium that incidentally reinforces the impression gained from Polycarp's letter to the Philippians of the lively literary activity of the Smyrnean church. Although the date of Polycarp's martyrdom and thus also of this letter (which was written soon after) has been repeatedly debated, the best arguments speak for sometime between 156 and 160.[96] The account of Polycarp's martyrdom was provided in response to a request from the Christians in Philomelium, who had asked for news of Polycarp's

death (20.1), and was sent as a letter "to the church of God of Philomelium and to all the communities of the holy and catholic church
in every place" (praescr.). The use of the latter address makes this a
catholic letter, though it is first addressed to the Philomelium church.
It was apparently left to that church to make the letter catholic in
practice, for in the conclusion there is the request: "When you have
learned about these things, send the letter on [ten epistolen diapemp-
sasthe] to more distant brothers in order that they too may glorify the
Lord" (20.1). Both the intention and the agent for broad circulation are
explicit here. *Diapempein* may signify either making and sending
copies on to other churches, or making and retaining a copy while
sending on the original to another church, which would then repeat
the procedure. Either way, the letter would have found a wide readership in little time. Possibly in the reference to "more distant brothers,"
that is, more distant than Philomelium to the *east* of Smyrna, there
lies the implication that the Smyrnean church would itself dispatch
an account to churches lying to the west.[97]

Particular interest and not a little difficulty attach to the matter
that is associated with the end of this letter in the manuscript tradition. This material, which is customarily designated as chapters 21
and 22, includes: a specification of the date of Polycarp's martyrdom
(chapter 21); a concluding farewell and doxology (chapter 22.1); and a
series of scribal colophons (22.2–4). None of this belonged to the
original letter from Smyrna to Philomelium, which comes to its obvious conclusion with the doxology and greeting of 20.2. The secondary
material is not all of a piece but was added at various points and for
different reasons early in the process of transmission. I limit my
attention to the scribal colophons, which read as follows:

> (22.2) *Gaius transcribed* [metegrapsato] *[this] from the papers of
> Irenaeus* [ek ton Eirenaiou], *a disciple of Polycarp. He also lived
> with* [sunepoliteusato] *Irenaeus.*
> (22.3) *And I, Socrates, transcribed* [egrapsa] *[it] in Corinth from
> the copy of Gaius* [ek ton Gaiou antigraphon]. *Grace be with all.*
> (22.4) *And I, Pionius, again transcribed* [egrapsa] *[it] from the
> copy mentioned above* [ek tou progegrammenou], *having sought
> it out in accordance with a revelation which the blessed Polycarp
> showed me, as I shall explain in the sequel, gathering it together
> when it was almost worn out with age, so that the Lord Jesus
> Christ might also gather me together with his elect ones into his
> heavenly kingdom, to whom be glory with the Father and the
> Holy Spirit forever. Amen.*

These notes, in which two copyists, Socrates and Pionius, speak in the first person and mention yet a third (Gaius), ostensibly document stages of one tangent of the early circulation of the *Martyrdom of Polycarp*. Do these scribal notes have any historical value? Their worth has been widely doubted, for two reasons. First, the reference in 22.2 to both Irenaeus and Polycarp has raised suspicion that the whole section, 22.2–4, is contrived to put even the copying of the letter "in a sort of succession extending back to Polycarp," and that 22.2–3 was "reformulated (or even invented)" by the person who added 22.4.[98] Second, 22.4, with its allusion to a "sequel," indicates that the *Martyrdom of Polycarp* was once transmitted as part of a larger collection of materials relating to Polycarp, including a *Life of Polycarp* by one Pionius. The Pionius intended is almost surely the Pionius martyred in Smyrna during the Decian persecution (250), but the name was pseudonymously used by a fourth-century writer who composed the *Life of Polycarp*.[99] Since the Pionian *Life of Polycarp* is unquestionably a fourth-century fabrication, the Pionian colophon (22.4) is often regarded as a fourth-century contrivance meant to lend credibility to the *Life* and coherence to the collection of Polycarpiana.

It would be rash to dismiss for these reasons the entire transmission history indicated in the colophons of 22.2–4. It is possible and perhaps likely that the scribal notes in 22.2–3 give reliable information. There is no reason to assume that the Gaius mentioned in 22.2 either was or was intended as the Roman presbyter in the time of Hippolytus (mentioned by Eusebius, *H.E.* 2.25.6), for the name was common and our sources make no connection between that Gaius and Irenaeus, and no distinguished pedigree could have been gained by the mere mention of the name. Gaius is said to have made a copy of *Martyrdom* from the text in Irenaeus's possession, Gaius having been a fellow citizen of Irenaeus, presumably in Gaul.[100] Similarly, in 22.3 the locale of Socrates' copying is mentioned, namely, Corinth. The name Socrates (or, in some manuscripts, Isocrates) does not summon any notable Christian or confer any special authority on the transcriptional history.[101] In short, the presumed inauthenticity of the Pionian colophon in 22.4 does not discredit the colophons in 22.2–3, which in the absence of a clear ulterior motive may be regarded as genuine.[102]

In that case it would appear that a copy of the Smyrnean account of Polycarp's martyrdom reached Gaul and was in the possession of Irenaeus or at least in the archives at Lyons. This copy was used as an exemplar by a certain Gaius, whose identity is unknown but who lived in Lyons and may perhaps have had a standing secretarial office in the church there. His transcription, presumably made in the last decades of the second century, made its way to Corinth, where it served in turn as an exemplar for the copy made by Socrates. It is impossible to say when this was, but it was probably sometime in the third century, perhaps early in the third. The Pionian colophon, pseudonymous though it is, may yet truthfully represent the use by its fourth-century author of a timeworn manuscript copied in Corinth a century earlier.

Several issues I have touched upon—letter collections, the potential for textual adulteration anticipated in the Apocalypse, the intentions and assumptions lying behind a catholic address, and the role attributed to Clement in Hermas—all come into play in connection with a notice of Eusebius concerning Dionysius, bishop of Corinth around 170. Eusebius says that Dionysius had made himself "useful to all in the catholic epistles which he drew up for the churches" (H.E. 4.23.1) and indicates that these were letters that Dionysius had written to various churches: in Lacedaemonia, in Athens, in Nicomedia, in Gortyna together with other churches in Crete, in Amastris together with other churches in Pontus, in Cnossus, and in Rome (H.E. 4.23.2–11). In addition to these seven letters to various churches, Eusebius also mentions the availability of a personal letter of Dionysius to the Christian woman Chrysophora (H.E. 4.23.13) and a letter from Pinytos, bishop of Cnossus, in reply to Dionysius's letter to that church (H.E. 4.23.8). It is puzzling that Eusebius dubbed as "catholic" letters that were obviously addressed to individual Christian churches or, in two cases, to several churches in a discrete area. The term normally signified letters of general rather than specific address. The explanation must lie not in the addresses of the letters but in the history of their circulation and transmission. In considering this, some interesting points come to light.

We know next to nothing about Dionysius beyond what Eusebius reports in this brief passage. He was apparently a widely known and respected man who sometimes exercised his teaching authority by writing letters on various topics to churches that lay beyond his own episcopal jurisdiction.[103] This is reminiscent of the activity attributed by Hermas to Clement of Rome, although Dionysius, a monarchical bishop, seems to write as an individual, while the author of 1 Clement writes on behalf of the presbyters of the Roman church. Like Clement, Dionysius illustrates the extent to which and the means by which Christian communities managed to be in touch over a broad area. Eusebius was undoubtedly acquainted with the letters of Dionysius as a collection, having found them transcribed together in a single codex or roll in the Caesarean library.[104] The statement of Dionysius, quoted by Eusebius (*H.E.* 4.23.12), indicates that the letters of Dionysius constituted a discrete collection: "When brothers [Christians] asked me to write letters I wrote them, and these the apostles of the devil have filled with tares, leaving out some things, and adding others. Woe be to them. Hence it is not surprising that some have set about falsifying even the scriptures of the Lord, when they have plotted against such inferior writings as these." Since this statement refers to the letters as a group, it must have accompanied a collection of the letters. It may have stood as (part of?) a preface, but most likely it was contained in the letter of Dionysius to Soter, bishop of Rome, from which Eusebius quotes twice in the preceding context (*H.E.* 4.23.10–11). In that case, the letter to Soter was probably a cover letter for the collection rather than another item in it. The presence of this note suggests both that the collection was made by Dionysius himself and that the motive for the collection was to counter the adulteration of the texts.

Whether the putative motive was the real one is open to speculation. It has been supposed that Dionysius would not have written to Rome about his letters, nor sent along a collection of them, unless some of his letters had been forwarded to Rome by others who complained about the views expressed in them, thus requiring Dionysius to defend himself to Soter.[105] This is conceivable, but whereas a collection of letters might serve to balance views expressed in only one or two, it is improbable that Dionysius could have rebutted a substantial complaint about his teaching merely by claiming textual corruption. Hence it seems likely that Dionysius was right to allege that some had contrived to emend his letters in support of views he did not himself hold.

The information offered by Eusebius seems to require a reconstruction like the following. Dionysius from time to time wrote to particular communities with instruction on a matter of current concern to them. At least some of those letters must have been individually circulated beyond their original recipients and therefore also copied, and it was in this process of copying that the texts of individual letters were corrupted by omissions and interpolations. Dionysius attributed this adulteration to "apostles of the devil," apparently believing that heretics were deliberately manipulating the texts of his letters in order to misrepresent his views. This may not have been unlikely, but, since Dionysius does not say what was added or omitted, or to what effect, it is possible that some of the corruptions arose merely through the copying process.[106] In either event the episode shows that an author's fears for the security of his text were warranted.

Dionysius tried to displace the defective texts by issuing an authorized edition, as it were, of his collected letters with their original texts. To work up this collection Dionysius must have used copies of the letters that he retained when he composed and dispatched them.[107] It was probably Dionysius himself who entitled the collection "catholic epistles" because, although the letters were addressed to specific churches, as a collection they were issued for circulation in the church as a whole.[108]

The fate of Dionysius's letters and the remedy he chose have many analogues in the larger literary world. Quintilian (*Inst. Or.* 1. pr. 7–8) mentions works circulating under his name that were based on notes taken at his lectures and published without his permission. He planned to displace them by publishing his ideas in a fuller and more accurate form. Arrian, as he explains in his introduction to the *Discourses* of Epictetus (1.1), was finally provoked to publish his own transcripts because unauthorized copies had somehow got into circulation and threatened to produce both misunderstanding of Epictetus as a teacher and criticism of Arrian as a writer. Galen (*De libr. prop.* praef.) preferred a limited, private circulation of his works among friends for fear that wider currency would result in the bowdlerization of his text and threaten his reputation. Not long after Dionysius's time, Origen was able to vindicate himself against an appeal to an interpolated manuscript by locating and producing the original manuscript from his own papers.[109] The currency of unauthorized, excerpted, or corrupted texts is so frequently given as the reason for publication that it is almost a topos in the literature of the period.[110] Once in circulation, a text could not be recalled, no matter how extensively corrupted it might have become. The republication of a text, however, if the new edition were known to be revised, enlarged, or otherwise preferable, had some chance of arresting, if not entirely supplanting, the currency of other forms of the text.

The publication history of another Christian document of the late second century and early third century, Tertullian's treatise *adversus Marcionem*, nicely illustrates this point. The work is known to us in what may be called its third edition, probably begun in 207 or 208.[111] At the beginning (1.1) Tertullian carefully informs the reader about earlier editions:

> *The first edition* [primum opusculum], *too hastily produced, I later withdrew, substituting a fuller treatment* [pleniore compositione]. *This too, before enough copies had been produced* [non-

dum exemplariis suffectam], *was stolen by one who was at the time a brother [Christian] but later became an apostate, and who copied excerpts very incorrectly and made them available to many people* [qui forte descripserat quaedam mendosissime et exhibuit frequentiae]. *Thus emendation was required. This occasion persuaded me to make some additions. Thus this composition, a third following a second, and instead of a third from now on the first, needs to begin by reporting the demise of the work it replaces in order that no one may be confused if in one place or another he comes across varying forms of it.*

There are several interesting points in this statement. Tertullian came to believe that the text of the first edition, written sometime between 198 and 204, was either too brief or careless, or both, and so he "withdrew" it *(rescideram)* to revise it. Under the circumstances, the withdrawal could scarcely have been more than a disavowal; he could not have taken the work out of circulation, for once out of his hands, an author had no control over it. Tertullian completed the revised version a year or two after the first edition, but publication was aborted when the text was pirated by a fellow Christian who transcribed parts of it and gave it out in a truncated and inaccurate form.[112] Tertullian says that the text was misappropriated *nondum exemplariis suffectam*. The sense of this phrase is not entirely clear, but considering the circumstances it may have been Tertullian's plan not simply to release the work for copying by any interested party, but to have a certain number of copies made at the outset and to distribute them. Such a procedure would have promoted its more rapid dissemination and helped to counter the currency of the first published version.[113] With the revised edition thus preempted and perverted, Tertullian decided to enlarge the work still more and completed it probably not before 211 or 212. No doubt he maintained a closer control of the text during the composition of this last version. The publication history of *adversus Marcionem* thus spanned about a decade and resulted in the currency of three different versions. The first was withdrawn by the author, but with limited practical effect since existing copies could not be repressed; the second, though without the author's permission and departing from his design, was widely disseminated; and the third, the author's considered composition, aimed to displace the previous two, and so far as we can see, succeeded in doing so.[114] Tertullian assumed that the third edition would have to compete with the other two, and that a reader might encounter all three and be confused. This obviously implies that the previous versions of the work were widely available and thus that dissemination had been rapid. The success of the third edition in displacing the earlier forms of the text probably depended on its initial production in a number of copies, a measure that seems to have been intended also for the second edition but not completed in time to be effective. If so, in this case publication would have involved more than the release of an exemplar for transcription by interested parties. Although it would be too much to speak of mass production, the production of multiple copies at the outset was the only way to give a later edition any advantage over an earlier one. We know nothing of the technical means by which this may have been accomplished, but they must have been considerable since the *adversus Marcionem* is a long treatise.[115]

This raises the important question of what resources were available for the physical production of Christian texts. On this subject we are so poorly informed for the first three centuries that any information at all is valuable. One of the earliest and fullest descriptions concerns the resources that were available to Origen in Alexandria early in the third century. We are told by Eusebius (*H.E.* 6.23.2) that Origen's wealthy patron, Ambrose, supplied Origen with a large staff in order to increase the speed and volume of his productivity and to distribute his works effectively: "As [Origen] dictated there were ready at hand more than seven shorthand writers *[tachygraphoi]* who relieved each other at fixed intervals, and as many copyists *[bibliographoi]*, as well as young women who were skilled in fine writing *[kalligraphein]*, for all of whom Ambrose provided without stinting the necessary means." The enormous volume of Origen's literary output was due in some measure to the services of this staff. His oral composition was transcribed by trained stenographers; their shorthand transcripts were then converted into full-text exemplars by copyists who could decipher stenographic notes; and from these exemplars female scribes produced fair copies in a good bookhand. Origen himself would have revised the exemplars before the copies were made.[116] Ambrose, who was intent not only on the rapid production of the great scholar's work but also on its wide availability to Christians of inquiring mind, would certainly have arranged for multiple copies to be made.[117] Otherwise such a large staff would have been unnecessary. Here for the first time in my survey are the details of something resembling a genuine publishing operation in the Christian setting.

Origen's "scriptorium" was, to be sure, unique within Christian circles in that it was privately sponsored and was designed to support the work of a single Christian writer.[118] There are good reasons to think that in other Christian centers, and at an earlier time, some systematic provision had been made for the production and dissemination of Christian texts. For example, in order to produce copies of the *adversus Marcionem* Tertullian must have been able to call upon a staff of trained copyists in Carthage. Irenaeus must likewise have had access to efficient resources in Gaul for the composition and circulation of the *adversus Haereses*, which was written in stages. The first two books were composed and sent to the friend who had proposed the work before the third book was written (*A.H.* 3, praef.), and the fourth and fifth books followed still later. Nevertheless, the work is known only as a whole, and as a whole it quickly made its way to Egypt and North Africa, where Tertullian used it.[119] We may also wonder whether the large body of theological works composed by Hippolytus in Rome would not have required scribal resources like those of his contemporary Origen.

It is difficult to determine just when Christian scriptoria came into existence. The problem is partly of definition, partly of evidence. If we think of a scriptorium as simply a writing center where texts were copied by more than a single scribe, then any of the larger Christian communities, such as Antioch or Rome, may have already had scriptoria in the early second century, and in view of Polycarp's activity something of the kind can be imagined for Smyrna. If we think instead of a scriptorium as being more structured, operating, for example, in a specially designed and designated location; employing particular methods of transcription; producing certain types of manuscripts; or multiplying copies on a significant scale, then it becomes more difficult to imagine that such institutions developed at an early date. Origen's scriptorium is the first for which we have clear evidence, and it is a special case. For the work of Cyprian a little later we can imagine something similar yet more official by dint of its attachment to episcopal authority and ecclesiastical activity. Certainly, there was a scriptorium attached to the Christian library in Caesarea by the early fourth century, when Eusebius was asked to produce fifty copies of the scriptures in short order, and it was probably already in operation when Pamphilus first began to build up the library in the third century. In antiquity a library of any appreciable size required scriptorial capacity.[120] Hence, it should be assumed that scriptoria were also to be found at that time in other Christian centers, most especially in those where there were libraries—such as Jerusalem, Rome, and Alexandria. It was only during the fourth and fifth centuries that the scriptoria of monastic communuities came into their own, also in association with monastic libraries.

We can only guess about the situation in the second century. It has been claimed that a Christian scriptorium with professional scribes "would have been an impossibility" before 200 c.e., and that up to that time "all manuscripts must have been copied privately by individuals."[121] Yet a few second-century manuscripts of scriptural texts may be scriptorial products, considering their calligraphy and correction against a second exemplar or considering the character of their texts.[122] The large number of Christian manuscripts found at Oxyrhynchus, including some that are both well written and early, may mean that there was a Christian scriptorium there by the late second or early third century.[123] If so, that is all the more reason to postulate scriptoria in Alexandria and other Christian centers at an earlier time.

Scriptorial activity can perhaps be glimpsed in Eusebius's quotation (H.E. 5.28.8–19) of a polemical fragment against a certain theological school in Rome in the last decades of the second century. This fragment is from a work called *Little Labyrinth*, which is sometimes attributed to Hippolytus.[124] It describes a group of Roman Christians, followers of Theodotus, who were devoted to the study of Euclid, Theophrastus, and Aristotle and were admirers of the contemporary physician and philosopher Galen.[125] One aspect of their attention to Greek learning was a critical interest in the text of scripture:

> *For this reason they did not fear to lay hands on the divine scriptures, claiming to have corrected them* [autas diorthokenai]. . . . *If anyone wishes to collect and compare with each other the texts of each of them he would find them highly divergent. The copies of Asclepiades do not agree with those of Theodotus, and it is possible to obtain many of them because their disciples have diligently written out copies corrected* [katorthomena], *as they say, but really corrupted* [ephanismena] *by each of them. Again, the copies of Hermophilus do not agree with these, and the copies of Apolloniades are not even consistent with themselves, for the copies prepared by them at first can be compared with those which later on were corrupted* [epidiastrapheisin] *yet again, and will be found to disagree greatly. . . . They cannot even deny that this crime is theirs, seeing that the copies were written in their own hand, and they did not receive the scriptures in this condition from their teachers, nor can they show originals* [antigrapha] *from which they made their copies* [metegrapsanto].

We see here the application to texts of Christian scripture—perhaps especially Gospel texts since the Theodotians sponsored an adoptionistic Christology—of the methods of textual and literary criticism developed by Greek scholarship to establish the texts of Greek literary and philosophical works.[126] The use of these methods in the Roman church appears to be parallel to but independent of the textual interests of Alexandrian Christian scholarship as represented by Origen. The polemic quoted by Eusebius is directed against the presumption of questioning the received text of scripture and especially against conjectural emendation *(diorthosis)*, which altered transmitted readings that did not meet ordinary standards of sense or style, and was a major aspect of textual criticism in antiquity. This work was pursued or sponsored by individual Christian teachers, apparently not as a joint project, for it seems that various recensions of the text were produced, each associated with a particular scholar—Theodotus, Asclepiades, Hermophilus, or Apolloniades. The work of each was current in many copies, so that copies were easily obtained and compared. It is unlikely that the ready availability of copies was due to purely private, individual copying. Despite its scholastic aspect, this textual work in Rome was not disinterested but stood in the service of exegesis and theological argument, which makes it still more probable that the emended texts were produced in numerous copies, the better to promote their wide use and thus sustain a particular theological viewpoint.

Complaints about the adulteration of texts are fairly frequent in early Christian literature. Christian texts, scriptural and nonscriptural, were no more immune than others from the vicissitudes of unregulated transmission in handwritten copies. In some respects they were more vulnerable than ordinary texts, and not merely because Christian communities could not always command the most competent scribes. Although Christian writings generally aimed to express not individual viewpoints but the shared convictions and values of a group, members of the group who acted as editors and copyists must often have revised texts in accordance with their own perceptions. This temptation was stronger in connection with religious or philosophical texts than with others simply because more was at stake. A great deal of early Christian literature was composed for the purpose of advancing a particular viewpoint amid the conflicts of ideas and practices that repeatedly arose within and between Christian communities, and even documents that were not polemically conceived might nevertheless become polemically useful.[127] Any text was liable to emendation in the interest of making it more pointedly serviceable in a situation of theological controversy. It is not surprising, then, to learn from Eusebius (*H.E.* 5.20.2) that Irenaeus, in concluding an antignostic work, *On the Ogdoad* (now lost), anticipated and sought to deter adventurous copyists: "I adjure you who will copy this book, by our Lord Jesus Christ and by his glorious advent when he comes to judge the living and the dead, that you collate [*hina antibales*] what you transcribe and that you correct it [*katorthoses*] against this copy [*antigraphon*] from which you transcribe, and very carefully, and that likewise you shall transcribe this oath and put it in the copy." Irenaeus, like anyone who dealt with texts, was well acquainted with the methods of their reproduction: transcription, collation, and correction. In admonishing prospective copyists Irenaeus was not chiefly worried about ordinary scribal errors that, though unwelcome, had to be tolerated under the conditions of ancient book production. His precaution was against copyists making deliberate, substantive revisions or excerptions of the text that perverted his meaning, an enduring concern of authors. Fully two centuries later Rufinus of Aquileia was no less anxious about it when he issued his Latin translation of Origen's *De principiis* and so affixed a still more intimidating warning:

> *Truly in the presence of God the Father and of the Son and of the Holy Spirit, I adjure and beseech everyone who may either transcribe or read these books, by his belief in the kingdom to come, by the mystery of the resurrection from the dead, and by that everlasting fire prepared for the devil and his angels, that, as he would not possess for an eternal inheritance that place where there is weeping and gnashing of teeth and where their fire is not quenched and their spirit does not die, he add nothing to what is written and take nothing away from it, and make no insertion or alteration, but that he compare his transcription with the copies from which he made it and make the emendations according to the letter and supply the punctuation, and not allow his manuscript to be incorrect or without punctuation, lest the difficulty of ascertaining the sense from the absence of the punctuation of the copy should cause greater difficulties to the reader.*[128]

There were problems enough, Rufinus well knew, interpreting what Origen had actually said without the introduction of distorting glosses and emendations by readers or of copies poorly produced by scribes. Rufinus's effort to repristinate Origen's reputation (which ironically depended on his own exercise of a certain freedom in translating

Origen's work) could only be hindered by a similar freedom among those who read or copied his translation.

Concern about the adulteration of texts was not unique to Christians, of course, but it was more characteristic of the scholastically minded than of those whose interests were purely literary. Artemidorus, a contemporary of Irenaeus, furnishes a close non-Christian parallel when he concludes his treatise on the interpretation of dreams with this request (*Oneir.* 2.70):

> I ask those who read my books not to add or remove anything from the present contents. For any person who is able to add points to my work would more easily write a work of his own. And if certain things that I have written in these books seem superfluous, the reader should use only those things that please him without discarding the rest of the books. For he should realize that it was out of obedience to Apollo, the overseer god and guardian of all things in addition to being my own native god, that I undertook this treatise. Apollo has encouraged me in the past, and now especially, when I have made your acquaintance, he clearly presides over my work, and has all but commanded me to compose this work.

If Artemidorus is content to make a polite request (though he too invokes a divine sanction), while Irenaeus and Rufinus issue minatory injunctions, it is undoubtedly because already by Irenaeus's time Christians had had some hard experience of the theological dangers latent in the malleability of texts.

Early Christian writers frequently accused heterodox teachers of a penchant for the willful revision of texts, especially scriptural texts.[129] The charge belongs to the stock repertoire of antiheretical polemics and should not be uncritically credited, for the heterodox were usually able to find their warrants at the level of interpretation, without resorting to textual emendation.[130] The fear, however, was not baseless. By the mid–second century a worrisome precedent had been set by Marcion, who was justly notorious for his recasting of texts. Having rejected the scriptures of Judaism, Marcion was among the first Christian thinkers to vest decisive theological authority exclusively in Christian texts. By emendation and chiefly by excision, however, he also made extensive revisions in the texts he held to be authoritative, namely, the letters of Paul and the Gospel of Luke. Yet it needs to be emphasized that in his time Marcion's editorial activity was not unique. During the second century Christian scriptural texts were still relatively fluid and subject to revision, even in mainline Christian circles. It was then, for example, that the Gospel of Mark was given its longer ending(s), the Pastoral Epistles were added to the corpus of Paul's letters, and the synoptic Gospels were harmonized with each other.[131] Moreover, Marcion's textual revisions were rather less numerous and extensive than was once supposed: many readings once regarded as Marcionite are now recognized as variants stemming from an earlier non-Marcionite tradition.[132] What is too little recognized, however, is that Marcion's editorial activity did not arise from caprice, nor from an overbearing ideology, but from his critical, scholastic judgment, however idiosyncratic that may have been. He had a theory of the history of the texts, and not unlike modern critics he suspected that the texts had been contaminated by glosses, interpolations, and redactions that obscured their original sense. His revisions aimed at nothing less than the critical reconstitution of a pure text. Although the results of his effort are unsatisfactory by modern standards, Marcion's attitude and approach to the texts were continuous with well-established traditions of philological criticism in Greco-Roman antiquity.[133] The same canons of textual and literary criticism can to some extent be observed before Marcion in Papias, in Tatian, who was Marcion's contemporary, afterward in the followers of Theodotus in Rome, and later still in Origen, Dionysius of Alexandria, and others.[134]

Marcion provides an exaggerated but not wholly misleading example of the extent to which Christians in the second century both invested authority in texts and revised texts with a view to their value in theological argument. The two concerns are closely correlative: the authoritative valuation of a document entails an interest in the accuracy and stability of the text. What is too little recognized is that in antiquity the conscientious reader was always interested in the correction of textual corruptions since, given the conditions of the production and transmission of texts, the accuracy of a text was necessarily an open question. The irony is that the attribution of authority to a document did not necessarily confirm the received text and ensure its careful preservation but, by heightening interest in its accuracy, opened the way for critical emendation.[135] In the absence of controlled transmission, an ancient text acquired stability not in proportion to the extent of authority lodged in it, but by the broad circulation of enough copies to establish and sustain a consistent, self-reinforcing textual tradition. This fact is somewhat obscured by the high positive correlation in early Christian literature between the authority conferred on a text and its proliferation in copies. Still, the history of the transmission of these documents also reflects this phenomenon in a general way. The texts that were preserved over time tended to be those that were most widely in use, thus generating a broad textual tradition in the early centuries. That not many heterodox texts survived into later periods or did so haphazardly is often taken as evidence that they were systematically repressed by an emerging orthodoxy. It is certainly true that the church increasingly discouraged the use of heterodox writings, but under the prevailing conditions of textual transmission, it was extremely difficult to repress a document already in circulation. From a bibliographic point of view it is far more likely that heterodox texts failed to survive because the limited circulation they enjoyed did not generate enough copies to establish a textual tradition that would sustain their transmission over time.[136] The immediate point is that the vesting of authority in a document did not of itself secure its text against emendation.

The correlation between the use and the replication of texts may be one of the reasons that so few works of another prolific Christian writer of the late second and early third centuries have survived. The remains of an ancient statue of Hippolytus of Rome (about 170–236), erected not long after his death, were discovered near Rome in 1551. Only the lower body is preserved, but on the back of the chair in which the figure is seated there is inscribed a list of Hippolytus's writings, most of them composed between 200 and 235. With the aid of this list and sundry references by later writers, the works of Hippolytus may be numbered at more than forty, covering almost all aspects of early Christian theological writing. Eight of these works are more or less fully extant, but the rest are either lost or preserved in small fragments. The poor survival rate of Hippolytus's works probably has two causes. First, he wrote in Greek, but in the same period when the Roman church was making a rapid transition to Latin. After Hippolytus the literature of Roman and western Christianity was wholly Latin, and Greek texts were not well preserved. What little of his work penetrated to the Greek-speaking eastern church was valued and preserved in Greek.[137] The part of his work that survived in pieces was preserved only because it was translated into provincial languages. Second, Hippolytus was caught up in the awkward politics of the Roman episcopacy. Having opposed the election of Callistus to the Roman see in 217, Hippolytus, as bishop of a splinter group, soon found himself outside the mainstream of Roman Christianity. Both factors conspired to sharply limit the circulation of Hippolytus's writings in the western church, but it was principally because he was on the cusp of a major linguistic change that his works were largely submerged.

A sharp contrast to the fate of Hippolytus's writings is provided by the works of Cyprian, bishop of Carthage (about 210–58). Though he wrote less than Hippolytus and was less centrally placed, Cyprian wrote in Latin. Virtually all the treatises and many of the letters of Cyprian have survived, and the means of their survival can be discerned. In the *Life of Cyprian*, written soon after his death by Pontius, who was Cyprian's contemporary and deacon, there is an apparently complete list of Cyprian's treatises, which are named in the same order that is found in the later manuscript tradition of Cyprian's works. For the list and its order Pontius seems to have depended on an already published collected edition of Cyprian's treatises. If so, the collected edition must have been available as early as 260 or 270, within scarcely more than a decade of Cyprian's death.[138] This is not at all implausible, given Cyprian's reputation among his contemporaries and the wide acquaintance with his work that he himself encouraged, as we can see from his letters.

The situation with the letters of Cyprian is different from that of the treatises, but is particularly interesting. Although the letters were not soon shaped into a comprehensive collection, there existed small collections of them in Cyprian's own time and indeed at his personal instance.[139] The letters themselves show that Cyprian encouraged and actively promoted the copying and circulation of many of them. For example, with some letters he enclosed or attached groups of other letters he had written: no fewer than thirteen accompanied one of his letters to the Roman clergy (*Ep.* 20.2), nine were enclosed with another (*Ep.* 27.3), and five, together with a treatise, were sent with a letter to Caldonius (*Ep.* 25).[140] Writing to the Carthaginian clergy (*Ep.* 32), he not only enclosed two of his letters to Rome and two letters from Rome to him, but remarked that "if any bishops from other churches, my colleagues, or presbyters or deacons should be present, or should arrive among you, let them hear all these matters from you; and if they wish to transcribe copies of the letters and to take them to their own people, let them have the opportunity of transcribing them; I have, further, given instructions to Saturus the reader, our brother, to give permission to copy them to any individual who wishes to do so." Thus Cyprian sponsored the wide circulation of his own letters during his lifetime, intending them to be read, copied, and disseminated, as he must also have done with his treatises. To this end he obviously retained copies of his letters, deploying them as addenda to still other letters to other parties, and permitting and encouraging others to make copies. It does not appear, however, that the various early small collections, or the later more inclusive ones, were derived from his own archives, for all the larger collections have substantial gaps. Rather, it must be supposed that the early compilations were small and diverse and owed their contents partly to the dossiers assembled and dispatched by Cyprian himself and partly to the special interests of his following. The larger collections emerged only later through a conglomeration of the smaller groups. Active as he was to publicize his ideas in writing, Cyprian likely continually required the services of copyists—no doubt they belonged to the clerical orders he supervised in Carthage—and maintained archives of his own and other works in Carthage.[141]

It is, incidentally, in connection with the works of Cyprian that we have the earliest of the most rare evidence of commercial dealing in Christian literature, though this is well after the time of Cyprian. Rufinus, writing near the end of the fourth century, mentions that certain heretics had inserted among the epistles of Cyprian, which had been collected and made available in a single codex, the treatise of Tertullian (sic: Novatian), De Trinitate, and arranged for the interpolated books to be sold in Constantinople at a price that would induce people to buy and read them, thus promoting a heretical tract by attaching it to the orthodox coattails of Cyprian.[142] Somewhat earlier, the compiler of the Cheltenham canon (about 360) listed the works of Cyprian, gave their stichometric totals, and added this explanation: "Since the index of verses [stichoi] in the city of Rome is not clearly given, and elsewhere too through greed for gain they do not preserve it in full, I have gone through the books one by one, counting sixteen syllables to the line, and have appended to each book the number of Vergilian hexameters." The writer, though not a Roman, was clearly acquainted with book production in Rome and its deceptive practices. The notice does not necessarily indicate that Cyprian's works were routinely sold in shops, for it may have been only copyists, not book dealers, who juggled the numbers for profit. However that may be, the works of Cyprian were apparently in high demand a century after his death.[143]

As ambitious and effective as Cyprian was in disseminating his writings, though the volume was greater, the activity itself is like that of Dionysius of Corinth (about which we should like to know more), Ignatius, and perhaps more typically, of Polycarp in the early second century. The traffic of letters to other communities, the making and retaining of copies, the forming of collections, the dispatching of texts to foreign parts through Christian couriers (often minor clergy), the encouraging of further secondary distribution—all was happening by the early second century. The activity of dissemination that is abundantly evident in Cyprian's letters appears to have been broadly typical of Christian practice long before his time.

Another index of the breadth of the dissemination of Christian literature in this period is the appearance of translations of Christian scriptural documents into a variety of provincial languages. Translations were repeatedly made in the ancient church, but I am concerned here only with the earliest phases and results of those efforts.[144] The spread of the Christian mission beyond Judaism and into the larger Greco-Roman world, a process that was under way before the middle of the first century, was greatly assisted by the circumstance that Greek was the lingua franca of the urban centers of the eastern Mediterranean region. Indeed, the first major effort to cope with the barrier of language is evident in that all the earliest extant Christian literature was written in Greek rather than Aramaic and it was the Septuagint rather than the Hebrew scriptures that constituted the Bible of the Christian mission outside Palestine. Yet as soon as Christianity began to emanate from urban centers into rural areas and provincial territories it encountered further linguistic obstacles.[145] The challenge of linguistic diversity within the Christian mission had probably already begun to be encountered in the late first century. The author of Acts anticipated it in his own way by claiming that the apostles, while still in Jerusalem, were invested by inspiration with an ability to preach in the provincial languages of "every nation under heaven" (2:1–13), and the same issue surfaces in a different way in the early and widespread tradition that Peter in his preaching relied on "interpreters."[146] The Christian communities that sprang up in provincial regions required access to Christian scripture, and it was this need that generated the non-Greek versions of Christian scripture.

There is no evidence that the creation of non-Greek versions of scripture was a systematic undertaking in the early church. The translation of Christian scripture into languages other than Greek must have taken place originally in the context of Christian worship. At first such translations were oral and ad hoc: in provincial congregations scripture was probably read aloud in Greek and then immediately rendered into the vernacular, just as in the synagogue service of Judaism the reading of scripture in Hebrew was followed by an Aramaic *targum.* Written translations would have developed gradually until at length the whole scriptural corpus became accessible in the local tongue. It is precisely because the versions developed in this uncoordinated, local way that they have value for my subject.

The earliest of such versions was the Latin—to be precise, the Old Latin, as distinct from the Vulgate. The first evidence for the existence of any Christian scripture in Latin comes not from Rome but from North Africa. In the earliest document of Latin-speaking Christianity, the *Acts of the Scillitan Martyrs,* written soon after 180, reference is made to the possession by Numidian Christians of "books and epistles of Paul." These must have been in Latin.[147] Nevertheless, we lack firm evidence for the quotation of Latin texts of Christian scripture in Africa before Cyprian.[148] Although it is not certain that the first Latin translations of Christian writings were made in North Africa—this could conceivably have happened in Rome or elsewhere in Italy—Old Latin texts were being produced by the last two or three decades of the second century. Doubtless, this was not a systematic effort. Augustine later complained of the variety and inaccuracy of Latin translations, saying that "in the early days of the faith everyone who obtained a Greek manuscript [of scripture] and imagined that he had some ability in both languages, however slight, undertook to make a translation [into Latin]" *(De doctrina christ.* 2.16). It was in view of this situation that Jerome was finally commissioned in 383 by Pope Damasus to produce a uniform and reliable Latin translation by revising the current Old Latin texts in light of the original Greek, which commission Jerome fulfilled with the Vulgate.[149]

Translations into Syriac were also being made by the late second century. The old Syriac is poorly preserved in manuscripts, less well than the Old Latin, but the second-century provenance of the Syriac versions is generally granted. Tatian's *Diatessaron,* whether or not composed in Syriac, was available in that language by the late second century. Not much later the translation of Christian scripture into Coptic (at least into the Sahidic and Boharic dialects) was under way.

These early versions have been valued and studied chiefly by textual critics for the light they shed on the history of the text of the New Testament, but they are eloquent witnesses to the breadth of the diffusion of Christian literature at an early time. Christianity's missionary penetration into the provincial hinterlands was accompanied as a rule by Christian texts. The early, diverse, and largely uncoordinated renderings of those texts into the vernacular attests to the importance that was attached to making those texts available to remote communities and fostered their spread and use into areas where other literature had little or no currency.

CHRISTIAN LITERATURE OF THE FOURTH AND FIFTH CENTURIES The momentous events of the early fourth century that brought about the toleration of Christianity and then bestowed upon it the benefits of imperial favor had profound effects on the life of the church, including the production, distribution, and use of Christian books. Not the least of these was an increase in demand. I have already mentioned Constantine's program of constructing churches, each having to be furnished with copies of the scriptures, the rapid production of which was assigned, at least in part, to Eusebius and the Christian library at Caesarea. The multiplication of copies of scripture at this time was more urgent because of the recent persecution of Diocletian, which had aimed at the systematic destruction of Christian books and sharply reduced their availability. The number of people coming into the church grew rapidly in the fourth century, and the new social and political standing of Christianity attracted ever more members of the upper class, among whom literacy and recourse to literature were the most common. As demand rose, it may have quickened the interest of the book trade in Christian texts, and we have seen that by the middle of the fourth century some Christian literature—Cyprian's works, for example—was being commercially distributed in Rome and Constantinople. Even so, evidence of commercial dealing in Christian literature remains meager in the fourth and fifth centuries. Though demand rose and opportunity increased, it does not appear that the methods of producing and circulating Christian texts changed with the coming of the peace of the church.

Christian writings of the fourth and fifth centuries yield much more information about the publication and circulation of Christian literature than do those of the earlier centuries.[150] Of course, there is no direct discussion of the subject, but much is said in passing that is helpful. It will suffice to identify those testimonies that are fullest and most representative of fourth- and fifth-century practices, many of which occur in the writings of Augustine and Jerome. Their comments indicate that the traditional procedure of the first three centuries remained in effect.[151]

Augustine in his letters and in the *Retractationes* intimates the way in which his writings were published and circulated. It was the responsibility of an author to see to the initial distribution of his work, and this was done by sending or releasing the work to a friend or friends, who arranged for its further distribution. Augustine appears to have published his early works by putting them in the hands of his longtime family friend and wealthy patron in Thagaste, Romanianus. Thus, writing to Paulinus of Nola (*Ep.* 27.4) in a letter carried by Romanianus himself, Augustine says that Romanianus is able to provide to Paulinus whatever he might wish of Augustine's works, for "he has everything I have written whether to those outside the church of God or to the brothers." In a later letter to Paulinus (*Ep.* 31), which was accompanied by three books (the treatise *De libero arbitrio*), Augustine remarks that these are not in the possession of Romanianus, "to whom I have given whatever I have been able to write for general circulation." Such comments suggest that at an early time Romanianus served, so to speak, as Augustine's literary agent: he was provided with exemplars of Augustine's work, which he made available for transcription or transcribed (probably at his own expense) for interested parties.[152]

Augustine gives more detailed information about the publication of two of his major treatises, *De Trinitate* and *De Civitate Dei*. Augustine began to compose *De Trinitate* about 398 but did not complete it until 418–19. The history of his effort is sketched in *Ep.* 174, written in 416 to Aurelius, bishop of Carthage:

> I had laid the work aside after discovering that it had been carried off prematurely or purloined from me before I had completed it or revised and corrected it as I had planned. I had intended to publish it [edere] not in separate books but all at once, because the subsequent books are connected to the preceding ones by a continuous development of the argument. Since my plan could not be carried out on account of the persons who got access to the books before I wished, I discontinued my interrupted dictation, thinking to make a complaint about this in some of my other writings, so that those who could might know that those books had not been published by me but filched from me before I thought them worthy of being published in my name. But now . . . I have devoted myself to the laborious task of finishing them. They are not corrected [emendatos] as I should wish, but as well as I could, so that the whole work might not differ too much from the parts which have been surreptitiously in circulation for some time. I send it now to Your Reverence by my

son and very dear fellow deacon, and I give my permission for it to be heard, copied, and read (audiendos, describendos, legendosque permisi) by any who wish. . . . There are some persons who have the first four or, rather, five books without the introduction and the twelfth without most of the last part. If they come to know of this edition they will make the corrections, provided they have the good will and the ability. I earnestly request that you order this letter to be used as a preface, separated from but standing at the head of those same books. (Compare also Retract. *2.41.)*

It is clear from this statement that in sending the treatise to Carthage Augustine was depositing an authoritative exemplar with Aurelius and that he expected Aurelius to make it available for transcription by interested parties. This constituted Augustine's publication of the work. With this action he initiated the process of circulation, knowing that the circulation of the authorized text, prefaced by this letter, would enable the unfinished and unauthorized text, which had become current without his consent, to be recognized and corrected. The circumstances remind us of those affecting Tertullian's publication of his *Adversus Marcionem* two centuries earlier, and the concerns voiced here by Augustine are like those expressed by Tertullian in his preface.

Further insight into the publication and circulation of Augustine's work comes from a letter that came to light only fifty years ago: Augustine's letter to Firmus (*Ep.* 1*A), written soon after 426, concerning *De Civitate Dei*.[153] Having sent the work to Firmus, Augustine advises him on the bibliographic disposition of the individual books: "There are twenty-two books [*quaterniones*] which are too bulky to bind into one volume [*unum corpus*]. If you want two volumes [*codices*] they must be divided so that one volume has ten books [*libros*] and the other twelve. . . . If, however, you prefer more than two volumes [*corpora plura quam duo*] then you must have five volumes [*quinque codices*] of which the first will contain the first five books . . . ; [and the second] the second group of five. The next three volumes [*tres alii codices*] which follow must have four books each." It is interesting to see Augustine's insistence that the bibliographic format of the work should correspond to the divisions of the subject matter and the phases of the argument. The physical form of the book is to follow its content. He goes on to say: "Concerning the work *On the City of God* which our brothers in Carthage do not yet have, I ask you kindly to give it to those who want to copy it. Do not give it to many at the same time, but only to one or two, and they will pass it on to others. You will make arrangements how to give it to your friends, whether they are Christians who want to learn [that is, catechumens] or people still held by some superstition from which they will seem to be able to be freed by the grace of God through this effort of mine." By placing a copy of the treatise in the hands of Firmus, Augustine intended to promote its circulation among Firmus's friends. Is this to be regarded as Augustine's act of "edition" or "publication," as was his deposit of an exemplar of *De Trinitate* with Aurelius?

In this case much has been made to depend on the identification of Firmus. It has commonly been supposed that the Firmus addressed here is none other than the African presbyter of this name who is often mentioned in Augustine's letters as a carrier of his correspondence.[154] Another and still more recently discovered letter (*Ep.* 2*) demonstrates that this Firmus is instead an unbaptized layperson, a catechumen of the Carthaginian leisure class who had requested a copy of *De Civitate Dei* simply from personal interest.[155] (*Ep.* 2* indicates that Firmus had previously obtained some of the books and, then, after hearing a reading of Book 18, importuned Augustine for the rest.) It is, of course, hardly conceivable that Augustine would have undertaken to publish *De Civitate Dei* simply by entrusting an exemplar to an unbaptized layperson. Publication for a specifically Christian readership must have been accomplished by some other means, whether by placing the text in the church library at Hippo or depositing an exemplar with the bishop of Carthage, or both. If Firmus is not therefore the one through whom the work was definitively released, Augustine nevertheless expected Firmus to assist in disseminating it, not to Christians in Carthage, but to Firmus's own friends, who were catechumens or pagans.[156] This was to be done in the usual way: Firmus was to make his text available for copying by someone, who would in turn allow his copies to be copied.

Does this evidence suggest that Augustine made a distinction between private copying and editions?[157] If so, the difference is unclear. To judge from a comparison of the cases of *De Trinitate* and *De Civitate Dei* as they appear in these letters (*Epp.* 174 and 1*A), an official or authorized edition was not necessarily distinguished by temporal priority. Firmus apparently had the full text of *De Civitate Dei* before it was current among the Christians in Carthage. Furthermore, Augustine had made part of the work, some thirteen books, available to the monks Peter and Abraham in 417, long before the whole was finished (*Ep.* 184A). Nor was an official edition marked by the production of several copies at once. In depositing an exemplar of *De Trinitate* with bishop Aurelius, Augustine did not expect him to multiply and distribute copies, but only to allow it to be transcribed by those who wanted a copy. Thus the juxtaposition of edition and private copying is an anachronism. It confuses the intention of circulation with the mode of circulation by presupposing that an edition involved the simultaneous multiplication of copies from a center. An edition was constituted simply by an author's deliberate release of a text— normally a completed and corrected one—to be copied and to enter into circulation. Whether the copying and circulation occurred privately, as it customarily did, made no difference. The author's concern was chiefly that it should be well placed for the purpose. Just as he had deposited an exemplar of *De Trinitate* with Aurelius, Augustine must also have deposited an examplar of *De Civitate Dei* in the church library at Hippo or Carthage, or both, and he alludes to that prospect in *Ep.* 1*A when he says that the brothers in Carthage do not yet have it. This constituted the edition of the work. It was obviously in order to reach a different readership more quickly that a copy was also given to Firmus, and yet this too was by definition an edition, though Augustine did not thereby intend to make the availability of the work depend entirely or mainly on Firmus.

The question is further complicated, however, in that sometimes an author might release a completed part of a larger work that was still in composition. That portion of the incomplete *De Civitate Dei* that had earlier been provided to Peter and Abraham was not an edition because the treatise was not complete, while the purloined copy of *De Trinitate* was not an edition because it circulated against Augustine's wishes and in incomplete and uncorrected form. There is evidence, too, that the treatise *De doctrina christiana* circulated for a time in only two books.[158] The Leningrad codex, apparently the oldest surviving manuscript of any of Augustine's writings, contains the same four works that are discussed at the beginning of Book 2 of the *Retractationes*, and it contains them in the same order. Of the *De doctrina*, which stands last, only the first two books are present. Hence it is interesting to observe that in the *Retractationes* (2.30) Augustine says: "When I discovered that the books *On Christian Instruction* were not completed I chose to complete them rather than to leave them as they were and go on to the re-examination of other works. Accordingly I completed the third book. . . . Then I added a new book, and so completed the work in four books." (Then he specifies some corrections for the second book.) Since in the *Retractationes* Augustine was reviewing the whole corpus of his published writings, it must be assumed that *De doctrina* had been published in its incomplete form, and this (though without the partially completed third book) is what is found in the Leningrad codex. For this and for paleographic reasons it would seem that this manuscript was written during Augustine's lifetime and indeed before the work was finally completed in the midst of the composition of the *Retractationes*.[159] The question whether a text of *De doctrina* in only two books constituted its first edition cannot really be answered. On the one hand, from the start the scope of the work was intended to be larger, so that a text in only two books would always have been incomplete; but, on the other hand, the work had apparently been corrected and given out for circulation. Hence it was not an edition in the modern sense—a complete, definitive text— but functionally it was an edition, for the work, though incomplete, was allowed to circulate and to be copied. This case shows how misleading the term *edition* can be when applied in the conditions under which texts circulated in antiquity. A text qualified as an edition only when it had been emended and released by the author for copying.[160]

The works of Augustine were published individually according to established convention. Each was initially sent in copy to a friend who would make its substance known and allow copies to be taken. Apart from Romanianus, Aurelius, and Firmus (compare also Darius, *Ep.* 230) we do not know who else may have served Augustine in this way. Jerome also made the texts of his writings available through a small group of his friends, particularly Paula and Eustochium, Marcella, Pammachius, and the priest Domnion. The last three were especially active as depositories and intermediaries in the diffusion of Jerome's works, but other individuals served him from time to time in these capacities.[161] Thus Jerome informed Desiderius (*Ep.* 47.3) that he might borrow copies (for transcription) of any of Jerome's works from Marcella or Domnion. Little that Jerome wrote went unpublished. He complained that whatever he composed was "at once laid hold of and published, either by friends or enemies" (*Ep.* 79), and sometimes therefore against his wishes. Moreover, he found it impossible to control his texts once they were published. Pammachius, who had been entrusted with the exemplar of *Adversus Jovinianum* in Rome, was later unable to suppress it at Jerome's request (*Ep.* 49.2). Jerome acknowledged the futility of the effort by quoting Horace ("Words once uttered cannot be recalled," *Ars Poet.* 390) and also by admitting that in any case the work was also in circulation in the East. Jerome must have released it there as well as through Pammachius, no doubt to promote its broad dissemination. To this end, then, a work could be published by releasing it to more than one party, as Augustine had done with *De Civitate Dei*.

It is striking that nowhere in the many remarks of Augustine and Jerome about the publication of their writings is there any mention of the commercial booktrade, of buying and selling of texts among Christians, or, for that matter, of any truly systematic method of diffusion. Their procedure of publication was consistently to deposit an exemplar with a sympathetic person (or persons) who was strategically placed to advertise the availability of the work and furnish it for private transcription.[162] This sufficed, however, for the rapid and broad dissemination of their works, although on some occasions the authors themselves, who also retained their own texts, made them available for copying or had copies made and provided them on request or at their own initiative.[163]

In the same letter in which Augustine refers Paulinus to Romanianus for copies of his works (*Ep.* 31), he asks Paulinus to send him a work Paulinus had written against the pagans and for some books written by Ambrose of Milan. Paulinus, moreover, was given the writings of Sulpicius Severus to distribute (*Dial.* 3.17). Hence it appears that Paulinus of Nola had a lively interest in Christian texts and played an active role in the diffusion of the works of Ambrose, Augustine, and Sulpicius. Sulpicius himself credits Paulinus with great success in the dissemination of his *Vita sancti Martini*, claiming soon after its publication that it was being read not only in Rome, where *libraii* (it is unclear whether commercial booksellers or copyists are meant) saw it as a highly profitable item, but also in Carthage and Alexandria (*Dial.* 1.23; compare 2.17). If this were a reference to the commercial book trade, it would be exceptional, but in the case of an edifying hagiographic work like this it would not be altogether implausible.[164] At best it might be the exception that proves the rule. Possidius concludes his biographical sketch of Augustine, written not long after Augustine's death, by appending a list of Augustine's works and commenting (*Vita Aug.* 18): "If anyone wants to make a copy of [any item] he should apply to the church in Hippo, where the best texts can generally be found. Or he may make inquiries anywhere else he can and should make a copy of what he finds and preserve it, and not begrudge lending it in his turn to someone else asking to copy it." It did not occur to Possidius to refer his readers to book sellers because the works of Augustine and of other ecclesiastical writers circulated through private, noncommercial channels. Possidius specifies as the best texts those that were held by the church in Hippo. Those were reliable, of course, because they were not derived from the process of transmission and had suffered none of its vagaries.

The works of another contemporary writer, Rufinus of Aquileia, also circulated chiefly through private copying. Rufinus is particularly interesting because, in addition to the usual method of private copying, he disseminated some of his works by means of monastic scriptoria and thus anticipates the circumstances under which texts would be principally copied and circulated in the medieval period.[165] The signs of transition may also be seen in the activity of Augustine's monastic brothers in the library and scriptorium in Hippo.

Both Augustine and Jerome relied heavily on stenographers and copyists.[166] For Augustine in particular, composing was always a matter of dictating *(dictare)*, and once a fair copy was transcribed from stenographic notes, of correcting *(emendare)*. Once transcribed and corrected, texts were *emendatiora exemplaria* (corrected exemplars), and it was from these that copies were made. As bishop of Hippo, Augustine was well furnished with stenographers and copyists.[167] Jerome, ensconced in a cave in the Judean desert, sometimes complained that he had no copyist and had to transcribe many of his compositions himself. When Jerome did have assistance, it was through the generosity of patrons.[168] This use of stenographers in the production of Christian literature was nothing new in the fourth century. Origen and his admirers relied upon stenographers two centuries earlier, and evidently they were in Christian service in the intervening period as well, for stenographic transcriptions were made of theological disputations and synodical proceedings in the third and fourth centuries. Of the episcopal convocation held in 244 to test the views of Beryllus of Bostra, Eusebius reports (*H.E.* 6.33.3) that "there are extant to this day records *[eggrapha]* of Beryllus and of the synod that was held on his account which contain at once the questions Origen put to him and the discussions that took place in his own community and all that was done on that occasion." He tells of a similar synod on the views of Paul of Somasata held in Antioch in 269, at which the interrogator, Malchion, "had stenographers to take notes *[episemeioumenon tachugraphon]* as he held a disputation with Paul, which [notes] we know to be extant to this day" (*H.E.* 7.29.2). Later councils routinely used stenographers to produce the minutes of their meetings.[169]

In this way, the church in its own proceedings was increasingly adopting the methods of the civil bureaucracy, with which Christianity had long been familiar. For instance, official protocols (*commentarii*) based upon stenographic court records of the trials of Christians were obtained by Christians for their own use and enshrined in various *acta martyrum*, some as early as the second century.[170]

The availability of scribes trained in stenography had another important result: it made possible the transcription and publication of homiletical material and so added another dimension to early Christian literature. By early in the third century Origen's public addresses were taken down in shorthand transcriptions and published (Eusebius, *H.E.* 6.36.1). This practice became widespread, and as a result the ex tempore words of the most gifted preachers of the Greek and Latin church have survived. The extensive homiletical remains of Christian *rhetores* like John Chrysostom and Augustine suggest the great interest and wide readership that attached to their sermons, though they were not intended for transcription or circulation and for the most part were not published by their authors.[171]

The evidence I have surveyed, though fragmentary and less abundant than I might wish, presents a consistent and coherent picture of the publication and circulation of Christian literature in the first five centuries. It indicates that Christian writings were virtually always published privately, through intramural Christian channels, and circulated thereafter by private copying.[172] The commercial booktrade is not mentioned in connection with Christian literature before the fourth century and then appears to have played a marginal role at most. The evidence also indicates that Christian writers had a readership in view from the beginning, and both anticipated and promoted the dissemination of their own work. The speed with which individual writings gained currency with readers across the Mediterranean world confirms the interest of that readership in Christian literature. The publication and circulation of Christian literature in the ancient church were fundamentally similar to that of non-Christian literature in the ancient world, for there too distribution by seriatim private copying was the established convention and apparently was never displaced by commercial efforts. In observing the similarity between Christian and non-Christian literature in the manner of its publication and circulation, however, one notes a major difference.Early Christian literature was disseminated more quickly and over a far wider area than were non-Christian writings and found a readership more numerous than the most ambitious pagan authors could have hoped for their works. The reasons are not difficult to discern.

First, Christian communities, though they were not more literate than society at large, and indeed were probably less so, were nevertheless strongly oriented toward the written word. For Christians, texts were not entertainments or dispensable luxuries, but the essential instruments of Christian life. One cannot imagine a Christian community in antiquity, even the earliest, that would not have relied upon texts, for like the Jewish synagogue, the literature of the faith was part of the raison d'etre of the community. Texts had a constitutive and regulative importance for Christian thought and action. This was preeminently and primitively true for the scriptural texts that Christianity appropriated from Judaism. It was hardly less true of those specifically Christian documents that were soon written for the instruction and administration of fledgling congregations by early Christian missionaries, and, later, those written in the service of communication and support among small, scattered churches in a large, unsympathetic, and hostile social environment. Unlike every other religious movement in the Roman world save Judaism and perhaps Orphism, Christianity was constitutionally oriented to texts. Though not every Christian could read, every Christian regularly heard reading. Texts were read aloud in worship, interpreted in preaching and catechesis, cited in apologetical debates, deployed in intramural theological disputes, and perused for personal edification—all the routine, practical activities of any Christian community. Books were essential to the ordinary life of a Christian congregation. Christians had a standing need for them, and produced, procured, and employed them accordingly.

This peculiar orientation to texts was never lost on its antagonists. Lucian of Samosata, mocking the career of Peregrinus in its Christian phase (about 120–40 C.E.), observed the importance Christians attached to books (*De morte Per.* 11): "He interpreted and explained some of their books, and even composed many, and they revered him as a god, made use of him as a lawgiver and regarded him as a protector." Later in the second century, Celsus knew that an effective attack on Christianity could not overlook the texts on which it depended, and he made it a point to become acquainted with them. A century later Porphyry devoted a significant part of his tract *Against the Christians* to a close criticism of Christian scripture.[173] At the beginning of the fourth century, Diocletian, seeking the most direct means of undercutting the church, aimed his first edict at the confiscation and destruction of Christian books (Eusebius, *H.E.* 8.2.4). In its proclivity for books, as well as in its preoccupation with doctrine and ethics, Christianity appeared to pagan observers more like a philosophical movement than a religious cult.[174]

Second, Christian texts had the advantage of circulation over non-Christian literature by virtue of the geographic dispersion of Christian communities and the relations that obtained between them. By the second half of the first century Christian congregations had been planted across Syria, Asia Minor, Greece, and Italy and could be found in most of the major urban centers of the Mediterranean world—Jerusalem, Alexandria, Antioch, Ephesus, Philippi, Corinth, and Rome. Soon thereafter the Christian mission successfully penetrated the provincial regions of Egypt, Syria, Gaul, and North Africa.[175] These numerous and far-flung Christian congregations, large and small, nevertheless retained a sharp awareness of their collective identity as the *ecclesia katholike* and affirmed their mutual relations through frequent communication.[176] The result was a highly reticulated system of local communities that spanned the Mediterranean world but preserved a strong sense of translocal unity and cultivated contacts with each other. Though it was not contrived for the purpose, this network was ideally suited to disseminate texts: it made up a large constituency requiring books and furnished efficient channels to distribute them. Thus, both the motive and the means for the circulation of Christian writings far exceeded those affecting the currency of non-Christian literature, and it was inevitable that the dissemination of Christian writings would outstrip in volume and speed the spread of other literature and more nearly approach something like mass circulation in the Christian setting than did non-Christian texts in society at large.

As I have shown, the circulation of Christian literature was private, being part and parcel of the constant intercourse between individual congregations. Transmission took place by letter and messenger (letters requiring couriers) throughout the first five centuries of the church. It is no less typical of Augustine in the fifth century than it was of Cyprian in the third century, of Polycarp in the second, or of Paul in the first, to mention only a few examples.[177] The travel of individual Christians or small delegations from one church to another, often over large distances, made the variety and breadth of Christian literature known to the congregations, thus increasing interest and demand, and also served as the efficient vehicle for the brisk movement of texts from one place to another.[178] The growing volume of Christian writings and the progressive consolidation of the church during the second and third centuries at once presupposed this process of the broad dissemination of Christian texts and gave it further stimulus.

One result of the production and broad distribution of Christian books was the gradual accumulation of Christian literature in certain centers and the emergence of Christian libraries. I turn to that subject in the following chapter.

IV — EARLY CHRISTIAN LIBRARIES

The importance to early Christianity of texts, and above all of the scriptures, meant that local communities, even small ones in provincial settings, took pains to acquire them and so came to possess collections of books. And these collections, however modest, formed the libraries that served the liturgical, catechetical, and archival needs of individual congregations. In addition to these congregational libraries, there grew up in certain Christian centers larger libraries, stocked with scriptural and nonscriptural texts, for the use of Christian scholars and teachers. Libraries were also found in monastic communities, and some individual Christians accumulated their own private libraries. These various libraries constitute a significant aspect of the history of early Christian literature: on the one hand, they were an important result of the publication and circulation of Christian literature, and on the other they were themselves part of that process, stimulating and furnishing resources for the further dissemination of texts. At the same time, their immediate purpose was to enable and promote the use of Christian texts, and in that role they shed light on the literary culture of the ancient church. Although studies have occasionally been devoted to this or that Christian library, the subject as a whole has not been adequately explored. As a dimension of the history of libraries in antiquity, and for what they may reveal about the history of early Christian literature and the literary culture of the early church, the topic of early Christian libraries invites a more thorough treatment than it has yet received.

All kinds of libraries—institutional and private, large and small— were familiar to the Mediterranean world well before the advent of Christianity, and the particular character of Christian libraries can be fully appreciated only by setting them in the context of established Greek, Roman, and Jewish libraries of the period. Still it is best to begin with early Christian libraries themselves and go on then to compare them with the non-Christian libraries of the ancient world. The sources yield a surprising amount of information about early Christian libraries. As much can be known about them as about other ancient libraries and so far as their contents are concerned, rather more. The evidence is diverse, however, and has to do with different types of libraries.

CONGREGATIONAL LIBRARIES   Congregational libraries, that is, collections of texts accumulated and retained in local Christian communities for liturgical and archival purposes, were the earliest, most numerous, and most characteristic of Christian libraries. Direct evidence being scant in the earliest period, however, it is necessary to begin with later accounts of them and to work backward from there.

The first explicit notices about congregational libraries appear in accounts stemming from the Great Persecution under Diocletian at the beginning of the fourth century. The persecution began with a series of edicts against Christians, the first of which, issued in 303, ordered Christian books to be confiscated and burned by imperial agents.[1] Several documents of this period dramatically portray the efforts of the state to enforce this edict in various local communities. In the *Gesta apud Zenophilum* there is a highly detailed account of the events that took place at the town of Cirta, capital of Numidia in North Africa:

> *Having arrived at the house where the Christians used to meet, the mayor said to Paul the Bishop,* "Bring out the writings of the Law [*scripturas legis*] and anything else you have here, according to the order, so that you may obey the command."

> *The Bishop:* The readers [*lectores*] have the scriptures [*scripturas*], but we will give what we have here.
> *The Mayor:* Point out the readers, or send for them.
> *The Bishop:* You all know them.
> *The Mayor:* We do not know them.
> *The Bishop:* The municipal office knows them, that is, the clerks Edusius and Junius.
> *The Mayor:* Leaving aside the matter of the readers, whom the office will point out, produce what you have.
> [There follows an inventory of the church plate and other prop-

erty, including large stores of male and female clothing and shoes, produced in the presence of the local clergy—three priests, two deacons, four subdeacons, and some grave diggers.]

The Mayor: Bring out what you have.

The Subdeacons Silvanus and Carosus: We have thrown out everything that was here.

The Mayor: Your answer is entered in the record.

[After some empty cupboards *(armaria)* had been found in the library *(in bibliothecis)*, Silvanus brought out a silver box and lamp which he said he had discovered behind a barrel.]

The Mayor's Clerk, Victor: You would have been a dead man if you had not found them.

The Mayor: Look more carefully, in case there is anything left here.

Silvanus: There is nothing left. We have thrown everything out.

[When the dining room was opened there were found there four bins and six barrels.]

The Mayor: Bring out the scriptures that you have so that we can obey the orders and command of the emperors.

[The subdeacon Catullinus produced one very large volume *[codicem unum pernimium majorem.]*

The Mayor: Why have you given one volume *[codicem]* only? Produce the scriptures that you have.

The Subdeacons Marcuclius and Catullinus: We have no more, because we are subdeacons; the readers have the books *[codices]*.

The Mayor: Show me the readers.

Marcuclius and Catullinus: We do not know where they live.

The Mayor: If you do not know where they live, tell me their names.

Marcuclius and Catullinus: We are not traitors. Here we are: order us to be killed.

The Mayor: Put them under arrest.

[The subdeacons nevertheless divulged the name of one reader, Eugenius, and when the mayor arrived at his residence Eugenius surrendered four books *(codices quatuor)*. The mayor then turned to the other two subdeacons, Silvanus and Carosus.]

The Mayor: Show me the other readers.

Silvanus and Carosus: The bishop has already said that Edusius and Junius the clerks know them all. They will show you the way to their houses.

Edusius and Junius: We will show them, sir.

[The mayor proceeded to visit the six remaining readers. Four of them produced their books as ordered: five volumes from the first, eight from the second, five large codices, and two small ones *(codices quinque majores et minores duos)* from the third, two codices and four fascicules *(quiniones)* from the fourth (who, incidentally, is identified as a *grammaticus)*. The fifth declared that he had no books. The last reader was not at home, but his wife produced six books that were in his possession, after which the mayor had the house searched. No other books being found, he again addressed the subdeacons.]

The Mayor: If there has been any omission, the responsibility is yours.[2]

This remarkable account offers surprising insights into one particular congregational library. It is striking in the first place that the congregation in Cirta possessed so many books: thirty-seven items are mentioned, including the one "very large volume" that was handed over by the subdeacon Catullinus, and a few smaller pieces, and there may well have been others that remained hidden. On any reckoning, this is a big collection of books for a Christian congregation in a provincial area. It is not said which books these were, although the mayor, in asking for "the writings of the law," apparently meant Jewish scripture, and the "one large volume" was probably a book of Gospels.[3] The fact that the house where the Christians met had a room identified as a library and that empty cupboards were found there also indicates that this congregation had a considerable collection of books. Under ordinary circumstances it must have been in these cupboards in this room that all or most of the community's books were kept. When the search was conducted, however, most of the books were in the hands of the readers. By this time, the reader was one of the so-called minor orders of the clergy.[4] In the Christian community of Cirta there appear to have been seven readers in all. If on this occasion all the books had been dispersed among the readers as a precaution against confiscation, it was probably not unusual for at least some of the community's books to be in their keeping: Marcuclius and Catullinus protest that they do not have books *because* they are subdeacons, implying that the readers are the custodians of the books and could be expected to have some of them in their homes. This is not surprising: public reading would have required study of the texts in advance, and that different readers should have different books may indicate that each reader was practiced only in certain texts.

Various *acta martyrum* from the same period bring other congregational libraries into view. The "Martyrdom of St. Felix" describes the impact of Diocletian's edict in the African town of Tibiuca, in 303.[5] At the summons of the magistrate to the elders of the Christian community the priest Aper and two readers, Cyril and Vitalis, appeared and were asked whether they had "the divine books" *(libros deificos)*. They replied that they did, but on being asked to hand them over they said the books were in the possession of the bishop, Felix, who was on a journey to Carthage. Upon his return Felix was hailed before the magistrate and ordered to surrender whatever "books or parchments" *(libros vel membranas)* he had, but he stubbornly refused. The bishop was then sent to the proconsul in Carthage, where again he refused to surrender the books, and so was condemned to be beheaded. In this case the bishop was the nominal custodian of the community's library, but whether he had taken the books under his care only to prevent their confiscation we cannot say. The reference to "books or parchments" envisions both rolls and codices, but the account reveals nothing of their number or content or where they were normally kept.

"The Martyrdom of Saints Agape, Irene, and Chione," recounting events at Thessalonica in Macedonia in March and April of 304, contains unusually detailed statements about the possession of books by a Christian congregation.[6] The prefect, Dulcitius, asked the women, "Do you have in your possession any records, parchments or books?" *(tina upomnemata e diphtherai e biblia)* (4.2). They denied that they did, claiming that officials had already confiscated them. Nevertheless, such writings were eventually discovered, for at a second hearing the prefect charged that Irene had "deliberately kept even until now so many parchments, books, tablets, small codices and pages" *(tosautas diphtheras kai biblia kai pinakidas kai kodikellous kai selidas)*, in spite of her previous denials (5.1). These texts were found hidden in the house where the women lived (5.4, 7) stored "in cabinets and chests" *(en tois purgiskois kai tois kibotiois)*" (6.1).

It is not entirely clear from this account whether it deals with a group of consecrated women or whether the books in question belonged to them or to a larger community. It is likely that the house was the home of at least one of the women (Irene) but also the meeting place of a larger Christian group, which is to say a "house church," and that the books were the property of the group and were kept in the house where they met. There is no mention of a discrete library room in the house but only of various cabinets and chests used to store books. The use of several storage cases, regardless of their location within the house, implies a goodly number of texts, as does the reference to a variety of formats: rolls, codices, tablets, and pages. Although there is no indication of the contents of these texts, save that they were all Christian writings, their contents were probably as diverse as their formats. Presumably they would have included items of Jewish scripture as well as some Gospels and epistles and probably other devotional and liturgical texts.

Another document that holds interest here is a fragmentary sheet of papyrus from the fourth century (P. Ash. Inv. 3) that carries a list of Christian writings together with marginal notes pertaining to what almost certainly are the holdings of a Christian congregational library.[7] We know the writings are Christian because of the titles listed. Fifteen entries survive, not all of which can be identified. Among the texts whose titles can be made out are *The Shepherd* of Hermas, several works of Origen (including his commentary on the Gospel of John), Leviticus, Job, the Acts of the Apostles, the Song of Songs, Exodus [and Numbers?], and a "Great Book" *(mega biblion)*, that is, a codex of the four Gospels.[8] To the left of each entry is the notation *derm[a]*, "skin" (parchment), indicating the material on which the texts are written.[9] All these works were, then, probably in codices, but the notations that they were written on parchment would have been unnecessary unless other works that were written on papyrus had also been listed, and those may have been either codices or rolls, but in a Christian library were more likely codices. It is uncertain whether this catalog, which was drawn up in the first half of the fourth century, pertains to the library of a Christian congregation, a monastic group, or an individual, but the items in it, mainly scriptural books and commentaries, may point to liturgical, and thus congregational, use.

As we have seen, empty cupboards were found in the library of the house where the Christian community of Cirta was accustomed to meet, and books were stored in cabinets and chests in the house of the martyr Irene in Thessalonica, again a place of Christian meeting. Comments like these suggest that the closest analogies to the libraries of local Christian communities should be sought among the private, domestic libraries of the ancient world. They also raise the question whether archaeological discoveries of places and spaces of early Christian worship might tell us something about Christian congregational libraries.[10] Unfortunately, no spaces that can be clearly identified as libraries have been found in the earliest known Christian meeting-houses. In the earliest period, when Christians met in private homes, the houses were not architecturally modified to fit the special needs of the group. Though certainly not all of these early house churches had a room that served purely as a library, in those that did the library probably housed the books of the community along with those of the patronal resident. Where there was no special room, books would have been kept in book boxes, chests, or cupboards. For the later period, when Christian congregations obtained residential property and modified the interior for congregational use, thus producing the *domus ecclesiae*, the architectural evidence allows no more than speculation about the housing of libraries.[11]

Together with the sources that have been cited, Diocletian's edict of 303 ordering the confiscation and burning of Christian books is itself important evidence, in both its assumptions and results. At the start of the fourth century, Diocletian took it for granted that every Christian community, wherever it might be, had a collection of books and knew that those books were essential to its viability. Thus the edict shows that congregational libraries were commonplace by the late third century, and that this fact was well known to non-Christians. As to the results of the edict, the relinquishing of Christian books to the civil authorities soon became a leading issue in the Donatist controversy. The Donatists regarded the handing over of the scriptures as an act of apostasy and branded clerics who had done so as "surrenderers" *(traditores)* who thereafter had no authority.[12] Whatever else this shows, it underlines the great value placed on the scriptures and the responsibility of priests and bishops as the custodians of Christian libraries.

What can be said of Christian libraries in the first three centuries? One further piece of evidence goes back to the late second century: it appears in the so-called Acts of the Scillitan Martyrs, the earliest dated document of the Latin-speaking church. The Scillitan martyrs, from the otherwise unknown village of Scillium in North Africa, were condemned and executed in Carthage on 17 July 180. According to this account, in the course of interrogating a group of Christians, "Saturninus the proconsul asked Speratus, 'What do you have in your case?" *[in capsa vestra].* Speratus answered, 'Books and letters of Paul, a just man' *[libri et epistulae pauli viri iusti]."*[13] The *capsa* was a container for texts, a "book bucket" (Greek: *teuchos*) made of wood or canvas. This one was portable, though it is unclear why it had been brought to the hearing.[14] It is a question whether the phrase *libri et epistulae* should be taken to mean "books and [also] letters" of Paul, or "books, that is, letters" of Paul. Either sense is possible.[15] Probabilities, however, speak for the former. The similar phrase in 2 Clement 14.2, "the books and the apostles" *(ta biblia kai hoi apostoloi)*, almost certainly means Jewish scriptures and apostolic writings, and among the latter Paul's letters in particular.[16] "Books" as distinct from Paul's letters may have designated Jewish scriptures or Christian Gospels or both.[17] Nothing suggests that these texts were Speratus's personal property; he was probably the custodian of books belonging to his community, perhaps in the capacity of a *lector* of the congregation.

If the "Acts of the Scillitan Martyrs" shows that by the late second century even small Christian groups in provincial towns had collections of books, that is a strong indication that larger congregations in urban settings also possessed libraries of Christian texts, and more extensive ones. There is little direct evidence to support this inference for the second century, but circumstantial considerations bear on it.

Since scriptural texts were used in Christian worship and catechesis, it must be supposed that individual congregations had at least some such texts at hand, and hence libraries, however small, consisting of parts of Jewish scripture and some Christian writings. Thus it is important to know how early and widespread the liturgical reading of scripture was in Christian worship. The earliest explicit allusion to the practice is found in the pastoral Epistles: in 1 Timothy "Paul" admonishes Timothy to "attend to the public reading of scripture, to preaching and to teaching" (4:13), and on this basis it can be assumed that at least by the early second century the liturgical reading of scripture was the established custom in Asia Minor. Near the middle of the second century a fuller reference to the practice appears in Justin's description of Christian worship (*Apol.* 1.67): "On the day which is called the day of the sun there is an assembly of all those who live in the towns or in the country, and the memoirs of the apostles or the writings of the prophets are read for as long as time permits. Then the reader ceases, and the president speaks, admonishing and exhorting us to imitate these excellent examples." Since Justin aims to give a typical description and was familiar with the usages of Asia Minor and Rome, the liturgical reading of scripture must have been common and perhaps universal by Justin's time. Most scholars assume that the practice was by then traditional and reached back well into the first century. Although it is not certain that the reading of scripture was an aboriginal or a universal feature of Christian worship in the first century, the practice can hardly be understood except as a borrowing from the liturgy of the synagogue, and thus it would have been widespread from an early time.[18] At any rate, the liturgical reading of scripture seems to have been the established custom of the churches by the early second century, and so a collection at least of scriptural texts was required by local Christian communities.

Furthermore, Christian writers from the middle to the end of the second century—Justin, Clement, Irenaeus and Tertullian, to name only major figures—knew and used a great many texts, scriptural and nonscriptural, Christian and non-Christian, and this invites the question where and how they had access to these books. It is scarcely conceivable that all the texts each used belonged to him individually; they must have relied heavily, if not exclusively, on collections in their local communities. Extensive collections of Christian books might be expected to have arisen early in prominent Christian centers like Rome, Antioch, Alexandria, and Carthage. The Christian schools of Justin, Marcion, and Valentinus that flourished in Rome by the middle of the second century required books, and so did the Alexandrian Christian scholarship that emerged about the same time among both gnostic and nongnostic teachers. It is not clear whether at that early time any distinction could be drawn between congregational libraries and the libraries that served Christian teachers. Yet teachers like Justin and Clement must have depended at least partly on texts accumulated by the Roman and Alexandrian churches. No such school activity is attested for Irenaeus in Lyons or for Tertullian in Carthage. If one can only assume that Irenaeus relied on a church library in Lyons, Tertullian hints at his resources in Carthage by mentioning documentary materials of the church—the membership roll *(census)*, the members of the clerical order *(ordo sacerdotalis)*, and the order of bishops *(ordo episcoporum)*—items that would normally have been kept in an ecclesiastical archive.[19] Tertullian, however, also had a wealth of pagan and Christian literature at hand upon which he drew freely. Some no doubt belonged to his personal library, but some, especially the works of ecclesiastical writers (including heterodox books), must have been in the library of the Carthaginian church.[20]

A few further points are at least suggestive in relation to congregational libraries in the second century. Ignatius, bishop of Antioch, writing to the Philadelphian church, recounts an exchange he had had with certain opponents (8.2): "For I heard some people saying, 'If I do not find it in the archives *[archeiois]* I do not believe it in the gospel.' And when I said to them, 'It is written,' they answered me, 'That is the point at issue.' But to me the archives *[archeia]* are Jesus Christ, the inviolable archives *[archeia]* are his cross and death and his resurrection and the faith that is through him." The sense of this anecdote has been much debated, but what is important for my purposes is the meaning of the term *archeion*. Its original sense is "governmental house" or "magistrate's office," whence it came to mean "records office" and could signify either the place where records were kept or the records themselves. Most commentators take the word to mean "the original records" and to refer to the Jewish scriptures regarded as "archival records" or "charter documents" of the church.[21] This is surely correct but does not necessarily exhaust the sense of this unique designation of Jewish scripture, for the word alludes to the *place* where such writings were deposited and available. Since its use by Ignatius's opponents has no clear ulterior motivation, all the more may it imply the existence of an archive or library of the Antiochene church where the Jewish scriptures, among other documents, were kept.[22]

Ignatius's remark proves nothing by itself, but it gains interest in connection with what is known of his friend and fellow bishop, Polycarp of Smyrna. Polycarp, as we know, was instrumental in the collection and dissemination of the letters of Ignatius and those of various churches. He also knew Jewish scripture, some letters of Paul, and probably also some Gospel literature. The availability of this material to Polycarp and the scribal work that was involved with his work on Ignatius's letters suggest that there was a library in the Christian community in Smyrna and that it went beyond strictly liturgical texts. Smyrna was an intellectual center in Ionia by the first century, and Strabo (14.646) mentions that one of its chief buildings was a civic library.[23] In such a setting neither the literary activity of Polycarp nor an accumulation of Christian texts by the church there would be surprising. There may have been a Christian library at roughly the same time in Hierapolis: Papias was familiar with several Gospel-type documents, other Christian texts, and a fund of Jewish texts. He also took a keen interest in the history of Christian texts and traditions and was himself engaged in writing a treatise on the sayings of Jesus. If Smyrna and perhaps Hierapolis had collections of Christian texts in the early decades of the second century, all the more should a Christian library be expected in Antioch at the same time.

Finally, the existence of congregational libraries in the early second century has also been inferred from an oblique angle, that is, from the titles of the Gospels.[24] Although the Gospels of the New Testament were issued anonymously and without titles, near the beginning of the second century they received titles that included the names of their putative authors. Why did this come about? The term *gospel* was familiar from the outset as a designation of the Christian proclamation, but it was subsequently applied to written narratives about Jesus, undoubtedly under the influence of the author of the Gospel of Mark, who introduces his work as "the beginning of the gospel of Jesus Christ" (1:1).[25] Yet when more than one Gospel narrative became available in a Christian community two problems emerged. The first was theological: it seemed inappropriate to speak of Gospels (in the plural), for traditionally the gospel was spoken of in the singular as the one Christian message. The second was practical: how these documents were to be distinguished from each other. The peculiar form of the titles of the Gospels—*the* gospel (singular) *according to (kata)* a putative individual author (Mark, Matthew, and so on)—may well have arisen for a practical reason: "the titles were necessary for arranging the Gospels in community libraries and for liturgical reading."[26] This explanation is appealing because it links the unusual titles of the Gospels to particular circumstances and needs and can account for the adoption of these titles before the formation, in the late second century, of a four-Gospel collection.

LARGER LIBRARIES IN CHRISTIAN CENTERS

Large Christian libraries that aimed to serve purposes beyond the liturgical or archival began to emerge by the early third century. The earliest Christian library that was not essentially liturgical and for which there is direct evidence was located in Jerusalem.[27] According to Eusebius (*H.E.* 6.20.1) this library was established by Alexander, bishop of Jerusalem from 212 to 250. Eusebius made use of it and mentions some of the documents he himself had found in it: works of Beryllus of Bostra, works of Hippolytus, and the Dialogue of the Roman churchman Gaius with the Montanist Proclus (*H.E.* 6.20.2). If Roman writers were found there, eastern writers would have been represented in much larger numbers, and copies of scriptural texts must be assumed. It also appears that the library's holdings were not limited to Christian texts, for a papyrus fragment of the *Kestoi* of Julius Africanus (P. Oxy. 412) suggests that a copy of the *Odyssey,* or at least an interpolated part of it, could be found there.[28] But beyond these sparse allusions nothing is known about the library in Jerusalem.

Did a similar library in Alexandria serve as the model for the Jerusalem library? Alexander of Jerusalem had been a student of Pantaenus and Clement in Alexandria (*H.E.* 6.14.9) and was an acquaintance of Origen. Some have thought that Alexander established the Jerusalem library on the advice of Origen, and that he may have been assisted in the task by Julius Africanus, who had previously assisted the emperor Alexander Severus in the formation of the library in the Pantheon and later was a resident of Emmaus (Nicopolis) in southern Judea. Neither possibility is implausible, and either would augur a serious bibliographic undertaking.[29] Apart from Eusebius's use of this library in the early fourth century, however, nothing is known of its subsequent history. Jerome, who might be expected to have used it during his Jerusalem period, never mentions it. If it was still in existence by the late fourth century its standing had probably been eclipsed by the reputation of the library in Caesarea in Palestine, easily the best known of early Christian libraries.

Like the library in Jerusalem, the library in Caesarea had its beginnings in the early third century. Its nucleus appears to have been the personal library of the Christian scholar Origen, who spent the second half of his career in Caesarea. Having been forced to leave Alexandria because of a dispute with its bishop, Demetrius, Origen took up residence in Caesarea in 231, formed a school there, and continued teaching, writing, and preaching until his death in 253. A well-educated and studious person, Origen had once possessed a personal library of mainly pagan literature, but, according to Eusebius (*H.E.* 6.3.8–9), upon assuming the leadership of the catechetical school in Alexandria, Origen had sold it off, "considering that the teaching of grammatical studies was incompatible with training in religious studies" and wishing to be self-supporting. Later in the course of his career Origen acquired another personal library that served him and his students. The description of the readings Origen prescribed given by Gregory Thaumaturgus implies that his library was large and diverse, containing many philosophical texts along with Christian ones.[30] At his death Origen left his library, including many of his own works, to the school he had established in Caesarea.

Jerome refers to the Caesarean library as "the library of Origen and Pamphilus" (*bibliotheca Origenis et Pamphili* [*De vir. ill.* 112]). If Origen's collection provided its initial stock, its subsequent development owed much to the energies and interests of Pamphilus, presbyter in Caesarea (d. 310), and later to the efforts of the Caesarean bishops Eusebius, Acacius, and Euzoius. Pamphilus, who was from an aristocratic family of Berytus (Beirut), had studied in Alexandria with the Christian scholar Pierius and then settled in Caesarea, where he was ordained to the priesthood. He lived simply and used his wealth to build up the library. Eusebius only briefly mentions the efforts of

Pamphilus to gather the works of Origen and other ecclesiastical writers (*H.E.* 6.32.3), probably because he had already given a full account of this activity in his "Life of Pamphilus," which is no longer extant. Jerome, who had read that work, remarks in a letter to Marcella (*Ep.* 34.1) that "when the blessed martyr Pamphilus whose life has been recounted in about three books by Eusebius, bishop of Caesarea, wished to equal Demetrius of Phaleron and Peisistratus in devotion to the sacred library, he eagerly searched throughout the world for examples that were true and eternal monuments of gifted writers. In particular he searched diligently for the works of Origen, which he dedicated to the church in Caesarea." Elsewhere, Jerome comments that "Pamphilus was so inflamed with love of sacred literature that he transcribed the greater part of the works of Origen with his own hand and these are still preserved in the library at Caesarea. I have twenty-five volumes of commentaries of Origen written in his hand" (*De vir. ill.* 75).

If Pamphilus had to search out works of Origen, not all of them were available in Caesarea. And he sought to acquire texts of other Christian writers as well. No doubt he also collected many non-Christian books, since Pamphilus was well versed in philosophy and gave instruction to many in a broad range of materials, pagan as well as Christian.[31] Through his efforts the Caesarean library grew to thousands of volumes.[32] Pamphilus apparently undertook also to catalogue its holdings, for Eusebius (*H.E.* 6.32.3) claims to have cited the "lists" (*pinakes*) of the library in his "Life of Pamphilus."[33] In his younger years Eusebius had assisted Pamphilus in the work of the library, and after Pamphilus's death became bishop of Caesarea (313) and continued his mentor's efforts. Eusebius's labor to enlarge the holdings of the library included gathering up from various sources more than a hundred letters of Origen (*H.E.* 6.36.3) and compiling a collection of "martyrdoms of the ancients" (*H.E.* 4.15.47, 5.1.2, 5.21.5), adding these, together with his own works, to the collection.

The contents of the library must be inferred from Eusebius. Unlike Pamphilus, Eusebius was a prolific writer who depended heavily on the resources of the library in composing his own works. In his *Church History* Eusebius shows acquaintance with an enormous variety of early Christian literature, and in his *Preparation for the Gospel* he reveals a familiarity also with a large body of Greek philosophical literature.[34] This acquaintance was gained principally in the libraries of Caesarea and Jerusalem. Apart from his explicit statements, it is not possible to distinguish between what he may have found in Jerusalem and what in Caesarea, but it is perhaps also unnecessary, since whatever he found in Jerusalem that was lacking in Caesarea he probably transcribed and added to the Caesarean collection.

The focus of the Caesarean library was of course on Christian literature, and particularly on the works of Origen, for both Pamphilus and Eusebius had the highest esteem for his intellectual and literary legacy. Pamphilus set about obtaining copies of all his writings, often transcribing them himself. The extant list of the titles of Origen's corpus (Jerome, *Ep.* 33.4.1–20), which was probably excerpted from the holdings list of the Caesarean library, attests Pamphilus's success. But the works of many other ecclesiastical writers were also collected. Among them were Apollinaris of Hierapolis, Clement of Alexandria, Dionysius of Alexandria, Hippolytus of Rome, Irenaeus of Lugdunum, Justin, Melito of Sardis, Tatian, and Theophilus of Antioch, and the Jewish writers Philo and Josephus. Beyond these were collections of letters by Ignatius of Antioch, Alexander of Jerusalem, Serapion of Antioch, Dionysius of Corinth, and Cornelius of Rome, among others, and a variety of synodical communications. Naturally the works of eastern Christian writers predominated in the Caesarean library, but some works of western provenance—by Irenaeus, Hippolytus, Tertullian, and Cyprian—had also been gathered.[35] In addition, the Caesarean library was rich in scriptural texts. The originals of Origen's Hexapla and Tetrapla were present, and many manuscripts of Christian scripture were also on hand, including some apocryphal texts.[36]

Some things about the disposition of the materials within the library can be made out from Eusebius's manner of using them. Often, after quoting a particular document, Eusebius cites the titles of other documents that he found in the same volume. Thus, for example, after quoting at length from the *Martyrdom of Polycarp* (*H.E.* 4.15.1–45), Eusebius mentions that "in the same document" he found a series of other martyrdoms (4.15.46). Or again, in his enumeration of the works of Philo (*H.E.* 2.18) there are peculiarities of order and attribution, as well as transitional comments by Eusebius, which suggest that the works of Philo were compiled in five different volumes. In the *Church History* there are many other instances of references to a given writer's works that indicate how Eusebius found them bibliographically disposed, so that to some extent it can be determined what materials were bound together in the various volumes he had at hand.[37] And Eusebius reveals something of the means and aims of bibliographic transcription when he says of his own collection of Origen's letters that he arranged them "in their own separate volumes *(en idiais tomon perigraphais)* so that they might no longer be dispersed" (*H.E.* 3.36.3). In observations like these we catch a glimpse of the library's work of arranging, cataloging, and binding its holdings.

However, the work of the library was not limited to collecting, arranging, and maintaining a large body of Christian literature. Like other major libraries, the Caesarean library engaged in the critical task of collating and revising texts, especially scriptural texts. Some manuscripts available today attest by colophons their descent from manuscripts of the library at Caesarea—manuscripts that had been corrected by Pamphilus and Eusebius themselves.[38] For example, the famous Codex Sinaiticus, transcribed in the fourth century, contains a subscription added in the sixth or seventh century to the book of Esther, stating that the manuscript was collated against "a very ancient manuscript that had been corrected by the hand of the holy martyr Pamphilus," and then goes on to quote the colophon found in that ancient manuscript: "Copied and corrected against the Hexapla of Origen, corrected by himself. The confessor Antoninus collated. I, Pamphilius, corrected the volume in prison."[39] Such colophons indicate that the Caesarean library was well stocked with biblical manuscripts, that from the beginning it sponsored a tradition of careful textual scholarship, and that it was highly respected as a repository of reliable texts.[40]

Beyond the critical constitution of texts, the library under Pamphilus's supervision also produced texts for distribution and use. Jerome refers to this activity in his *Apology against Rufinus* (1.9) by quoting a passage from Eusebius's *Life of Pamphilus:*

> *What lover of books was there who did not find a friend in Pamphilus? If he knew any who were in want of the necessities of life, he helped them to the full extent of his power. He would not only lend copies of the Scriptures to read, but would give them most readily, and not only to men, but to women too if he saw that they were given to reading. He therefore kept a store of manuscripts* [multos codices praeparabat] *so that he might be able to give them to those who wished for them whenever occasion demanded.*

The acquisition, criticism, and production of texts required, of course, a scriptorium, and doubtless there was one attached to the Caesarean library from the outset.[41] The clearest proof of the scriptorium, its capacity and repute, is Constantine's commission to Eusebius to provide promptly for the churches of Constantinople fifty copies of the sacred scriptures, well written on parchment by professional scribes (*Vita*

Const. 4.36). Eusebius says that Constantine's orders "were followed by the immediate execution of the work itself, which we sent him in magnificent and elaborately bound volumes *trissa kai tetrassa*" (*Vita Const.* 4.37). The last phrase is difficult to interpret. Although it has usually been taken to mean books written in three and four columns to the page (of a codex), the more likely meaning is that the volumes were sent off to the emperor "three or four at a time."[42] It is also a question, as noted earlier, what the content of these "volumes of sacred scripture" was. It has been widely assumed that they were complete Bibles, in which case producing fifty of them in a short time would have been a truly monumental technical enterprise, notwithstanding the emperor's promise of all necessary resources. Since the scope of the Christian Bible was still variable in the early fourth century, however, and since even in later periods manuscripts of the entire Greek Bible were unusual, it is more likely that these were volumes of the four Gospels only, as were commonly produced from the third century on.[43] That Constantine's order was promptly met, and with magnificently produced volumes, bespeaks the efficiency and technical capacity of the Caesarean library's scriptorium in the early fourth century.

Further insight into the operations of the scriptorium is offered by Jerome's notice that under Eusebius's successors in the Caesarean episcopate, Acacius (340–66) and Euzoius (369–76), an effort was made to preserve the holdings of the library by transcribing them from papyrus onto more durable parchment *(in membranis instauare)*.[44] The work must have been done by the scriptorium, but it is not clear whether the retranscription was projected for the whole library or only for those parts that were in poor condition and liable to be lost altogether, or whether the deterioration was due to age, use, or other causes. The conversion of the whole library from papyrus to parchment would have been daunting, even if its holdings were smaller than has often been supposed. Whatever the scope of the restoration, however, it helped insure the preservation of many items of early Christian literature.

Since the library of Pamphilus at Caesarea was not a congregational library of liturgical and archival material but an actual research library, it is a question what relation it had to the Caesarean church. During Pamphilus's time it must have been under his direct supervision, although, since he was a presbyter and not a bishop, it would ultimately have been under episcopal control. It appears to have come directly under episcopal control with Eusebius and his successors. It is unclear also where the library was located in relation to the church.

Since the library at Caesarea escaped the persecution of Diocletian, it has been suggested that it was housed in a building not associated with the church.[45] It is equally possible, however, that the library went unscathed because the persecution was pressed less energetically in the East than in the West. Archaeological explorations in Caesarea have not identified the site of the library, although a building whose remains contained several inscriptions (including Romans 13.3) and a statue of Jesus *criophorus* has sometimes been thought to have housed it.[46] Of the ultimate fate of the Caesarean library nothing is known. Jerome knew it well, but he is its last true witness. It might have been visited by Hilary of Poitiers during his exile to the East (356–61): Jerome comments (*De vir. ill.* 100) that Hilary wrote his *Commentary on the Psalms* in imitation of Origen, though adding some original matter. He also notes (*De vir. ill.* 96) that Eusebius of Vercelli worked up a Latin version of Eusebius's commentaries on the Psalms. Possibly both men became acquainted with these works in Caesarea.[47] After the fourth century, however, there are no reliable attestations of the library, and it was probably destroyed in the Arab invasion of the seventh century.

The importance of the Caesarean library is difficult to overestimate: its significance for the history of early Christian literature has been compared to that of the Alexandrian library for classical literature.[48] Many early Christian works now lost are known only through notices of their presence there, and many others probably owe their perseverance to having been disseminated from it.[49] It played an especially prominent role in the transmission of scriptural literature. In the fourth century Caesarea was instrumental in the production and distribution of biblical texts to replace those destroyed elsewhere in the persecution of Diocletian, and so exercised great influence on the textual tradition of the Christian Bible. Thus concerning the Septuagint, Jerome noted that while Hesychius was the editor of the text used in Alexandria and Egypt, and while Lucian of Antioch's text was in use from Constantinople to Antioch, "the provinces between these read the Palestinian manuscripts prepared by Origen and widely promoted by Eusebius and Pamphilus."[50] It is uncertain whether a similarly distinctive "Caesarean text" of the New Testament or parts of it were sponsored by the library. Colophons in some New Testament manuscripts point that way, and many scholars have sought to identify a Caesarean text type.[51] Though no such recension has been isolated, there may well have been one.

In addition to the libraries at Jerusalem and Caesarea, it is usually assumed that there was also a major Christian library in Alexandria, and that its beginnings must have antedated those at Jerusalem and Caesarea and reached well back into the second century. There is, however, no direct evidence for a library in Alexandria, and its existence in the second and third centuries can only be inferred. By the last decades of the second century, the so-called catechetical school at Alexandria was flourishing under Pantaenus as a school of higher Christian studies (Eusebius, *H.E.* 5.10), and it continued to prosper later on under Clement and Origen (Eusebius, *H.E.* 6.3.3, 6.14.9).[52] From what we know of the broad intellectual interests of these men, the programs of studies they supervised, and the texts to which they refer, they must have had access to a rich collection of Jewish, Christian, and gnostic books that could have been found only within the Christian community, that is, a Christian library. It may be that Pantaenus and Clement, like Origen (*H.E.* 6.3.9), had personal libraries to put at the use of their students, but by Origen's time it is likely that a Christian library had taken shape, as the school itself acquired a more structured and institutional form. As the center of Greek scholarship, Alexandria set the pace for the Greek world in the development of libraries and in the criticism and production of texts, and it would be surprising if the Christian scholarship carried on there were indifferent to the availability of textual resources. Indeed, the evidence of Clement's and Origen's work shows that it was not. Origen's work went unimpeded when he unburdened himself of his private library, so he must have had recourse to another collection. Further, when Christian libraries were established in the third century in Jerusalem and Caesarea, Alexandria already held preeminence as a center of Christian learning, and the founders of those libraries, Alexander and Pamphilus, had both studied there. We may assume that they took as their model a Christian library in Alexandria. Later on, when the emperor Constans requested Athanasius to furnish "codices of the divine scriptures" *(puktia ton theion graphon)* for use in Italian churches, a scriptorium and hence a library were presupposed.[53] Thus despite the absence of direct early testimony, there are sound reasons to suppose that a sizable Christian library existed in Alexandria no later than the beginning of the third century.

CHRISTIAN LIBRARIES IN THE POST–CONSTANTINIAN PERIOD In the time after Constantine there is evidence of the development of Christian libraries in Rome and Constantinople. For Rome the evidence is slight until late in this period. Episcopal libraries in Rome, precursors of the great Vatican library, are first attested in the fourth and fifth centuries.[54] Yet Rome was already an important Christian center by the early second century, a place where Christian literature accumulated and from which it was disseminated. The school activity around Justin, Marcion, Valentinus, and, somewhat later, the work of the Theodotians, Gaius, and Hippolytus presuppose substantial collections of Christian texts in Rome in the second and early third centuries. Certainly in that period the various titular churches of the city had their own congregational libraries and archives, but it is unclear where larger, more scholastic collections may have been held.

The first allusion to a papal library comes from Julius I (337–52), who directed the clergy to settle certain legal matters not in the civil courts but in the *scrinium sanctum in ecclesia*.[55] The use of the singular suggests a central library, whether in the Lateran or in the episcopal church. There is evidence that a little later Damasus I (366–84) rebuilt the basilica of the church of Saint Laurence (San Lorenzo in Prasina) to better house a library. A dedicatory hexameter inscription that once stood over the entrance to the basilica is preserved in a codex of the Vatican library. It reads:

> *archivis fateor volui nova condere tecta addere*
> *praeterea dextra laevaque columnas*
> *quae Damasi teneant proprium per saecula nomen.*[56]

This library, however, was probably not the central ecclesiastical library at Rome, for the Lateran Palace had been the official residence of the pope and the center of ecclesiastical administration since the time of Sylvester (315–335), and it is more likely that the papal library, including the central archives, was located there.[57]

Excavations carried out at the beginning of the twentieth century in the Capella Sancta Sanctorum, the only surviving part of the ancient Lateran Palace, discovered among the foundations of the chapel the remains of a room of the earliest Lateran library. On one wall was a fresco of a reader, apparently Augustine, seated at a desk, an open codex before him. Beneath it was a legend referring to the writings of the fathers (see fig. 6).[58] Clearly this library contained theological literature, not merely archives. The painting dates from the fifth or early sixth century, but the room was probably a library much earlier. Although the *Liber pontificales* lists a series of popes, beginning with Celestine I (422–32), who contributed to the growth of the Lateran library, little is known of its scope and contents before the seventh century. The proceedings of the Lateran Council of 649 include an extensive list of books the council requested from the library in order

6. A sixth-century fresco, discovered in excavations beneath the Lateran Chapel in Rome, depicting a Christian reader (probably Augustine) with a codex on a reading desk. The wall where the fresco is found was probably part of the Lateran library. Photo used courtesy of Letouzey et Ane, Paris.

to document the issues, a list that includes a great variety of theological texts, orthodox and heretical, deriving from both the Greek and the Latin church.[59] If this list reflects the actual or approximate holdings of the library, it held an extensive collection of theological literature at least by the middle of the seventh century.[60]

We know of the establishment of another library by Hilary (461–68), who built at the church of Saint Laurence on the Via Tiburtina (San Lorenzo fuori le mura) a cloister, a bath, a residence, and two libraries *(bibliothecas II)*.[61] "Two libraries" probably means one library in two sections, one for Greek and one for Latin literature, following the Roman convention.

Apart from the Lateran library the major churches in Rome developed their own libraries, and these often held more than liturgical materials. In these libraries were many copies of biblical texts that Jerome used in translating the New Testament and the Psalms into Latin *(Ep. 112.19)*, and at least some of these libraries contained theological literature as well. Writing to Pammachius in Rome *(Ep. 48.3)*, Jerome suggested that he "consult the commentaries of the above-named writers [Origen, Dionysius, Pierius, Eusebius, and others] and take advantage of the church libraries" *(ecclesiarum bibliothecis)*. Some incidental evidence about church libraries is furnished by Paulinus, bishop of Nola in southern Italy. Early in the fifth century, Paulinus, who was a wealthy and literary man, built a basilica in Nola in honor of St. Felix. In the basilica, which was constructed in the triple apse style, the left apse was set apart as a library, and over its entrance Paulinus placed the inscription, "Whoever is moved by the holy desire to reflect on the scriptures, Here at peace can sit and engage in the pious perusal."[62] This library obviously served not only as a book storage area but as a reading room, encouraging the private use of the books.[63] Similar basilical designs are attested at Rome and Naples, and in those churches one of the side apses may regularly have been set aside as a library.

Apart from church libraries, there is evidence of at least one Christian academic library in Rome, and although it falls near the end of the period of our interest it should not be overlooked. This is the library built by Pope Agapetus (535–36) at the instance, it would seem, of Cassiodorus. Cassiodorus wished to establish in Rome, with the assistance of Agapetus, a school of Christian higher studies comparable to those in Alexandria and in Nisbis.[64] Although turbulent political conditions aborted this plan, Agapetus did establish a substantial library in his residence on the Caelian Hill. Excavations have brought to light the remains of this library, including an inscription that reads, *Bibliotheca Agapeti I a. DXXXV DXXXVI.*[65] In design it closely resembled the library at Timgad in North Africa: it consisted of a large rectangular hall (about thirty by twenty-two meters) at the head of which was a semicircular apse fourteen meters in diameter. The walls of the apse provided five broad niches for bookshelves or cupboards. This building was eventually incorporated into the monastery established by Gregory the Great in his family residence on the same Caelian Hill. An inscription stood in the library of the Gregorian monastery:

> *A venerable company of saints sits in a long line*
> *teaching the mystical precepts of the divine law.*
> *The priest Agapetus is appropriately seated among them.*
> *He has built with art this beautiful place for books.*[66]

Here we glimpse a Christian appropriation of the classical practice of decorating library rooms with busts, paintings, or mosaics of revered authors. The inscription refers to a fresco that must have run along the wall of the apse above the bookcases, depicting the Christian writers whose works were shelved below. As the founder of the library, Agapetus was given an honored place among them, though the construction of the library, let alone the acquisition process, cannot have taken place under him alone. Given the influence of Cassiodorus, it is likely that the library acquired both secular and Christian literature. Nothing, however, is known about the actual holdings or operations of the library or about its ultimate fate.[67]

The Christian library in the West about which the most is known was in neither Rome nor Italy, but belonged to Augustine's church at Hippo in North Africa.[68] In his sketch of Augustine's life, Possidius, who was Augustine's friend as well as his biographer, makes two important statements about the library at Hippo. He says, first, that

> *as for all he dictated and published* [dictata vel edita], *and all the debates in the church that were transcribed and revised* [excepta atque emendata], *some were against heretics and some were expositions of the canonical books. . . . There are so many that there is scarcely a student who has been able to read through and become acquainted with them all. However, not to be thought to fail those who are especially eager for the words of truth, I have decided to append to this little work of mine a catalogue* [indiculum] *of these books, tracts, and letters* [librorum, tractatuum, et

epistolarum]. *Whoever reads it and cares more for God's truth than for earthly riches will be able to choose for himself which books he wants to read and learn. If he wants to make a copy of it for himself, he should apply to the library of the church at Hippo* [bibliotheca Hipponensis ecclesiae] *where the best texts* [emendatiora exemplaria] *can be found, or he may inquire elsewhere and copy* [describat] *what he finds and keep it, and not begrudge lending it to another who asks to copy it.*[69]

Later in the same work Possidius remarks that

[Augustine] made no will since, as one of God's poor, he had nothing to leave. But he always laid it down that the library of the church and all the books [ecclesiae bibliothecam omnesque codices] *were to be carefully preserved for posterity. . . . He left to the church an adequate number of clergy, and monasteries of men and of women full of celibates and their superiors, together with libraries containing books and tracts by himself and other holy men, by which, thanks be to God, his stature in the church is known, and in these he will always live among the faithful.*[70]

The first comment concerns the library of the church at Hippo *(bibliotheca ecclesiae),* which was housed in the *episcopium* or episcopal residence.[71] It contained the works of Augustine in their master copies. Although copies of these works could be found elsewhere, their authoritative exemplars could be consulted only in Hippo. This same library is referred to in the second comment, which goes on to mention also small collections that belonged to the monastic houses. These monastic libraries contained "books and tracts by himself and other holy men"—scripture mainly, together with devotional and disciplinary works.[72]

Whether or not Augustine established the library of the church at Hippo, during his episcopate there was no distinction made between his library and the library of the church. It was he who built it up, contributing to it the books he had when he came to Hippo, adding his own works as they were composed, and acquiring for it the works of others. It was his own working library.[73] Yet the phrase *ecclesiae bibliothecam omnesque codices,* "the library of the church and all the codices," is not redundant, but means that "the codices" should be differentiated from the library proper and taken to refer to scriptural books, some or most of which were housed not in the library but in the basilica, where they were convenient for liturgical use.[74]

The scope and contents of the church library at Hippo are only partially known. Possidius says that it contained Augustine's own works, which Possidius classified under three heads—*libri, tractatus, epistolae*—the total fixed in the *indiculum* at 1,030. It also contained scriptural books in many copies, works of other Latin Christian writers, and works of Greek Christian writers in Latin translations.[75] Possidius does not mention non-Christian literature, but the library must have contained some. Augustine used the works of a large number of pagan writers, and he surely had a place for them in the library at Hippo.[76] The library also contained records of synodical proceedings, disputations, official decrees, and the like. Augustine often refers to archival materials, but neither he nor Possidius mentions an ecclesiastical archive as such or as distinct from the library of the church. If it is certain that these records were available locally, it remains unclear where they were housed and what relation they had to the library proper.[77] Given Augustine's use of them—some are transmitted among his own works—it seems likely that archival material was retained in the library as a special collection.

The contents of the library were apparently catalogued.[78] The *indiculum* that Possidius appended to his biography of Augustine shows that the library kept close track of Augustine's works. Possidius anticipated that readers of his life of Augustine would want to know what Augustine had written and where those works might be found and copied. Yet Augustine himself was familiar with the catalogue and must have participated in devising it. He referred to his own works under the same categories as Possidius used (*Retract.* 2.41), and he was able to specify in the *Retractationes* the time and circumstances of his compositions, which suggests that the catalogue was not just a list but included specific information. In fact, the nature and possibility of a work like the *Retractationes* presupposes such a catalogue. Thus there is good reason to think that the catalogue presented by Possidius is based on Augustine's own system of cataloging his writings. It may be that the systematic bibliographic effort reflected in the *indiculum* of Augustine's works was not confined to Augustine's corpus but extended to the library as a whole, in which case there would have been other parts of the catalogue dealing with the works of other Christian writers, with non-Christian texts, and with scriptural texts.

Little is known about the operation of the church library in Hippo. It was by no means public but served those who, like the clerics who shared his residence, were engaged along with Augustine in scholarly study. Though permission could be obtained to make transcriptions, it does not seem that books were loaned out.[79] Sometimes copies, mainly of Augustine's works, were made in the library and sent to individuals, either at their own request and expense or as gifts, and in the same way books were acquired by gift as well as by the transcription of borrowed copies. This copying of books in the library for acquisition or distribution, coupled with Augustine's habit of composing by dictation, which resulted in stenographic transcriptions to be converted to fair copies and corrected, gives ample evidence of a scriptorium and numerous skilled *notarii* and scribes associated with the library.

Although it escaped destruction in the Vandal invasion, the fate of the church library at Hippo and its valuable contents is unknown. Such a well-developed and closely organized library was not common in provincial towns like Hippo, which owed the substance and repute of its ecclesiastical library to the presence of its prolific and scholarly bishop.

Eastern Christian libraries in the post-Constantinian period are less well attested than those in the West, and mostly by late sources.[80] It is widely supposed that Constantine founded an imperial library in Constantinople soon after the government was transferred there in 330. The supposition is plausible if indeed Constantine sought to make the city a "new Rome," but there is no direct evidence that he established a library there.[81] Constantinople emerged as a center of intellectual life only somewhat later, under Constantius II (337–361). The first indication of an imperial library in Constantinople comes from Themistius, who in an oration delivered in 357 congratulates the emperor on having undertaken to reconstitute and collect in Constantinople the literary heritage of ancient hellenism by having the works of ancient authors, including minor ones, transcribed by a cadre of professional scribes working at imperial expense (*Or.* 4.59–61). Such a scriptorium and such a task presuppose a library, and the library, if not established by Constantius, owed its character and early development to him.[82] Subsequently, according to Zosimus (*Hist. nov.* 3.11.3), the emperor Julian (361–63) lent his patronage to the library and enlarged its holdings with his own. The Theodosian code (14.9.2) informs us that in 372 the emperor Valens ordered the employment of seven copyists *(antiquarii)*—four for Greek and three for Latin texts— and some assistants to maintain and repair the books of the imperial library. Thus we know that the library housed both Greek and Latin texts, but not necessarily in separate libraries, as was the practice in Rome. In 425 Theodosius II (408–50) formally established the school of higher studies in literature and philosophy, a kind of imperial university of the Byzantine empire. It would follow that the imperial library was intended to be the central library of the empire.[83] The twelfth-century epitomist Joannes Zonaras relays an old and possibly accurate estimation that in 475 when the library was damaged by fire it contained 120,000 volumes, which suggests that the library grew steadily during the first century after its founding.[84]

The imperial library was not a Christian library in the strict sense, although it must have contained Christian literature along with non-Christian. The comment of Nicephorus (*H.E.* 4.3) that Theodosius II collected texts of Christian scripture and commentaries on them from far and wide may well signify their presence in the library. It is not clear who made use of the library. At first it must chiefly have served the imperial family, the civil servants who worked in the palace precincts, and a select group of scholars, but after the academy of literary and philosophical studies was reorganized by Theodosius II it would also have served as the library of the academy. The library was restored after the fire of 475 but was apparently destroyed when Leo the Isaurian dissolved the school in 726.

There is disappointingly little information about church libraries in the East in the fourth and fifth centuries. When Anianus, however, writing in the early fifth century, says in the preface to his Latin translation of Chrysostom's homilies on Matthew that the works of Chrysostom could be found in "all the church libraries of the Greeks" *(omnes ecclesiasticae graecorum bibliothecae)*, he confirms that they were numerous and contained patristic as well as biblical texts.[85]

There are a few indications of the furnishings and decorations of early Christian libraries. Beyond the literary testimony, some of the earliest pictorial representations of Christian books show them stored in freestanding bookcases *(armaria)*. The lunette of St. Laurence found in the mausoleum of Galla Placidia in Ravenna, which was built in the first half of the fifth century, shows an open *armarium* containing a copy of each of the Gospels.[86] The frontispiece of Codex Amiatinus, written in the early eighth century on the basis of an earlier archetype, represents Ezra writing the Law before an open *armarium*.[87] The fresco found beneath the Lateran chapel shows a reader seated before a codex on a reading desk. This and the inscriptions from the library in the basilica in Nola and from the library of Pope Agapetus prove that by the fifth century Christian libraries were decorated with paintings and inscriptions. In all these ways Christian libraries followed the conventions of Greek and Roman libraries, and although none of this evidence precedes the fifth century, Christian libraries large enough to be housed in a special room probably always followed established conventions of storage and decoration. Before I turn to Greek and Roman libraries, two further types of Christian libraries, the monastic and the personal, should be examined.

EARLY MONASTIC LIBRARIES   Monastic libraries are attested as early as the fourth century in the Christian East. The monastic impulse in Christianity first took root in the East, and the best documentation of its early development comes from Egypt. The eremitic tradition emerged there in the late third century and the cenobitic in the early fourth, largely under the respective influence of two contemporary figures, Anthony (about 251–356) and Pachomius (about 290–346). Pachomius established the first known cenobitic monastery at Tabennesi in Upper Egypt (about 320–25), followed by others at Phbow and at Chenoboskia. He later took under his supervision monasteries that he himself had not founded, and at his death he directed no fewer than nine monasteries for men and two for women. The monastic rules of Pachomius, which do not survive in their original form, and the various versions of the *Life of Pachomius*, show that books played a significant role in Pachomian communities.[88]

Although early monasticism took no interest in learning or scholarship, scripture was important to the devotional life of the monks. Novices were required to learn some psalms, epistles, and Gospel texts, and those who came as illiterates were taught to read.[89] Community worship included extensive readings from scripture, and scripture was recited and reflected upon throughout the day according to the rule.[90] If all monks were expected to read and to know scripture, there must have been texts available within the community, and this is confirmed by a variety of allusions in the Pachomian literature to the use of books. Pachomius admonished the monks to beware of "the splendor and the beauty of this world in things like good food, clothing, a cell, or a book outwardly pleasing to the eye"—a warning not to avoid books but to appreciate their content rather than their appearance.[91] Books were readily accessible to the monks: "In each house . . . the books, which were in a niche, were under the care of [the housemaster and his assistant]." They could be borrowed by a monk and returned in the evening or borrowed by one house from another for up to a week.[92] The books were not limited to scriptural texts. Pachomius discouraged the reading of Origen's works and also various apocryphal books, and so we must assume that these were present, either in the house libraries or through general circulation.[93] The Pachomian literature also alludes to scribal activity among the monks, and there are good indications that eventually there was a monastic scriptorium.[94]

The interest of Pachomian monasticism for early Christian libraries lies not only in these notices in Pachomian literature but more in the recovery in 1945 of a cache of Coptic codices in the immediate environs of the first three Pachomian monasteries—the so-called Nag Hammadi library. The discovery consisted of twelve codices and part of a thirteenth, comprising in all fifty-two separate texts of forty-six documents (four texts being present in duplicate, and one in triplicate), all in Coptic, forty of which were previously unknown. All were found together in a large jar sealed by a bowl and buried beneath a boulder at the base of cliffs on the right bank of the Nile, some six miles northeast of the town of Nag Hammadi and within sight of the ruins of the Pachomian monastery at Phbow.[95] The discovery of this ancient, well-preserved collection of books provoked questions that continue to be debated today: What sort of collection is this? To whom did it belong? When and why did it come to be buried?

The texts are a varied lot: some are Christian, some are gnostic, some are Christian-gnostic, some are Hermetic, and two are philosophical—the *Sentences of Sextus* and a fragment of Plato's *Republic*. They derive from many provenances. Most, perhaps all, were translated from Greek. For these reasons the term *library* should be used with care; this does not appear to be a library in the narrow sense of a homogeneous and carefully organized group of writings, but only in the sense of a collection of books.[96] The initial conjecture, based on the content of the texts, was that this was the library of a group of Egyptian gnostics.[97] But the Christian coloration of many of the texts rules out a purely gnostic setting and has led most scholars to think the collection belonged to a Christian group with gnostic proclivities. The site of the discovery, near Pachomian monastic settlements and close to their center at Phbow, creates the presumption that this group of texts stands in some relation to Pachomian monasticism. Although their paleographical and codicological features do not prove that the codices were produced or used in the Pachomian monasteries, they do confirm that the texts belonged to the same period and locale.[98]

If a connection between the Nag Hammadi codices and the Pachomian monasteries is assumed, what is it? Pachomius and the movement he fostered are reputed to have been highly orthodox, whereas some of these texts clearly are not. Consequently, it has been argued that if the monks owned the codices, they would have used them only for reference, as documentation of positions the Pachomians rejected.[99] This explanation, however, has little to commend it. The bindings of the codices are well made and decorated, suggesting that the texts they enclosed were valued, and the way they were wrapped in a cloth and buried in a covered jar indicates that they were not discarded but carefully stored away.[100] Moreover, the great heterodox movements of the fourth century that strongly affected Egypt—the Manichaen, Arian, Origenist, and Melitian movements—and the ones that normally figure in the *Lives of Pachomius*—Arianism and Meletianism—find no representation among these texts, and in any case only some of the texts are clearly heterodox. Besides, there is no independent reason to think that Pachomian monks, at least in the early period, were studious heresiologists.

Another and more widely held view is that Pachomian monks copied and used the Nag Hammadi texts for their own spiritual edification.[101] If that is so, Pachomian monasticism was not so rigidly orthodox as has been assumed, and the sources that stress its orthodoxy are either idealized or from a later period.[102] Heterodox elements aside, the Nag Hammadi texts emphasize ascetic practice, visionary experience, and esotericism, all of which interested the Pachomian monks. Thus the possibility that the early Pachomian communities of the area owned and used these books cannot be excluded. The site of the finds, the dating of the texts, the extent of their compatibility with monastic interests, and everything otherwise known about the production, storage and use of books in Pachomian communities all conspire to show that these codices were possessed and used by Pachomian monks, if not as scripture then as devotional literature.[103] Whatever their use, if these codices indeed belonged to Pachomian monks there is a reason for their eventual disposal. In 367 Athanasius, bishop of Alexandria, issued his famous 39th Festal Letter announcing which books might be read by Christians and which were to be avoided. This letter, like others of its type, was publicized in the Pachomian communities, and it is entirely possible that the Nag Hammadi texts were removed in deference to the bishop's direction.[104]

Besides the Nag Hammadi texts, other ancient manuscripts, principally the so-called Bodmer Papyri but also some items in the Chester Beatty Library, throw light on Pachomian libraries. Though clearly Egyptian, the specific provenances of these documents remained obscure long after their discovery. Now there is reason, however, to think that they came from a single find, made in 1952 near the Egyptian town of Dishna, about twelve kilometers east of the site of the Nag Hammadi discovery and five kilometers northeast of the Pachomian monastery at Phbow.[105] Consequently these manuscripts are now often collectively designated as the Dishna papers. An inventory of the original find, items of which are now dispersed among various repositories, counts the remains of thirty-eight books comprising both codices and rolls and including classical, Christian, scriptural, and documentary materials.[106] In addition to these there were copies of letters of Pachomius and other abbots of the Pachomian Order, nine items altogether, and it is their presence that indicates that the find as a whole constituted a library of a Pachomian monastery. The paleographical evidence of the letters, the latest of which were copied in the sixth and seventh centuries, suggests that the cache was buried in the seventh century.[107]

Taken together, the Dishna papers provide important insights into an early monastic library. First, the range of materials is astonishing: included are classical texts (nine items, mainly parts of Homer but Menander and Cicero as well), scriptural texts (twelve items with Old Testament materials, six with New Testament materials, and three with some of each), a few apocryphal and pseudepigraphical texts, some liturgical, homiletical, grammatical, and documentary items, and of course the letters of Pachomius and other abbots. Second, the manuscripts are in several languages: most are written in Coptic, but some are Greek and two are Greek-Latin bilingual manuscripts, thus illustrating in bibliographic terms the multilingualism of the Egyptian context. Third, the manuscripts were written at various points over several centuries: the earliest about the end of the second century (P 66 [Papyrus Bodmer II]), the latest in the seventh century (Horsiesios's letter 3); and they vary considerably in the quality of their production. This broad range of dates in the transcription of the manuscripts indicates a long period during which they were collected. Fourth, the manuscripts permit inferences about the actual development of the collection. The collection cannot have begun before the founding of the Pachomian Order in the early fourth century, and most of the Christian codices in it may be paleographically dated from the early fourth to the early fifth century. Some of the codices, however, are considerably earlier and must have been brought into the monastic setting from outside, presumably soon after the founding of the order. It is probably for this reason that many of the best-produced manuscripts of the whole find, whether they contain Christian or classical texts, are older than the order itself, while many of the later manuscripts are more poorly produced—written in less practiced hands or using inferior materials or left incomplete.[108] Thus it appears that the collection was developed with difficulty, with a decline in standards of transcription, and with a sharp decrease in acquisitions after the early fifth century.

The likely identification of the Dishna manuscripts as the remains of a Pachomian monastic library and the probability that the Nag Hammadi texts belonged to a Pachomian monastery nearby greatly illuminate the formation and character of early Christian libraries in the monastic setting. They show that by the early fourth century highly ascetic and remote Christian groups were accumulating, transcribing, storing, and using extensive collections of books. If so, Christian libraries in this period must have been widespread, and any appreciable Christian community must have had one.

The monastic collections also afford some insight into the contents of Christian libraries. Of course, neither the Nag Hammadi codices nor the Dishna materials can be taken to typify the contents of Christian libraries generally. The peculiar character of the Nag Hammadi texts is such that they could only have been a part of a monastic library. The Dishna texts are doubtless more representative. The preponderance of scriptural texts (not necessarily all canonical) and other liturgical material (homilies, hymns, scriptural catenae), some ecclesiastical records, and at least a few pieces of non-Christian literature: all this might be expected also in congregational book collections. And although there are no commentaries among the Dishna texts, these too would have found a place in many congregational libraries from the third century onward.[109]

PRIVATE LIBRARIES OF
INDIVIDUAL CHRISTIANS

I proposed above that some of the early fathers—Justin, Clement, and Tertullian, for example—had their own collections of texts, ecclesiastical resources not withstanding, and there is direct evidence that some later Christian writers kept personal libraries. We have seen that Origen early in his life disposed of his library of pagan texts, but soon thereafter acquired another collection of books to serve him in research and teaching, a library that he ultimately left to the church in Caesarea, where it became the original stock of the library built up by Pamphilus. Similarly, the nucleus of the library in Hippo was the personal library of Augustine, and the whole of it remained in some sense his own throughout his episcopate, such that upon his death he bequeathed it to the church. In addition to these, Jerome possessed a large personal library, of which he says, "I had collected [it] for myself at Rome by great care and effort."[110] His library, centered on Latin works, must already have been extensive before he left Rome. Jerome refused to be without it and had it transported on his travels until he finally installed it in his monastic quarters in Bethlehem. Nevertheless, he was continuously enlarging and diversifying it, soliciting copies of books, mostly Christian, from friends and busily transcribing copies for himself of books he borrowed from friends or found in libraries in Rome, Caesarea, and elsewhere.[111] Occasional fits of conscience over the propriety of reading pagan literature tortured Jerome, and he was once temporarily deterred from it by a harrowing nightmare. Yet he could not permanently forego this pleasure or the collection of books that allowed him to indulge it.[112] Over many years Jerome's library must have grown large and contained in the end far more Christian than pagan books.[113] Its fate, like that of so many, is unknown; it was perhaps destroyed in 416 when an unruly mob consumed with Pelagian zeal set fire to Jerome's monastic residence in Jerusalem.[114]

Beyond the personal libraries of these prominent Christian writers there is an interesting notice about a library that belonged to George of Cappadocia, the Arian bishop who supplanted Athanasius in Alexandria in 356. When George was killed in a riot in Alexandria in 361, the emperor Julian wrote to Ecdicius, prefect of Egypt, ordering that George's library be salvaged and sent to him: "See that all the books of George be sought out. For there were at his residence many philosophical works, many rhetorical works, and many of the doctrine of the impious Galileans, which we could wish were all destroyed, but lest with these the more useful be made away with, let them also be carefully sought for. But let your guide in this search be the secretary (notarios) of George himself. . . . I am myself acquainted with the books of George, for he lent me many, though not all, when I was in Cappadocia, for transcription, and then had them back again."[115] In another letter, to Porphyrius, written about the same time and with the same request, the emperor calls George's library "very large and important" and says that it contains "the works of philosophers of every sort and of many commentators and above all numerous Christian books of all kinds."[116] Julian's acquaintance with George's library dated from his adolescent years (342–48), which he spent at Macellum when George was still in Cappadocia. Clearly the collection was, as Julian regarded it, a private, not an ecclesiastical library and a remarkably good one. Julian's description of its contents is valuable and probably applies equally well to many other private Christian libraries. Why was Julian so anxious to obtain it? If, as some claim, he wanted to fold it into the imperial library in Constantinople, which Julian was enlarging and moving to a building he had constructed to house it, why would he request that the library be sent to him in Antioch? It is more likely that Julian wanted George's library because the Christian books in it would be especially useful for the tract he was then writing against the Christians.[117]

During the fourth and fifth centuries, as increasing numbers of the intellectual class became Christians, extensive private libraries would have been found as often among Christians as they had always been among pagan scholars and literary men. Almost every Christian teacher and writer must have accumulated a working library, usually comprising a good selection of pagan literature along with Christian texts. Among those scholars and teachers who converted to Christianity—men like Justin in the second century, Cyprian in the third, and Augustine in the fourth—pagan literature would have constituted the original stock of their libraries, to which Christian literature was added. As a rule, these private libraries appear to have been more diverse than congregational libraries and perhaps more diverse even than the great institutional Christian libraries found in Caesarea, Alexandria, and Rome.[118]

THE LARGER CONTEXT: GREEK, ROMAN, AND JEWISH LIBRARIES By the time of Christian origins the ancient world held many Greek and Roman libraries and some Jewish libraries, and the literary and archaeological evidence attests that all these varied as much one from another as Christian libraries did. With few exceptions, little information survives about any particular non-Christian library. Nevertheless, the evidence offers a good general picture by which to better our understanding of early Christian libraries. Many good studies of Greek and Roman libraries are already available.[119] It will suffice for our purposes to consider in general the history and types of ancient non-Christian libraries, together with some examples.

Greek Libraries Little is known about Greek libraries before the Hellenistic period. Although there is mention of private collections as early as the fifth century B.C.E.—Euripides, Euthydemos, Eucleides of Athens, and Plato were all said to have been collectors of books—nothing is known about the scope or substance of their collections.[120]

Private collections became more numerous in the fourth century but were hardly commonplace. The best known and best attested was Aristotle's, which had a long and interesting history. Aristotle passed his collection on to his successor as head of the Lyceum, Theophrastus, who in turn bequeathed it to Neleus, apparently on the assumption that Neleus would be the next head of the Lyceum. This indicates that, although the collection was private, it served as the library of the school. When Strato succeeded Theophrastus instead of Neleus, Neleus returned to his home in Skepsis, taking the library, or the better part of it, with him. Disused and poorly stored by Neleus's heirs, it was purchased by the bibliophile Apellicon of Teos, who took it to Athens and inexpertly tried to restore the damaged parts. When Sulla conquered Athens in 86 B.C.E. he seized Apellicon's library as his personal booty and carried it to Rome. There Tyrannios the grammarian worked over the texts, probably making copies for himself, and on the basis of his texts Andronicus of Rhodes, later the head of the Peripatetic school, shaped an edition of Aristotle. Sulla housed the library at his estate near Cumae, and upon his death it was inherited by Faustus Cornelius Sulla. There Cicero made use of it and was happy to purchase some rare items from it when the estate was later auctioned.[121] Although direct evidence is lacking, it is plausible to suppose that Plato's own collection, though undoubtedly smaller than Aristotle's, served as the library of the Academy just as Aristotle's did for the Lyceum, and that other philosophical schools or their leaders also held collections.[122]

Greek libraries came to prominence in the hellenistic age, when private libraries were overshadowed by the appearance of the great institutional libraries, principally those at Alexandria and Pergamum. Established by hellenistic rulers as symbols and instruments of Greek culture, these were libraries on a new scale. Not only was their scope vastly larger than any earlier library; they were royal foundations, institutions of the state, richly funded, carefully organized, accessible to scholars, and intended for the patronage of learning.

Of the famous library at Alexandria, the greatest in the ancient world, far more has been conjectured than known.[123] Its founding is usually associated with Ptolemy Philadelphus (Ptolemy II, 283–246), but, although Philadelphus was active in promoting the development of the library, it probably originated under Ptolemy Soter (Ptolemy I, 367–282). Aspiring to make Alexandria the center of Greek learning, Ptolemy Soter built a Museion and brought outstanding scholars to Alexandria. Among others, Ptolemy attracted Demetrius of Phaleron, the Athenian statesman and man of letters who had been the out-standing student of Theophrastus at the Lyceum. Demetrius was in-strumental in the organization of the Museion and probably had a hand in planning the library.[124]

The Museion in Alexandria, like those in other Greek cities, was a cult center for the worship of the Muses. These shrines were often the meeting place of literary persons and the setting of literary competi-tions, but philosophy too was associated with the Muses as early as the time of Pythagoras, and both the Academy of Plato and the Lyceum of Aristotle were organized like cult associations, fostering a communal life among the members.[125] Through Demetrius, the Alexandrian Mu-seion was indebted to these models, especially to the Lyceum, though the members of the Museion were not philosophers but men of letters and science who constituted a sort of royal academy of arts and sci-ences. According to Strabo (17.1.8), who saw the Museion in the time of Augustus, "it has a covered walk, an arcade with recesses and seats and a large house, in which is the dining hall of the learned men of the Museion. This association of men shares common property and has a priest of the Muses who used to be appointed by the kings but is now appointed by Caesar." Located within the palace precinct, the Mu-seion was funded by the royal treasury, and the scholars immediately associated with it were provided a stipend, a common meal, and per-haps residential quarters as well.

The Museion was dedicated to research. If scientific subjects were prominent at the beginning, literary-philological studies had found an equal place by the time of Ptolemy Philadelphus and eventually became its primary focus. Research depends on resources, so the Mu-seion required a library: virtually from the beginning books must have been on hand. Yet of the library as an institution—its location, organi-zation, and holdings—the evidence is incomplete and often incon-sistent. The best, though relatively late, evidence indicates that there were actually two libraries. The Byzantine monk John Tzetzes (about 1110–1180), drawing on earlier sources, mentions a library "outside the Palace (precinct)" and another "within the Palace (precinct)." In discussing the translation of Jewish scripture into Greek, Epiphanius (about 315–403) says that when the translation was finished it was placed "in the first library" in the royal quarter, but he goes on to mention that later there was another, smaller library in the Serapeum, which he calls "the daughter of the first one."[126] The larger "first library" appears to have been housed in the Museion, not in a sepa-rate building.[127] The Museion was large enough to accommodate the library, and its scholars needed to have books close at hand. If the library outgrew the space in the Museion, that would explain why a second library was housed in the Serapeum. But the nature of this daughter library and its relation to the first remain unknown.

From the time of Ptolemy Philadelphus the Alexandrian library was supervised by a royally appointed librarian *(prostasia tes bibliothekes)* who was often the tutor of the royal house as well.[128] The identities and the chronology of the librarians are not certain, but normally the librarian was a prominent intellectual of the Museion.[129] His responsibilities, which are nowhere described, must have included, along with acquisitions and cataloging, a concern for the types and qualities of texts and for the substance and resources of various bodies of knowledge.

The library was reputed to be immense. No doubt it was large, but testimonies about its size vary widely and are hard to interpret. Tzetzes states that the main library in the palace precincts contained no fewer than 490,000 rolls, of which 400,000 were *summigeis* (mixed), and 90,000 *amigeis* (unmixed) or *haplai* (single), and that the outer library of the Serapeum held another 42,800 rolls.[130] A collection of roughly half a million rolls, however, can hardly be credited, even at the height of the library's development, much less in the time of Ptolemy Philadelphus. The relatively small amount of literature available for collection and the arduous tasks of acquisition, criticism, emendation, and transcription make it almost inconceivable that the library's holdings were ever so vast.[131] Given that these proportions are not widely attested, that figures like these are notoriously unreliable, and that the reputation of the library stimulated imagination, the library's contents were probably much less extensive than Tzetzes indicates. Even so, the library apparently did aspire to create a complete collection of Greek literature.[132] It also procured elements of other national literatures so far as they were available in Greek: some Jewish, native Egyptian, and Persian works were represented, and we can assume that Latin literature eventually found a place as well.[133]

As to how the library acquired its texts, there is little to go on save a few anecdotes furnished by Galen in his comments on the history of the works of Hippocrates.[134] Discussing how a copy of the *Epidemics* owned by Mnemon of Sides came to Alexandria during the reign of Ptolemy Euergetes, Galen says that Euergetes was so concerned to enlarge the library that he ordered all books found on ships docking at Alexandria to be seized and copied, the copies being returned to the ships and the originals retained for the library. Galen is also the source of the well-known story that Euergetes borrowed the official Athenian texts of Sophocles, Euripides, and Aeschylus in order to transcribe them, depositing with the Athenians the huge sum of fifteen talents as security. After the library made fine copies, Euergetes returned the copies but kept the originals, forfeiting his deposit. Such extreme measures must have been only occasionally used to supplement the conventional methods of purchasing texts or borrowing them for transcription. Indirect evidence of purchase also comes from Galen, who claims that books were forged on a large scale in order to profit from the competition that arose when the library at Alexandria found itself in rivalry with the library instituted at Pergamum by the Attalids. In any event, money was no obstacle, and agents of the Ptolemies busily sought out texts in foreign parts.[135]

Once acquired, texts were processed before being placed in the library for use. Galen mentions depositories *(apothekai, oikoi)* where books were initially stored, each labeled according to its provenance: its previous owner, its editor, or its place of derivation.[136] This information was important for cataloguing, of course, but also for the work of textual and literary criticism, which aimed to distinguish textual traditions and to establish authoritative texts. The tasks of bibliography and criticism were closely connected: texts not only had to be transcribed and catalogued, but critically constituted by means of collation, emendation, and restoration. An effort was also made to establish uniformity of format and perhaps also of inscription and to secure a high standard of production. These technical tasks required both scholarly and scribal resources: the philological expertise of the scholars of the Museion and a well-organized scriptorium were equally essential to the creation and operation of such a library.[137]

The Alexandrian library was without peer in the third century B.C.E., and it sustained its preeminence for centuries against much adversity. The library at Pergamum, for example, mounted a determined challenge to Alexandrian supremacy early in the second century B.C.E. Then, around 145 B.C.E., the persecution of Alexandrian scholars and their disciples by Euergetes II resulted in an emigration of academic talent from the Museion and a loss of distinction in its librarians. Still another misfortune was Caesar's war with Alexandria in 48 B.C.E., during which, according to Livy, many books were accidentally destroyed by fire.[138] Though less is known about the final fate of the Alexandrian library than about its beginnings, it was probably destroyed along with the palace quarter in 273 C.E., when the emperor Aurelian overpowered the rebel Firmus.[139] Yet the fate of the Serapeum library was not sealed until 391 C.E., when the Christian patriarch Theophilus, against violent popular resistance but with imperial support, converted the temples of Alexandria into churches.[140] Pagan scholars took flight, and, although the library is not mentioned in the reports, it seems likely that its contents were dispersed or destroyed.

The only other Greek library of the time to attain more than local importance was the great library at Pergamum. We know less about the history of the Pergamene library than the Alexandrian one, but more about its physical setting. The third ruler of Pergamum, Attalus I (241–197), was a patron of literature, science, and the arts who attracted scholars to Pergamum—Antigonus of Carystus, Crates of Mallos, and Apollonius of Perge among them—and he may have initiated the library project. It was, however, his successor, Eumenes II (197–159), who constructed the library and other buildings in the city (Strabo, 13.4.2). Excavations of ancient Pergamum have revealed the library's location and layout.[141] It was associated with the Temple of Athena and consisted of a series of four rooms standing behind its north stoa. The largest of these was either a common room for scholars or a festival room, and the books were stored in the three smaller adjacent rooms.[142] The northern arcade just outside these may have been used as a reading area along with the common room.

The administration and operation of the library at Pergamum are largely obscure. Little is known of those who served as its librarians. Eumenes was unsuccessful in his effort to recruit Aristophanes of Byzantium, who was the librarian in Alexandria, and only one later librarian of Pergamum is identified in the sources, the Stoic scholar Athenodorus Cordylion of Tarsus.[143] According to a story first recorded by Pliny the Elder, parchment was invented at Pergamum during the reign of Eumenes because Ptolemy, to prevent the library from competing with the library at Alexandria, had restricted the export of papyrus.[144] Although this story cannot be credited, Pergamum probably did refine the production of parchment, and it must have been characteristic of Pergamum to use it as a writing material. The use of parchment instead of papyrus suggests that, like the library at Alexandria, the library at Pergamum was interested in the technical aspects of book production and sponsored some bibliographic innovations. It also followed Alexandria in designating the provenances of its texts, distinguishing between mixed and unmixed rolls and devising a catalogue.[145]

The Pergamene library enjoyed a high reputation in antiquity as a major repository of books, but there is only one explicit allusion to its size: Anthony is said to have made a gift to Cleopatra (sometime after 41 B.C.E.) of two hundred thousand volumes taken from the library at Pergamum.[146] Even if this poorly attested tradition is accurate, it is unclear what portion of the library these rolls represented. The gift is often thought to have been the entire stock of the library, but nothing suggests that the library was thereby depleted, and if it had been, later Pergamene scholars like Teleus the grammarian and the physician Galen could not have carried out their research there. Two hundred thousand rolls, however, would have constituted a large collection, and the figure should be treated with reserve.[147] Still, the holdings of the library at Pergamum must have been substantial for it to rival its Alexandrian counterpart.

There were, of course, other libraries in the Greek world before the Roman period. Some, like the smaller library in Alexandria and the Pergamene library, were associated with temples.[148] Others were connected with educational institutions. In 275 B.C.E. Ptolemy Philadelphus established a gymnasium in Athens, the Ptolemaion, and a library must have been associated with it since inscriptions of the first century B.C.E. attest that the *epheboi* added one hundred rolls each year to the collection.[149] Inscriptional evidence shows that the gymnasium in Pergamum also had a library, that large donations were made to a library in Cos that was probably attached to a gymnasium, and that gymnasial libraries existed in Rhodes, Halicarnassus, and Teos, among other places.[150] It seems that by the second century B.C.E. it was commonplace for gymnasia, at least those in larger cities, to have libraries.

Two other Greek libraries, but of the Roman period, were related to institutions of higher learning: the library of Celsus in Ephesus, which was probably associated with the Museion of that city, and the Hadrianic library in Athens. The library of Celsus, Roman consul and then proconsul of Asia, was established in his honor by his son early in the first century C.E. and provided with a fine building, decoration, works of art, a supply of books, and a considerable fund for further acquisitions.[151] Its remains are relatively well preserved. Behind a beautiful facade with three doors lay a large room (approximately eleven by seventeen meters) in which two tiers of colonnades topped by a gallery ran along three walls, broken only by a large apse opposite the main door, where there once stood a statue, probably of Athena. At regular intervals along the walls at all three levels there were niches approximately three meters high, one meter wide, and half a meter deep to accommodate wooden shelves on which rolls were stored. Yet of the contents or operation of this library nothing is known.

In 131 C.E. the emperor Hadrian founded a Museion and a library in Athens that were later supported also by Antoninus Pius and Marcus Aurelius.[152] Excavations have uncovered a magnificent stoa of a hundred columns and at its eastern end the remains of a large building. The huge central room (twenty-three by fifteen meters) that opened onto the stoa was undoubtedly the library: its rear wall contains a large central niche and two stories of three smaller niches to each side where books were shelved.

Roman Libraries Roman libraries, whether in Rome or in the western half of the empire, show both continuity and change in the evolution of libraries.[153] Roman libraries were deeply indebted to the Greek heritage; indeed, the first significant book collections in Rome were private Greek libraries plundered in eastern campaigns. These included the library of Aristotle, brought, as noted earlier, to Rome by Sulla as booty from the sack of Athens in 86 B.C.E., the royal Macedonian library seized at Pella by Aemelius Paullus in 168 B.C.E., which upon being transferred to Rome became the first private library at Rome, and the library of Lucullus, which had come into his hands in the Mithridatic wars.[154]

The Romans took a strong interest in the establishment of state libraries, following, no doubt, the model of the Greek kingdoms. The first in Rome was planned by Julius Caesar, and in 47 B.C.E. he appointed the great Roman scholar Varro its librarian-designate.[155] The plan went unfulfilled with Caesar's death, but when Asinius Pollio defeated the Illyrians in 39 he used the spoils to build the library Caesar had planned, in the Atrium Libertatis beside the Forum.[156] Little is known of this library except that, in an arrangement that was to become typical of Roman libraries, its holdings were divided into separate Greek and Latin sections.

The ambitious building programs of Augustus included the construction of libraries.[157] Early in his principate he established a library in the temple of Apollo on the Palatine. Like Greek libraries it was associated with a cult sanctuary, but its division into Greek and Latin sections was a Roman innovation.[158] Largely destroyed in the great fire of 80 C.E., this library was restored by Domitian and remained a prominent institution until at least the middle of the fourth century.[159] Augustus established a second library in the Porticus Octaviae, adjoining the temple of Jupiter and Juno in the Campus Martius.[160]

Later emperors continued to build libraries. Tiberius built a temple to the deified Augustus and ensconced a library in its precincts.[161] Destroyed by fire sometime before 79, it was rebuilt by Domitian, but of its later history there is no record. Vespasian erected a Temple of Peace and installed a library there. The best-known and most frequently mentioned imperial library was built by Trajan in the second century. The remains of the library of the temple of Trajan, later known as the Ulpian library, may be seen today beneath the Via dell'Impero.[162] Two large, identical buildings (twenty-seven by seventeen meters), one for Greek and one for Latin books, faced each other across a large rectangular court, onto which each opened through a rank of columns. In each building, on the wall opposite the opening, there was a large central niche for a monumental statue. On either side of this niche and along the two adjoining walls there ran a low podium, mounted by steps between columns that supported a gallery above. In the walls behind the podium are rectangular niches into which wooden cabinets were built for the books. This library had a long life, and the collection was still in use in the fifth century.[163]

Libraries were also among the facilities of some Roman baths. One has been identified in the Baths of Trajan, where there can be seen two levels of niches in the walls of a semicircular area in one corner of the larger complex. A large (twenty by forty meters) library room has also been identified in the Baths of Caracalla, built in 216. It opened through a rank of columns onto a courtyard. On the wall opposite the opening is a large central apse, on either side of which, as well as along the adjoining walls, there are niches surmounting a low podium.[164] The presence of libraries in these locations is a useful reminder that Roman baths had many functions: there Romans "washed themselves, took exercise, spent their leisure time, were exposed to art and cultural programs, made business and political contacts, and conducted their social activities."[165]

The last state library in Rome for which there is good evidence was built in the precincts of the Pantheon by Alexander Severus (222–235). This library is especially interesting in connection with Christian libraries because Severus entrusted its design to the Christian scholar Sextus Julius Africanus.[166] Africanus had served as an officer in the army of Septimus Severus and lived in Emmaus (Nicopolis) in Palestine, and he was a friend and correspondent of Origen. Though nothing is known of the holdings of the Pantheon library, it is likely to have contained some Christian and Jewish along with Greek and Latin literature, given Severan syncretistic interests and the role of Africanus in the construction of the library.[167]

Elsewhere in Italy and the western provinces there were other Roman libraries. Pliny the Younger founded a library in Como as a benefaction to his native community.[168] An inscription attests a library in Arunca, the *bibliotheca Matidiana,* named after Hadrian's deified mother-in-law.[169] There are well preserved remains of a library in Nimes that, judging from its architectural features, belonged to the Hadrianic period, and of another at Timgad in North Africa that was constructed about the middle of the third century.[170] Also in North Africa a library at Carthage is attested by Apuleius and possibly another at Oea (Tripoli).[171] Libraries established in the East in the Roman period have already been mentioned.

These various libraries have customarily been called public. It is better to call them institutional, for we have little information about who may have had access to them. A few ancient sources seem to suggest that some of these libraries were public, but what this meant is not entirely clear.[172] Some poets of the Augustan age thought their works would be more accessible if they were placed in a library that was not purely personal,[173] but this need not imply either unrestricted access or a large public that frequented libraries. It indicates instead the value to an author of being able to place his work in a central location rather than rely on its informal and haphazard dissemination. The few references in ancient literature to the actual use of institutional libraries speak of individuals, and they may have exercised special privileges.[174] In considering the question of access, several things need to be kept in mind. First, statements like Suetonius's that Julius Caesar sought "to open to the public the greatest possible libraries of Greek and Latin books" (*Iul.* 44.2) must be interpreted with a view to a society whose large majority was illiterate. The constituency of readers who could have been the "public" users of an institutional library was a small percentage of the public at large and consisted mainly of aristocrats. Thus even without formal restrictions there were narrow de facto limits of literacy and leisure on potential users. Second, the Romans established libraries in imitation of the Hellenistic kingdoms, where large libraries had become such prestigious ornaments of the state that no aspiring power could omit them.[175] The political and cultural symbolism of institutional libraries was a primary value to their founders, independently of their use. Third, the social structure of literary culture and activity under the empire has bearing on the creation of these libraries. The emperor was the preeminent *patronus* of literary culture, and state libraries were a way to exercise his patronage toward his *amici* and his urban *clientes.*[176] These were the real public served by institutional libraries. Libraries established by individual benefactors in towns and cities were apparently no more accessible to the general public but served the constituency of gymnasia. In all, there is little reason to think that any ancient libraries were public in the modern sense.

Besides institutional libraries, there were many private Roman libraries.[177] The archaeological remains of some are found in imperial residences in Rome and in aristocratic homes in Pompeii and Herculaneum. Because they were domestic libraries and because they were much smaller than institutional libraries, they resemble more closely the sorts of libraries that arose in Christian circles, and so are especially interesting to us.

The library in the house of Augustus in Rome consisted of twin rectangular rooms on either side of the central hall *(tablinum)* and opening onto the peristyle.[178] Each of the side walls of these rooms had three niches to accommodate book cupboards or shelves. A wider niche, perhaps intended to hold a statue, was centered in the wall opposite the main entry. In the eastern room there are traces of fresco paintings in some niches, suggesting the use of open shelves rather than cupboards. The two rooms are relatively large (9.6 by 4.6 meters), more spacious than necessary for storage, so that freestanding cupboards, desks or statues may have stood in them. The private library thus conceived is no mere repository of books but an environment for books and reading. The two nearly identical rooms almost certainly held separate Greek and Latin collections, and this division was to become the mark of the Roman library.

The house of Augustus is dwarfed by the grandiose Domus Aurea, begun but never completed by Nero. On its southern facade was a large, five-sided central courtyard onto which the library opened.[179] The room, notable for its apsidal form, was approximately four by six meters. A large recess at the head of the apse had a small statuary niche. Two cabinet niches faced each other across this recess, and two others stood in each flanking wall of the apse. Two small rooms adjacent to the library may have been reading or writing rooms.

Private libraries in imperial residences are not typical, of course.[180] The remains of two other domestic libraries are more representative, if still aristocratic. At Pompeii, a library was found in the House of Menander, named by archaeologists for the poet whose portrait graces a wall there.[181] Along the south side of the peristyle lies a series of four exedral areas, two semicircular and two rectangular. The central rectangular room, the largest of the four exedra, was probably a reading room. One wall holds the portrait of Menander handling a scroll, and the opposite wall bears another portrait of an unidentified but presumably literary figure. The library itself was close by the reading room at the southeast corner of the peristyle. It has no wall niches, but holes in two of its walls suggest that shelving was attached, and panels of the mosaic floors outline places where cabinet pieces once stood, probably filled with books, against the south and east walls.

By far the most interesting of all ancient private libraries is the library of the Villa of the Papyri at Herculaneum, which like Pompeii was buried in the eruption of Mount Vesuvius in 79 c.e. In the course of excavations carried out from 1750 to 1765, among the smaller rooms of this sumptuous suburban villa a library was found.[182] There was no doubt about the nature of the room for it was discovered nearly intact: open-shelf bookcases lined the walls and a two-sided bookcase stood in the middle of the room.[183] Many papyrus rolls still lay in them, and many others were scattered about the room and nearby. Altogether there were nearly eighteen hundred manuscripts, eight hundred of them complete rolls.[184] The collection was specialized, consisting mostly of Epicurean philosophical works, principally those of Philodemus of Gadara (died about 40 b.c.e.) The vast majority were written in Greek. During the first century b.c.e. the villa was the property of L. Calpurnius Piso, father-in-law of Julius Caesar and a patron and friend of Philodemus, who lived with Piso for a time, and it remained in the hands of Piso's heirs until the volcano destroyed it.[185]

The library room was quite small, slightly more than three meters square. It was located in the living quarters of the villa and opened onto a peristyle bordering a courtyard, and thus it followed Greek design. Most of the papyrus rolls were found here: some on the shelves against the walls (vertical dividers on the shelves indicate that rolls were stored in groups) and more still in the freestanding two-sided cupboard in the middle of the room. Eighteen others were tied together in a cylindrical box (*capsa* or *scrinium*), and still others lay on the floor, tied together and wrapped in papyrus.[186] A small adjacent room was probably used for reading and writing. Thin metal plates that may originally have been inscribed were found in and around the library; perhaps they were labels, used on the library shelves.

The history of the library of the Villa of the Papyri can be partially reconstructed on paleographic grounds.[187] Its earliest manuscript was a copy of Epicurus's *On Nature* that goes back to the third century and was presumably brought to Herculaneum by Philodemus. To this were added the works of Demetrius Laco, the teacher of Philodemus, but the major expansion of the collection took place with the addition of the works of Philodemus himself. The Herculaneum manuscripts appear to have been copied between the third century B.C.E. and the early decades of the first century C.E. Only a few were transcribed after about 40 B.C.E., and none in the decades preceding the destruction of the library. Some of the latest manuscripts were copies of early works of Epicurus. Clearly this was the library of one who was particularly interested in Epicureanism and its rival philosophical schools, especially Stoicism. The heavily Epicurean content of the texts, the various marginalia and commentaries among the manuscripts, and the presence of duplicate texts of works by Epicurus and Philodemus all indicate that this was a working library. Given the vitality of Epicureanism in southern Italy at this time, these same features indicate that the villa was probably a center of Epicurean activity, the gathering place of an Epicurean circle whose philosophical purpose was served by such a library.[188]

The Villa of the Papyri is the only Greek or Roman library whose contents are well known, and we can only estimate the size and scope of other Greek and Roman libraries. The great institutional libraries at Alexandria and Pergamum could have held tens of thousands of books. No other Greek library rivaled them in size or reputation, and neither did any Roman libraries, though they grafted the stock of Latin literature onto the Greek. It is also difficult to estimate the size of private libraries.[189] Some were large. Atticus's library, which we would expect to be among the largest, is said to have contained twenty thousand rolls, but larger ones are reported: Epaphrodites, Greek secretary to Nero, reportedly had a library of thirty thousand rolls, and the third-century poet Serenus Sammonicus, a massive collection of sixty-two thousand![190] Whether or not we credit these figures, large personal collections were the exception. The private libraries of aristocratic literary men, scholars, or status seekers probably only rarely exceeded one or two thousand rolls.[191] For most collectors, the difficulty of obtaining good exemplars and reliable scribes, together with the expense of acquisition and limited storage space, were prohibitive. Thus the process of accumulation was slower in most cases and its results more modest than some reports suggest.[192]

A few summary comments about the architecture and arrangements of Greek and Roman libraries remain before I turn to Jewish libraries and then back to Christian ones. The Greek institutional library was not an independent building but a series of rooms attached to a stoa of a larger court, often of a temple. These included a common room for reading or discussion and adjacent smaller rooms where the books were stored. The earliest known Roman libraries continued to be connected to a *porticus* and associated with temples, but several changes in library design occurred in the Roman setting. First, the common room was enlarged and the books stored within it, so that adjacent storage rooms became superfluous. Second, the walls were constructed with large rectangular niches into which wooden bookcases were built.[193] These bookcases *(armaria)* were more often cabinets with doors, not open shelves.[194] Third, the library was made freestanding, and the *stoa* or *porticus*, having lost its significance through the enlargement and elaboration of the main library room, was either converted into an entry hall or omitted altogether in favor of a richly decorated facade.

Private, domestic libraries show less regularity of design. Some of the grander private libraries, like those in imperial residences, had some of the same features, housing Greek and Latin collections separately or having wall niches with cabinetry for book storage.[195] More commonly, a small room opening onto a peristyle or central hall was used to store books and an adjacent room for reading. Vitruvius's advice (6.4.1) that private libraries should be oriented to the east to take advantage of the light and inhibit dampness was not closely followed: known domestic libraries vary widely in orientation and in relation to other rooms of the house. In private libraries, open shelves *(pegmata)* along the walls and freestanding cabinets *(loculamenta)*, not book cabinets built into the walls, provided the storage.[196] Institutional or private, large or small, Greek and Roman libraries were decorated with statues and paintings and sometimes with inscriptions. Institutional libraries usually contained a monumental statue of a divine figure (Athena or Minerva) or of an emperor in a large central niche and elsewhere displayed busts or paintings of famous authors, as private libraries often did.[197] In short, Greek and Roman libraries were designed not only to store books but to evoke the literary tradition and to inspire the reader.

Jewish Libraries Evidence about the accumulation, storage, and use of book collections in Judaism during the early Christian period is most important to our subject, for Christianity shared with Judaism a religious interest in texts, and the Jewish collections known to us were compiled by religious communities and employed for religious purposes. As far as we know, Jewish libraries were not institutions in their own right, and we know of no discrete Jewish buildings that served as libraries. Indeed, though evidence is scant, those Jewish libraries that come to our attention bear little resemblance to Greek and Roman libraries.

The first Jewish libraries to mention, because they were the most widespread, are those that belonged to synagogues. By the time of Christian beginnings the synagogue was a central institution in Palestine and the Diaspora, and the focal point of the religious life of Jews. Although the synagogue served many functions in Judaism, it was above all a place for prayer and the reading of scripture.[198] Hence it is not surprising that, despite a broad architectural diversity among ancient synagogues, one consistent feature is the Torah shrine.

The Torah shrine was a receptacle in which the sacred books were placed. Located on the wall facing Jerusalem, where it provided the point of focus for the congregation, the shrine had two components: a niche, *aediculum*, or apse centrally located in the wall, and a chest, or "ark," that contained Torah scrolls.[199] Typically the shrine, reached by a short flight of stairs, had a decorated facade of two or four columns supporting an arch or gable ornamented with a conch. No chest survives, but ancient depictions portray it as a wooden cupboard with double doors that were paneled, carved, or both. The shrine itself was covered by a *paroket*, or curtain, shielding its contents from view. It is unclear whether the chest was always housed in the shrine or kept elsewhere and introduced into the shrine on occasions of worship. By the same token, it is uncertain whether the Torah scrolls were always kept in the chest or were stored elsewhere and placed in the chest only for liturgical use. Practice may have varied from place to place, but there is also evidence that it developed and changed.

Although the reading of Torah was a central element of synagogue liturgy from the beginning, the Torah shrine was not an aboriginal architectural feature of the synagogue. In the remains of the few extant pre-70 C.E. synagogues there is no evidence of a permanent Torah shrine, and in other ancient synagogues permanent shrines were clearly later additions to the initial construction. This indicates that in the early period of synagogue worship the chest was portable, brought into the assembly hall on occasions of worship but otherwise stored in an adjoining room.[200] Only later, in the Talmudic period, did the permanent Torah shrine become the norm. This architectural development expresses an increasingly reverent cultic regard for the Torah, but also, after the destruction of the Jerusalem temple, it represents the incorporation into the synagogue of architectural and artistic allusions to the temple. This development is reflected also in a change of name for the container of the Torah scrolls. Early rabbinic sources typically designate it as the *tebah* (*tebah shel sepharim*, "chest of books"), but later, against some opposition, the preferred term came to be *aron* (*aron hakkodesh*, "ark of holiness"). The change signifies the provision of a sanctuary or shrine for the Torah, which recalled the ancient "ark of the tabernacle" (for example, Ex. 25:10; 37:1–9; 1 Kings 8:21).[201]

Literary and achaeological evidence shows that the Torah chest held from two to nine books but might contain as many as twenty-one.[202] Its central position underscores the extent to which the synagogue was oriented to books and reading, and so necessarily retained collections of books. There are other, broader indications of this. The synagogue was not only a place of worship but also of study. Philo stresses the didactic function of synagogues, comparing them to schools (*didaskaleia; Vita Mos.* 2:215–16), while Josephus says that the weekly gathering aims at "the learning of our customs and law" (*Ant.* 16.43, compare *Contra Ap.* 2.175).[203] Second temple and rabbinic sources speak of a *bet sepher* (house of the book) and a *bet midrash* (house of study), which were either housed in or closely connected with the synagogue building itself.[204] The nature of these enterprises before the third century C.E. is hard to determine. They are often regarded as schools, the former as a lower or elementary school, the latter as a secondary school. Since the primary education of children, especially in reading, often took place at home or in the home of a teacher, it may be that the *bet sepher* was not so much a school as a place of study, where texts were read and discussed. Whether we think of schools or of settings for study, the availability there of books was essential, and the name "house of the book" assumes no less. Besides the Torah scrolls, the books of the Prophets and the Writings must have been present, and probably pieces of nonscriptural Jewish literature as well. Archival materials were also kept in synagogues, for it was not only a place of worship and study but also a kind of town hall where the community met to deliberate public, judicial, financial, and religious questions, and so necessarily kept rolls and records.[205] The genizah found in the typical synagogue also points to the accumulation of texts. The genizah was a place of storage—a room or chest or cavity in the floor—where worn or otherwise damaged and unusable books and ritual objects were kept until they could be disposed of without profanation, which was normally achieved by burial. The provision of a genizah presupposes a high rate of use for a considerable number of texts.[206] Taken together, these several observations indicate that most synagogues, and certainly all larger ones, had libraries— collections of texts for liturgical, educational, and archival purposes, stored either in a room of the synagogue itself or in a closely adjoining structure.

The most notable Jewish library known to us, however, did not belong to a synagogue but to the sectarian Jewish community settled at Khirbet Qumran at the northwestern corner of the Dead Sea from about 150 B.C.E. to about 70 C.E. In speaking of Qumran, scholars often use the term *library* in a broad way to refer to the large number of manuscripts that were discovered, beginning in 1947, in the caves close by the settlement site.[207] In the enormous body of scholarly literature generated by this manuscript find, the question of whether these manuscripts once constituted a library in the narrower sense of a collection of texts purposefully gathered, organized, stored, and used by a particular community has received little attention.[208]

The scrolls were found in eleven different caves around the remains of the settlement. More than eight hundred manuscripts have been identified, including biblical texts (about two hundred of the manuscripts, covering all biblical books save Esther), nonbiblical (apocryphal and pseudepigraphic) texts, a number of sectarian documents—liturgical, commentarial, and disciplinary—and many fragments that have yet to be identified.[209] On the basis of the scrolls and the early results of the excavation of the site, a broad consensus arose that the settlement was inhabited by a sectarian Jewish community composed of Essenes and that the scrolls constituted its library. The presence of the scrolls in caves has been taken to indicate that they were hidden there for safekeeping by the sect, presumably when it found itself threatened by Roman forces during the first Jewish revolt against Rome in 66–73 C.E.

This long-standing consensus has recently been challenged at several points. It has been argued, for example, that the scrolls found in the caves near Qumran did not belong to the sectarians who inhabited the site but to libraries in Jerusalem, including the library of the temple, and were secreted in the desert when Jerusalem came under threat of Roman assault.[210] This theory would account for some peculiarities of the find: the presence among the scrolls of manuscripts that are paleographically dated as early as the middle of the third century B.C.E., long before the establishment of the community at Qumran; the absence among the scrolls of such original documentary materials as deeds, letters, contracts, and other archival sorts of materials, and possibly also of authorial autographs; and the relatively small proportion of heterodox sectarian writings among the total fund of manuscripts. Nevertheless, this theory is not finally convincing because it neglects the Qumran community itself and does not take adequate account of the ideological coherence of the sectarian texts, of the storage of some of the manuscripts in jars of the same kind found in the ruins of the settlement, or of the close correspondence between the paleography of the manuscripts and the main period of the occupation of the site.[211] Thus there is still good reason to think that the scrolls were in fact the property of the community that inhabited the settlement at Khirbet Qumran.[212] The identity of that community, however, and the nature of the settlement at Qumran cannot be as confidently determined as they were at first. This was possibly an Essene community, but a different or more precise identification may yet be shown. Fortunately, that issue need not be decided for the purposes of this discussion.

The vast majority of the scrolls were found in the caves numbered 1, 4, 6, and 11. Of these, cave 4 contained by far the richest trove— nearly six hundred manuscripts, which suggests that cave 4 contained the main library of the community.[213] It is usually supposed, however, that neither this cave nor any other was the normal venue of manuscripts and that texts ordinarily kept elsewhere in the settlement— though in the state of the archaeological remains no such place can be identified—had been hastily sequestered in them.[214]

There are several reasons to think that cave 4 was itself the library, not just a hiding place. First, cave 4 is the closest and most accessible of the caves to the settlement site and thus conveniently located to serve as a library. Second, cave 4 is one of six caves carved out of the marl terraces, but the only one to contain a large number of manuscripts.[215] Furthermore, in the walls of cave 4 there are a number of holes, man-made, that could serve to anchor wooden shelving for manuscripts, although no shelves survive. Fourth, no jars were found in cave 4 and few sherds. Because it is unlikely that large numbers of individual manuscripts were normally kept in jars, the absence of jars in cave 4 may well mean that the many manuscripts found there had not been prepared for hiding but were regularly available for use there. In addition, the pattern of deterioration in those manuscripts indicates that they were not damaged in antiquity, either before or after they were put in the cave, but that they have simply decayed in situ, in accordance with natural forces in the environment, after they had fallen down on themselves.[216] Chiefly important is the large concentration of texts in this cave, which far outstrips in number and variety the contents of all the other caves combined. All these observations are well explained if cave 4 was the library of the Qumran community. Since it is certain that some of the caves were used as residences by the sectarians, there would be nothing peculiar in the use of a cave as the regular depository of books.

It is not persuasive to claim that the manuscripts found in caves in the immediate vicinity of the settlement, and especially cave 4, are too numerous and diverse to have constituted the library of the Qumran community. The community had a lengthy history on the site, and the sectarians' interest in texts and their rigorous devotion to the reading and interpretation of biblical texts in particular are well documented in the scrolls themselves. The availability of so many manuscripts and the presence among them of a large number of texts—especially of biblical but also of sectarian texts—in multiple copies is less an indication of the remains of several libraries than of a single collection accumulated and used for intensive study.[217]

Still, it is a question how these texts were collected and, more specifically, how they were produced. At least the few that date from the third century B.C.E. were brought to the community from elsewhere. Most are paleographically dated to the period of the occupation of the site, and many of these, if not all, must have been copied there. Early investigators of the site believed that the main building complex once contained a scriptorium. There were remains of several plaster tables and benches that appear to have been permanent fixtures in a long, narrow second-floor room that had collapsed into the ground floor; two inkwells were found in the same debris.[218] However, scribes are not known to have used writing tables until a much later period, and, apart from the inkwells, no writing implements or fragments of leather or papyrus were found in the debris. Besides, there is no sign of any provision for shelving in the remains of the room.[219]

The absence of archaeological evidence for a scriptorium does not mean that texts were not copied on site or that most or all of the scrolls were brought from elsewhere. Indeed, there is good reason to think that most of them were copied at Qumran and by members of the community. It has been shown on paleographic grounds that the Qumran scrolls can be rather neatly divided into two groups.[220] The first group is characterized by a particular orthographic system and grammatical forms that may be termed Qumranic; the second group is characterized by the absence of this system and these forms. It is striking that the obviously sectarian documents belong to the first group and not to the second. Although some biblical scrolls and other nonsectarian texts appear in each group, the second group consists mainly of biblical scrolls. The manuscripts written in the Qumranic orthography must have been written at Qumran by scribes of the community. These include all the sectarian texts, some biblical texts, and some apocryphal works. The other texts, mostly biblical, must have been written elsewhere and brought to Qumran from the outside.[221] Since in antiquity books were normally acquired not through purchase but by transcription from a borrowed exemplar, the large accumulation of texts at Qumran presupposes extensive copying. Though not all of this transcription was necessarily done at the site, much of it must have been, for in some cases the same scribes copied different manuscripts,[222] and the sectarian documents are not likely to have been composed or copied elsewhere. Thus even without proof of a scriptorium, there can be little doubt that there was lively scribal activity at Qumran.

Consequently, in the Qumran texts and especially in the large cache of cave 4 we have a library of religious literature that was developed and used over a period of about two centuries by a sectarian Jewish community. The state in which it was found allows its contents to be known and suggests where it was housed. Moreover, the ideas and practices of the community, not least its intense interest in texts, reflected in its sectarian documents demonstrate the importance that such a collection of books must have had for its life.

Of other Jewish libraries little is known. Was there a library associated with the temple in Jerusalem, as is often supposed? A temple library is implied by several sources of the second temple period.[223] For instance, in 2 Macc. 2:13–15 it is said that "[Nehemiah] founded a library and collected the books about the kings and prophets, and the writings of David, and the letters of kings about votive offerings. In the same way Judas also collected all the books that had been lost on account of the war that had come upon us, and they are in our possession. So if you have need of them, send people to get them for you." These statements appear in the second of two letters at the beginning of 2 Macc. (1:1–9; 1:10–2:18) that were ostensibly sent by "the people of Jerusalem" to Aristobulus, a Jewish teacher in Alexandria. A temple library is also implied by the Letter of Aristeas (176–7), which mentions manuscripts brought from Jerusalem (presumably from the temple, since the delegation was sent by the high priest) to Alexandria for the translation of the Torah into Greek. Since both 2 Maccabees and the Letter of Aristeas have propagandist aims, what they suggest about a temple library is not above suspicion. Yet it accords with evidence from Josephus and rabbinic sources that the temple was a center for the collection and dissemination of texts. Copyists and correctors worked in the temple to furnish scriptural texts for use in Israel and the Diaspora, using the "book of the [temple] court" as the authoritative exemplar.[224] This evidence is sketchy, but cumulatively it creates a strong presumption of the existence of a library and archives in the Jerusalem temple, though it does not provide any clear idea of what the library was like. It would stand to reason that the temple held Torah scrolls and other scriptural books, and archival materials (such as priestly genealogies and the courses of Levites) related to the various cultic, financial, and administrative functions of the temple. From this it is a short step to the existence of a library. The least that can be said is that a temple library was entirely conceivable to Jews of the period and, in the case of Josephus, to someone in a good position to know of it.

CHRISTIAN LIBRARIES IN CONTEXT
Considering the number and variety of ancient libraries, it may seem unremarkable that Christianity too should have created libraries. We can make comparisons between early Christian libraries and other libraries of the ancient world, but the comparisons will be limited by the evidence and by the nature of the case. There is no archaeological evidence for Christian library buildings before the fifth century to compare with the remains of Greek and Roman libraries, and none is to be expected because the earliest Christian libraries were housed not in discrete structures but in house churches, monastic buildings, and later in basilicas. Moreover, though the contents of Greek and Roman libraries are poorly known, obviously there was a wide disparity between them and Christian collections. Nevertheless, much that is interesting emerges when early Christian libraries are placed in their larger context.

We have seen that Greek and Roman libraries were often dependencies on temple buildings and that Jewish synagogues had their collections of texts. Libraries architecturally associated with temples were not, however, specifically for religious use, as synagogue collections were. Greco-Roman religious movements did not as a rule produce or use religious literature, let alone collect it. Some pagan temples, or their priesthoods, must have kept at least a few texts for ritual and archival purposes, although such collections are rarely intimated.[225] Early Christian libraries, on the other hand, belonged to religious communities and consisted primarily of religious texts used for religious purposes, a phenomenon closely paralleled in the Greco-Roman world only by Judaism. Granting this fundamental resemblance with Judaism, some important distinctions need to be drawn.

It was ultimately to Judaism that early Christianity owed its orientation to texts, but Christianity developed this proclivity much more strongly than Judaism. Whereas Judaism, reconstituted after 70 C.E. along rabbinic lines, relied chiefly on oral tradition for teaching and for the interpretation of sacred texts, Christianity from the beginning generated a tradition of literature that grew exponentially in volume and diversity. Moreover, the nature of the relations and communications among Christian communities and the religious and theological issues that engaged them gave this literature a distinct importance for Christian thought and practice. The church depended more heavily on literature than any other religious movement of the ancient world, including Judaism, which is why we frequently hear of Christian collections of books but rarely of such collections among other religious groups.

In both Jewish and Christian congregational libraries the books belonged to religious communities, served the needs of the group, and were put to liturgical use. Christian congregational libraries were larger and more diverse, adding Christian scriptures to Jewish and often including a variety of nonscriptural texts: commentaries on scripture, controversial tracts, homilies, martyr acts, episcopal letters, synodical communications, and so forth. Nothing resembling an ark or shrine is attested for the storage of Christian books, even scriptural ones, which supports the bibliographic indications that the attitude of early Christianity toward religious texts was more practical than sacral.

In the first three centuries Christian congregational libraries were retained in domestic settings, first in the house church, then in the *domus ecclesiae*, and only later in church buildings, and this together with their modest size brings them into relation not with Judaism, but with the domestic libraries of the Greco-Roman world. Domestic libraries were private collections, but some of them were magnets for literary or philosophical circles that gathered in those homes to cultivate their mutual interests. The library of the Villa of the Papyri in Herculaneum, the best-known domestic library of the ancient world, is the one most aptly compared to the Christian congregational library. It was, as noted earlier, a specialized collection of philosophical texts, mainly Epicurean, and though housed in a private residence, it was apparently used by a group of Epicurean friends who formed a close-knit philosophical community that gathered in the villa through the generosity of its owner. The setting and constituency were aristocratic, but otherwise the situation at Herculaneum parallels that of the small Christian congregation, which also held a special collection of literature belonging to an ongoing tradition of thought and practice, a collection housed in a private residence and used by a group that assembled there out of devotion to that tradition for the purpose of assimilating the tradition by reading, study, and discussion and of actualizing it in their common life. As in its concern with doctrine and ethics and in its lack of a traditional cult, so also in its concern with texts Christianity bore a closer resemblance to Greco-Roman philosophical movements than to pagan religious cults.

The larger Christian libraries, Caesarea being the best known, are not to be understood as overgrown congregational libraries. They are best compared, though not in size, to the great institutional libraries of the ancient world. Not only were they larger than congregational libraries and of more than local significance; they held relatively systematic collections, employed technical methods, and served scholastic rather than liturgical purposes. By the third century, if not earlier, there were Christians who had the minds not only of scholars but of bibliographers and librarians—and it must be emphasized how closely conjoined these interests were in the ancient world. Figures like Origen, Pamphilus, Eusebius, and Augustine knew the qualities and uses of a good collection of books, recognized the need to accumulate Christian literature for scholarship and teaching and appreciated the value of book collections for the Christian cause. Libraries like the one at Caesarea replicated in the Christian setting the institutional type of non-Christian library and employed the critical and bibliographic techniques that had become conventional in Greek and Roman libraries. The Caesarean library was assiduously developed to become precisely what Constantine took it to be, an institutional Christian library that held a large number of excellent texts and was able to reproduce them.

THE LEGACY OF EARLY CHRISTIAN LIBRARIES

The preservation and transmission of Greek and Roman literature owes no small debt to the Christian monastic libraries of the Middle Ages, and it is fitting to conclude this discussion by considering one monastic library that was instrumental to the preservation of Greco-Roman literature and learning, the library created by Cassiodorus for his monks.[226] After a distinguished political career, Cassiodorus returned late in life to his family estates at Scyllacium in Calabria, southern Italy, and sometime between 527 and 554 he established there a cenobitic monastery, the Vivarium. From the outset the Vivarium bore the peculiar stamp of its founder. Frustrated in his earlier effort to establish at Rome, with Agapetus, a theological school like those at Nisbis and Alexandria, Cassiodorus now sought to incorporate systematic theological study into monastic life. Against the tendency of earlier monasticism to confuse ignorance with otherworldliness and to foster a narrowly clerical culture, Cassiodorus insisted that liberal learning was essential to theological studies, especially to the comprehension of scripture, and so he aimed to enrich monastic culture with the heritage of classical literature and scholarship. To that end he brought together in the monastery a large library of Christian and classical texts and prescribed a curriculum for the monks.

The theory, materials, and methods of this undertaking are set out in Cassiodorus's *Institutiones divinarum et saecularium litterarum*, in two books.[227] The first book *(divinarum litterarum)* gives a syllabus of readings in Christian texts, surveying the books of scripture together with patristic commentaries and offering notes on various Christian treatises and advice about how to study them. The second book *(saecularium litterarum)* describes a course of study in the liberal arts and sciences, which Cassiodorus thought were just as important to Christian scholarship as they had been to pagan. Thus the *Institutiones* is a largely bibliographic work. Though not a library catalogue, as a practical guide to monks for their studies it indicates the contents of the library, since the works it recommends must have been available on site.

The collection consisted mainly of Latin texts: they were the more easily had, and few of the monks were literate in Greek. Greek manuscripts were on hand, but not many; according to Cassiodorus, all of them were stored in a single *armarium*, namely, the eighth.[228] The far more numerous Latin manuscripts were stored in other *armaria*, probably arranged according to subject matter. They included biblical texts, biblical commentaries, church histories, dogmatic works, and hagiographic and monastic literature, among other materials. Many of the Latin texts were Greek works, Christian and non-Christian, that were available in Latin translation or were translated at Vivarium.[229] The focus of the library was theological, but many non-theological and pagan works—on grammar, rhetoric, cosmology, geography, agriculture, medicine, and mathematics—were present.[230] A collection this large was created with difficulty: the texts had to be found, purchased or borrowed for transcription, and in many cases translated.[231]

The community at Vivarium was engaged not only in the study of books but in producing them as well. The work of translating, editing, and copying was intense: here the scriptorium that became typical of medieval monasteries was already hard at work. Most of the monks worked as scribes *(antiquarii, librarii)* in the transcription of texts; the editorial work of collation, criticism, annotation, and punctuation was reserved to a few *notarii*. Cassiodorus emphasized copying with meticulous accuracy and careful orthography, and shortly before he died he wrote a treatise, *De orthographia,* for the guidance of the monastic scribes. Cassiodorus aimed wherever possible to bring together writings on the same subject in a single omnibus codex.[232] Bindings were designed to make books as beautiful on the outside as the clarity and beauty of the script made them inside.[233]

Because the basis of theological study was scripture, Cassiodorus took a particular interest in biblical texts, carefully gathering and collating manuscripts and producing some notable editions of the Bible. One he called the *codex grandior,* a pandect of the Old Latin version, offering seventy books in ninety-five quaternions.[234] Another was an edition of the Vulgate produced in nine separate volumes *(novem codices)* reproducing Augustine's arrangement in seventy-one books, and written in sense lines *(per cola et commata).*[235] Still another was a Vulgate pandect in fifty-three gatherings of six leaves each, transcribed in a small hand *(minutiore manu)* and following Jerome's division of the text into forty-nine books.[236] Besides accurately constituting the text of scripture in its current versions and several arrangements, Cassiodorus aimed to make it as intelligible as possible by incorporating various aids for the reader: the texts were divided into sections *(capitula),* brief summaries *(tituli* or *breves)* of their content were provided, punctuation was supplied, and, in the case of the nine-volume edition, the text was transcribed in sense lines.[237]

There are no accounts of the history of the library at Vivarium after the death of its founder, but it did not disappear without trace. Many later medieval manuscripts reveal an indebtedness to books produced and held there. The seventh century Codex Amiatinus, one of the best ancient manuscripts of the Vulgate, is an example. It includes (folio 2v-3r) a painting of the tabernacle of the Temple of Jerusalem. Cassiodorus had such an illustration painted and affixed it to the beginning of his *codex grandior,* and Bede refers to this picture

7. The frontispiece of Codex Amiatinus, representing Ezra (or Cassiodorus?) inscribing a codex. Note that the *armarium* holds nine codices.

as belonging to a pandect of Cassiodorus.[238] We also know from Bede that the Codex Amiatinus was copied in the late seventh century at the English monastery at Yarrow, from an archetype brought to Yarrow from Rome.[239] The Codex Amiatinus also carries a frontispiece depicting Ezra the scribe seated in front of an *armarium* containing nine codices, the titles of which are clear: they are shelved exactly in the order followed in Cassiordorus's Bible in *novem codices* (see fig. 7). This illustration probably stood at the beginning of Cassiodorus's nine-volume Bible.[240] The text of Amiatinus is the Vulgate text arranged by sense lines, like the text of Cassiodorus's nine-volume Bible, whereas the pandect of Cassiodorus containing the illustration of the temple carried the Old Latin text. Thus Cassiodorus's Old Latin *codex grandior* and his *novem codices* Vulgate were both available at Yarrow and were used in the transcription of Amiatinus. Since it is certain that the *codex grandior* came from Rome, it is likely that the nine-volume Bible did also. Some nonbiblical manuscripts, commentaries, church histories, and dogmatic works are also derived from Vivarium, all by way of the Lateran library in Rome, which appears to have been the starting point of a broad distribution of manuscripts from Vivarium. The library at Vivarium must have been incorporated into the papal library in Rome near the end of the sixth century, although the circumstances are obscure.[241]

Cassiodorus's emphasis on the value of liberal learning to biblical and theological studies was novel in monastic culture, but as to its library and its work in book production what we see at Vivarium was not new. Non-Christian and non-theological works may have been more numerous at Vivarium, but the scope and volume of the Christian literature collected there were probably about equal to the holdings of the library at Hippo in the early fifth century or (allowing for a preponderance of Greek texts) to the Caesarean library in the early fourth. The scribal and editorial work carried on at Vivarium continued a tradition that reached back to the third century to the work of Pamphilus and earlier still to Origen. Though Christian literature was continuously written and the pool of potential acquisitions grew ever larger, there is little perceptible evolution in the history of Christian libraries in antiquity. The methods of their creation and operation—including all the special tasks of acquisition, organization, storage, use, and book production—remained broadly constant throughout the period.

Thus the monastic libraries of the early middle ages were the direct legatees of Christian libraries of the first five centuries, which, though they chiefly aimed to gather Christian literature, did not dispense with pagan literature. The heritage of classical literature persisted largely because of the interest in Christian literature and through the agency of the Christian libraries that were devised to collect and preserve it.

THE USES OF EARLY
CHRISTIAN BOOKS

ooks are written to be read, but they are read for many purposes and in many contexts, and the act of reading varies accordingly. I want now to consider how early Christian books were read: in what circumstances, for what reasons, and in what manner books were used by Christians of the ancient period. But before asking the particular question of Christian reading, it is necessary to consider the nature of reading itself as it was generally practiced in antiquity.

The most important thing to be said is that in the Greco-Roman world virtually all reading was reading aloud; even when reading privately the reader gave audible voice to the text.[1] Thus, apart from the context, the difference between private and public reading was not in a contrast between silent reading and reading aloud, but in levels of projection. The principal reason for audible private reading was the manner in which texts were written, namely, in "continuous script" *(scriptio continua)*—with no division between words, sentences, or paragraphs, and no punctuation. A familiar passage in English becomes suddenly cryptic when deployed in this way:

> *theearthisthelordsandthefulnessthereoftheworldandthosewhod wellthereinforhehasfoundedituponthe seasandestablisheditupon theriverswhoshallascendtothehillofthelordandwhoshallstandin hisholyplacehewhohascleanhandsandapureheartanddoesnotlift uphissoultowhatisfalseanddoesnotsweardeceitfully*

If a familiar text is surprisingly difficult, an unfamiliar one would present a far greater challenge. The relentless march of characters across the lines and down the columns required the reader to deconstruct the text into its discrete verbal and syntactical components.

The best way to decipher a text written in this way was phonetic: sounding the syllables as they were seen and organizing them as much by hearing as by sight into a pattern of meaning.

All reading is interpretive, but a text written scriptio continua presented a greater range of interpretive options and demanded more hermeneutical decisions of the reader than modern texts do. When it is up to the reader to determine what groups of syllables form a word, what groups of words make up phrases and clauses and sentences, and to decide what group of sentences rounds up an idea into a paragraph, then the reader is obliged to constitute the sense of a text in a far more active and extensive way than we, who are assisted by word division, punctuation, capitalization, paragraph division, italicization, and other conventions of modern texts. Yet if reading was necessarily more active in antiquity, it cannot be said whether it was appreciably more difficult. A text presented in scriptio continua is perplexing to the modern reader, but the ancient reader was accustomed to it and had developed the skills to approach it. A practiced reader would have developed an eye for patterns of characters, and by sounding those patterns aloud could grasp words by ear before distinguishing them by sight.

Thus, in reading aloud the written was converted into the oral. Correspondingly, in the composition of a text the oral was converted to the written. In antiquity a text could be composed either by dictating to a scribe or by writing in one's own hand.[2] Yet when an author did write out his own text, the words were spoken as they were being written, just as scribes in copying manuscripts practiced what is called self-dictation. In either case, then, the text was an inscription of the spoken word. Because authors wrote or dictated with an ear to the words and assumed that what they wrote would be audibly read, they wrote for the ear more than the eye. As a result, no ancient text is now read as it was intended to be unless it also heard, that is, read aloud.[3]

In addition, the public reading of texts was far more common in antiquity than it is today.[4] Because only a small minority were literate, official documents directed to the general public had to be read out, if they were also posted, and there were other occasions as well for public reading. Among the literate, the premiere performance of works of poetry and prose was often a public reading—a *recitatio*—before the actual publication of the text. These oral performances of texts were rooted in the close relation between the written and the oral modes. Since not only reading but also composition in writing had an aural component, the sense was most fully brought out when the text was read aloud, either by its author or by someone else. But good public reading required familiarity with the text. The initial reading of any text was inevitably experimental because it had to be decided, partly in retrospect, which of the possible construals of scriptio continua best rendered the sense. If public reading were not to be halting, tentative, or misleading, those decoding judgments had to be made in advance through rehearsals of the text.

This fact of ancient reading practice had another and broader consequence. It was claimed earlier that the large majority of Christians, like the large majority of non-Christians in the ancient world, were illiterate, so that books were of no immediate or private use to them. Yet even among the literate, it was as common to be read to as to read for oneself, and the illiterate were as capable as the literate of *hearing* books read. Thus the absence of literacy had limited consequences in the context of public reading.

THE PUBLIC READING OF CHRISTIAN BOOKS

The public reading of Christian books took place for the most part in assemblies for worship. Justin Martyr, describing the procedure of Christian assemblies in the middle of the second century, says:

> And on the day which is called the day of the sun there is an assembly of all those who live in the towns or in the country, and the memoirs of the apostles or the writings of the prophets are read for as long as time permits. Then the reader ceases, and the president speaks, admonishing and exhorting us to imitate these excellent examples. Then we all rise together and pray and, as we said before, when we have completed our prayer, bread is brought, and wine and water, and the president in like manner offers prayers and thanksgivings according to his ability and the people assent with Amen; and there is a distribution and partaking by all of that over which thanks have been given, and to those who are absent a portion is sent by the deacons. And those who are prosperous and willing give what each thinks fit, and what is collected is deposited with the president, who gives aid to orphans and widows and those who are in want on account of illness or any other cause, and to those also who are in prison and to strangers from abroad, and, in a word, cares for all who are in need (Apol. 1.67).

The reading mentioned here as a vital part of the weekly assembly was by that time an established and probably universal Christian liturgical custom. Near the beginning of the second century the author of 1 Timothy admonished "Timothy," a church leader, to "attend to the reading of scripture, to preaching, and to teaching" (4:13), all of which belonged to assemblies for worship. For the earlier period the evidence is limited. Late in the first century the author of Revelation anticipated the public reading of his own book to Christian congregations when he pronounced a blessing upon "the one who reads . . . and those who hear" (1:3). Earlier still, the author of Colossians also assumed this practice: "And when this letter has been read among you, have it read also in the church of the Laodiceans, and see that you read also the letter from Laodicea" (4:16). In making this request the pseudonymous author took it for granted that Pauline letters were commonly read aloud in the congregational setting. Indeed, Paul himself had expected his letters to be read out to the group he addressed when it gathered for worship: "I adjure you by the Lord that this letter be read to all the brothers" (1 Thess. 5:27).[5] At that early time, however, the reading of apostolic letters was a liturgical act only in the sense that it occurred in a liturgical context; the texts themselves were not liturgical, since neither Paul nor those to whom he wrote regarded his letters as scripture. In Paul's day the church's scriptures were those of Judaism, but by the time Colossians was written Paul's letters had probably begun to acquire a scriptural aspect. Certainly a scriptural authority had accrued to them and to some other early Christian writings as well by the middle of the second century.[6]

If before the mid–second century some texts were publicly read in Christian assemblies, it is still difficult to determine just how early this practice began or how widely it was followed. Neither do we know just which texts it was the practice to read. The earliest reports about Christian liturgical gatherings yield no clear evidence on these points and leave uncertain much else about the occasions and character of early Christian worship. Nevertheless, they have relevance in my attempt to determine the place of texts and reading in early Christian worship.

The earliest evidence is offered by Paul, who gives extended attention to problems of Christian worship in 1 Corinthians 11–14. Discussing the celebration of the Lord's supper in 11:17–34, Paul cites the tradition of the eucharistic words of Jesus but says nothing about the reading of scripture. In his characterization of Christian assemblies in chapter 14, where the chief issue is tongue-speaking, Paul makes no mention of the common meal but speaks of each having "a hymn, a lesson, a revelation, a tongue, or an interpretation" (1 Cor. 1:26). A "lesson" *(didache)* or an "interpretation" *(hermeneia)* may allude to reading but not necessarily. The differences between these two treatments may indicate two different kinds of meetings, and, indeed, a distinction is indicated by the fact that the presence of nonbelievers is assumed for one (1 Cor. 14:20–25) but the eucharistic gathering was limited to believers.[7] For these reasons it is often thought that Paul and his communities knew two different kinds of Christian assembly, one for the common meal, the other for a "service of the word."

In contrast to Paul, the passing allusions to Christian worship in Acts do not suggest different types of Christian gatherings. Acts broadly characterizes Christian meetings as occasions of "devotion to the apostles' teaching and fellowship, to the breaking of bread, and the prayers" (Acts 2:42) and refers to them simply as "breaking bread," that is, the community meal (2:46, 20:7), yet does not exclude other elements (20:7–12). The statements of Pliny the Younger about Christian worship in Bythinia in Asia Minor in the early second century are also relevant. Pliny says that the Christians he had interrogated

> *claimed that the whole of their guilt or error was this: that they gathered regularly on a fixed day before sunrise when they sang antiphonally a song to Christ as to a god, and bound themselves by a solemn oath, not to commit any wicked deeds, but rather never to commit any fraud, theft, or adultery, never to break their word, nor to deny a trust when called upon to deliver it over; after which it was their custom to disperse and then reassemble to share food—but food of an ordinary and innocent kind. (Ep. 10.96.7)*

Here it is obviously a matter of two different gatherings on the same day, an early morning one devoted to things spoken and sung and an evening one to the meal. Yet the public reading of texts is not mentioned.

Finally there is the description of Christian worship by Justin, quoted above, who characterizes the service as a single weekly gathering that included public reading, exhortation, prayer, and the celebration of the eucharist (*Apol.* 1.67).

The meaning of each of these reports could be debated. It is also a question whether they could be fitted together to form a consistent picture of early Christian worship or whether indeed such a picture should be sought, given that customs may have varied over time and from place to place. It is a widespread opinion among historians of early Christian worship that at the beginning Christianity sponsored two separate and independent occasions of worship, one a "service of the word," at which there was prayer, the reading of scripture, and preaching, and the other an assembly for the community meal. On this view, the single assembly incorporating both elements, "word" and "sacrament," that is clearly attested by Justin in the middle of the second century is the result of a development that unified what were originally two types and occasions of worship.[8] This is not implausible. The postulation of two distinct forms of primitive Christian worship corresponds to the distinction in Judaism between the worship of the synagogue, comprising prayer, scripture reading, and preaching, and the worship of the temple, consisting in cultic sacrifice. It also recognizes what appear to be different occasions and constituencies of worship in Paul's letters and accounts for a development of the eucharistic celebration from a community meal into a discrete sacramental ritual that could be combined with the service of the word. Nevertheless, it has been argued to the contrary that from the beginning the form of Christian worship was a single weekly gathering for the celebration of the meal, and that teaching and sacrament were inseparably combined within the framework of the meal.[9] On this interpretation what we find in Justin is not a development by combination but only by refinement, the spontaneous expressions of the spirit (1 Cor. 12–14) having been eliminated and the meal reduced to ritual.

It does not seem necessary for present purposes to adjudicate between these theories. Both recognize that the shape and substance of early Christian worship, whatever its distinctiveness, stood under the influence of Jewish liturgical practice. The influence of the synagogue could hardly have been escaped in any case, since Christianity arose as a sectarian movement within Judaism, where the synagogue was the weekly context of popular worship. Early (Jewish-) Christians continued for a time to participate in ordinary synagogue worship, and when they constituted themselves separately they probably convened as sectarian synagogues.[10] Many individual elements of early Christian worship appear to be indebted to the liturgy of the synagogue.[11] One of these is the public reading of scripture.

THE READING OF SCRIPTURE IN THE SYNAGOGUE   Most of the evidence about the synagogue liturgy comes from the second century and later.[12] It cannot be assumed that what is attested for the second and later centuries was already in effect in earlier times, for practice was increasingly regulated and standardized after the destruction of the temple, when the synagogue became the sole locus of corporate Jewish worship. Consequently, the shape of synagogue worship in the period of Christian beginnings is obscure, and allowance must be made for variations. It is beyond doubt, however, that the reading of scripture was a central, if not the only, feature of synagogue worship by the first century of the common era.[13]

By the second century the fixed elements of the synagogue service were three: prayer, readings from scripture, and a homily. The service began with the Shema', the recitation of which was bracketed by blessings *(berakot)*. The Shema' was followed by the *Tephilla*, a series of benedictions, then came the reading of scripture and the homily, which was based on it. The homily concluded with the recitation of the Aramaic prayer, the *Kaddish*.

In the principal service on the sabbath morning the reading of scripture was in two parts—one from the Torah and the next from the Prophets (*Haphtarah*, "conclusion"), the latter selected with a view to the first.[14] The Mishnah and Tosephta, in tractate Megillah, lay down detailed prescriptions for the reading of scripture in the synagogue.[15] The reading was done by lay members of the congregation, and in the rabbinic period a minimum of seven persons read at the sabbath morning service, each being required to read at least three verses from the Torah (M. Meg. 4.4).[16] The first reader recited a benediction before reading, the last a benediction after reading (M. Meg. 4.1–2). The scripture was read as it was written, in Hebrew, but, because the vernacular was Aramaic, the practice arose of accompanying the reading with an Aramaic translation or paraphrase *(targum)*, provided by the *methurgeman* (translator).[17] The protocol for the translation is specified in M. Meg. 4.4: "He who reads the Torah is not to read less than three verses; he may not read to the methurgeman more than one verse [at a time], or in [a reading from] the Prophets more than three. But if these three are three separate sections he must read them out one by one. They may leave out verses in the Prophets, but not in the Torah. How much may they leave out? Only so much that he leaves no time for the *methurgeman* to make a pause." Thus the translation was closely correlated with the reading, but in such a way that no confusion should arise between what constituted the reading and what belonged to the translation. The methurgeman had to be someone other than the reader, and it was forbidden for the methurgeman to read the translation from a written text. Nor could the translation be given in a louder voice than the reading itself. In this way the sacred text was fully respected and the translation marked off as such.[18] Still, the translation given by the methurgeman was not individually creative but largely traditional.[19] In the Greek-speaking synagogues of the Diaspora, however, the scriptures were apparently always read in Greek, and no translation was required.[20]

Whether these rabbinic stipulations about the reading of scripture in the synagogue merely codified earlier practices or reshaped them in important ways remains a question. So too does the related issue of whether there was a schedule of readings, a lectionary system, and if so of what sort. The Mishnah already assumes a sequential reading *(lectio continua)* of the Torah in the synagogue, a practice that by the end of the second century must therefore have been followed.[21] Still, this does not necessarily mean (and the Mishnah does not say) that a fixed lectionary system was in place by then. There were, however, two lectionary systems in use in the early centuries of the common era. One was the Babylonian system, one that prescribed a particular section *(parasha)* of the Torah for each sabbath (fifty-four *parashiyyot* in all) so that the entire Torah was read through in one year. This annual cycle, which persists in modern Judaism, became generally authoritative in Judaism along with the Babylonian Talmud. There was another system, however, which divided the Torah differently, into 154 *sedarim*, to provide for the consecutive reading of the entire Torah over a period of three (or three and a half) years. This system was followed in early Palestinian practice.[22] Still, there is no compelling evidence that there was a single, uniform triennial system or that either annual or triennial systems were in effect in the earliest period of the common era. Early rabbinic traditions acknowledge local variations in the length and occasions of the readings and therefore in the schedule of reading the Torah.[23] Both the annual and the triennial lectionary systems appear to have developed after the principle of the continuous, sequential reading of Torah had been established and the sabbath morning readings had been accorded decisive importance in the sequence. These determinations were not made before the late second century, and the two lectionary systems then arose as different ways of adapting the liturgical reading of the Torah to these basic principles.[24] Before the late second century there was a greater diversity of practice in how Torah was read. The prophetic readings were never subject to the same degree of regularization as the Torah readings but were more freely selected, and with a view to their pertinence to the Torah readings.

The early diversity of synagogal reading customs does not, however, cast doubt on the prominent place of scripture reading in the synagogue in the first century, and the absence of a fixed system does not mean that early reading practices were arbitrary or fundamentally discontinuous with later, systematic programs. Reading from the Torah was clearly the established custom by the first century (Josephus, *C. Ap.* 2.175, Acts 13:14–15, 15:21), and a prophetic lection was at least sometimes conjoined to it (Acts 13:14–15; compare Lk. 4:16–30). It also appears that before the introduction of lectionary systems the Torah was read in accordance with traditional sections and in the order of the books, and thus generally by lectio continua, at least in Palestine.[25] On the other hand, it is not likely that all the detailed Mishnaic prescriptions reflect traditional customs. For example, the requirement of seven readers for the Torah scarcely mirrors early or general practice: there are indications of single readers, and in small synagogues there may not have been many readers available.[26] And although it is probable that reading was early accompanied by translation, there is no evidence for the methurgeman or rules for translating before the late second century. Apart from the fact of the practice, few details are known about the reading of scripture in the synagogue in the first century.

THE READING OF SCRIPTURE IN EARLY CHRISTIAN WORSHIP As we have seen, the evidence for the reading of scripture in the setting of early Christian worship also belongs mostly to the second and later centuries. By then Jewish scripture and some Christian writings were regularly given public reading in the context of the liturgy. Yet it is difficult to reconstruct first century Christian practice on this point. It is easily assumed that the early church simply transposed synagogue practice into its own context, but this cannot be taken for granted. No explicit evidence attests the liturgical reading of either the Torah or the prophets in Christian assemblies of the first century. Moreover, early Christianity's approach to scripture, since it was determined by its christological confession and oriented more to the prophets than to the Torah, differed from that of synagogal Judaism. In addition, when it arrives on the field of historical vision Christianity is already fully wedded to the Septuagint, not to the Hebrew scriptures. The question of synagogue influence is further complicated by the diversity of Christian communities in the first century. Some Jewish-Christian communities remained for a time within the orbit of the synagogue and are likely to have persisted in the liturgical customs of the synagogue after they left it. The customs of the hellenistic synagogue must have been followed to some extent in Hellenistic Jewish-Christian communities, but it is uncertain how synagogue services in the Greek Diaspora differed from those in Palestine, except that the scriptures were known and used in Greek. It is less clear whether strictly Gentile Christian communities of the first century, though they were often spawned from hellenistic-Jewish missions, adopted synagogue usages. For these reasons it cannot be uncritically assumed that scripture reading belonged from the outset to specifically Christian worship or, if it did, that it played the same role that it did in the synagogue. In the absence of explicit testimony, the question of the liturgical use of scripture in first-century Christianity can be approached only indirectly by considering some features of the earliest Christian literature.

The letters of Paul offer some provocative evidence. Paul, a Pharisaic Jew, was closely acquainted with synagogal usages both in Palestine and the Diaspora (whether or not he sought converts in synagogues, as Acts maintains), and in his letters, written to predominantly or exclusively Gentile Christian communities, Paul makes frequent appeals to the scriptures of Judaism. Although these facts suggest prima facie that the scriptures of Judaism were publicly read in the Pauline churches, the opposite conclusion has sometimes been drawn. A. von Harnack observed that Paul's appeals to scripture are confined to the four letters he wrote to communities that stood under some Jewish influence, whether by constituency or instruction, namely, Galatians, 1 and 2 Corinthians, and Romans, whereas in letters to Gentile Christian communities, where there was apparently little Jewish influence (Philippians, 1 Thessalonians, Philemon), Paul scarcely appeals to scripture at all. From this Harnack concluded that the scriptures of Judaism were not commonly used in Gentile churches established by Paul, either in liturgical or other settings.[27] Agreeing with Harnack, W. Bauer went further to assert the improbability of any liturgical use of Jewish scripture in Gentile Christianity in the apostolic period.[28] These conclusions, however, are drawn entirely from silence, and there is much to be said for a different view.[29]

Paul's use of the scriptures of Judaism in his letters takes the most varied forms, from direct quotation to passing allusion, from using a text as a simple proof to developing intricate midrashic arguments, from typological appeals to allegorical interpretations. There is scarcely a basic element of Christian teaching that Paul does not refer to scripture. This is not to say that scripture is the basis of Christian preaching and teaching for Paul, but he does take it as an indispensable correlate and witness. The frequency, variety, and subtlety of Paul's recourse to scripture presumes not only that the communities he addressed acknowledged the authority of Jewish scripture, but also that they were sufficiently familiar with it to understand and appreciate his appeals to it, subtle and diverse as they were. More than that, Paul emphasizes as a principle not merely the value of scripture but its specific pertinence to the Christian community: it was written "entirely for our sake" (1 Cor. 9:10), "for our instruction, upon whom the end of the ages has come" (1 Cor. 10:11); indeed, "whatever was written in former days was written for our instruction, so that by steadfastness and the encouragement of the scripture we might have hope" (Rom. 15:4). How might these communities be instructed in scripture or experience its encouragement if not in the service of worship?[30] The fact that Paul expected his own letters to be read in the liturgical assembly shows that he envisioned the Christian gathering for worship as an appropriate setting for public reading; it is likely he assumed that reading was customary, not confined to the rare occasion of a letter from him. It is probably not fortuitous that the first explicit mention of the liturgical reading of scripture in Christianity (1 Tim. 4:13) appears in a letter that stands in the Pauline tradition and presupposes the practice of churches in the Pauline mission field.

Paul's letters are the best evidence for the question of the public reading of scripture in first-century Christianity (though he never mentions the subject) because he wrote to communities that were exclusively or predominantly Gentile, and if churches composed mainly of Gentiles were familiar with Jewish scripture, then all the more was that to be expected among Christian communities with larger Jewish constituencies. The fact that virtually all the earliest Christian writers were deeply interested in Jewish scripture and gave it theological use presumes that their readers too were aware of scripture, acknowledged its authority, and knew its substance. To say that the use of scripture belonged to theological argument but not to liturgical practice is to introduce a distinction that was foreign to the concrete life of the early church.

Given that the church originated within Judaism, it is likely that the customs of the synagogue influenced Christian liturgical practice, and the presence by the mid–second century of prayer, scripture reading and homily in the *synaxis* of Christian assemblies, mirroring both the structure and the elements of the synagogue service, would bear this out. Precisely how the liturgical reading of scripture was taken up into Christian use we cannot determine. We do not know whether it belonged, with prayer and preaching, to a distinctive Christian service of the word (a Christian version of synagogue worship) or whether it was incorporated into a single eucharistic occasion of worship. This obscurity is due to the paucity of evidence, but probably also to a certain variety and flexibility of early Christian liturgical practice. What we do know is that by the second century the public reading of scripture was a fixture of the church's worship. So we go on to ask just what was read, by whom, and how.

The Content of Public Reading A complication arises in speaking of the liturgical reading of scripture in the first several centuries: in neither Judaism nor Christianity was there yet a canon of scripture, that is, a fixed and closed list of religiously authoritative documents. Nevertheless, from the time of Christian beginnings the Jewish writings that would eventually compose the Christian Old Testament canon were broadly known and used and recognized as authoritative, and hence were scriptural, though not yet canonical, for Jews and Christians alike. Peculiarly Christian writings, however, only later and gradually acquired the status of scripture. In that process, liturgical reading was an important factor.

During the late first and early second centuries the books that were read in Christian assemblies were principally the scriptures of Judaism. The question is in what form they were available in early Christian communities. It is not likely that in this early period all churches would have possessed full collections of Jewish scripture. The scriptures of Judaism comprised not a single book but a collection of scrolls, five of the Torah and more of the prophetic books. These books were relatively costly, and their availability even to all synagogues cannot be taken for granted.[31] Even if the books were available outside the synagogue and could be afforded, small Christian congregations probably had only a select group of Jewish texts. Under the circumstances it may be that Christians for a time found it convenient or necessary to use only extracts or "testimonies" drawn from Jewish scriptures, instead of volumes of continuous texts.[32] During the same period Christian writings were still making their way into circulation and had not gained the status of scripture. Nevertheless, their instructional value for Christian congregations was surely recognized, and a given church would have used whatever Christian books had come to hand and proved to be helpful. In this way Christian writings began to be read in the same setting as the Jewish scriptures.

It was common practice at least by the middle of the second century to read Christian as well as Jewish texts in Christian services.

Justin says that at the beginning of the service "the memoirs of the apostles" or "the writings of the prophets" were read. By the former he undoubtedly has Gospels in mind, though other apostolic writings are not necessarily excluded.[33] And for Justin, "prophetic writings" may have been an inclusive designation for Jewish scripture, bringing the Torah, Psalms and Prophets under the rubric by which Justin himself typically understood them. It is unclear whether Justin regarded Christian texts ("the memoirs of the apostles") as scripture on a par with the "writings of the prophets." But soon afterward Irenaeus, Clement of Alexandria, and Tertullian all speak of the Gospels, the Pauline letters, and some other early Christian texts as scripture and accord them fully as much authority as Jewish scripture. Thus Tertullian, describing Christian worship at the end of the second century (*Apol.* 39.3), can speak of the reading of "the books of God" without differentiating between Jewish and Christian writings, and he certainly intended both.

If in the first and early second century Christians made liturgical use primarily of Jewish scripture and whatever Christian texts they might have, by the late second century the situation had changed, for a great many Christian texts had been widely disseminated and were generally available. Once this happened, Christian communities were confronted with the question of exactly *which* books to read publicly in assemblies for worship. It was in this context that the process of determining the scope and contents of the Christian canon of scripture began, though it took several centuries to be completed. When the term *canon* was first applied to Christian texts, it did not mean "norm" but simply "list," namely, a list of those books that were acceptable for public reading.[34] Thus the questions that were raised about the theological substance or religious authority of individual Christian books were not abstract, but had practical liturgical correlatives. Consider the incident reported by Eusebius (*H.E.* 6.12.2) about Serapion, bishop of Antioch, who was confronted with the question whether the Gospel of Peter should continue to be publicly read in the church at Rhossus. Initially Serapion saw no difficulty and said "Let it be read," but later forbad it because he found it to contain heretical ideas. A little later, in Rome, some objected to the Gospel of John and Revelation because they were being put to heterodox use (Eusebius, *H.E.* 3.28.2, Irenaeus, *A.H.* 3.9). The debate was framed in terms of content and authorship, but the practical issue was whether those documents should be publicly read. Similarly, when Irenaeus (*A.H.* 3.8–9) insisted on the exclusive authority of only four Gospels it was not just a matter of their authority in religious controversy; what he intended was that only those Gospels should be acknowledged in the church, and the mode of such acknowledgment was public reading. Liturgical reading was the concrete setting from which texts acquired theological authority, and in which that authority took effect. In this light it is not surprising that when Eusebius in the early fourth century took stock of "the writings of the new covenant," that is, Christian texts that had scriptural authority, he considered chiefly whether they had been used by earlier ecclesiastical writers and whether they had been publicly read *(dedemosieumene)* in all or most churches.[35]

During the second and third centuries the scope of materials that were publicly read was fluid. The Gospels of Mark, Matthew, and Luke and the letters of Paul were certainly among the earliest Christian texts to be circulated and must also have been among the earliest Christian writings to be read along with Jewish scripture in Christian assemblies.[36] The fact that the authority of these documents was never called into question but was everywhere taken for granted by the late second century is itself the strongest indication that they were established in liturgical use long before. Most of the other texts that were eventually included in the canon came into liturgical use somewhat later or in a more limited area. Yet not every document that was liturgically read became canonical: according to Eusebius (*H.E.* 3.3.6; 3.16; 4.23.11) *The Shepherd* of Hermas and the letter of Clement of Rome were often read in Christian assemblies in the second and third centuries, yet neither found its way into the canon.[37] In questionable cases a variety of criteria might be brought to bear—whether, for example, a given writing had an apostolic connection or was orthodox or had general (catholic) relevance. But these considerations usually had only negative force. What counted the most was whether the church, in whole or large part, was accustomed to hearing the document read in the service of worship.[38]

The reading practices of the church did not all develop at once, and the course of development is difficult to reconstruct. Not until the third and fourth centuries can we begin to see clearly and in detail what its results were, and then there are regional variations. Some things, however, can be made out about the earlier period as well. Justin indicates that the service began with the reading of scripture, apparently without preliminaries, and that this proceeded while the congregation assembled.[39] He mentions first "the memoirs of the apostles" and then "the writings of the prophets," which may reflect the order of the readings, but not necessarily. Justin also says that these texts were read "as long as time permits," indicating that there was as yet no lectionary system appointing segments of texts for reading. As much as possible was read in the time available.

The number and the choice of readings, as they come into focus in the third and fourth centuries, show wide regional variations.[40] Justin mentioned only two lessons, but there were usually more later on. By the fourth century the Antiochene church took two lessons from Jewish scriptures, one each from the Law and the prophets as was customary in the synagogue, and two lessons from Christian scripture, one from Acts or the epistles and one from the Gospels.[41] The oldest western liturgies, however, had only one lesson from the Old Testament and two from the New, and this pattern was widely followed. Yet Roman practice, at least in its developed form, included only two lessons, both from Christian scripture, the first from the (Pauline) epistles, the second from the Gospels.[42] No matter how many readings there may have been in a given area (though there were always at least two), it was the rule that Gospel reading should stand in the final, culminating position. Yet just how early these several customs developed it is impossible to say.

Very likely it was the practice of the church from an early time to read the scriptures by lectio continua, just as the synagogue read the Torah. The text of a book or of a series of books was read through consecutively, being taken up each Sunday where it had concluded on the previous Sunday. This practice may already be signaled by Justin's statement that scripture was read "as long as time permits." For the third century and later the custom of lectio continua is demonstrated less by explicit statements than by the nature of patristic commentaries on scripture. These often consist of a series of homiletical expositions that had originally been delivered on a text being read consecutively from beginning to end over a series of Sundays. Commentaries of Origen, Chrysostom, Ambrose and Augustine, among others, were composed, or perhaps wc should say compiled, in this way. By means of lectio continua the congregation not only heard most of the scriptures read over time but were able to grasp sequences of events and the logic of arguments in scripture and to know the sweep of the biblical story.[43]

As the concept of the "ecclesiastical year" developed, the consecutive reading of scripture began to be interrupted at the great seasonal festivals of the church. Though the practice is not well attested for an earlier time, by the fourth century there are good indications that especially at Easter, Ascension, Pentecost, and Epiphany certain texts were selected as particularly appropriate for liturgical reading—the resurrection narratives of the Gospels at Easter, the ascension story in Acts at Ascension, and so forth.[44] These readings came to be called proper, that is, belonging to the occasion. The prescription of texts for feast days—which probably began in connection with Easter and was extended to other feast days—led ultimately to the creation of lectionaries prescribing readings for the entire ecclesiastical year. The first complete lectionaries, with readings for all days, date from the seventh century, but there were partial lectionaries in the fifth century, and some lectionary texts survive from the sixth.[45] During the first five centuries, then, the church operated without a fixed lectionary system and read the scriptures quite freely.

Public reading was sometimes given to texts that were not scriptural. Thus public reading alone did not imply that a text had the authority of scripture, and such reading was not necessarily liturgical, though it occurred in the Christian assembly for worship. An example is the letter of the Roman bishop Soter, of which Dionysius of Corinth says in his letter to Soter, "Today we observed the holy day of the Lord, and in the observance we (publicly) read your letter, which we shall continue to read (publicly) from time to time for our admonition" (Eusebius, *H.E.* 4.23.11). Besides the episcopal letters or synodical communications that were effectively published by being read to congregations, it became the custom to read from the acts of martyrs on their feast days.[46] This practice was sanctioned by the Council of Carthage in 397 (canon 36), and Augustine often cites such readings in his sermons, but the reading of martyr acts began much earlier, possibly in the second century.[47] Of course, the reading of official communications or martyr acts was never confused with the reading of scripture.

The Reader By the end of the second century there had arisen within the church a specific office of "reader" *(anagnostes, lector)*, and this office is the oldest of the so-called minor orders of the clergy.[48] The office is first attested by Tertullian for North Africa at the end of the second century *(Praescr. 41)*, and Hippolytus attests it for Rome only a little later *(Apost. Trad. 1.12)*. By the middle of the third century it was well established everywhere. Eusebius *(H.E. 6.43.11)* preserves part of a letter from the Roman bishop Cornelius to Fabius, bishop of Antioch, that includes a list of Roman clergy in the middle of the third century and mentions, besides the bishop, "forty-six presbyters, seven deacons, seven subdeacons, forty-two acolytes, fifty-two exorcists, readers and porters, and more than fifteen hundred widows and distressed persons." In the same period Cyprian of Carthage often speaks of the office of the reader, mentions several readers by name in various letters, and indicates that the office was a lesser order but closely coordinated with the clergy.[49] It can be seen in the several eastern church orders, the *Didascalia Apostolorum*, the *Apostolic Church Order*, and the *Apostolic Constitutions*, that the office of the reader was also well known in the East in the third and fourth centuries.

Though the office is not certainly attested before the end of the second century, the function of public reading in the church was established early, reaching back to the first century, where its history can be only sketchily reconstructed. The early allusions suggest some diversity in the status and responsibilities of those who read. The two earliest pose an interesting question. The first is found in Rev. 1:3, which pronounces a blessing upon "the one who reads" and upon "those who hear." This reader has no official capacity, for the participle *anaginoskon*, "the one who reads," rather than the noun *anagnostes*, "the reader," is used. The other of the allusions is found in 1 Tim. 4:13, which admonishes Timothy to attend "to the (public) reading, to preaching and to teaching" *(te anagnosei, te paraklesei, te didaskalia)*. Here the responsibility for reading, preaching, and teaching all accrue to the community leader, or bishop, represented by "Timothy." Both texts come from Asia Minor and belong to roughly the same period, but they assign the prerogative of reading completely differently: in the first case it is not an official capacity, in the second it is.

The problem is further complicated by another allusion in 2 Clement 19.1, written perhaps toward the middle of the second century: "Therefore brothers and sisters, following the God of truth, I am reading to you an exhortation to pay attention to that which is written, that you may save both yourselves and the one who reads *[ton anaginoskonta]* among you." This apparently refers to a reading from scripture ("that which is written") followed by a homily ("exhortation") upon it.[50] The statement is nonetheless especially interesting because it suggests that 2 Clement is itself the exhortation that is meant, in which case 2 Clement was a homily composed and read *by the reader*, though the author does not seem to be a member of the clergy proper.[51] Thus it would seem that at least in some churches the responsibility of the reader was not only to read the scripture but also to deliver the homily that interpreted and applied the scripture he had read. This would make the reader's role prominent indeed, even if not official. The situation here differs from that in 1 Timothy, where reading, teaching and preaching are the sole prerogatives of the bishop. In contrast with both 1 Timothy and 2 Clement, Justin's account of Christian worship represents the reading as the task of a reader but the delivery of the exposition as the task of the "president" (proestos), presumably the bishop or an elder who presided in his place.

If these several early references to readers and public reading do not yield a consistent picture, that is probably an accurate reflection of diverse practices in churches of the late first and early second century. We might expect variations in the way individual communities arranged to meet their practical needs, before any uniform system of church order had developed. In any congregation only a small number of persons could read at all, and fewer could read publicly. In the early period, and long afterward in small communities, there may have been no more than one or two who had the ability. The task of reading inevitably fell to the literate, and because the congregation depended upon them for its access to texts, a great importance accrued to them. Like others who served to edify and instruct the congregation as a whole, the capacity to read was appreciated as one of the manifold gifts of the spirit—a charisma.[52] Gradually, however, what had been free charismatic activities were assimilated to particular offices and came to be exercised with fixed authority, a tendency that was already well under way, if unevenly, by the end of the first century. By the middle of the second century the church had largely achieved a structured form of governance vested in bishops, presbyters, and deacons. Yet the old charismatic ministries did not disappear; some were taken up among the prerogatives of office and ceased to be freely exercised, while others continued for a time alongside established offices.[53] The evolution of the role of the reader within this larger development is impossible to trace in detail, but its general lines can be discerned.

Early on, the task of reading fell to any member of the congregation who was capable of it, and the ability to read was reckoned a spiritual endowment. As fixed offices arose, the responsibility for reading was often assumed by a bishop, presbyter, or deacon, for reading was an interpretive activity, and the interpretation of scripture was increasingly a concern to those who governed the church and administered its teaching. On the other hand, the qualifications for church office were chiefly moral and spiritual and did not necessarily include literacy. It is likely that in some congregations the officeholders were not able to read or could not read well and thus relied upon literate members of the congregation to read under their official auspices.[54] If the responsibility for public reading may have varied like this with the circumstances of individual congregations and with developing patterns of church order, then the inconsistencies in the early allusions to readers and reading become intelligible.

Liturgical practice is inherently conservative. The emergence of a formal office of reader by the late second century was not an innovation but simply the regularizing of a by-then long-standing function and coordinating it with other functions that had become official. This happened in different ways in different regions of the church, as we can see from early references to the appointment of readers. The earliest is found in Hippolytus's *Apostolic Tradition* (about 230), which stipulates that "the reader is ordained when the bishop gives him the book, for hands are not laid upon him" (1.12). In not having hands laid upon him the reader is differentiated (along with widows, virgins, subdeacons, and healers) from the clergy proper (bishops, presbyters, and deacons). This already implies the distinction between "major" and "minor" orders: in the major orders spiritual endowment occurs with the laying on of hands, whereas in the minor orders persons are formally acknowledged for the exercise of gifts they already possess. Another and different description of the appointment of a reader occurs in the *Apostolic Constitutions* (8.22): "Ordain a reader by laying your hands upon him, and pray to God saying, 'Do now look down upon your servant, who is to be entrusted to read your holy scriptures to your people, and give him your holy spirit, the prophetic spirit. You who instructed your servant Ezra to read your Law to the people [compare Neh. 8] do now also at our prayers instruct your servant and grant that he may without blame perfect the work committed to him, and thereby be declared worthy of a higher degree.' " Here, in contrast to Hippolytus's rule, the reader is subject to the laying on of hands, and the readership is a recognized order of the clergy—a lower order from which one might advance into the higher ranks. We find here no clear division between major and minor orders, but a continuum among all orders. The prayer of ordination ascribes to the reader a special endowment of the divine, prophetic spirit, which perhaps preserves an early recognition of the charismatic aspect of the reader's activity.[55] A similar conception belongs to one of the main sources of the *Apostolic Constitutions*, the *Didascalia Apostolorum*, a church order of the third century preserved entire only in Syriac. In treating the portions of the offerings that are to be allotted to the clergy, the Greek text specifies (2.28) that "if there is also a reader, let him too receive with the presbyters [a double portion] in honor of the prophets." Here too is the association of the reader with the prophets, implying that the reader's function has a charismatic dimension. It should also be noticed that here the reader does not belong to the minor orders, which are unknown as such in the *Didascalia*, but stands fully among the clergy, in a position not inferior to the presbyter and deacon, with whom he receives an equal portion.

These two traditions about the ordination and status of the reader reflect different developments in the western and the eastern church and embody different conceptions of the rank and role of the reader. In the western church the reader was understood as a functionary responsible for a particular action in the liturgy. As such, he receives no special spiritual endowment but is merely given the object of his duty, the book. The eastern ritual conveys a higher estimate of the reader: a spiritual endowment is invoked by prayer and bestowed through the laying on of hands, just as for the other orders. Thus the reader has full standing among the clergy, and his role is divinely sanctioned. Both the western and the eastern conceptions are rooted in the work of the reader in the earliest period, when, by virtue of possessing a valuable skill, the reader was understood to exercise a spiritual gift. The difference arose as a matter of emphasis—whether the ability to read was conceived primarily as a human competence or as a divine gift.

Most of the minor orders of the clergy that had developed by the third century arose from the order of deacons. Subdeacons, exorcists, acolytes, and porters came into being by way of dividing and delegating tasks that had originally belonged to deacons but eventually required more people. Consequently, there was never any uncertainty about the rank of these orders in relation to the major orders. Yet the office of the reader was an exception to this rule: the responsibility for reading did not originally belong to the diaconate, and it was not the prerogative of elders or bishops, but had an independent early origin.[56] Once the various orders had arisen it was uncertain where the readers should be placed among them, and the sources express different views, some placing them among the major orders, others relegating them to minor rank. Thus whereas the other minor orders were derived from the diaconate, in the case of readers the process was the reverse: the function that had originally belonged to them was progressively absorbed by the higher orders, and the prominence of the reader was gradually reduced.

A symptom of this can be seen in stipulations about what the readers were expected to read. Originally the reader was responsible for all of the readings in the service. Justin says that both the "writings of the prophets" and the "memoirs of the apostles" (presumably the

Gospels) were recited by the reader. In the third century, Cyprian attests that in Carthage it was the privilege of the reader to read the Gospel.[57] By the fourth century in both the Eastern and the Western church the reading of the Gospel, reckoned a special privilege, had been taken over by deacons and presbyters. Thus Jerome comments, "You were often reading the gospel of Christ as if you were a deacon" (*Ep.* 147.6). The *Canons of Basil* (97) prescribe that "only a deacon or presbyter should read the gospel in a catholic church; no one should overstep his rank." The *Apostolic Constitutions* stipulate that "a deacon or a presbyter will read the Gospel" (2.57.5). Thus the reader came to be restricted to the reading of the Old Testament and the Epistle and, where there were only two readings, to the Epistle alone.

As the readership devolved into a minor order, it became a point of entry into the clergy and a proving ground for advancement to the higher ranks. It is not surprising then that lectors were always male.[58] They were chosen from among the faithful, and generally not from the catechumenate.[59] Literacy naturally remained a prerequisite, but more than ordinary literacy was needed. A list of qualifications are spelled out in the *Apostolic Church Order* (3): "For reader, one should be appointed after he has been carefully proved: no babbler, nor drunkard, nor jester; of good morals, submissive, of benevolent intentions, first in the assembly at the meetings on the Lord's Day, of plain utterance *(euekoos)*, skillful in exposition *(diegetikos)*, mindful that he functions in the place of an evangelist." Of course, in addition, one who was to be effective in reading publicly had to be articulate and capable of communicating clearly the sense of what he read.[60] Those who satisfied these desiderata were inevitably few in most congregations and would have been among the most obvious prospects for clerical service. Given the prominence of the reader before the congregation, the moral and spiritual qualifications of a reader were by no means undervalued. Cyprian (*Ep.* 39.2) exploited the public prominence of the reader when he appointed the confessors Celerinus and Aurelius to that post:

> It seemed right for [Aurelius] to start with the office of lector
> since nothing was more becoming to the voice which confessed
> God with glorious praise than also to sound him forth through
> the celebration of the divine readings, after the sublime words
> which bespoke martyrdom for Christ: to read the Gospel of
> Christ whence martyrs are made, to come to the pulpit after
> the scaffold; to have been conspicuous there to a multitude of

Gentiles, to be conspicuous here to the brothers; to have been heard there to the marvel of the people standing around, to be heard here to the joy of the brotherhood.

Concerning Celerinus he declared (*Ep.* 39.5), "There is nothing in which a confessor may be a greater help to his brothers than that, while the evangelical reading of the gospel is heard from his lips, whoever hears may imitate the faith of the reader." Here the exemplary faith of the readers is as important as their capacity for reading.

Cyprian speaks of these as young men "deserving of higher ranks" but not yet qualified for them by age. For the office of lector there was apparently no stipulated age, but the necessary skills and deportment meant that readers were usually at least in late adolescence, between the years of sixteen and twenty.[61] Later on, near the end of the fourth century, when the liturgical function of the reader had been sharply diminished, the practice developed of ordaining readers at younger ages, sometimes even in infancy. Ambrose speaks of "the voice of the young reader" *(lectoris parvuli)*; Augustine mentions a group of *lectores infantuli*; Paulinus of Nola says of a lector that "he served in his first years" *(primis lector servivit in annis)*; Sidonius Apollinaris says of John, bishop of Chalon, that he began as a lector *ab infantia*; and some inscriptions indicate readers who were a mere five years old.[62] The impetus to ordain preadolescents as readers perhaps lay in the idea that "childish innocence was considered best suited to lift the word of God from the sacred Book and offer it, unadulterated, to the congregation."[63] But in the cases of exceptionally young readers there was no intention that they should actually read. It was the role of the readership as an entry to clerical orders that was at work here: as a training ground in which an early start was advantageous, talented children or children from devout or influential backgrounds were enrolled as lectors. This is plain in the comment of Siricius of Rome (*Ep.* 1.13) that "whoever has vowed himself for submission to the church from his infancy ought to be baptized before the age of puberty and united to the ministry of lectors."[64] Those who were made readers as children were, however, given literary and religious instruction by the church to prepare them for the responsibilities of reading and, later, of higher clerical office.[65]

The Manner of Reading Liturgical reading in the early church was performed from a particular place: the reader stood facing the congregation on a raised platform. This was the established practice by the middle of the third century, for Cyprian alludes to the reader standing on a *pulpitum* (*Ep.* 38.2) and compares the place of the reader to a lamp upon a lampstand (*Ep.* 39.5). Since this was well before the construction of Christian basilicas, it must be supposed that the place where Christians met (housechurch or *domus ecclesiae*) was furnished with such a platform (*bema*, or *ambo*). Indeed, one can be seen in the early third-century housechurch at Dura Europus: at the eastern end of the room that served as the assembly hall there was a small raised platform that must have been the place from which reading and preaching were done. Often, perhaps usually, a desk stood upon it to hold the book and probably a lamp. When Christian basilicas began to be constructed they normally contained an ambo.[66] More than a simple platform, the ambo was an elevated podium located in the nave, but off-center. Usually it was a freestanding structure, but sometimes it was built onto the choir or was linked to the altar area by a *solea*, a raised walkway. The ambo was made of wood or marble, had a balustrade and lectern, and was often richly decorated with carving or mosaics.[67] Though sometimes used for other purposes, the ambo was primarily the place for the reading of scripture.[68] The use of a bema or ambo for reading would have arisen simply because it enabled the reader to be more easily heard. It may have had its immediate model in the similar platform commonly found in synagogues and used for the same purpose (the *bima, migdal*), but there are pagan analogues too.[69]

Stationed upon the bema, the reader, who carried the book with him, announced what he would read and proceeded to read it. There are no clear indications from the earliest period about how the reading was rendered, but there is every reason to suppose that it was not given in a speaking voice but was intoned, that is, chanted to a simple inflection. At any rate, this was the practice by the fourth century, and it probably goes back to a much earlier time. No clear distinction between speech and singing was made in antiquity. To read a poetic text was, in a sense, not merely to read but to sing, and the rendering of prose texts too, especially in public or in ceremonial contexts, could have a singing quality.[70] Several impulses conspired to promote a stylized manner of reading the scripture. Chanting is, among other things, a means of amplifying and projecting the voice and, like the placement of the reader on a raised podium, it served to make the reader's voice more articulate and audible. Chanting is also a solemn reading style, and in the case of the reading of scripture may have been thought more suitable to the content and occasion than an ordinary reading voice. Moreover, chanting is more effective than ordinary speech in impressing what is read upon the memory. Perhaps most important, chanted reading, with its intonations, pauses, and rhythms provided a way to orally parse the text for the hearers.

A cantillated type of reading was developed early in Judaism for the reading of scripture, and there can be little doubt that it antedated the rise of Christianity. The Talmud records the opinion of Rabbi Johanan that "anyone who reads the scripture without melody or recites the mishnah without a tune, to him applies the scriptural verse, 'And I also gave them statutes that were not good' [Ezek. 20:25]" (B. Meg. 32a). Since the statutes themselves could hardly be thought to lack merit, the phrase "not good" is taken to refer to the manner of recitation.[71] It is unknown just what sort of cantillation was employed in synagogue reading at this early time and unlikely that there was complete uniformity in the practice. The biblical chant used in Judaism must originally have been in the style of a simple recitative, marked by cadence and monodic tone, but with little musical adornment. While the systems of cantillation that are in use now in various traditions of Judaism and Christianity cannot be traced with any certainty beyond the medieval period, it is striking that they all rely on a fundamental recitation note for the rendering of each clause, the recitation note being introduced and concluded by a brief and simple melodic phrase.[72] This type of cantillation, which is neither speech nor song but a rhythmo-melodic recitation (Sprechgesang), is "logogenic": the musical element is generated by the words, is dependent on the verbal and syntactical structure of the text, and is subordinated to the oral communication of the text.[73] Hence the elements of rhythm and melody do not comprise an autonomous musical form but remain entirely at the service of the words. The biblical chant as it was developed in Judaism was originally devised and used not for musical purposes but to provide for the oral punctuation of a text that otherwise lacked clear indications of how it was to be read, that is, interpretively rendered.[74] It was the task of the reader to discriminate between the syntactical and semantic units of the text and thus enable its structure and sense to be grasped by the hearer. This was a matter chiefly of the oral subdivision of the text into its constituent clauses by means of melodic cadences.

It is another indication of the close and interactive relation of the oral and the written modes that Jewish biblical texts eventually came to be equipped with systems of accents (te'amim) to govern their liturgical reading according to certain melodic conventions. The developed systems of Masoretic written accents, which represent in a detailed way the melodic motifs according to which the biblical texts were chanted in public reading, are relatively late, the earliest dating from the late fifth or early sixth century.[75] Still, the Masoretic systems were not fundamentally innovative; rather, they elaborated, systematized, and transcribed traditions of the reading and interpretation of scripture that had much earlier origins and were for a long time taught and transmitted orally. There are some very early Jewish manuscripts of biblical texts, both in Greek and in Hebrew, that are transcribed with a view to reading by using spacing to signify the pauses necessary in recitation for marking out the semantic units. In all probability this method of transcription was associated with an early and relatively simple kind of cantillated reading.[76]

At least some early Christian communities would have been accustomed to cantillated reading from the synagogue, and in Jewish-Christian settings the manner of reading scripture would have been taken over along with the Jewish scripture itself and the practice of reading it in worship. Diaspora synagogues, which read the scriptures in Greek, must also have used some form of cantillation, and Gentile Christian congregations, which also knew and used scripture only in Greek, must have heard the scriptures chanted. The systems of cantillation that are well attested in later Christian sources do in fact have interesting affinities with Jewish usage, but it is hard to demonstrate that the former originated in the latter, although this is widely believed to be the case.[77] Whether scripture reading took the form of a chant in the setting of Christian worship does not finally depend on deciding whether this practice was directly appropriated from Judaism. What makes it likely that early Christians read and heard the scriptures in a cantillated style is the necessity, in the public reading of any text, especially of a religiously authoritative text, that the text be clearly articulated and properly interpreted. It was noted earlier that in the absence of word division, punctuation, and other decoding aids to read *was* to interpret. Although the text was fixed, its sense was not unambiguously given in the characters but was, so to speak, conferred in the act of reading itself. Knowing how to read was knowing how to understand, and to read rightly was to give the proper interpretation. When a text was read publicly, the communication of its semantic substance depended entirely on the oral gestures of pause, tone, rhythm, and cadence, which compose the chant-style and make it an effective hermeneutical medium.

Although the first several centuries provide no direct evidence about the Christian scriptural chant, it is presupposed by the phenomenon of Christian psalmody. It has commonly been thought that psalmody, as distinct from the reading of scripture, was one of a number of elements taken over by the church from Judaism and was therefore characteristic of Christian worship from the earliest time. Yet there are reasons to doubt this: there is no mention of psalmody as such in Jewish sources until the fifth century, and references to Christian psalmody, which are sparse during the first three centuries, become plentiful in the fourth and fifth.[78] In psalmody we have to do, of course, with scriptural texts, but the Psalms came to be rendered in a more fully musical form than other parts of scripture. Exactly when and how the psalms came to be differentiated from the reading of scripture, accorded a distinct though related place in worship, and given musical elaboration beyond simple cantillation is to some extent obscure.[79] This was apparently a gradual development during the second and third centuries, but its results were complete by the early fourth century when we begin to hear frequently of the singing of Psalms as an established element in Christian worship. More or less concurrently with the development of Christian psalmody we begin to hear no longer merely of the reader but also of the singer (psaltes).[80] Before the fourth century there was no need to distinguish between a reader and a singer, for the reader was responsible for and capable of the cantillation of all the lessons, including the psalms, and even when the practice of psalmody was in place it was often the reader who "sang" the psalms.[81] The emergence of a separate office of singer or cantor appears to belong to the last half of the fourth century and is correlative with the development of Christian psalmody as distinct from the reading of scripture.[82] It attests a heightening of the difference between the cantillation of readings and the singing of psalms and recognizes the more properly musical skills required by psalmody, skills that did not necessarily belong to a competent reader.[83] The emergence of psalmody in both Christianity and Judaism presupposes the cantillation of scripture and grew out of it.

The chant, then, was the way the public reading of scripture was done in the early church, and it served primarily the hermeneutical purpose of making the semantic structure and substance of the text accessible to the hearer. Hence the public reading of scripture required real skills on the part of the reader, who had to acquire a familiarity with the text, parse it for himself, and then orally convey not merely the words but their meaning to the congregation. One who performed the public reading was necessarily in some sense a student of scripture. In this light it is not surprising that in the report of the confiscation of scriptural books in Cirta at the beginning of the fourth century the books were for the most part to be found in the homes of the lectors.[84] There they were no doubt studied in preparation for public reading. The delicacy of this responsibility can be gauged by a remark of Irenaeus, who says that some heretics "do not know how to read Paul": failing to observe that Paul often transposes the order of words and clauses, they derive mistaken conclusions from Paul's letters. He gives as an example 2 Thess. 2:8, which is grammatically capable of two very different interpretations, and says (*A.H.* 3.7.2): "If then one does not attend to the [proper] reading [of the text] and if he does not exhibit the intervals of breathing as they occur, there will be not only incongruities but he will utter blasphemy when reading, as if the advent of the Lord could take place according to the working of Satan. So, therefore, in such passages the transposition *(hyperbaton)* must be exhibited by the reading and the apostle's meaning preserved accordingly." It does not matter whether Irenaeus is referring here to private or public reading; the point is that the way a text is read—whether the clauses are properly distinguished and related by pause and cadence—makes all the difference in what it is taken to mean. Texts written in scriptio continua were inevitably subject to some ambiguity of sense. The resolution of those ambiguities—the rescue of sense from syllables—took place in the very act of reading. In the case of publicly read scriptural texts this could be no small matter.

Because reading was known to be a matter of interpretation and because it was so important to convey the right interpretation in public reading, early manuscripts of scriptural texts are often written in a somewhat larger hand, with fewer letters to the line and fewer lines to the page, than other texts and were more often furnished with reading aids.[85] The same considerations resulted eventually in the practice of transcribing scriptural texts *per cola et commata*, that is, in sense lines, each semantic unit (phrase *[comma]* or clause *[colon]*) being written on a separate line (yet still without separating words). Such colometric transcription was a departure from the more common stichometric method of scriptio continua, according to which the lines of text were written out to a standard number of syllables, regardless of the sense units comprised by them. The colometric method attended closely to sense, while the stichometric was merely a matter of space. The transcription of a manuscript in sense-lines anticipated and obviated some of the main difficulties of reading and especially of public reading: a good part of the reader's normal work was done by the manuscript itself, which showed the reader exactly what the sense units were and prescribed the pauses or breaths between.[86] Thus the arrangement of a text in sense-lines aimed above all to assist the reader, and manuscripts transcribed in this way must have been intended particularly for public reading. A number of ancient biblical manuscripts that are written colometrically have survived, and they indicate that this method of transcription came into some vogue in Christianity in the fourth century, if not earlier.[87] Jerome applied colometry in principle to his Latin translation of the Bible, but there is no doubt that it was used earlier for Greek texts. It is probably because colometric writing required much more space and was therefore more expensive that it did not become standard and displace the stichometric method.

The best-known colometric manuscripts of Christian scripture are also bilingual, presenting the Greek and Latin texts in parallel columns, either on the same page or on facing pages. This raises another question in connection with the public reading of scripture in Christian worship: was the text read in its original language and then read in translation? We noted previously that this was common practice in the synagogue: the reading of the Hebrew text was immediately followed by an Aramaic translation. All the scriptural texts of Christianity were in Greek, and the need to translate would have arisen only in areas that were not Greek-speaking, or at any rate in congregations that were bilingual. There are various indications that in these settings translation often followed the reading. Egeria attests the practice in Jerusalem in the late fourth century: "The lessons that are read in the church have to be read in Greek, but there is always someone at hand to translate them into Syriac so that the people will understand," and she adds that for those who speak Latin the lesson is translated into Latin (*Peregrin.* 47.4). Early in the fourth century Eusebius tells of a martyr, Procopius of Scythopolis, who had served as a reader and also as a translator of Greek into Syriac (*De Mart. Pal.* 1.1). Epiphanius refers to the office of translator of the lessons and homilies (*De fide* 21), and the *Euchologium* of Serapion of Thumis contains a prayer (11.4) "for the readers and translators" *(anagnoston kai hermeneon)*. All these allusions refer to bilingual or polyglot communities. If in the fourth century the reading of the scriptures in Greek was often followed by a rendering in the vernacular, the intelligibility of public readings in Greek must sometimes have been a problem much earlier than this.[88] In provincial areas where Greek was little known the immediate solution was just to give the readings in the vernacular. It was in response to this need that the ancient versions of scripture began to be produced, beginning in the second century with the Latin and Syriac. But in congregations in which some knew Greek and others did not it is likely that the scripture readings were often given in both Greek and the vernacular. It was no doubt for such situations that bilingual manuscripts were produced, making it possible to give the readings in both languages.[89] Though Greek was the traditional language of Christianity, Christianity never regarded Greek as a sacred language in the way that Judaism valued Hebrew and had no scruples about written translations of scripture into provincial vernaculars. Thus both the production of non-Greek versions of scripture and the use of bilingual manuscripts are rooted in the liturgical reading of scripture and witness the effort to make the sense of scripture accessible to all.

THE PRIVATE USE OF CHRISTIAN BOOKS

Outside the public reading of scripture in the setting of worship we must also reckon with the private uses of Christian books. The little evidence there is on this subject has never been adequately examined.[90] The private use of Christian literature in the ancient church was necessarily qualified by three factors: the extent of literacy, the availability of books, and the cost of books. As to the first, private reading was possible only for the small minority of Christians who could read, a minority that probably never exceeded 15–20 percent in the first few centuries, as we have noted. If the private use of Christian books was limited, it was for this practical reason. Second, we have observed that as a rule Christian literature was not produced or distributed through the commercial book trade. Like most other literature, it had to be acquired through private transcription, and that required locating the text and gaining permission to copy it. The third factor, cost, was probably the least important. The only expense lay in the cost of materials and the services of a scribe, and economies could be obtained by copying the text on the back of an existing roll (an opisthograph) or in an erased roll or codex (a palimpsest), or by transcribing the text personally instead of employing a professional scribe. Moreover, in some Christian centers books could be had more or less for the asking: Pamphilus, on the evidence of Eusebius as cited by Jerome, not only lent books but readily gave them away, and he kept a stock of manuscripts for the purpose.[91] Pamphilus was a bibliophile, of course, but making Christian texts available to individual readers must have been thought a good thing to do wherever the circumstances allowed it. Thus the only major barrier to the private acquisition and use of Christian books was the capacity to read them.

The social fact of limited literacy goes a long way toward explaining why relatively little is said in early Christian literature about the private reading of Christian books. The first explicit notice appears in Hippolytus's *Apostolic Tradition* (36): "If on any day there is no instruction [in the Christian gathering], let each one at home take the scriptures and read sufficiently in passages that he finds profitable." Too much should not be inferred from this admonition: only some could read, and it can hardly be supposed that every Christian had personal copies of scripture.[92] But if the statement reflects an ideal rather than an actual circumstance, it would have been completely pointless unless copies of scriptural texts were in the private possession of some, naturally of some who were literate. It was about the same time, according to Eusebius (*H.E.* 4.26.12), that Melito, bishop of Sardis, responded to a request from a layman, a certain Onesimus, to provide to him "extracts *(eklogai)* from the Law and the Prophets concerning the Savior." These were not, to be sure, books as such but a collection of passages ("testimonies") culled from the scripture of Judaism, yet the case indicates that religious texts were wanted and obtained by individual Christians who were both literate and inquiring. Clement of Alexandria (*Paed.* 2.10.96) advises that the Christian husband and wife should spend the day in prayer, reading, and good works, and elsewhere (*Strom.* 7.7.49) he recommends "readings in the scriptures before meals"—and thus apparently presumes the availability and use of scriptural texts in at least some domestic settings.[93]

Evidence for the private use of Christian books becomes more abundant in the third and later centuries. Origen in various homilies speaks of the importance of reading the scriptures at home, recommending it as a daily exercise of at least a few hours.[94] His admonitions were provoked by the indifference, indeed aversion, of some to the private reading of scripture; they complained of the *taedium verbi divini*—the irksomeness of the private study of scripture.[95] Origen certainly does not assume the literacy of all Christians, but he does presuppose the availability of texts to those who could read. For those who find the task difficult, he proposes a kind of graduated syllabus whereby one begins with the most intelligible books (Esther, Judith, Tobit, or the Wisdom of Solomon), moves on to the Gospels, Epistles, and Psalms, and only later tackles difficult and seemingly unrewarding texts like Leviticus or Numbers.[96]

No early Christian teacher was more insistent on the importance of the private reading of scripture than John Chrysostom, the bishop of Constantinople.[97] Besides delivering a homily on the theme "That the [Private] Reading of Scripture is Useful" (*Hom. in princip. Act.* 3), he repeatedly encouraged his hearers to study the scriptures at home. "I wish to ask one favor of you all," he begins one homily, "that each of you take in hand that section of the Gospels which is to be read among you on the first day of the week, or on the sabbath, and before the day arrives that he sit down at home and read it through, and carefully consider its contents, and examine all its parts well, what is clear, what is obscure, what seems to be contradictory but is not really; and when you have tried, in a word, every point, then go to hear it read" (*Hom. in Joh.* 11.1). Just as the scriptures are "a chest of medicines" capable of relieving ailments of the soul, so the ignorance of scripture is "the cause of all evils" (*Hom. in Col.* 9). Chrysostom frequently reproached his hearers for their unwillingness to study it privately: "Who among you, if required, could recite one Psalm or any other part of divine scriptures? No one" (*Hom.in Matt.* 2. 9). For the dearth of private reading Chrysostom had heard many excuses: a lack of leisure, a lack of the books, a lack of interest, even "I am not a monk."[98] Elsewhere (*Hom. in Joh.* 32) Chrysostom complains that not very many Christians had books of scripture: "Which of you when at home takes some Christian book in hand, goes over its contents and searches the scriptures? None can say that he does, but with most we shall find draughts and dice, but books nowhere, except among a few. Even those few have the same dispositions as the many, for they tie up their books and keep them always put away in cases, and all their care is for the fineness of the parchments and the beauty of the letters, not for reading them." Apparently the problem was not that Christian books were especially difficult or expensive to procure for private use, but that few troubled to obtain them, and fewer still to read them.

Indifference to the private study of Christian texts is addressed by the *Apostolic Constitutions,* which gives the well-to-do Christian specific advice (2.4–6) about reading:

> *If you are in good circumstances and do not need to work for your living, do not wander here and there wasting your time, but be always zealous to visit your brothers in the faith. Meditate with them, and instruct yourself in the living word. If not, stay at home and read in the Law, in the book of Kings and the Prophets, and in the Gospel which is their fulfillment. But keep far from yourself all pagan books. . . . What do you find wanting in the*

word of God that you should rush to pagan stories! If you want to read history, you have the book of Kings; if works of wise men and philosophers, you have the prophets . . . ; if you desire poetry, you have the Psalms of David; if you want information about the beginnings of the world, you have Genesis, written by the great man Moses; if laws and ordinances, you have the Law. . . . If you read in this way, you will grow greatly and increase in the faith.

The passage assumes the availability of scriptural texts for private use, at least among the affluent who could afford them and had the leisure to read them. The concern here, however, is an indifference toward the private reading of the scriptures that resulted from the diverting appeal of non-Christian literature. The claim that the books of Christian scripture constitute a veritable literary omnibus, offering a full sampling of authors, subject matters, and genres and providing reading that is not only informative but edifying, suggests that the reading of other literature is superfluous. This argument, made on literary grounds, was directed to people who would read in any case: the question being not whether to read, but what. Of course, the highly literate people—those who not only could read but who valued good literature —were often the hardest to persuade to read scripture: they were put off by its uncultivated style, its obscurities, and its peculiar conceptuality. Christian teachers and writers, cultivated men themselves, were well aware of these obstacles to would-be readers of scripture and regularly sought to overcome them.

The exercise of literacy in private reading was clearly a two-edged sword in the early church. So far as literacy existed among the faithful, it was valued as a means to spiritual development and fuller understanding through the private reading of Christian books. But literacy also provided access to texts that might subvert the reader's Christian conviction, and private reading was beyond any close regulation. Thus, if literate Christians were encouraged to read Christian books, the scriptures above all, they were often also warned against other reading. Non-Christian literature, suffused with elements of Greco-Roman religion and mythology, was widely thought to endanger spiritual health. At least as great a danger was perceived in those Christian books that were found to be religiously defective—whether merely misleading or flagrantly heterodox—and therefore unsuitable for Christian reading. Many such books enjoyed wide currency in the first several centuries of the church and were privately accessible to the literate, and for just that reason caveats were issued against their use.

Athanasius in his famous 39th Festal Letter, issued in 367, enumerated the canonical books of the old and new covenants. In addition to the canonical books—"scripture proper"—he mentions "other books besides these which have not indeed been put in the canon but have been appointed by the fathers as reading matter for those who have just come forward and wish to be instructed in the doctrine of piety," namely, the Wisdom of Solomon, Sirach, Esther, Judith, Tobit, the *Didache*, and *The Shepherd* of Hermas. Altogether disallowed, however, are the "apocrypha," which are not specifically named but are described as "fabrications of the heretics." It was not Athanasius's sole purpose to stipulate what might be publicly read in the church—indeed, by this time the likelihood that a heretical book would be publicly (that is, liturgically) read was very small. He also meant to stipulate what might be read privately, for he speaks of the canonical books as "the springs of salvation, in order that he who is thirsty may refresh himself with the words contained in them." Another early canon list, the Muratorian fragment, though mainly concerned with what books could be publicly read, nevertheless casts a glance at private reading by remarking of *The Shepherd* of Hermas that "it ought to be read, but it cannot be publicly read in the church" (lines 77–78).

The regulation of private reading was problematic not just because it was private but because the ostensibly Christian books whose use was discouraged were numerous, too numerous to be proscribed individually. Hence the safest rule for private reading was the strictest one: in the formulation of Cyril of Jerusalem, "What is not read in the church should not be read privately" (*Catech.* 4.36).[99] This principle, which presumes the availability of many texts, simultaneously excludes both non-Christian books and noncanonical Christian books. There were, to be sure, protests against such narrow strictures, and claims that wider reading was valuable,[100] but we can see in these early dilemmas spawned by private reading the ultimate roots of the *Index librorum prohibitorum*.

Modern manuscript finds offer corroboration and illustration of private reading in the early church. Some manuscripts were obviously produced for private use, though it must often remain uncertain whether a given manuscript was publicly or privately used. There is a special category of ancient manuscripts that consists of miniature codices, roughly analogous to modern pocket books, and clearly produced for private reading.[101] Appreciably smaller than ordinary codices, they range in size from about ten centimeters by fifteen down to a diminutive five centimeters by six and a half. As a rule they contain fewer pages than ordinary codices, though some are remarkably long.[102] In all, some fifty-five miniature codices are known, of which forty-five are parchment and ten papyrus; all belong to the third and later centuries; and most contain only one document or parts of one.

There are two striking things about these miniature codices. First, the large majority (forty-seven of fifty-five) contain Christian texts, which indicates that the miniature format was if not a uniquely Christian phenomenon, one heavily favored by Christians, and that literate Christians could and did possess books for private reading.[103] Chrysostom makes an interesting allusion to Christian ladies who wore little Gospel books hanging from their necks, thus keeping their devotional reading close at hand. This custom perhaps goes back to the second century, for the *Acts of Andrew* (23) describes Trophime as having "the Gospel on her bosom." Second, the preponderance of Christian writings found in these small codices are apocryphal. Although scriptural texts are among them—Exodus, Joshua, John, Galatians, and frequently the Psalms, for example—we also find, especially among the earlier examples, *The Shepherd* of Hermas (P. Oxy. 1783, 1828), the *Acts of John* (P. Oxy. 850), the *Acts of Peter* (P. Oxy. 849), the *Acts of Paul and Thecla* (P. Ant. 13), the *Didache* (P. Oxy. 1782), an apocryphal Gospel (P. Oxy. 840), the *Protevangelium of James* (P. Grenf. 8); and some other texts that were at least arguably apocryphal, for example, the Apocalypse (P. Oxy. 1080), Tobit (P. Oxy. 1594), 4 Ezra (P. Oxy. 1010), and Bel (Bodl. gr. bib. 2d). This underscores the popular nature of the apocryphal literature by showing its use for edifying private reading, and it also shows that official efforts to control what was read privately, whether by drawing up lists or formulating a general principle, were responses to the currency, especially in private hands, of apocryphal books.

In addition to pocket codices, opisthographs shed a little light on private reading. Although there are many opisthographs among the papyri, it was unusual to transcribe a text in this way, the only reason for doing so being economic. Most opisthographic manuscripts were either school texts or private copies made by or for persons of limited means. Not many early Christian texts were transcribed on rolls rather than in codices, but of those that were, most are opisthographs. Good examples are a copy of Hebrews written on the back of a roll containing an epitome of Livy (P. Oxy. 657 + P. S. I. 1292), a copy of the Apocalypse on the back of a roll of Exodus (P. Oxy. 1075), and a copy of *The Shepherd* of Hermas (P. Mich. 130) on the back of a documentary text. Such texts were probably private copies made for personal use.

Although they varied a great deal in quality, from the poor man's copy on a used piece of papyrus to the well-written and decorated miniature parchment codex adorning the breast of a matron, Christian books for private reading were often well produced. Chrysostom dismisses the value of fine parchments beautifully written in letters of gold if the texts are not read and understood (*Hom. in Joh.* 32). Jerome must stress the importance for private reading of the accuracy of the text above "gilding, Babylonian parchment, and arabesque decoration" (*Ep.* 107.12) and bemoans the fact that "parchments are dyed purple, gold is melted for lettering, and manuscripts are decked with jewels," while the needy are neglected (*Ep.* 22.32). Just as Roman bibliophiles were often satirized for collecting books for show, so some Christians sought to display their piety, as well as their wealth, in fancy copies of scripture that went unread.

From these various bits of evidence several general conclusions can be drawn. It seems clear that literate Christians were able to obtain Christian texts for private reading. Because the matter of their cost almost never comes up, expense does not appear to have been an obstacle.[104] Some cost was involved, no doubt, but it was not prohibitive for most. It should probably be assumed that texts were obtained by private transcription, since in all the allusions to private reading there is no mention of a commercial trade in Christian books. Moreover, the church strongly encouraged its literate members to religious cultivation through the private reading of Christian books.[105] The value of private reading, however, depended on what was read, and the currency of apocryphal and heretical texts as well as the persistent aesthetic appeal of pagan literature meant that private reading would not be endorsed as an unqualified good. Yet the worry about what Christians might read privately is itself a telling indication that Christian texts were available in great variety and number.

THE MAGICAL USE OF CHRISTIAN BOOKS

Apart from public and private reading, though ultimately in consequence of it, Christian books, particularly scriptural texts, were also employed for magical purposes. Superstition is no respecter of ethnic, social, religious, or intellectual distinction, and it was inevitable that magical ideas and practices, which were widespread in the ancient world, would find a place among Christians too.[106] In a society in which few could read, texts were esoteric objects to many, and if spoken words were powerful, so were inscribed words, for they had the advantage of duration and secrecy.

Texts of certain words or formulae were readily believed to have an intrinsic power that could be appropriated to the advantage of the individual, and the trove of magical amulets and magical papyri surviving from antiquity shows how firmly potency might be lodged and used in written form.

The magical use of Christian texts was a function of the sanctity, authority, and indeed power attributed to the "divine words" they contained. It would be a mistake to think that the attribution of power to written words was a merely popular predilection. The learned Origen, urging Christians to attend closely to scripture and to struggle to understand obscure passages, suggested that even when there is no comprehension of the sense, the very sound of sacred words in the ear is somehow beneficial: if words have power in pagan magic, how much more powerful must be the truly divine words of scripture![107] When, later, John Chrysostom described the scriptures as "divine charms" *(theiai epodai)* he was not merely coining a metaphor, for in the same context he alludes without dissent to the popular conviction that "the devil will not dare approach a house where a Gospel-book is lying, much less will any evil spirit or any sort of sin ever touch or enter a soul which bears about with it such sentiments as it contains" (*Hom. in Joh.* 32). Elsewhere Chrysostom mentions that it is the practice of some to "suspend [extracts from] Gospels from their necks as a powerful amulet *(anti phulakes megales)* and carry them about in all places wherever they go."[108] Augustine, later still, considered it permissible in case of a headache to sleep with a copy of the Gospel of John under one's pillow.[109] In these instances it is not that what is read and understood confers power on the reader (however much the fathers desired and promoted that), but that the texts themselves or the words as written or spoken are effective objects.

The popularity of magical uses of scripture is more amply documented by ancient papyri than in literary sources, for among the papyri are many texts that were transcribed for use as amulets.[110] Most of these date from the fourth century and later, but a few are earlier. A diversity of texts are excerpted in Christian amulets. There is a preponderance of excerpts (forty-two) from Psalm texts, among which the initial verse of Psalm 90 (91) was frequently used. In addition, the Lord's prayer was transcribed for this purpose; a few amulets bring together the opening words (incipits) of each of the (four) Gospels; in others various verses that had some prophylactic connotation are brought together. The widespread use of scriptural amulets is indirectly attested by the canons of the Council of Laodicea (360), which prohibit the clergy from following the practice (canon 36).

Some have suggested that the Christian use of scriptural texts on amulets may have been influenced by the Jewish practice of wearing *tephillin* (phylacteries) in obedience to Deut. 6:4–9 and 11:13–21, and Ex. 13:1–10, 11–16, which were understood to require that the divine commandments be bound onto one's person. The tephillin, small leather boxes tied to the head and left arm, contained the scripture passages that warranted the practice. The question of Jewish influence arises mainly from the fact that the Palestinian Talmud permits the use of Psalm 90 (91) as a prophylactic text, and that this Psalm frequently appears in Christian amulets (though the relevant passages from Exodus and Deuteronomy do not). Yet the Psalms were so much read in early Christianity, and Psalm 90 (91) is so appropriate as a prophylactic text that it seems unnecessary to seek here any dependence on Jewish practice. Apotropaic formulae were widely used in antiquity, often written on papyrus and carried as amulets. Hence it is better to see in Christian scriptural amulets only a specifically Christian manifestation of a broad cultural disposition.

This is clearly the case with a different kind of magical use of scripture, namely, the practice of bibliomancy, divination from a book. The most famous instance of Christian bibliomancy is furnished by Augustine's account of his conversion (*Conf.* 8.12.29). Seated in the garden at Cassiciacum, Augustine, in a state of spiritual torment, heard the sing-song voice of a child from a nearby house say, "Take and read, take and read," which he concluded could only be "a divine command to open my book of scripture and read the first passage on which my eyes should fall." He did so, opening a codex of Paul's epistles and striking on Rom. 13:13–14, which resolved his nagging doubts and brought him to full commitment to Christianity.[111] In this very narrative, and by way of explaining his response to the child's voice, Augustine recalled how Anthony, the Egyptian monk memorialized by Athanasius, "happened to be present at a Gospel reading, and took it as an admonition to himself when the words were read, 'Go, sell all you have, give to the poor, and you shall have treasure in heaven; and come, follow me'" (Mt. 19:21; compare Athanasius, *Vita Ant.* 2), and so Anthony was converted. A variety of similar instances of bibliomancy can be cited in the fourth and later centuries, whereby either the chance overhearing of a scriptural text was taken as a personal omen *(kledon)* or a scriptural book was randomly consulted for a personal directive or prediction.[112]

There was nothing especially Christian in this practice except the books from which omens were sought. Greeks were well acquainted with the *sortes Homericae,* and Romans with the *sortes Vergilianae—*

that is, opening at random poetic books (inspired by the Muses) and taking the first words to catch the eye as an omen of immediate personal relevance.[113] Bibliomancy was also practiced by Jews—and thus we have *sortes Biblicae*.[114] The popular Christian use of the scriptures, both the Old Testament and the New, for oracular purposes thus followed a well-trodden path. It was not the product of any particular influence, but only a Christian version of a broad tendency in popular culture. Christian bibliomancy, like Jewish, sprang from a high regard for scripture and more particularly a strong conviction of its inspired quality. Christianity, of course, had from the beginning placed a high theological value on the prophetic character of scripture, but bibliomancy appears to have had little or nothing to do with that. Instead, it shows only how far a prophetic understanding of scripture was capable of being generalized, personalized, and trivialized in popular and private use. Some patristic writers protested against divination by scripture. Augustine, for whom it had once proved decisive, expressed his reservations (*Ep.* 55.37): "Regarding those who draw lots from the pages of the Gospel *(de paginis evangelicis sortes legunt)*, although it could be wished that they would do this rather than run about consulting demons, I do not like this custom of wishing to turn the divine oracles to worldly business and the vanity of this life, when their object is another life."

There was yet another method than bibliomancy for using the books of scripture in fortune-telling. A number of manuscripts dating from the fourth through the seventh centuries present on each page, after the scriptural text, a brief statement introduced by the word *hermeneia* (interpretation).[115] Because they are introduced in this way these statements have sometimes been thought to represent an incipient type of biblical commentary. But far from interpreting the scriptural text, these statements are answers to questions, and some typical answers are, "You will receive joy from God"; "Expect a great miracle"; "After ten days it will happen." Although the questions are not preserved in any early Christian books, we can tell what kind of fortune-telling system this was from its close resemblance to an ancient Greek oracle book known as the *Sortes Astrampsychi*, probably composed in Egypt during the third century C.E.[116] That work provided ninety-two questions, and then sets of ten possible answers to each question, and an introductory letter giving instructions on the use of the system. The inquirer selected a numbered question and then chose another number from one to ten ("God will put the number into his mouth," say the directions). These two numbers were used to find in the tables of answers the relevant response to the question. Here, then, is an oracular method that does not make use of the text of scripture but was sometimes inserted into scriptural books, and some early Christian manuscripts present a Christian adaptation of this system. Nevertheless, that scriptural books were made its bibliographic vehicle presupposes that scripture itself had already come to be viewed and used as an oracular resource.[117]

If these various personal, magical employments of scripture seem peculiar or perverse, they nevertheless attest the grip these books had taken on Christian imagination and the many capacities that were attributed to them as "divine writings" containing "divine oracles" *(ta theia logia)*. But behind the sundry magical uses of these books lies the regular solemn reading and hearing of scripture in Christian worship, in which the power of scripture was experienced and emphasized as the source of divine revelation—a power that belonged to words, but no less to the books in which they stood.

ABBREVIATIONS

The following abbreviations are used in the notes.

AB	Anchor Bible
ABD	*Anchor Bible Dictionary*
ACW	Ancient Christian Writers
AGB	*Archiv für Geschichte des Buchwesens*
AJA	*American Journal of Archaeology*
AJPhil	*American Journal of Philology*
AKG	Arbeiten zur Kirchengeschichte
ANRW	*Aufstieg und Niedergang der römischen Welt*, ed. H. Temporini and W. Haase, Berlin, 1972–
ANTF	Arbeiten zur neutestamentlichen Textforschung
APF	*Archiv für Papyrusforschung*
ArchStenog	*Archiv für Stenographie*
ASNU	Acta seminarii neotestamentici upsaliensis
AusBibR	*Australian Biblical Review*
BA	*Biblical Archaeologist*
BASOR	*Bulletin of the American Schools of Oriental Research*
BETL	Bibliotheca ephemeridum theologicarum louvaniensium
BHT	Beiträge zur historischen Theologie
Bib	*Biblica*
BibTrans	Bible Translator
BJRL	*Bulletin of the John Rylands Library*
BR	*Biblical Research*
BSOAS	*Bulletin of the School of Oriental and African Studies*
BZ	*Biblische Zeitschrift*
CBQ	*Catholic Biblical Quarterly*
CBQMS	Catholic Biblical Quarterly Monograph Series
CErc	*Cronache Ercolanesi*
CIJ	*Corpus inscriptionum iudaicarum*, ed. J. B. Frey
CIL	*Corpus inscriptionum latinarum*
CJ	Classical Journal

CP	*Classical Philology*
CQ	*Classical Quarterly*
CR	*Classical Review*
CSEL	Corpus scriptorum ecclesiasticorum latinorum
CW	*Classical World*
DACL	*Dictionnaire d'archéologie chrétienne et de liturgie*, ed. F. Cabrol, 1907–53
DJD	Discoveries in the Judean Desert
EL	*Ephemerides Liturgica*
EvQ	*Evangelical Quarterly*
EvTh	*Evangelische Theologie*
ExpT	*Expository Times*
FC	Fathers of the Church
FRLANT	Forschungen zur Religion und Literatur des Alten und Neuen Testaments
GCS	Griechischen christlichen Schriftsteller
GR	*Greece and Rome*
GRBS	*Greek, Roman and Byzantine Studies*
Greg	*Gregorianum*
HeythJ	*Heythrop Journal*
HNT	Handbuch zum Neuen Testament
HSCP	*Harvard Studies in Classical Philology*
HTR	*Harvard Theological Review*
HUCA	*Hebrew Union College Annual*
IDB	*Interpreter's Dictionary of the Bible*
IDBSup	*Interpreter's Dictionary of the Bible Supplementary Volume*
IEJ	*Israel Exploration Journal*
Int	*Interpretation*
JAC	*Jahrbuch für Antike und Christentum*
JBL	*Journal of Biblical Literature*
JCE	*Journal of Christian Education*
JEA	*Journal of Egyptian Archaeology*
JEH	*Journal of Ecclesiastical History*
JETS	*Journal of the Evangelical Theological Society*
JHS	*Journal of Hellenic Studies*
JJS	*Journal of Jewish Studies*
JLH	*Journal of Library History*
JQR	*Jewish Quarterly Review*
JR	*Journal of Religion*
JRH	*Journal of Religious History*
JRS	*Journal of Roman Studies*
JSJ	*Journal for the Study of Judaism*
JSNT	*Journal for the Study of the New Testament*
JTS	*Journal of Theological Studies*
MH	*Museum Helveticum*
NHS	Nag Hammadi Studies
NovT	*Novum Testamentum*
NovTSupp	Supplements to Novum Testamentum

NTAbh	Neutestamentliche Abhandlungen
NTS	*New Testament Studies*
NTTS	New Testament Tools and Studies
PBA	*Proceedings of the British Academy*
PG	*Patrologia graeca*, J. Migne
PL	*Patrologia latina*, J. Migne
QD	Quaestiones Disputatae
RAC	*Reallexikon für Antike und Christentum*, ed. Th. Klauser
RB	*Revue biblique*
RBén	*Revue bénédictine*
RE	*Real-Encyclopädie der classischen Altertums Wissenschaft*, ed. A. Pauly and G. Wissowa
REA	*Revue des études anciennes*
RevScRel	*Revue des sciences religieuses*
RGG	*Die Religion in Geschichte und Gegenwart*
RHE	*Revue d'histoire ecclésiastique*
RhM	*Rheinisches Museum für Philologie*
RHPR	*Revue d'histoire et de philosophie religieuses*
RHR	*Revue de l'histoire des religions*
RQ	*Revue de Qumran*
RSR	*Religious Studies Review*
SBA	Sitzungsberichte der (königlichen) bayerischen Akademie der Wissenschaften
SBLDS	Society of Biblical Literature Dissertation Series
SBLMS	Society of Biblical Literature Monograph Series
SBLSBS	Society of Biblical Literature Sources for Biblical Study
SBS	Stuttgarter Bibelstudien
SBT	Studies in Biblical Theology
SC	Sources chrétiennes
SMSR	*Studi e materiali di storia delle religioni*
SNTSMS	Society for New Testament Studies Monograph Series
SP	*Studia Papyrologica*
SPAW	Sitzungsberichte der preussischen Akademie der Wissenschaften
StD	Studies and Documents
StEv	*Studia Evangelica*
STh	*Studia Theologica*
StPat	*Studia Patristica*
SUNT	Studien zur Umwelt des Neuen Testaments
TAPA	*Transactions of the American Philological Association*
TDNT	*Theological Dictionary of the New Testament*, ed. G. Kittel and G. Friedrich
ThRev	*Theologische Revue*
ThZ	*Theologische Zeitschrift*
TLZ	*Theologische Literaturzeitung*
TR	*Theologische Rundschau*
TRE	*Theologische Realenzyklopädie*, ed. G. Krause and G. Muller, 1977–

TS	*Theological Studies*
TU	Texte und Untersuchungen
VC	*Vigiliae christianae*
WMANT	Wissenschaftliche Monographien zum Alten und Neuen Testament
WUNT	Wissenschaftliche Untersuchungen zum Neuen Testament
YCS	*Yale Classical Studies*
ZKG	*Zeitschrift für Kirchengeschichte*
ZKT	*Zeitschrift für katholische Theologie*
ZNW	*Zeitschrift für die neutestamentliche Wissenschaft*
ZPE	*Zeitschrift für Papyrologie und Epigraphik*
ZTK	*Zeitschrift für Theologie und Kirche*

NOTES

CHAPTER I: LITERACY AND LITERARY CULTURE
IN EARLY CHRISTIANITY

1. *Contra Celsum* 1.62. Trans. H. Chadwick, *Origen: Contra Celsum* (Cambridge: Cambridge University Press, 1965).

2. One can only agree with G. Stanton, "Form Criticism Revisited," in *What about the New Testament? Essays in Honor of Christopher Evans*, ed. M. D. Hooker and C. Hickling (London: SCM Press, 1975), 13–27, when he comments (25, n. 13) that "we urgently need a full-scale study of the extent of literacy and of the uses to which writing was put in Judaism and Hellenism in the first century AD" in order to have a context for estimating literacy and its uses in early Christianity. See also William Harris, *Ancient Literacy* (Cambridge: Harvard University Press, 1989), which, though full of important observations for the larger Greco-Roman context, deals specifically with Jewish and Christian literacy only in passing.

3. A good instance is A. von Harnack, *Bible Reading in the Early Church*, trans. J. R. Wilkinson (London: Williams and Norgate, 1912), who did not address this question directly but, in arguing that the private reading of scripture by the laity was a normal and widespread practice from the earliest times, assumed there was something close to mass literacy among Christians of the first five centuries.

4. On the problem of definition, see Harris, *Ancient Literacy*, 3–8.

5. Ibid., 10–24.

6. P. Oxy. 2673, on which see further below in text.

7. Harris, *Ancient Literacy*. Harris provides an extensive bibliography of earlier studies, but see also R. Thomas, *Oral Tradition and Written Record in Classical Athens* (Cambridge: Cambridge University Press, 1989), esp. 15–34; E. Meyer, "Literacy in Late Antiquity" (Ph.D. diss., Yale University, 1988); and R. McKitterick, ed., *The Uses of Literacy in Early Mediaeval Europe* (Cambridge: Cambridge University Press, 1990), which, though it concerns a later period, offers many important observations on the phenomenon of literacy generally.

8. Harris acknowledges unrepresentative divergences on both sides of the

average. Thus, in some Hellenistic cities, most notably Teos, the rate of literacy might have reached 20–30 percent (141; cf. 329: 30–40%) owing to unusual educational foundations aimed at general education (130–33), whereas it is "unlikely that the overall literacy of the western provinces [of the Roman empire] even rose into the range of 5–10" (272).

9. Harris, *Ancient Literacy*, 323–37 (337).

10. It might be claimed, for example, that, by striving toward a quantification of the extent of basic literacy, the approach pays inadequate attention to the substance of the written tradition, differences in reading and writing skills, the levels (commonly different) of facility in them, the uses and functions of literacy, variations in the significance of literacy from one culture to another, and the complexity of literacy in bilingual or multilingual contexts. For many of the right questions, see the introductory essay of McKitterick in *Uses of Literacy*, 1–10.

11. For the mistaken inference from the centrality of scripture that the extent of literacy was greater among Christians than non-Christians, see, e.g., von Harnack, *Bible Reading*; J. Leipoldt and S. Morenz, *Heilige Schriften: Betrachtungen zur Religionsgeschichte der antiken Mittelmeerwelt* (Leipzig: Harrasowitz, 1953), 106–22; H. I. Marrou, "L'école dans l'antiquité tardive," in *La scuola nell'occidente latino dell'alto medioevo* (Spoleto: Presso la sede del Centro, 1972), 127–43 (136).

12. Among many modern studies, see esp. E. A. Judge, *The Social Pattern of Christian Groups in the First Century* (London: Tyndale, 1960); and "St. Paul and Classical Society," *JAC* 15 (1972): 19–36; G. Theissen, *The Social Setting of Pauline Christianity: Essays on Corinth*, trans. John H. Schutz (Philadelphia: Fortress Press, 1982); A. J. Malherbe, *Social Aspects of Early Christianity* (2d ed.; Philadelphia: Fortress Press, 1983); W. A. Meeks, *The First Urban Christians: The Social World of the Apostle Paul* (New Haven: Yale University Press, 1983); for the second and third centuries, see D. J. Kyrtatis, *The Social Structure of the Early Christian Communities* (London: Verso, 1987).

13. Meeks, *First Urban Christians*, 72–73, concluding an excellent survey of the social level of Christians in the Pauline churches and pointing to interesting indications that "the most active and prominent members of Paul's circle are people of high status inconsistency (low status crystallization). They are upwardly mobile; their achieved status is higher than their attributed status."

14. Harris, *Ancient Literacy*, 315, comments that it is most difficult to reach definite conclusions about the extent and level of literacy among shopkeepers and craftspeople, who constituted "a partly literate, partly semi-literate, partly illiterate social stratum in the high Empire."

15. Harris offers a good concise discussion of education in the late republican and early imperial periods (ibid., 233–48). Fuller but in some respects overly optimistic appraisals are given in S. F. Bonner, *Education in Ancient Rome* (Berkeley: University of California Press, 1977); H. I. Marrou, *A History of Education in Antiquity* (New York: Mentor, 1964); M. L. Clarke, *Higher Education in the Ancient World* (London: Routledge and Kegan Paul, 1971). See also A. D. Booth, "Elementary and Secondary Education in the Roman

Empire," *Florilegium* 1 (1979): 1–14; and "The Schooling of Slaves in First-Century Rome," *TAPA* 109 (1979): 11–19.

16. A useful overview is given in G. L. Espermann, *The Attitude of the Early Christian Latin Writers toward Pagan Literature and Learning* (CUA Patristic Studies; Cleveland: Zubal, 1984). Espermann also takes account of Greek Christian views and provides an extensive bibliography. See also H. Hagendahl, *Latin Fathers and the Classics* (SGLG, 6; Goteborg: Elanders, 1958); and E. A. Judge, "The Reaction against Classical Education in the New Testament," *JCE* 77 (1983): 7–14.

17. Note, however, that according to Eusebius (*H.E.* 6.3.8), Origen at one time engaged in "the teaching of letters" *(ten ton grammatikon logon didaskalian)*, i.e., grammatical studies, but gave it up.

18. Origen is an example (Eusebius, *H.E.* 6.2.7–10), but his family seems to have been reasonably well off.

19. On this issue, see J. Lebreton, "Le déssaccord de foi populaire et de theologie savante," *RHE* 19 (1923): 481–506; H. J. Carpenter, "Popular Christianity and the Theologians in the Early Centuries," *JTS*, n.s., 14 (1963): 294–310; and N. Brox, "Der einfache Glaube und die Theologie: Zur altkirchlichen Geschichte eines Dauerproblems," *Kairos* 14 (1972): 161–87.

20. Harris, *Ancient Literacy,* 281–82, too hastily dismisses interest in literacy among the Jews.

21. *Contra Apion.* 2.204, *Ant.* 4.211; cf. T. Levi 13.2; Philo, *Ad Gaium* 115, 210.

22. P. T. Megillah 3.73d, P. T. Ketuboth 13.35c. The town of Beitar was said to have had five hundred schools with no fewer than five hundred students in each (!) soon after 70 C.E. (P. T. Taanith 4.69a). On the development of Jewish schools, see M. Hengel, *Judaism and Hellenism* (Philadelphia: Fortress Press, 1974), 1:78–83; and on the organization and methods of Jewish schools, see S. Safrai, "Education and the Study of the Torah," in *The Jewish People in the First Century* (Compendia Rerum Iudaicarum ad Novum Testamentum, sec. 1), ed. S. Safrai and M. Stern (Philadelphia: Fortress Press, 1976), 2:945–70.

23. Early ordinances concerning schooling are attributed to Simeon ben Shetah (103–76 B.C.E.) and to Joshua ben Gamala (ca. 65 C.E.) in P. T. Kebuoth 8.32c and T. B. Baba Batra 21a. Hengel, *Judaism and Hellenism,* 1:82, remarks that "without a considerable number of Jewish elementary schools, the rise of the Rabbinate, the extension of the popular Pharisaic movement and even the establishment of the basic institution of the synagogue, which presupposes a basic stock of people knowledgeable in the law in particular places, would be inconceivable." On Jewish elementary schools, see B. Gerhardsson, *Memory and Manuscript: Oral Tradition and Written Transmission in Rabbinic Judaism and Early Christianity* (ASNU 22; Lund: C. W. K. Gleerup, 1964), 56–66.

24. Safrai, "Education," unguardedly asserts that "everyone" had the ability to read (954) but by his own accounting recognizes that this was not so: females normally did not attend schools, and the rural population had little opportunity.

25. On Greek in Palestine, see esp. J. N. Sevenster, *Do You Know Greek? How Much Greek Could the First Jewish Christians Have Known?* (NovTSup 19; Leiden: Brill, 1968); and Hengel, *Judaism and Hellenism,* 1:58–65. On the

concurrence and interplay of languages in Palestinian Judaism in the period, see J. Fitzmyer, "The Languages of Palestine in the First Century A.D.,," in *A Wandering Aramean: Collected Aramaic Essays* (Missoula: Scholars Press, 1979), 29–56; and J. Barr, "Hebrew, Aramaic, and Greek in the Hellenistic Age," in *The Cambridge History of Judaism*, ed. W. D. Davies and L. Finkelstein (New York: Cambridge University Press, 1989), 2:79–114. For Greek aspects of Jewish (including rabbinical) education, see S. Liebermann, *Greek in Jewish Palestine* (New York: Feldheim, 1965), 1–67; and Hengel, *Judaism and Hellenism*, 1:65–78.

26. See E. Rawson, *Intellectual Life in the Late Roman Republic* (London: Duckworth, 1985), 50–53.

27. On the appearance of the illiterate in the papyri, see esp. H. C. Youtie, "Agrammatos: An Aspect of Greek Society in Egypt," *HSCP* 75 (1971): 161–76; "Because They Do Not Know Letters," *ZPE* 19 (1975): 101–8; and "Upographeus: The Social Impact of Illiteracy in Graeco-Roman Egypt," *ZPE* 17 (1975): 201–21.

28. Justin, in the prologue to the *Dialogue with Trypho*, says that he was converted to Christianity by hearing preaching in which the argument from prophecy played a large role.

29. On the liturgical reading of Christian texts, see ch. 5.

30. Later Christian writers often recall this description of the apostles: e.g., Origen, *Contra Celsum* 8.47; Jerome, *In Matt.* 4.19–20; Augustine, *De civitate dei* 18.49.

31. See esp. E. Wipzycka, "Le degré d'alphabétisation en Egypt byzantine," *REA* 30 (1984): 279–96, esp. 288–95. The Apostolic Canons (third century) entertain the possibility that in Egypt a bishop might be illiterate. The famous case of the illiterate lector in the Egyptian village of Chysis at the beginning of the fourth century (P. Oxy. 2673) is not a contradiction in terms if he was illiterate in Greek but not in Coptic. For alternative explanations, see E. Wipzycka, "Un lecteur qui ne sait pas écrire ou un chrétien qui ne veut se souiller?" *ZPE* 50 (1983): 117–21; and G. W. Clarke, "An Illiterate Lector?" *ZPE* 57 (1984): 103–4. More problematic is a certain Aurelius, appointed lector in Carthage (Cyprian, *Ep.* 38), who elsewhere (*Ep.* 27.1) is said not to have known his letters. On congregational readers, see ch. 5.

32. Thus Pachomius provided (*Praecepta*, 139–40) that all postulants be taught to read. Cf. Basil, *Regulae*, 15. On the place of books and reading in Pachomian monasticism, see also ch. 4.

33. This in contrast to the claims of Harnack, *Bible Reading*. On the private reading of Christian literature, see ch. 5.

34. The same ambiguity belongs to the term *literature* itself, which is sometimes taken to mean "everything in print," but at other times it refers only to such works as are "notable for literary form or expression." For a discussion of the problem, see R. Wellek and A. Warren, *Theory of Literature* (3d rev. ed., London: Jonathan Cape, 1966), 20–28.

35. "Über die Anfänge der patristischen Literatur," *Historische Zeitschrift* 48 (1882): 417–72; reprinted separately by Wissenschaftliche Buchgesellschaft, Darmstadt, 1954. Subsequent references are to the original publication. To my knowledge the essay has never been translated.

36. Ibid., 429. Overbeck is speaking here specifically of the letter, but the idea is valid for his conception of Urliteratur generally.

37. Ibid., 423.

38. See Ph. Vielhauer, "Franz Overbeck und die neutestamentliche Wissenschaft," in *Aufsätze zum Neuen Testament* (TB 31; Munich: Kaiser, 1965), 235–52 (=*EvTh* 10 (1950–51): 193–207). For the importance of the concept of "forms" in Overbeck's work, see also M. Tetz, "Über Formengeschichte in der Kirchengeschichte," *ThZ* 17 (1961): 413–31.

39. "Anfänge," 428–32.

40. Ibid., 443.

41. Ibid.: "To that extent [Christian literature] can be termed, if not purely Christian, purely religious."

42. Ibid., 444.

43. Ibid., 436. For a fuller exposition of *Urgeschichte*, see Overbeck, *Christentum und Kultur*, ed. C. A. Bernoulli (Darmstadt: Wissenschaftliche Buchgesellschaft, 1963), 20–24. On the conception, see E. Guttgemanns, *Candid Questions Concerning Form Criticism*, trans. W. D. Doty (Pittsburgh: Pickwick, 1979), 155–57; and J.-C. Emmelius, *Tendenzkritik und Formgeschichte: Der Beitrag Franz Overbecks zur Auslegung der Apostelgeschichte im 19. Jahrhundert* (FKD, 27; Göttingen: Vandenhoeck und Ruprecht, 1975), 162–71.

44. Ibid., 436–38. Overbeck speaks (437) of the formation of the New Testament canon as the *Totenschein* (death certificate) of Urliteratur. Cf. Vielhauer, who comments that for Overbeck the notion of Urliteratur "is not a formal-temporal concept for the delimitation of a literary epoch, but an expression for the demise of the forces that created it—for a process that we designate by way of anticipation as the end of *Urgeschichte*" ("Franz Overbeck und die neutestamentliche Wissenschaft," 248).

45. "Anfänge," 432: "And indeed, they are absent in [the church's] literature from this time on not only in fact, *but because there was no possibility of their further cultivation*" (emphasis added). Although these genres do appear in the later apocryphal literature (much more of which has come to light since he wrote), Overbeck avers that "already the designation of this literature as apocryphal shows that in history it has, so to speak, only an illegitimate existence, and even that its recognition depends only on the fiction" of a primitive origin (ibid.). That is, Overbeck thought that the production of apocryphal literature presupposed that the genres it employed were peculiar to an earlier and now concluded period.

46. Overbeck clearly overstated the generic peculiarity of early Christian writings. Furthermore, his appeal to the formation of the New Testament canon as a function and symptom of the transition from Urgeschichte to Geschichte, and so also from Urliteratur to Literatur, presumes that canon formation occurred in the second century, whereas modern canon studies locate it rather in the fourth and fifth centuries. Thus, the distinction between canonical and apocryphal literature arises much later than he supposed. Further, Overbeck overdraws the contrast between primitive and "historical" Christianity by taking imminent eschatology and otherworldliness as the distinctive features only of the former and ignoring the dialectical dimension in earliest Christianity's attitude toward the world. Indeed, by positing such

a sharp break between Urgeschichte and Geschichte that any continuity between the two is lost altogether, his conception becomes essentially unhistorical.

47. Citations are made from the English translation, *Light from the Ancient East: The New Testament Illustrated by Recently Discovered Texts of the Graeco-Roman World*, trans. L. R. M. Strachan (London: Hodder and Stoughton, 1927), 4th German ed., rev. and enlarged, 1923.

48. *Light from the Ancient East*, 10.

49. Ibid., 62; cf. 69: "The New Testament has proved to be, as a whole, a monument of late colloquial Greek, and in the great majority of its component parts the monument of a more or less *popular* colloquial language" (emphasis in original).

50. Ibid., 247, 246. Throughout his long chapter on "The New Testament as Literature" (146–251) Deissmann attends almost exclusively to the letters of Paul, offers only three pages of comment on other New Testament documents, and leaves the Gospels and Acts out of account.

51. *RGG* (2 ed., 1929), 3:1681.

52. K. L. Schmidt, "Die Stellung der Evangelien in der allgemeinen Literaturgeschichte," in *Eucharisterion: Studien zur Religion und Literatur des Alten und Neuen Testaments Hermann Gunkel zum 60 Geburtstag*, ed. H. Schmidt (Göttingen: Vandenhoeck und Ruprecht, 1923), 50–134; cf. also K. L. Schmidt, *Der Rahmen der Geschichte Jesu* (Berlin: Trowitzsch, 1919), 76, 125; R. Bultmann, *The History of the Synoptic Tradition*, trans. J. Marsh (New York: Harper and Row, 1963), 4; M. Dibelius. *From Tradition to Gospel*, trans. B. L. Woolf (London: Nicholson and Watson, 1934), 1–6.

53. M. Dibelius, *From Tradition to Gospel*, 3–4; cf. R. Bultmann, *History of the Synoptic Tradition*, 321–22.

54. As characterized by Dibelius, the aim of form criticism is "to rediscover the origin and the history of the particular units [of tradition] and thereby to throw some light on the history of the tradition *before* it took literary form" ("Zur Formgeschichte der Evangelien," *TR* n.f. 1 [1929], 185–216 [187; emphasis added]; the statement is quoted by Bultmann, *History*, 4).

55. Bultmann, *History*, 4: "The literature in which the life of a given community, even the primitive Christian community, has taken shape, springs out of quite definite conditions and wants of life from which grows up a quite definite style and quite specific forms and categories. Thus every literary category has its 'life situation' (*Sitz im Leben*: Gunkel), whether it be worship in its different forms, or work, or hunting, or war. The Sitz im Leben is not, however, an individual historical event but a typical situation or occupation in the life of a community. In the same way, the literary 'category,' or 'form' through which a particular item is classified is a sociological concept."

56. Guttgemanns, *Candid Questions*, 127; cf. 189–93.

57. Ibid., 178–89, for a sketch of the history of the idea.

58. Dibelius, *From Tradition to Gospel*, 1.

59. Ibid., 9 (emphasis added).

60. On oral tradition, see below in text.

61. For useful surveys of noncanonical Jewish literature, see G. W. E. Nickelsburg, *Jewish Literature between the Bible and the Mishnah: A Historical*

and Literary Introduction (Philadelphia: Fortress Press, 1981); M. E. Stone, *Jewish Writings of the Second Temple Period* (Philadelphia: Fortress Press, 1984); R. A. Kraft and G. W. E. Nickelsburg, eds., *Early Judaism and Its Modern Interpreters* (Atlanta: Scholars Press, 1986), esp. pt. 3, "The Literature."

62. See, e. g., Dibelius, *From Tradition to Gospel*, 10–11, and the discussion of this point by Guttgemanns, *Candid Questions*, 136–39.

63. N. Perrin, "The Evangelist as Author: Reflections on Method in the Study and Interpretation of the Synoptic Gospels and Acts," *BR* 17 (1972): 5–18. The literature on redaction criticism is by now enormous. See the still useful survey of J. Rohde, *Rediscovering the Teaching of the Evangelists* (London: SCM Press, 1968), esp. 16–21, 37–38, on the role of the evangelists as authors.

64. That texts were both produced and copied at Qumran is indisputable, even if a scriptorium cannot be archaeologically identified. See F. M. Cross, *The Ancient Library of Qumran and Modern Biblical Studies* (Garden City, N.Y.: Doubleday, 1961), 66–67, and ch. 4.

65. See Guttgemanns, *Candid Questions*, 130–35, noting that the written character of apocalyptic tradition and the authoritative study of scripture were "an inalienable element of Jewish apocalyptic" (134) and that apart from the absence of a historical analogy in Judaism, the form critical assumption of a natural antinomy between imminent end expectation and literary activity is a "quite general *psychological* conclusion from analogy" (131, emphasis in original) that has no historical basis. The modern study of Jewish and Christian apocalypses has amply demonstrated that they are self-consciously literary and spring from an intensive literary tradition rich in established forms and conventions. See esp. J. J. Collins, "Toward the Morphology of a Genre," *Semeia* 14 (1979): 1–20.

66. Noteworthy are Malherbe, *Social Aspects*, ch. 2, "Social Level and Literary Culture"; and Loveday Alexander, "Luke's Preface in the Context of Greek Preface-Writing," *NovT* 28 (1986): 48–74, with some of the results of her Oxford dissertation of 1977, now published as *The Preface to Luke's Gospel: Literary Conventions and Social Context in Luke 1.1–4 and Acts 1.1* (SNTSMS 78; Cambridge: Cambridge University Press, 1993). The discussion by W. C. van Unnik, "First Century A.D. Literary Culture and Early Christian Literature," gives only passing attention to social questions.

67. See esp. Ph. Vielhauer, *Geschichte der urchristlichen Literatur* (Berlin: de Gruyter, 1975); H. Koester, *Introduction to the New Testament*, vol. 2, History and Literature of Early Christianity (Philadelphia: Fortress Press, 1982); E. Hennecke, *New Testament Apocrypha*, ed. W. Schneemelcher, trans. R. McL. Wilson et al., 2 vols. (Philadelphia: Westminster, 1963–66); and more broadly, A. von Harnack, *Geschichte der altchristlichen Literatur bis Eusebius* (2d ed.; Leipzig: Hinrichs, 1958); O. Bardenhewer, *Geschichte der altkirchlichen Literatur* (repr. Darmstadt: Wissenschaftliche Buchgesellschaft, 1962); and E. J. Goodspeed, *A History of Early Christian Literature*, rev. by Robert Grant (Chicago: University of Chicago Press, 1966).

68. The attempt by J. A. T. Robinson, *Redating the New Testament* (Philadelphia: Westminster, 1976), to argue for a pre-70 date for most of the New

Testament literature usefully challenges the consensus by showing the tenuous basis of many of its claims, but the alternatives he proposes are not convincing.

69. For arguments toward an early dating of these see, e.g., J. D. Crossan, *Four Other Gospels* (Minneapolis: Winston, 1985).

70. For the classic statement of the Q hypothesis see B. H. Streeter, *The Four Gospels* (London: Macmillan, 1924), 150–292. The discovery of the Gospel of Thomas, which exhibits the very form that Q was supposed to have had—namely, a collection of sayings without narrative context—at least confirmed that such a literary genre was current in the early church. On the genre of Q see J. M. Robinson, "Logoi Sophon," in J. M. Robinson and H. Koester, *Trajectories through Early Christianity* (Philadelphia: Fortress Press, 1971), 71–113. Recent and intensive work on Q not only supports its written form, but envisions successive recensions of it over a period of time. See esp. J. S. Kloppenborg, *The Formation of Q* (Philadelphia: Fortress Press, 1987), who also provides a convenient statement of the arguments in favor of the documentary character of Q (41–51).

71. On the (written) sources behind the Gospels, see esp. the discussion by H. Koester, *Ancient Christian Gospels: Their History and Development* (Philadelphia: Trinity International, 1990), 253–55 (on the passion narrative), 286–89 (on Mark); and 250–67 (on John), with references to relevant studies. (To the same general point, but by a highly speculative route, cf. J. C. O'Neill, "The Lost Written Records of Jesus' Words and Deeds behind Our Records," *JTS* 42 [1991]: 483–503.)

72. See, respectively, H. D. Betz, *Essays on the Sermon on the Mount* (Philadelphia: Fortress Press, 1985); and D. Wenham, *The Rediscovery of Jesus' Eschatological Discourse* (Sheffield: JSOT Press, 1984).

73. Note that Matthew speaks of the "book *(biblos)* of the genealogy of Jesus Christ" (1:1). Even if this means "birth record," a documentary form is implied. Cf. R. Brown, *The Birth of the Messiah* (Garden City: Doubleday, 1977), 58–59, with 69–70 (Matthew drew upon two preexisting genealogical lists, which had possibly already been joined); and 93–94 (Luke adopted and adapted a genealogical list current among Greek-speaking Jews).

74. See 1QS 6:6–7, CD 8:6, 9:8. On scripture interpretation at Qumran there is an enormous volume of literature. See, e.g., F. F. Bruce, *Biblical Exegesis in the Qumran Texts* (London: Tyndale, 1959); O. Betz, *Offenbarung und Schriftforschung in der Qumransekte* (Tübingen: Mohr, 1960); and G. Vermes, *Post-Biblical Jewish Studies* (Leiden: Brill, 1975), 35–56. See also S. D. Fraade, "Interpretive Authority in the Studying Community at Qumran," *JJS* 44 (1993): 46–69. On the library at Qumran, see ch. 5.

75. See, e.g., 1 Cor. 15:3–4; Acts 2:30–31; 3:18. Still useful on this point is C. H. Dodd, *The Apostolic Preaching and Its Developments* (London: Hodder and Stoughton, 1936). See more recently B. Lindars, "The Place of the Old Testament in the Formation of New Testament Theology," *NTS* 23 (1976–77): 59–66; and T. Holtz, "Zur Interpretation des Alten Testaments im Neuen Testament," *TLZ* 99 (1974): 19–32.

76. Scripture is explicitly cited approximately a hundred times in the Pauline epistles, although the citations are not evenly distributed among them:

especially high concentrations are found in Galatians and Romans, while quotations are absent in Philippians, 1–2 Thessalonians, Colossians, Titus, and Philemon. For the role of scripture in the Pauline letters, see esp. E. E. Ellis, *Paul's Use of the Old Testament* (Grand Rapids: Eerdmans, 1957); D.-A. Koch, *Die Schrift als Zeuge des Evangeliums: Untersuchungen zur Verwendung und zum Verständnis der Schrift bei Paulus* (BHT 69; Tübingen: Mohr, 1986); and R. B. Hays, *Echoes of Scripture in the Letters of Paul* (New Haven: Yale University Press, 1989). For a concise discussion, see D. M. Smith, "The Pauline Literature," in *It Is Written: Scripture Citing Scripture: Essays in Honor of Barnabas Lindars*, ed. D. A. Carson and H. G. M. Williamson, (Cambridge: Cambridge University Press, 1988), 265–91.

77. C. H. Dodd, *According to the Scriptures: The Substructure of New Testament Theology* (London: Nisbet, 1952); K. Stendahl, *The School of St. Matthew and Its Use of the Old Testament* (Uppsala, 1954; reprinted [with a new introduction] Philadelphia: Fortress Press, 1968); and B. Lindars, *New Testament Apologetic: The Doctrinal Significance of the Old Testament Quotations* (London: SCM Press, 1961). For a general discussion, see R. N. Longenecker, *Biblical Exegesis in the Apostolic Period* (Grand Rapids: Eerdmans, 1975); J. A. Fitzmyer, "The Use of Explicit Old Testament Quotations in Qumran Literature and in the New Testament," *NTS* 7 (1960–61): 297–333 (=Fitzmyer, *Essays on the Semitic Background of the New Testament* [London: Chapman, 1971], 3–58); and D. M. Smith, "The Use of the Old Testament in the New," in *The Use of the Old Testament in the New and Other Essays: Studies in Honor of W. F. Stinespring*, ed. J. M. Efird (Durham, N.C.: Duke University Press, 1972), 3–65.

78. See Lindars, *New Testament Apologetic*, 17–31, for a clear exposition of the phenomena and their significance.

79. Stendahl, *The School of St. Matthew*, esp. 13–35, emphasizing the scribal, rabbinical, and catechetical features of Matthew, and 194–202. Cf. G. Strecker, *Der Weg der Gerechtigkeit* (Göttingen: Vandenhoeck und Ruprecht, 1962), 83–84.

80. The hypothesis was first developed by J. Rendel Harris, *Testimonies*, 2 vols. (Cambridge: Cambridge University Press, 1916, 1920). For the idea, see earlier, E. Hatch, *Essays in Biblical Greek* (Oxford: Oxford University Press, 1889), 203, who spoke of the likelihood that Greek-speaking Jews would have among other books "collections of *excerpta*," manuals that "would consist of extracts from the Old Testament," and considered that "the existence of composite quotations in the New Testament, and in some of the early Fathers, suggests the hypothesis that we have in them relics of such manuals." The term *testimonia* was first used for such collections by F. C. Burkitt, *The Gospel History and Its Transmission* (Edinburgh: T. & T. Clark, 1907). For a survey of the history of scholarship on this question, with an extensive bibliography, see R. Hodgson, "The Testimony Hypothesis," *JBL* 98 (1979): 361–78.

81. *According to the Scriptures*, 28–60. In this respect the work of R. Hays, *Echoes of Scripture*, has some resemblance to Dodd's.

82. See James Barr, *Old and New In Interpretation: A Study of the Two Testaments* (London: SCM Press, 1966), 142–43, expressing the view "that the concept of 'context' was not normally present" so that "interpretation was

generally done as if true results could be obtained whether context was noticed or not."

83. Dodd, *According to the Scriptures*, 110: "It was Jesus Christ himself who first directed the minds of His followers to certain parts of the scriptures as those in which they might find illumination upon the meaning of His mission and destiny." Lindars, *New Testament Apologetic*, 30, rightly dissents.

84. These texts were published originally by J. M. Allegro, "Further Messianic References in Qumran Literature," *JBL* 75 (1956): 182–87, and "Fragments of a Qumran Scroll of Eschatological Midrashim," *JBL* 77 (1958): 350–54, and were given definitive edition in J. M. Allegro, *Qumran Cave 4: I (4Q158–4Q186)* (DJD 5; Oxford: Clarendon, 1968), with the sigla 4Q175 (=4QTest) and 4Q174 (=4QFlor). In 4QFlorilegium, unlike 4QTestimonia, the texts are not merely cited but are interwoven with midrashic commentary. The texts extracted in 4QTestimonia are Deut. 5:28 and 18:18–19; Num. 24:15–17; Deut. 33:8–11; Josh. 6:26 (this last has a midrashic interpretation attached to it). 4QFlorilegium adduces 2 Sam. 7:10–14; Ps. 1:1 and Ps. 2:1f. 4QFlorilegium is not a list of testimonies in the strict sense, because the quotations are accompanied by midrashic comments, but it nevertheless stands in a close relation to 4QTestimonia.

85. C. H. Roberts, *Two Biblical Papyri in the John Rylands Library, Manchester* (Manchester: Manchester University Press, 1936), 47–62 (=P. Ryl. Grk. 460). The scriptural texts are Is. 42:3–4, 66:18–19, 52:15, 53:1–3, 53:6–7, 53:11–12 (an unknown verse), Gen. 26:13–14, 2 Chron. 1:12, and Deut. 29:8, 11. Roberts regarded the fragments as part of a Christian book of testimonies.

86. On ancient anthological works, see esp. H. Chadwick, "Florilegium," *RAC* 7 (1969): 1131–59.

87. J. A. Fitzmyer, "4QTestimonia and the New Testament," *TS* 18 (1957): 513–37 (534), repr. in Fitzmyer, *Essays*, 59–89. This essay is an excellent survey of the issue and the literature.

88. Interestingly, D.-A. Koch, *Die Schrift als Zeuge des Evangeliums*, who rejects the testimonia hypothesis in its traditional forms (247–56), nevertheless finds it necessary in view of Paul's own citations to suppose that Paul himself had made a collection of testimonia on the basis of his own reading of scripture and drew on this in the composition of his letters (253).

89. On the availability of books within early Christianity, see ch. 3. On the availability of Jewish scripture in Christianity, it is a relevant consideration that the earliest Septuagintal manuscripts that can be identified as Christian products come from about the middle of the second century.

90. See also O. Skarsaune, *The Proof from Prophecy: A Study in Justin Martyr's Proof-Text Tradition* (SuppNovT 56; Leiden: Brill, 1987), arguing that Justin used a collection of testimonies. This has also been argued for the Epistle of Barnabas by R. A. Kraft, "Barnabas' Isaiah Text and the 'Testimony Book' Hypothesis," *JBL* 79 (1960): 336–50, and 80 (1961): 371–73; and P. Prigent, *Les testimonia dans la christianisme primitif: L'épitre de Barnabe I–XVI et ses sources* (Paris: Gabalda, 1961).

91. Note, e.g., the programmatic emphases of Lk. 24:27, 46; Jn. 20:9; 2 Cor. 3:14–15.

92. M. Parry, "Studies in the Epic Technique of Oral Verse-Making, I: Homer

and Homeric Style," *HSCP* 41 (1930): 73–147; and "Studies in the Epic Technique of Oral Verse-Making, II: The Homeric Language as the Language of Oral Poetry," *HSCP* 43 (1932): 1–50; M. Parry and A. B. Lord, *Serbocroatian Heroic Songs* (Cambridge: Harvard University Press, 1954); and A. B. Lord, *The Singer of Tales* (New York: Athenaeum, 1960). See, more recently, A. B. Lord, "Perspectives on Recent Work in Oral Literature," in *Oral Literature: Seven Essays*, ed. J. J. Duggan (Edinburgh: Scottish Academic, 1975).

93. Influential in this development is the article by J. Goody and I. Watt, "The Consequences of Literacy," in *Literacy in Traditional Societies*, ed. J. Goody (Cambridge: Cambridge University Press, 1968), 27–68. For the theory of fundamental disparity between oral and literate modes and of the sociocultural and intellectual results of the displacement of orality by literacy, see esp. E. A. Havelock, *The Literate Revolution in Greece and Its Cultural Consequences* (Princeton: Princeton University Press, 1982); and *The Muse Learns to Write: Reflections on Orality and Literacy from Antiquity to the Present* (New Haven: Yale University Press, 1986); W. J. Ong, *The Presence of the Word: Some Prolegomena for Cultural and Religious History* (New Haven: Yale University Press, 1967), and *Orality and Literacy* (London: Methuen, 1982).

94. *The Oral and the Written Gospel: The Hermeneutics of Speaking and Writing in the Synoptic Tradition, Mark, Paul and Q* (Philadelphia: Fortress Press, 1983), esp. 1–43 and the summary statements, 207–11.

95. Though Kelber allows that among theorists "the manner and degree of difference is controversial" (14), he himself proceeds to draw the contrast sharply (esp. 90–131).

96. Invaluable as a counterpoint to theories of a "great divide" between orality and literacy are the studies of R. Finnegan: "How Oral Is Oral Poetry?" *BSOAS* 37 (1974): 52–64; *Oral Poetry: Its Nature, Significance, and Oral Context* (Cambridge: Cambridge University Press, 1977); "What Is Orality—If Anything?" *Byzantine and Modern Greek Studies* 14 (1990): 130–49; and *Literacy and Orality: Studies in the Technology of Communication* (Oxford: Blackwell, 1988). See also B. V. Street, *Literacy in Theory and Practice* (Cambridge: Cambridge University Press, 1984).

97. See W. S. Green, "Romancing the Tome: Rabbinic Hermeneutics and the Theory of Literature," *Semeia* 40 (1987): 147–68. For a concise but careful discussion of the coexistence and interplay of oral tradition and texts in the rabbinic setting, see H. L. Strack and G. Stemberger, *Introduction to the Talmud and Midrash*, trans. M. Bockmuehl (Edinburgh: T. & T. Clark, 1991), 35–49 (with literature); and M. Jaffee, "How Much Orality in 'Oral Torah'? New Perspectives on the Composition and Transmission of Early Rabbinic Tradition," *Hebrew Studies* 10 (1992): 53–72. The close relation of the oral and the written in rabbinic Judaism was also recognized in the work of B. Gerhardsson, *Memory and Manuscript*.

98. See, e.g., the important recent studies of R. Thomas, *Oral Tradition and Written Record in Classical Athens* (Cambridge: Cambridge University Press, 1989), and T. M. Lentz, *Orality and Literacy in Hellenic Greece* (Carbondale, Ill.: Southern Illinois University Press, 1989).

99. Kelber seems to recognize this. For example, he admits that the passion

narrative manifests a heavy reliance on scripture but argues that "much of scripture, like much literature in antiquity, was mentally accessible to an oral mode of appropriation. Obviously, orality derived from texts [?] is not the same as primary orality, which operates without the aid of texts. The passion narrative is largely built on texts and texts recycled into the oral medium, that is, secondary orality" (197). Such formulations serve to insulate the theory from the inconvenience of the data. Elsewhere, however, Kelber acknowledges that the situation was complex, that in some instances "the lines of orality and textuality were indeed blurred," and that we may never know the "precise shadings and degrees of interplay between the [oral and written] media" (23).

100. See L. Hurtado, "The Gospel of Mark: Evolutionary or Revolutionary Document?" *JSNT* 40 (1990): 15–32; C. Breytenbach, "Das Problem des Übergangs von mündlicher zu schriftlicher Überlieferung," *Neotestamentica* 20 (1986): 47–58; and J. Halverson, "Oral and Written Gospel: A Critique of Werner Kelber," *NTS* 40 (1994): 180–95.

101. Kelber (210–11) represents the destruction of Jerusalem as the "trauma" that catalyzed the conversion of the synoptic tradition from orality into textuality. But Q, and likely other presynoptic documents (see ch. 3), must have been available beforehand.

102. On the malleability of handwritten texts, see ch. 3. Kelber himself subsequently recognized this in passing in his essay, "Narrative as Interpretation and Interpretation of Narrative: Hermeneutical Reflections on the Gospels," *Semeia* 39 (1987): 107–34 (122–23).

103. The point is well developed not only in criticism of Kelber but with reference to modern biblical criticism generally by T. E. Boomershine, "Peter's Deinial as Polemic or Confession: The Implications of Media Criticism for Biblical Hermeneutics," *Semeia* 39 (1987): 47–68. Along similar lines, see P. Achtemeier, "*Omne Verbum Sonat*: The New Testament and the Oral Environment of Late Western Antiquity," *JBL* 109 (1990): 3–27, and the remarks of M. A. Tolbert, *Sowing the Gospel: Mark's World in Literary-Historical Perspective* (Minneapolis: Fortress Press, 1989), 43–46. On ancient reading habits, see also ch. 5.

104. On the Christian literature available to Papias, see U. H. J. Körtner, *Papias von Hierapolis: Ein Beitrag zur Geschichte des frühen Christentums* (FRLANT 133; Göttingen: Vandenhoeck und Ruprecht, 1983), 173–76.

105. A. F. Walls, "Papias and the Oral Tradition," *VC* 21 (1967): 137–40.

106. For what follows, see the valuable study of L. Alexander, "The Living Voice: Skepticism towards the Written Word in Early Christian and in Graeco-Roman Texts," in *The Bible in Three Dimensions*, ed. D. J. A. Clines (Sheffield: JSOT Press, 1990), 221–47.

107. Alexander, "The Living Voice," 226–27, citing Quintillian, *Inst.* 2.2.8 and Pliny, *Ep.* 2.3.

108. Ibid., 230–37, citing Seneca, *Ep.* 6.5 and 33.9, among other texts. She points out the value of a tradition of first-hand oral instruction in respect of its authenticity and its capacity for revision and development over time and changing circumstances. No great distinction should be made between the methods of philosophical instruction and training in the crafts, at least insofar as in this period training in philosophy was training in a way of life and so

entailed for the student a kind of "apprenticeship in living" to a philosophical teacher. On this point, see also R. L. Wilken, "Alexandria: A School for Training in Virtue," in *Schools of Thought in the Christian Tradition*, ed. P. Henry (Philadelphia: Fortress Press, 1984), 15–30.

109. Alexander, "Living Voice," 242–45. This is also true of Clement of Alexandria when he undertakes at the beginning of the *Stromateis* (1.1) to justify his commitment of Christian teaching to writing. On Clement, see also E. F. Osborn, "Teaching and Writing in the First Chapter of the *Stromateis* of Clement of Alexandria," *JTS* 10 (1959): 335–43.

110. Galen, after approvingly citing the proverb about the living voice, goes on to say that "those who are studious and naturally intelligent often gain no common advantage from reading books that are clearly written" and expresses his confidence that his own book will be useful to many—sentiments that were surely shared by Papias and Clement of Alexandria. More generally on the reluctance of early Christian writers to set pen to paper, see L. Vischer, "Die Rechtfertigung der Schriftstellerei in der alten Kirche," *BZ* 12 (1956): 320–36. That reluctance was variously motivated, but never by any opposition to texts as such and was, of course, overcome in every case.

111. It is important, however, to distinguish the preference for direct personal instruction such as we see in Papias and collateral witnesses from the idea of esoteric philosophical teachings that are under no circumstances to be written. The well-known statement of opposition to writing found in Plato's *Phaedrus* (274b-277a) is focused on the difference between oral and written teaching. The argument there is not against writing and books as such, but against the idea that manuals are an adequate substitute for dialogical personal teaching. This view was undoubtedly shaped by the increasing use of writing in pedagogical contexts in the fourth century B.C.E. and aimed to affirm that interpersonal discussion was more valuable for teaching and learning than texts. This is taken further in Plato, *Ep.* 7, which rejects the idea that serious philosophical ideas can be, or ought to be, committed to writing and sets up in the developing Platonic tradition (cf. *Ep.* 2) the notion of secret "unwritten doctrines," which are not to be found in any text. See the comments of Alexander, "The Living Voice," 237–42, with literature.

112. For good histories of scholarship on the nature of New Testament Greek, see G. Friedrich, "Prehistory of the Theological Dictionary of the New Testament," *TDNT* 10, 613–61; and, more recently and more fully, J. W. Voelz, "The Language of the New Testament," *ANRW* 2.25.2: 893–977. Pointed remarks are made by S. Brown, "Philology," in *The New Testament and Its Modern Interpreters*, ed. E. J. Epp and G. W. MacRae (Atlanta: Scholars Press, 1989), 127–47. A concise discussion that emphasizes the value of linguistic evidence for social level and literary culture is given by Malherbe, *Social Aspects*, 35–41.

113. *Light from the Ancient East.*

114. See, in addition to *Light from the Ancient East*, his *Bible Studies: Contributions Chiefly from Papyri and Inscriptions to the History of the Language, the Literature, and the Religion of Hellenistic Judaism and Early Christianity*, trans. A. Grieve (Edinburgh: T. & T. Clark, 1909). J. H. Moulton and J. Milligan later drew the full lexical implications of Deissmann's view

with their *Vocabulary of the Greek New Testament* (London: Hodder and Stoughton, 1930). The systematic extension of Deissmann's ideas to the field of grammar was made by J. H. Moulton, *A Grammar of New Testament Greek* (3 vols.; Edinburgh: T. & T. Clark, 1906–63).

115. Very important for the enumeration and discussion of Semitisms in the New Testament is W. H. Howard's appendix to J. Moulton and W. F. Howard, *Grammar of New Testament Greek* (Edinburgh: T. & T. Clark, 1920), 2:412–85.

116. The most influential advocate of this position has been N. Turner, whose views are stated in a variety of essays; but see esp. "Second Thoughts VII: Papyrus Finds," *ExpT* 76 (1964): 44–48, and the third volume, "Syntax" (by Turner) of J. Moulton, *Grammar* (Edinburgh, 1963), 4–5. For criticism of this view, see E. V. McKnight, "Is the New Testament Written in 'Holy Ghost' Greek?" *BibTrans* 16 (1965): 87–93; and "The New Testament and Biblical Greek," *JBR* 34 (1966): 36–42.

117. See esp. K. Beyer, *Semitische Syntax im Neuen Testament* (Göttingen: Vandenhoeck und Ruprecht, 1962); and M. Wilcox, *The Semitisms of Acts* (Oxford: Oxford University Press, 1965). In the case of the Gospels and sayings of Jesus in particular, appeal is still made, following the tradition of Dalman, Burney, and others, to Aramaic influence: see esp. M. Black, *An Aramaic Approach to the Gospels and Acts* (2d ed.; Oxford: Oxford University Press, 1954).

118. See, e.g., A. Wifstrand, "Stylistic Problems in the Epistles of James and Peter," *STh* 1 (1948): 170–82; W. C. van Unnik, "The Teaching of Good Works in 1 Peter," *NTS* 1 (1954): 92–110, and "A Classical Parallel to 1 Peter 2:14–20," *NTS* 2 (1956): 198–202; and, more generally, N. Turner, "The Literary Character of New Testament Greek," *NTS* 20 (1974): 107–14.

119. *Fachprosa, vermeintliche Volkssprache und Neues Testament: Zur Beurteilung der sprachlichen Niveauunterschiede im nachklassischen Griechisch* (Acta Univ. Upsaliensis, Studia Graeca Upsaliensis, 5; Uppsala, 1967). Curiously, Voelz takes no account of Rydbeck's study.

120. Ibid., 14, 177, 190.

121. Ibid., 177, 190, and cf. fig. 1 on 179.

122. Ibid., 195–96.

123. For Rydbeck's criticism of Deissmann's use of the rubric popular *(volkstümlich)* for both the papyri and the New Testament texts, see *Fachprosa*, 194–96.

124. *The Preface to Luke's Gospel: Literary Convention and Social Context in Luke 1:1–4 and Acts 1.1* (SNTSMS 78; Cambridge: Cambridge University Press, 1993). Cf. the summary in "Luke's Preface in the Context of Greek Preface-Writing," *NovT* 28 (1986): 48–74.

125. E.g., *Light from the Ancient East*, 248–49, though Deissmann discriminates even here: Luke-Acts remains among the popular books even though it marks a "transition to the popular books in which the cosmopolite tone prevails," while Hebrews is characterized as "an intruder among the New Testament company of popular books," since it alone shows "an endeavor to attain beauty of form."

126. For the tendency to call "spoken" the forms of Koine known only in

texts, see, e.g., Voelz, "The Language of the New Testament," 933–34. For a protest, see Rydbeck, *Fachprosa,* 186–89, 194–96.

127. For a useful discussion of this paradigm, see W. L. Wonderly, "Some Principles of 'Common-Language' Translation," *BibTrans* 21 (1970): 126–37. He rightly calls attention also to the "situational variety" of language use: persons at any given socioeducational level vary their speech in different social situations from the formal to the casual and intimate.

128. Pioneering work in the modern rhetorical criticism of early Christian texts has been done by G. Kennedy, *New Testament Interpretation through Rhetorical Criticism* (Chapel Hill: University of North Carolina Press, 1984); and *Classical Rhetoric in its Christian and Secular Tradition from Ancient to Modern Times* (Chapel Hill: University of North Carolina Press, 1980). A useful discussion of the developments to date is provided by B. L. Mack, *Rhetoric and the New Testament* (Minneapolis: Fortress Press, 1990). For extensive bibliography on rhetorical studies of the literature of the New Testament, see D. F. Watson, "The New Testament and Greco-Roman Rhetoric: A Bibliography" *JETS* 31 (1988): 465–72; and "The New Testament and Greco-Roman Rhetoric: A Bibliographical Update" *JETS* 33 (1990): 513–24.

129. See, e.g., E. A. Judge, "Paul's Boasting in Relation to Contemporary Professional Practice," *AusBibR* 16 (1968): 37–50; W. Wuellner, "Greek Rhetoric and Pauline Argumentation," in *Early Christian Literature and the Classical Tradition,* ed. W. R. Schoedel and R. L. Wilken (Paris: Beauchesne, 1979), 177–88; H. D. Betz, "The Literary Composition and Function of Paul's Letter to the Galatians," *NTS* 21 (1975): 353–79; and "The Problem of Rhetoric and Theology according to the Apostle Paul," in *L'apôtre Paul: Personnalité, style et conception du ministère,* ed. A. Vanhoye, *BETL* 73 (1986): 16–48; and R. Jewett, "Romans as an Ambassadorial Letter, *Int* 36 (1982): 5–20. A good overview of scholarly literature on Pauline rhetoric is given by F. W. Hughes, *Early Christian Rhetoric and 2 Thessalonians* (JSNTSup 30; Sheffield: JSOT Press, 1989), 19–30 ("The Rhetoric of Letters"); see also T. Schmeller, *Paulus und die "Diatribe"* (Munster: Aschendorff, 1987).

130. See, e.g., H. D. Betz, "The Sermon on the Mount: Its Literary Genre and Function," *JR* 59 (1979): 285–97; G. A. Kennedy, "An Introduction to the Rhetoric of the Gospels," *Rhetoric* 1 (1983): 17–31; V. K. Robbins, *Jesus the Teacher: A Socio-Rhetorical Interpretation of Mark* (Philadelphia: Fortress Press, 1984); B. L. Mack and V. K. Robbins, *Patterns of Persuasion in the Gospels* (Sonoma: Polebridge, 1989); J. L. Staley, *The Print's First Kiss: A Rhetorical Investigation of the Implied Reader in the Fourth Gospel* (SBLDS 82; Atlanta: Scholars Press, 1988); and Tolbert, *Sowing the Gospel.*

131. Two useful surveys that give particular attention to genre, as well as furnish fulsome references to the relevant literature, are K. Berger, *Formgeschichte des Neuen Testaments* (Heidelberg: Quelle & Meyer, 1984) (cf. also his "Hellenistische Gattungen im Neuen Testament," *ANRW* 2.25.2: 1031–1432); and David E. Aune, *The New Testament in Its Literary Environment* (Library of Early Christianity; Philadelphia: Westminster, 1987).

132. The best short statement of this view to date is H. Cancik, "Die Gattung Evangelium: Das Evangelium des Markus im Rahmen der antiken Historiographie," in *Markus-Philologie,* ed. H. Cancik (Tübingen: Mohr,

1984), 85–114. Also valuable in this connection are other studies in the same volume: Cancik, "Bios und Logos: Formengeschichtliche Untersuchungen zu Lukians *Leben des Demonax*," 115–30; M. Reiser, "Der Alexanderroman und das Markusevangelium," 131–64; and G. Luderitz, "Rhetorik, Poetik, Kompositionstechnik im Markusevangelium," 165–204. See also A. Dihle, "Die Evangelien und die biographische Tradition der Antike," *ZTK* 80 (1983): 33–49. A valuable overview is given by D. Dormeyer and H. Frankemölle, "Evangelium als literarische Gattung und theologischer Begriff: Tendenzen und Angaben der Evangelienforschung im 20-Jahrhundert, mit einer Untersuchung des Markus Evangeliums in seinem Verhältnis zur antiken Biographie," *ANRW* 2.25.2: 1543–1704. Two recent important monographs on the genre of the Gospels are D. Dormeyer, *Evangelium als literarische und theologische Gattung* (Darmstadt: Wissenschaftliche Buchgesellschaft, 1989); and R. A. Burridge, *What Are the Gospels?* (SNTSMS 70; Cambridge: Cambridge University Press, 1992). A useful survey of the issue is given by Aune, *New Testament*, 17–76.

133. On Greco-Roman and early Christian letters, see esp. S. K. Stowers, *Letter Writing in Greco-Roman Antiquity* (Library of Early Christianity; Philadelphia: Fortress Press, 1986), and J. L. White, "New Testament Epistolary Literature in the Framework of Ancient Epistolography," *ANRW* 2.25.2: 1730–56.

134. A. Malherbe, "Ancient Epistolary Theorists," *Ohio Journal of Religious Studies* 5 (1977): 3–77 (esp. 15), republished with revisions as *Ancient Epistolary Theorists* (SBLSBS 19; Atlanta: Scholars Press, 1988).

135. For a helpful discussion, see E. R. Richards, *The Secretary in the Letters of Paul* (WUNT 42; Tübingen: Mohr, 1991), 211–16 (app. G, "The 'Literary or Non-Literary' (Deissmann) Debate: The Problem of Classifying the Letters of Paul"). On the nature and functions of early Christian letters see also the comments of H. Koester, "Writings and the Spirit: Authority and Politics in Ancient Christianity," *HTR* 84 (1991): 353–72.

136. See n. 128. The standard older studies are those of J. Weiss, "Beiträge zur paulinische Rhetorik," *Theologische Studien. Herrn Wirk: Oberkonsistorialrath Prof. D. Bernhard Weiss zu seinem 70-Geburtstage dargebracht* (Göttingen: Vandenhoeck und Ruprecht, 1897), 165–274; and R. Bultmann, *Der Stil der paulinischen Predigt und die kynisch-stoische Diatribe* (Göttingen: Vandenhoeck und Ruprecht, [1910] 1984).

137. For a survey of the discussion of the genre of Acts, see Aune, *New Testament*, 77–157; for the apocryphal Acts, see J.-D. Kaestli, "Les principales orientations de la recherche sur les Actes apocryphes," in *Les Actes Apocryphes des Apôtres*, ed. F. Bovon et al., (Geneva: Labor et Fides, 1981), 57–67. The question of the genre of Acts is complicated by the issue of whether the Gospel of Luke and the Acts of the Apostles need to be taken together or considered separately. See the comments of I. H. Marshall, "Acts and the 'Former Treatise,'" in *The Books of Acts in Its First Century Setting*, 1, "The Book of Acts in Its Ancient Literary Setting," ed. B. W. Winter and A. D. Clarke (Grand Rapids: Eerdmans, 1993), 163–82.

138. R. Mortley, "The Title of the Acts of the Apostles," *Lectures anciennes de la Bible* (Cahiers de Biblia Patristica 1; Strasbourg: Centre d'analyse et de documentation patristiques, 1987), 105–12.

139: Still, there is a diversity of views: Aune, *New Testament* 77–157, speaks of Luke-Acts as a "general history"; D. W. Palmer, "Acts and the Ancient Historical Monograph," in *The Book of Acts in Its First Century Setting*, 1, "The Book of Acts in Its Ancient Literary Setting," 1–29, calls Acts a "historical monograph"; R. Maddox, *The Purpose of Luke-Acts* (Edinburgh: T. & T. Clark, 1982) designates Luke-Acts as a "theological history"; and G. E. Sterling, *Historiography and Self-Definition: Josephus, Luke-Acts, and Apologetic Historiography* (Leiden: Brill, 1992), calls Luke-Acts "apologetic historiography." Cf. R. J. Dillon, "Previewing Luke's Project from His Prologue (Luke 1:1–4)," *CBQ* 43 (1981): 205–27; and C. J. Hemer, *The Book of Acts in the Setting of Hellenistic History* (WUNT, 49; Tübingen: Mohr, 1989), esp. 30–100. L. Alexander, *The Preface to Luke's Gospel*, regards Luke-Acts as a "technical treatise" in the scientific tradition, but this does not necessarily deny historiographic interest.

140. See R. Soder, *Die apocryphen Apostelgeschichten und die romanhafte Literatur der Antike* (Stuttgart: Kohlhammer, 1932); and, more recently, R. Pervo, *Profit with Delight: The Literary Genre of the Acts of the Apostles* (Philadelphia: Fortress Press, 1987), who also considers the canonical Acts as a historical romance.

141. On the issue of genre, see the various articles in J. J. Collins, ed., *Apocalypse: The Morphology of a Genre*, Semeia 14 (1979); and A. Y. Collins, ed., *Early Christian Apocalypticism: Genre and Social Setting*, Semeia 36 (1986). On Jewish apocalyptic generally, see J. J. Collins, *The Apocalyptic Imagination: An Introduction to the Jewish Matrix of Christianity* (New York: Crossroads, 1984); and C. Rowland, *The Open Heaven: A Study of Apocalyptic in Judaism and Early Christianity* (New York: Crossroads, 1982).

142. For a broadly inclusive discussion, see D. E. Aune, *Prophecy in Early Christianity and the Ancient Mediterranean World* (Grand Rapids, Mich.: Eerdmans, 1983).

143. See the remarks of E. D. Hirsch, *Validity in Interpretation* (New Haven: Yale University Press, 1967), 68–126, emphasizing the importance for interpretation of genre and its recognition (esp. 74–76).

144. Harris, *Ancient Literacy*, 227, cf. 126: "Any assumption that the intellectually less demanding genres of Hellenistic literature aimed at, or reached, a truly popular audience of readers should be resisted. . . . Popular culture had little to do with reading."

145. Ibid., 228. See in addition D. N. Levin, "To Whom Did the Ancient Novelists Address Themselves?" *Rivista di studi classici* 25 (1977): 18–29; B. P. Reardon, "Aspects of the Greek Novel," *Greece and Rome* 23 (1976): 118–31 (130); and esp. B. Wesseling, "The Audience of the Ancient Novels," *Groningen Colloquia on the Novel* 1 (Groningen: E. Forsten, 1988), 67–128. Cf. B. E. Perry, *The Ancient Romances: A Literary-Historical Account of Their Origins* (Berkeley: University of California Press, 1967); and G. Schmeling, *Chariton* (New York: Twayne, 1974), who envision a broad middle-class readership (though Schmeling has revised his view in *Xenophon of Ephesus* [Boston: Twayne, 1980], 131–38).

146. T. Hagg, *The Novel in Antiquity* (Berkeley: University of California Press, 1983), 90–101; cf. Wesseling, "The Audience," 76: "Intellectuals in the first place, but not exclusively."

147. It is along these lines that Tolbert proposes to understand the Gospels and in particular Mark, as "popular literature, composed in such a way as to be available to wide spectrum of society": *Sowing the Gospel*, 48–79.

148. See the pointed remarks of J. Dummer, "Die Stellung der griechischen christlichen Schriften im Rahmen der antiken Literatur," in *Das Korpus der griechischen christlichen Schriftsteller. Historie, Gegenwart, Zukunft*, ed. J. Irmscher and K. Treu (TU 120; Berlin: Akademie, 1977), 65–76.

CHAPTER II: THE EARLY CHRISTIAN BOOK

1. An interesting but not entirely successful effort to draw out the significance of early Christian papyri for church history was made by the late C. H. Roberts, *Manuscript, Society, and Belief in Early Christian Egypt* (Schweich Lectures of the British Academy, 1977; London: Oxford University Press, 1979). That the papyri have not yet received the attention they merit even from New Testament textual critics has been noted by E. J. Epp, "The New Testament Papyrus Manuscripts in Historical Perspective," in *To Touch the Text: Biblical and Related Studies in Honor of Joseph A. Fitzmyer, S. J.*, ed. M. P. Horgan and P. Kobelski (New York: Crossroads, 1989), 261–88.

2. On these issues, see esp. D. F. McKenzie, *Bibliography and the Sociology of Texts* (Panizzi Lectures, 1985; London: British Library, 1986); together with the review essay of G. T. Tanselle, "Textual Criticism and Literary Sociology," in *Studies in Bibliography*, ed. F. Bowers (Charlottesville: University Press of Virginia, 1991) 44:83–143.

3. There is a rich literature on this subject. Mention is made here only of especially important or particularly useful discussions: classic and influential studies are those of Th. Birt, *Das antike Buchwesen in seinem Verhältnis zur Litteratur* (Berlin: Hertz, 1882); W. Schubart, *Das Buch bei den Griechen und Römern*, 3d ed., by E. Paul (Heidelberg: Schneider, [1922] 1962; K. Dziatzko, *Untersuchungen über ausgewählte Kapitel des antiken Buchwesens* (Leipzig: Teubner, 1900); and F. G. Kenyon, *Books and Readers in Ancient Greece and Rome*, 2d ed. (Oxford: Clarendon, 1951). A useful recent contribution has been made by H. Blanck, *Das Buch in der Antike* (Munich: Beck, 1992). Relatively brief but current overviews may be found in P. E. Easterling and B. M. W. Knox, "Books and Readers in the Greek World," in *Cambridge History of Classical Literature*, 1, "Greek Literature," ed. Easterling and Knox (Cambridge: Cambridge University Press, 1985), 1–41; and E. J. Kenney, "Books and Readers in the Roman World," *Cambridge History of Classical Literature*, 2, "Latin Literature," ed. Kenney (Cambridge: Cambridge University Press, 1982), 3–32.

4. The terms *biblos* and *biblion* were derived from the name of the city of Byblos (and so were originally spelled *byblos*). Strictly, the word *biblion* is a diminutive (little book), but the nuance was lost as this word became more general than *biblos*. (The designation of Jewish or Christian scripture as the Bible is taken from the Greek, *ta biblia*, "the books.") The Latin word *volumen*, with the literal sense of "something rolled," designated the book as a physical object. The Latin *liber*, which originally meant "bark," was sometimes used synonymously with *volumen* and sometimes to indicate a literary unit of a larger work (thus as an equivalent of the Greek *tomos*). The Latin *libellus* (little book) retained its proper sense, but the Greek *biblion* did not.

5. The most thorough and authoritative discussion is given by Naphtali Lewis, *Papyrus in Classical Antiquity* (Oxford: Clarendon, 1974), with corrections and expansions in *Papyrus in Classical Antiquity: A Supplement* (Papyrologica Bruxellensia, 23; Brussels: Fondation Egyptologique Reine Elisabeth, 1989).

6. Thus, Lewis, *Papyrus*, 37, 41–51, reflecting the traditional view. Pliny claims, apparently mistakenly, that Nile water was the adhesive agent. Water was probably used, but only to keep the material sufficiently moist during the manufacturing process.

7. Thus I. H. M. Hendriks, "Pliny, Historia Naturalis XIII, 74–82 and the Manufacture of Papyrus," *ZPE* 37 (1980): 121–36. See also the responses of E. G. Turner in *ZPE* 39 (1980): 113–14, and N. Lewis in *ZPE* 42 (1981): 293–94; and Hendrik's further comments, "More about the Manufacture of Papyrus," *Atti del XVII Congresso Internazionale di Papyrologia*, 1 (Naples: Centro Internazionale per lo Studio dei Papyri Ercolanesi, 1984), 31–37. For Lewis's fuller response, see *Papyrus in Classical Antiquity: A Supplement*, 16–21.

8. Pliny (*Nat. Hist.*, xiii, 78) indicates that there were different grades and sizes of manufactured sheets, but the only dimension he notes is width. The omission of any mention of height is logical if the breadth of sheets (unlike their height) is an aspect of their quality: the wider the sheet, the fewer joins had to be made in manufacturing a roll, and thus there were fewer imperfections in the surface (W. A. Johnson, "Pliny the Elder and Standardized Roll Heights in the Manufacture of Papyrus," *CPhil* 88 [1993]: 46–50). Among surviving examples the standard range of height is twenty-five to thirty-two centimeters.

9. On the uses and difficulties of this terminology, see E. G. Turner, "The Terms Recto and Verso: The Anatomy of the Papyrus Roll," *Actes du XV congres international de papyrologie*, pt. 1 (Papyrologica Bruxellensia, 16; Brussels: Fondation Egyptologique Reine Elisabeth, 1978). Strictly speaking, the side that is inscribed (or first inscribed if writing is on both sides) is the recto, but normally in a roll this was the side with the fibers running horizontally.

10. Pliny (*Nat. Hist.* 13.77) claimed that there were never more than twenty sheets in a roll. Lewis, *Papyrus*, 54–55, considers it likely that this was the standard length. See also T. C. Skeat, "The Length of the Standard Papyrus Roll and the Cost Advantage of the Codex," *ZPE* 45 (1982): 169–75, esp. 169–72, who estimates the actual length of such a roll at 3.2–3.6 meters, or an average of 3.4 meters (a little over eleven feet). But as Lewis notes (55) Pliny, since he is speaking about raw materials, may have meant only that no more than twenty sheets could be made from a single stalk of papyrus. In that case, the standard length of a manufactured roll may have been considerably longer than 3.4 meters.

11. See Pliny, *Nat. Hist.* 13.78–79; Cicero, *Att.* 16.6.4; and Horace, *Serm.* 1.10.92.

12. Pliny says that the valued characteristics of papyrus were fineness, firmness, whiteness, and smoothness *(tenuitas, densitas, candor, levor)*.

13. There are instances in classical literature attesting the use of papyrus materials hundreds of years old, without any indication that the material had significantly deteriorated (see, e.g., Pliny, *Nat. Hist.* 13. 83, Galen 18[2]. 630).

An impressive indication of the strength and durability of papyrus is to be seen in the fact that one of the leather rolls found at Qumran (4QSam a) was reinforced by gluing a strip of papyrus on its verso side.

14. See R. R. Johnson, "The Role of Parchment in Graeco-Roman Antiquity" (Ph.D. diss., University of California, 1968), 3–21. Most Qumran scrolls are leather or parchment, and only a small percentage are papyrus.

15. Pliny (*Nat. Hist.* 13.70), relying on Varro, claimed that parchment was invented in Pergamum in the reign of Eumenes II (197–158 B.C.E.) owing to a shortage of papyrus caused by an Egyptian embargo allegedly imposed by an Egypt that had grown jealous over the growing repute of the library at Pergamum. This time of origin is refuted by evidence of an earlier use of parchment, and the alleged cause and motive are certainly fanciful. For an analysis of the tradition, see Johnson, "The Role of Parchment," 22–51, and "Ancient and Medieval Accounts of the 'Invention' of Parchment," *California Studies in Classical Antiquity* 3 (1970): 115–22, which canvasses most of the literary testimony about parchment.

16. For the technical and scientific aspects of parchment production, see esp. the detailed discussion by R. Reed, *The Nature and Making of Parchment* (Leeds: Elmet, 1975), and, more generally, *Ancient Skins, Parchments, and Leathers* (London: Seminar Press, 1972), and M. L. Ryder, "The Biology and History of Parchment," in *Pergament: Geschichte, Structur, Restaurierung, Herstellung*, ed. P. Ruck (Simarigen: Thorbecke, 1991), 25–33.

17. Johnson, "The Role of Parchment," 113–18, surveys this question, which he deems "fruitless." Although the relative costs cannot be judged, he rightly distinguishes between various grades of parchment and considers that the lesser grade(s) would have been "moderately priced" but that the finer ones were "quite expensive" (116). As to papyrus, Lewis, *Papyrus*, 133–34, considers that "a roll of papyrus cost the equivalent of one or two days' wages, and it could run as high as what the labourer would earn in five or six days," such that "in social milieux more elevated than that of a prosperous Egyptian villager the purchase of papyrus is not likely to have been regarded as an expenditure of any consequence."

18. Kenyon, *Books and Readers*, 54. This was the original reference of the dictum: "A big book is a big evil" (Callimachus). Longer rolls are known, but they are uncommon, and the very long rolls that have turned up in Egypt are ceremonial burial rolls, not meant to be read by the living.

19. For the evidence, see Th. Birt, *Die Buchrolle in der Kunst. Archaologisch-antiquarische Untersuchungen zum antiken Buchwesen* (r.p. New York: Olms, 1976); H. Immerwahr, "Book Rolls on Attic Vases," in *Classical, Mediaeval, and Renaissance Studies in Honor of B. L. Ullman*, ed. C. Henderson (Rome: Edizione de storia e letteratura, 1964), 1:17–48, and "More Book Rolls on Attic Vases," *Antike Kunst* 16 (1973): 143–48.

20. See F. G. Kenyon, "Book Divisions in Greek and Latin Literature," in *William Warner Bishop: A Tribute*, ed. H. M. Lydenberg and A. Keogh (New Haven: Yale University, 1941), 63–75; and more recently J. van Sickle, "The Book-Roll and Some Conventions of the Poetic Book," *Arethusa* 13 (1980): 5–42, esp. 6–12. Of course, single rolls might also contain shorter *tomoi*, on which see Lewis, *Papyrus*, 76–7, inc. n. 9.

21. There are instances when both sides of a roll are inscribed. Such a roll is known as an opisthograph (literally, also "written behind" or "on the back"). The reason is almost always a wish to conserve material. Pliny the Younger (*Ep.* 3.5.17) says that his uncle left him 160 notebooks written in a very small hand on both sides *(commentarios centum sexaginta mihi reliquit, opisthographos quidem et minutissimis scriptos).* These were personal notebooks. No well-produced roll was written on both the front and back. In almost all extant opisthographs the writing on the back is in a different hand than is the writing on the front, and the text was inscribed on the back when the text on the front was no longer valued or used. A rare example of an opisthograph that was written by the same scribe on both the front and back is the Isocrates fragment in the Beinecke Library of Yale University.

22. Turner, "Recto and Verso," 20–24.

23. Top margins ranged from three to four centimeters, bottom margins from three to five. On the characteristic features of the papyrus roll book, see the close analysis of W. A. Johnson, "The Literary Papyrus Roll: Formats and Conventions. An Analysis of the Evidence from Oxyrhynchus" (Ph.D. diss., Yale University, 1982), and his unpublished paper kindly shared with me, "The Aesthetic of the Luxury Book Roll." On scripts themselves, see below in the text.

24. On punctuation and other sigla, including critical signs, see E. G. Turner, *Greek Manuscripts of the Ancient World*, ed. P. Parsons (2d ed. rev. and enlarged; London: University of London Institute of Classical Studies, 1987).

25. See H. Zilliakus, "Boktiteln i antik litteratur," *Eranos* 36 (1938): 1–41; and R. P. Oliver, "The First Medicean MS of Tacitus and the Titulature of Ancient Books," *TAPA* 82 (1951): 232–61.

26. For title tags, see Turner, *Greek Manuscripts*, 34, with pl. 6–8, and T. Dorandi, "Sillyboi," *Scrittura e civiltà* 8 (1984): 185–99, with plates. Cf. the remarks of Ovid, *Pont.* 4.13.7, and Cicero, *ad Att.* 4.4a.1, 5.4 and 8.2.

27. See W. Luppe, "Rückseitentitel auf Papyrusrollen," *ZPE* 27 (1977): 89–99. These are in a hand other than the scribe's and presumably were supplied by the owner of the book.

28. For detailed discussion, see S. Besslich, "Die 'Horner' des Buches: Zur Bedeutung von cornua im antiken Buchwesen," *Gutenberg Jahrbuch* (1973): 44–50.

29. See, e.g., Lucian, *Adv. Indoct.* 8, 16; Martial, 3.2.10, 8.72, 9.93.3.

30. See C. Sirat, "Le livre hébreu dans les premiers siècles de notre ére: Le témoignage des textes," *Les débuts du codex*, ed. A. Blanchard (Bibliologia, 9; Brepols: Turnhout, 1989), 115–24. On the question of material, see also J. P. Hyatt, "The Writing of an Old Testament Book," *BA* 6 (1943): 71–80; and M. Haran, "Book Scrolls in Israel in Pre-Exilic Times," *JJS* 33 (1982): 161–73 (with an addendum in *JJS* 35 [1984] 84–85). The large majority of the Qumran scrolls are on skin, mainly leather rather than parchment. On this aspect of the Qumran materials, see J. B. Poole and R. Reed, "The Preparation of Leather and Parchment by the Dead Sea Scrolls Community," *Technology and Culture* 3 (1962): 1–26.

31. For descriptive catalogues of early Christian manuscripts, principally papyrus, see esp. J. van Haelst, *Catalogue des papyrus littéraires juifs et*

chrétiens (Paris: Publications de la Sorbonne, 1976); and K. Aland, *Repertorium der griechischen christlichen Papyri*, I, Biblische Papyri (Patristische Texte und Studien, 18; Berlin: de Gruyter, 1976). Reports on new accessions may also be found in a series of essays by K. Treu, "Christliche Papyri," appearing periodically in *APF*, and in the report by K. Aland in the annual *Bericht der Hermann Kunst-Stiftung zur Forderung der neutestamentlichen Textforschung* (Munster, 1982–).

32. See the statistical table given by C. H. Roberts and T. C. Skeat, *The Birth of the Codex* (London: Oxford University Press, 1983), 37. Statistics in such a matter are somewhat tricky since the evidence survives fortuitously and since paleographers by no means always agree on the date of individual manuscripts. Still, the evidence is extensive enough to be representative, and differences in paleographic dating do not fundamentally change the general picture.

33. This began to be recognized by Kenyon, *Books and Readers*, 94–99, but was argued in detail and influentially by C. H. Roberts, "The Codex," *Proceedings of the British Academy* 40 (1954): 169–204, now revised and expanded in Roberts and Skeat, *Birth*. Among the earlier literature, see also C. C. McCown, "Codex and Roll in the New Testament," *HTR* 34 (1941): 219–50, and "The Earliest Christian Books," *BA* 6 (1943): 21–31. It has been urged, especially by Roberts, that the Christian predilection for the codex pertains especially to scriptural materials, but this distinction is hard to sustain in the state of the evidence. It seems likely that the codex was the preferred though not exclusive medium for all Christian writings.

34. This is confirmed in the curious opinion of Seneca (*de brev. vit.* 13) that Claudius Caudex (consul in 264 B.C.E.) was the first to persuade the Romans to board ships and was so named because "among the ancients a structure formed by joining boards together was called a *caudex*, whence also the tables of the law are also called *codices*, and, in the old fashion, boats that carry provisions up the Tiber are even now called *codicariae*." Among the Greeks, the term *kodix* (the only form of the word actually attested) was eventually borrowed but even then did not mean "book." See the discussion of B. Atsalos, *La terminologie du livre-manuscrit a l'époque byzantine* (Thessaloniki: 1971), 144.

35. For wooden tablets, see the discussion in Roberts and Skeat, *Birth*, 11–14 (with literature), and add the discussions provided by M. Sirat, P. Cauderlier, and R. Pintaudi in *Les débuts du codex*, ed. A. Blanchard (Bibliologia, 9; Brepols: Turnhout, 1989). Also note the unusual "concertina" Roman writing tablets discovered in England, on which see A. K. Bowman, "The Vindolanda Tablets and the Development of the Book Form," *ZPE* 18 (1975): 237–52; and A. K. Bowman and J. D. Thomas, *Vindolanda: The Latin Writing Tablets* (London: SPRS, 1983), suggesting that this might represent an intermediate stage in the development from wooden tablets to a leaf book. Turner ("Recto and Verso," 51–53) would relate these more closely to the roll written *transversa charta* than to the codex.

36. Pliny the Younger (*Ep.* 3.5.14–15) speaks of his uncle dictating notes to his slave, who jotted them down in shorthand on wax tablets (*pugillares*). Horace's suggestion (*Sat.* 1.10.72–73) that if the stylus is frequently inverted (for erasure) one is more likely to write something worth reading obviously

applies to drafts written on wax tablets. On note-taking in connection with lengthy compositions, see T. Dorandi, "Den autoren über die Schulter geschaut: Arbeitsweise und Autographie bei den antiken Schriftstellern," *ZPE* 87 (1991): 11–33.

37. A sheet or manuscript from which writing has been removed and that is then used again for writing is called a palimpsest (from the Greek *palimpsestos*, "rubbed [or washed] again"). Although the word has come to be associated almost exclusively with parchment, both papyrus and parchment could be and were recycled in this way.

38. Quintilian's statement reads: "It is best to write on wax because of its ease of erasure, though weak sight may make it desirable to use parchment *(membranarum)* instead." The term *membranae* in such close conjunction with the mention of wax tablets indicates that a parchment codex is meant. The earliest surviving example of a parchment notebook comes from the second or third century. Ostensible allusions and extant examples are fully discussed by Roberts and Skeat, *Birth*, 15–23.

39. For detailed discussion, see Roberts and Skeat, *Birth*, 24–29.

40. *Epigrams* 14. 184 (Homer), 186 (Vergil), 188 (Cicero), 190 (Livy), and 192 (Ovid).

41. For the list, see J. van Haelst, "Les origines," 13–35 (esp. 23, 25). There is naturally disagreement about the dating of some of these manuscripts, but the differences are not great and affect only a few items.

42. For particulars, see J. Mallon, "Quel est le plus ancien codex latin?" in *De l'écriture: Recueil d'études publiées de 1937 à 1981* (Paris: Editions du CNRS, 1982), 209–12. Although the original editors dated the manuscript "no earlier than the third century," they did so for reasons now invalid. Mallon (211) puts the date at the end of the first or near the beginning of the second century.

43. E. G. Turner, *The Typology of the Early Codex* (Philadelphia: University of Pennsylvania Press, 1977), 38.

44. Mallon, "Codex latin?" 208, thinks this codex has a Roman origin. See also van Haelst, "Les origines," 26.

45. *Das Archiv des Petaus* (Pap. Colon., 4), ed. U. Hagedorn and D. Hagedorn and L. C. Youtie and H. C. Youtie (Cologne: Westdeutscher Verlag, 1969), 156–57. See the also the comments of E. G. Turner, *The Papyrologist at Work* (GRBM 6; Durham, N.C.: Duke University, 1973), 37–38; and van Haelst, "Les origines," 21–23. Although this letter was found among the Petaus materials, it seems to have no substantive connection to the archives.

46. L. Koenen, "Ein Monch als Berufsschreiber zur Buchproduktion im 5.6. Jahrhundert," in *Festschrift zum 150-jährigen Bestehen d. Berl. ägypt. Museum* (1974), 351, n. 20, but against Turner and van Haelst, who seem to think that Dius dealt only in parchment codices.

47. The evidence is compiled and discussed by Turner, *Typology*, 13–54.

48. Van Haelst, "Les origines," 32–34, appealing to the later dates assigned to some of the manuscripts by E. G. Turner, *Typology*. The dates given by Aland, *Repertorium*, accord closely with those used by Roberts and Skeat.

49. Van Haelst, "Les origines," 34.

50. A good discussion of these is given by Roberts and Skeat, *Birth*, 45–53, and what follows summarizes their points except where otherwise indicated.

51. T. C. Skeat, "Length of the Standard Papyrus Roll," 175, concludes a saving of 26 percent.

52. A modern advocate of this view is G. Cavallo, ed., *Libri, editori, e pubblico nel mondo antico* (Bari: Laterza, 1975), 83–85; cf. also his review of *The Birth of the Codex* in *Studi italiani di filologia classica,* ser. 3, 3 (1985): 118–21.

53. See ch. 1. In addition, Roberts and Skeat, *Birth,* 69–70, point out that so-called popular literature was usually transcribed in rolls.

54. Ancient literature preserves no outright complaints about the inconvenience of rolls. E. G. Turner (*Greek Papyri* [Oxford: Clarendon, 1968], 7) points out that some Athenian vase paintings depict readers who have allowed a roll to become twisted or have lost a grip on it, and that Pliny (*Ep.* 2.1.5) tells of Verginius Rufus fracturing his hip while trying to recover a dropped roll. The fact that a good many extant rolls appear to have been torn in two could be either the reason for or the result of their being thrown away. See also T. C. Skeat, "Two Notes on Papyrus: I, Was Rerolling a Papyrus Roll an Irksome and Time-Consuming Task?" in *Scritti in onore di Orsolina Montevecchi* (Bologna: Clueb, 1981), 373–76 ("No.").

55. Special weight and new arguments are given to this feature of the codex by M. McCormick, "The Birth of the Codex and the Apostolic Life-Style," *Scriptorium* 39 (1985): 150–58.

56. Most of the very early Christian codices appear to have contained only individual texts and not particularly long ones. The earliest codices, Christian or not, tended to be of the single quire variety, with a maximum capacity of around two hundred pages.

57. Similarly, the columns in rolls were not normally numbered, and the number of columns in a given text depended on how the individual manuscript was written. Turner (*Typology,* 75) notes that pagination "would not seem to have been integral with the invention of the codex, otherwise one would have expected to find it as a part of every codex," and that in many codices where pagination is present, it has been secondarily added. This suggests that "pagination originated in book consultation rather than in book production" (M. McCormick, "Typology, Codicology, and Papyrology," *Scriptorium* 35 [1981] 334).

58. Roberts, "The Codex," 187; cf. Roberts and Skeat, *Birth,* 53.

59. Ibid., 187–91.

60. Ibid., 189. P. Katz, "The Early Christians' Use of Codices Instead of Rolls," *JTS* 46 (1945): 63–65, claimed that Christians adopted the codex simply to differentiate Christian from Jewish books, but it is not obvious why such a differentiation should have been thought necessary or desirable. On Roberts's reconstruction, the various alleged practical advantages of the codex over the roll are entirely discounted, and everything is mortgaged to the authority of the document itself.

61. Among manuscripts that can be dated before the fourth century, only 2 represent Mark, while Matthew and John are represented in 12 each, and Luke in 4. Roberts later acknowledged that this was a problem for his hypothesis (*Manuscript, Society, and Belief,* 59, 61). For criticism of Roberts' theory, see also van Haelst, "Les origines," 29–31.

62. Roberts and Skeat, *Birth*, 57–61.

63. For such a practice, see the comments of S. Liebermann, *Hellenism in Jewish Palestine* (New York: Jewish Theological Seminary, 1962), app. 3, "Jewish and Christian Codices," 203–8, who says that the use of a codex was the most appropriate way to make it clear "that they were writing the Oral Law for private, or unofficial use, and not for publication" (205).

64. Roberts and Skeat, *Birth*, 59.

65. Ibid., 59–60. It must, however, have been a Greek-speaking Christian community, since Roberts and Skeat appeal in this connection also to the nomina sacra, a Christian convention in the transcription of certain Greek terms, and draw a close connection between this convention and the origin of the codex.

66. The point is well made by van Haelst, "Les origines," 31–32. *Apopirin* in M. Kelim 24.7 does not mean a papyrus codex, but a wooden tablet.

67. Roberts and Skeat, *Birth*, 60.

68. Having rightly rejected the theories of Roberts and Skeat, van Haelst immediately concludes "the impossibility of finding a satisfying hypothesis" and proceeds to revise the evidence in order to reduce the need for one ("Les origines," 32). Still, even on his terms an explanation is needed for the far greater speed for the transition to the codex in Christianity.

69. An earlier version of the following argument was presented several years ago at an National Endowment for the Humanities conference in Dallas and was subsequently published as "The Pauline Corpus and the Early Christian Book," *Paul and the Legacies of Paul*, ed. W. Babcock (Dallas: Southern Methodist University Press, 1990), 265–80. I am indebted to participants in the conference for stimulating my further reflections on it.

70. Although traditions about Jesus, and perhaps especially the sayings of Jesus, did have a primitive and preeminent authority in Christianity, that authority was by no means exclusive of other authorities (e.g., scripture or apostolic figures), and it did not automatically accrue to written Gospels. The uses of Jesus-traditions in early-second-century literature may suggest that oral tradition was often preferred to written Gospels. See H. Koester, *Synoptische Überlieferung bei den apostolischen Vätern* (TU 65; Berlin: Akademie Verlag, 1957).

71. On the knowledge and use of Paul's letters by these and other early Christian figures, see D. Rensberger, "As the Apostle Teaches: The Development of the Use of Paul's Letters in Second Century Christianity" (Ph.D. diss., Yale University, 1981); A. Lindemann, *Paulus im ältesten Christentum: Das Bild des Apostels und die Rezeption der paulinischen Theologie in der frühchristlichen Literatur bis Marcion* (Tübingen: Mohr, 1978); and E. Dassmann, *Der Stachel im Fleisch: Paulus in der frühchristlichen Literatur bis Irenaeus* (Munster: Aschendorff, 1979). Their positive assessments contradict the previously influential view of W. Schneemelcher, "Paulus in der griechischen Kirche des 2. Jahrhunderts," *ZKG* 75 (1964): 1–20. On the early circulation and valuation of Paul's letters, see also ch. 3.

72. For a concise survey of the main theories, see H. Gamble, *The New Testament Canon: Its Making and Meaning* (Philadelphia: Fortress Press, 1985), 36–41 (with literature); and E. H. Lovering, "The Collection, Redaction,

and Early Circulation of the Corpus Paulinum" (Ph.D. diss., Southern Methodist University, 1988).

73. Tertullian, *adv. Marc.*, 5. Tertullian considers Philemon after Philippians, and so presumably as the last letter in Marcion's collection (5.21–22). According to Epiphanius, however, in Marcion's collection Philemon followed Colossians and stood before Philippians (*Pan.* 42.9.4, 11.8, 12). The placement of Philemon turns out to be important.

74. P 46 almost certainly did not contain the personal letters or at any rate not Timothy (1–2) and Titus, for the number of leaves missing from the end of the codex were not sufficient to have contained them. See F. G. Kenyon, *The Chester Beatty Biblical Papyri*, fasc. 3, suppl. (London: Emery Walker, 1936), x–xi. P 46 does contain Hebrews (between Romans and Corinthians), but it is unlikely that Hebrews formed part of any primitive edition of Paul's letters.

75. For this theory and its witnesses, see Th. Zahn, *Geschichte des neutestamentliche Kanons*, 2 vols. (Erlangen: Deichert, 1892), 2:73–75; K. Stendahl, "The Apocalypse of John and the Epistles of Paul in the Muratorian Fragment," in *Current Issues in New Testament Interpretation*, ed. W. Klassen and G. F. Snyder (New York: Harper and Row, 1962), 239–45; and N. A. Dahl, "The Particularity of the Pauline Epistles as a Problem in the Ancient Church," in *Neotestamentica et Patristica* (NovTSup 6; Leiden: Brill, 1962), 261–71.

76. The evidence for such an order is assembled by H.-J. Frede, "Die Ordnung der Paulusbriefe und der Platz des Kolosserbriefs im Corpus Paulinum," *Vetus Latina* 24/2 (Freiburg: Herder Verlag, 1969), 290–303. Cf. J. Finegan, "The Original Form of the Pauline Collection," *HTR* 49 (1956): 85–104.

77. Thus Frede, "Die Ordnung der Paulusbriefe," 292; Finegan, "Original Form"; and N. A. Dahl, "The Origin of the Earliest Prologues to the Pauline Letters," *Semeia* 12 (1978): 233–77, esp. 253, 263.

78. Dahl, "Particularity," 261–71.

79. Ibid. For further discussion, see ch. 3.

80. What is often called the "Marcionite order" of the Pauline letters, which is a distinguishing characteristic of the edition of the collection used by Marcion, is not exclusively associated with Marcion in the ancient evidence. The sequence Galatians-Corinthians-Romans, etc., is also found in the old Syriac, as witnessed by the Catalogus Sinaiticus and the commentary of Ephrem, on which see, respectively, A. S. Lewis, ed., *Studia Sinaitica*, 1, "Catalogue of the Syriac MSS in the Convent of St. Catherine on Mt. Sinai" (London: Clay, 1894), 13–14; and Th. Zahn, "Das Neue Testament Theodors von Mopsuestia und der ursprungliche Kanon der Syrer," *NKZ* 11 (1900): 788–806, esp. 798–99. The evidence is summarized by Frede, "Die Ordnung der Paulusbriefe," 295–97, but cf. J. Kerschensteiner, *Der altsyrische Paulustext* (Louvain: Secrétariat du Corpus SCO, 1970), 172–76, with some reservations.

81. This was seen already by A. von Harnack, *Marcion: Das Evangelium vom fremden Gott* (2d ed. rev.; Leipzig: Hinrichs, 1924), 168–69, also noted by J. Knox, *Marcion and the New Testament* (Chicago: University of Chicago Press, 1942), 60–70.

82. Additional confirmatory evidence of this is to be found in the so-called Marcionite prologues to the Pauline letters, and above all if they are not in fact

Marcionite. That they are catholic and not Marcionite products has been persuasively argued by H.-J. Frede, *Altlateinische Paulus-Handschriften* (Freiburg: Herder, 1964), 165–78, and in still greater detail by Dahl, "Earliest Prologues." Careful analysis of the prologues (Dahl, 246–51) shows that only six of those now available are original, and that a seventh (for Laodiceans/Ephesians) was at some point replaced. This means that the original set of prologues, which undoubtedly derives from the second century and a Greek archetype, represented ten letters of Paul (including Philemon) as letters to seven churches. It is a germane fact too that the prologues characteristically concern themselves with the communities that were addressed, rather than with the letters as such.

83. See Knox, *Marcion*, 43–45, and *Philemon among the Letters of Paul* (rev. ed.; New York: Abingdon Press, 1959), 83–86. This would comport with the evidence of Epiphanius. In any case, the present prologue for Philemon is patently secondary, which indicates that Philemon must have been reckoned with Colossians in the original set of prologues.

84. Clarity requires emphasizing that the seven churches edition taken up by Marcion was itself not identical to the original seven-churches edition, but a secondary variation on it. The order of the letters in Marcion's collection is not at all likely to have been his innovation, contrary to the common view. That order is much more easily comprehended as chronologically rather than dogmatically conceived (see Frede, *Altlateinische Paulus-Handschriften*, 165–66). An early placement of Romans in an ostensibly chronological scheme was permitted by the absence of chapters 14–15 in the text of Romans belonging to that edition. That Marcion simply took over a preexisting edition of Paul's letters, without modifying its order, is also supported by the character of its text. See the helpful treatment of this subject by J. J. Clabeaux, *A Lost Edition of the Letters of Paul. A Reassessment of the Text of the Pauline Corpus Attested by Marcion* (CBQMS 21; Washington, D.C.: Catholic Biblical Association, 1989).

85. This observation was made by E. J. Goodspeed on behalf of his own theory of the original Pauline letter collection, which, however, he took to consist of seven letters, not of letters to seven churches. See his *New Solutions of New Testament Problems* (Chicago: University of Chicago Press, 1927), 1–64.

86. On the early history of the Pauline letters before their collection, see also ch. 3.

87. Skeat, "Length of the Standard Papyrus Roll," 169–70.

88. Of a (presumed) manufactured roll of about 26 meters, Skeat (170) comments that it would be "much too long to be handled in one piece."

89. It is surprising how little attention has been given to the possibility that the Pauline letter collection was initially made available in a codex. I am able to cite only Finegan, "Original Form," 88; and G. Zuntz, *The Text of the Epistles: A Disquisition upon the Corpus Paulinum* (London: British Academy, 1953), 15. Both of these simply take it as a supposition but do not argue the case, though Finegan seems to recognize that a fixed order of the letters could not be secured in any other way.

90. I owe this formulation to a 1987 conversation with Peter Zaas of Siena College.

91. Thus, even though it may be true that practical advantages alone do not adequately explain the broad adoption of the codex in early Christianity (Roberts and Skeat, *Birth*, 53), those advantages cannot be simply disregarded when trying to determine why the codex was initially employed for whatever Christian document it was that served to popularize the codex for Christian literature generally.

92. Roberts, "The Codex," 187–88.

93. See ch. 1.

94. For a rather more speculative argument to this effect, see K. P. Donfried, "Paul as *Skeinopoios* and the Use of the Codex in Early Christianity," in *Christus bezeugen*, ed. K. Kertelge, T. Holtz, and C.-P. Marz (Leipzig: St. Benno-Verlag, 1989), 1:249–56. Observing that Paul's craft was leatherworking, Donfried suggests that Paul specialized in making parchment codices (!) and employed them himself to record both testimonia and Christian traditions, and to write his own letters.

95. But see the discussion by T. C. Skeat, " 'Especially the Parchments': A Note on 2 Timothy iv.13," *JTS* 30 (1979): 173–77, who favors the second sense against the lexical authorities and most commentators.

96. For the view that the Pastoral Epistles, though on the whole pseudonymous, nevertheless embody some authentic fragments, see P. N. Harrison, *The Problem of the Pastoral Epistles* (London: Oxford University Press, 1921). For the calculated use of personal notices to create an impression of authenticity in pseudonymous writings, see W. Speyer, *Die literarische Fälschung im heidnischen und christlichen Altertum* (HKAW 1.2; Munich, 1971), 44–84, and more briefly, N. Brox, *Falsche Verfasserangaben. Zur Erklärung der frühchristlichen Pseudepigraphie* (SBS 79; Stuttgart: Katholische Bibelwerk, 1975), 57–62.

97. McCormick, "Codex and Apostolic Life-Style," *Scriptorium* 39 (1985): 155.

98. See ch. 1 on early Christian testimonia collections. McCormick, "Codex and Apostolic Life-Style," 156–57, rightly calls attention to the importance from the beginning of Jewish scripture, "the first book the first Christians needed and used" (156), but his conception of Jewish scripture as a book and his apparent assumption that Christians would have undertaken early on to produce copies of whole books, are anachronistic.

99. See van Haelst, "Les origines," esp. 32–35.

100. For the list see Roberts and Skeat, *Birth*, 71, or van Haelst, "Les origines," 23–25 (who adds the dates proposed by Turner).

101. See van Haelst, "Les origines," 26, and McCormick, "Codex and Apostolic Life-Style," 157. McCormick takes these early non-Christian codices to be essentially the books of doctors and teachers and finds the common feature of these two groups in their mobility. This leads him to suggest that these groups were drawn to the codex because of its portability.

102. For the sizes and shapes of early codices, see especially Turner, *Typology*, 13–34.

103. Turner, *Typology*, comments (58) that "the relatively early character of this make-up is a striking fact" but considers (98–99) that the evidence does not suffice to prove that the earliest codices must have been made up in single

quires. It is potentially relevant that no known parchment codex is made up in a single quire; this method seems restricted to papyrus. All but one of the Nag Hammadi codices are of the single-quire variety, in spite of the fact that by the time these codices were constructed the multiple-quire method had become widespread. The largest number of pages among the Nag Hammadi codices is 156. For particulars see J. M. Robinson, "On the Codicology of the Nag Hammadi Codices," in *Les textes de Nag Hammadi*, ed. J. Ménard (Nag Hammadi Studies, 7; Leiden: Brill, 1975), 15–31, and (more fully) *The Facsimile Edition of the Nag Hammadi Codies: Introduction* (Leiden: Brill, 1984), 24–44.

104. See the studies of B. van Regemorter: "La reliure des manuscrits grecs," *Scriptorium* 8 (1954): 3–23; "Le codex relie depuis son origine jusqu'au Haut Moyen-Age," *Le Moyen Age* 61 (1955): 1–16; and *Some Early Bindings from Egypt in the Chester Beatty Library* (Chester Beatty Monographs, 7; Dublin: Hodges Figgis, 1958). Yet none of the codices she treats is as early as the third century.

105. A detailed analysis is given by J. M. Robinson, "The Construction of the Nag Hammadi Codices," in *Essays on the Nag Hammadi Texts in Honor of Pahor Labib*, ed. M. Krause (Nag Hammadi Studies, 6; Leiden: Brill, 1975), 170–90; and *The Facsimile Edition of the Nag Hammadi Codices*, 71–86 (superseding the studies of B. van Regemorter, "La reliure des manuscrits gnostiques decouverts a Nag Hammadi," *Scriptorium* 14 [1960]: 225–34; and J. Doresse, "Les reliures des manuscrits gnostiques coptes," *Revue d'Egyptologie* 13 [1961]: 27–49). Robinson shows that the covers can be distinguished by different types of manufacture.

106. Such a cover is preserved with the miniature Glazier manuscript (fourth or early fifth century) of the Pierpont Morgan Library containing part of Acts in Coptic, which is, incidentally, the earliest extant complete vellum codex and provides the earliest surviving cover for a vellum codex. Its cover is made of wooden boards joined with a leather strip on the spine and has straps with bone pegs at their ends, which wrapped around the closed codex. See J. S. Kebabian, "The Binding of the Glazier Manuscript of the Acts of the Apostles," in *Homage to a Bookman: Essays on Manuscripts, Books and Printing Written in Honor of Hans P. Kraus* (Berlin: Mann, 1967), 25–29.

107. Only a few papyrus codices were written in two columns a page. Among the Christian ones are P 4 + 64 + 67, P 8, P 50, P 78, and P. Oxy. 3527.

108. Turner, *Typology*, 37.

109. *Greek Literary Hands 350 B.C.–A.D. 400*, xi.

110. One of the best and most carefully nuanced discussions of Greek hands is given by Turner, *Greek Manuscripts*, 1–23. On the payment of scribes, the only explicit evidence is the edict of Diocletian of 301 C.E. (*De pretiis rerum venalium* 7.39–41 [CIL 3:381]), setting rates per hundred lines (*stichoi*) at twenty-five denarii for writing of the first quality and twenty denarii for writing of the second quality.

111. On informal round script, see the discussion of Turner, *Greek Manuscripts*, 20–21. The fullest discussion of script in specifically Christian manuscripts is given by Roberts, *Manuscript, Society, and Belief*, 14–23.

112. See Turner, *Greek Manuscripts*, 15.

113. This later became a characteristic feature of medieval manuscripts,

where the initial letter is often not only enlarged but elaborately worked and frequently done in red ink ("rubricated"). These developments are not found in Greek literary papyri. There are, however, a few examples in Christian papyri dating from the fourth and fifth centuries.

114. A good treatment of these factors is given by A. Dain, *Les manuscrits* (3d ed. rev.; Paris: Les Belles-Lettres, 1975), 15–55.

115. For intentional changes in the transmission of early Christian scriptural texts, see C. S. C. Williams, *Alterations to the Text of the Synoptic Gospels and Acts* (Oxford: Clarendon, 1951); K. W. Clark, "Textual Criticism and Doctrine," in *Studia Paulina in honorem J. de Zwaan* (Haarlem, 1953), 52–65; M. Karnetzki, "Textgeschichte als Überlieferungsgeschichte," *ZNW* 47 (1956): 170–80; and B. D. Ehrman, *Orthodox Corruptions of Scripture* (New York: Oxford University Press, 1993). See also ch. 3.

116. On the habits of the scribes of some of the earliest Christian books, see E. C. Colwell, "Scribal Habits in Early Papyri: A Study in the Corruption of the Text," in *The Bible in Modern Scholarship*, ed. J. P. Hyatt (Nashville: Abingdon, 1965), 370–89; J. R. Royse, "Scribal Habits in Early Greek New Testament Papyri" (Ph.D. diss., Graduate Theological Union, 1981), summarized in Royse, "Scribal Habits in the Transmission of New Testament Texts," in *The Critical Study of Sacred Texts*, ed. W. D. O'Flaherty (Berkeley Religious Studies Series, 2; Berkeley: Graduate Theological Union, 1979), 139–61; P. M. Head, "Observations on Early Papyri of the Synoptic Gospels, Especially on the 'Scribal Habits,'" *Bib* 71 (1990): 240–47; and more generally K. Junack, "Abschreibpraktiken und Schreibergewohnheiten in ihrer Auswirkung auf die Textüberlieferung," in *New Testament Textual Criticism: Its Significance for Exegesis, Essays in Honor of Bruce M. Metzger*, ed. E. J. Epp and G. D. Fee (Oxford: Clarendon, 1981), 277–95.

117. An interesting example is P 66, an early copy of the Gospel of John. The scribe, although possessing a good and well-practiced hand, proved in this case to be a careless copyist. See, on this manuscript, in addition to the studies in the preceding note, G. D. Fee, "The Corrections of Papyrus Bodmer II and Early Textual Transmission," *NovT* 7 (1965): 247–57; and E. F. Rhodes, "The Corrections of Papyrus Bodmer II," *NTS* 14 (1968): 271–81.

118. Turner, *Typology*, 84–87. The manuscript that especially caught his eye was the Chester Beatty codex IX–X (Ezekiel, Daniel, Susanna, Bel, and the Dragon), which offers 49–54 lines to a page and 17–23 letters to a line, while comparable Greek prose texts in codex manuscripts tend to have a few more lines to the page and significantly more letters to the line. The observation holds also for P 66 and P 75, among other early Christian manuscripts.

119. See Turner, *Greek Manuscripts*, 144, on P. Oxy. 3533 (Menander). Some more notable examples among early Christian manuscripts are: P. Bad. 456 (Exodus-Deuteronomy), P. Mich. 130 (Hermas), P. Ryl. 1.1 (Deuteronomy), Chester Beatty IX (Esther), and P. Yale 3 [P 50] (Acts). On lectional aids in early Christian manuscripts, see also the comments of Roberts, *Manuscript, Society, and Belief*, 21–22. For the practice of the public reading of Christian texts, see ch. 5.

120. The original study of this phenomenon was made by L. Traube, *Nomina Sacra: Versuch einer Geschichte der christlichen Kürzung* (Munich: Beck,

1907). It has been repeatedly discussed, but without great progress, in many subsequent studies. See esp. A. H. R. E. Paap, *Nomina Sacra in the Greek Papyri of the First Five Centuries A.D.: The Sources and Some Deductions* (Leiden: Brill, 1959); S. Brown, "Concerning the Origin of the *Nomina Sacra*," *SP* 9 (1970): 7–19; G. Howard, "The Tetragram and the New Testament," *JBL* 96 (1977): 63–83; and most recently, C. H. Roberts, *Manuscript, Society, and Belief,* 26–48.

121. Aland, *Repertorium,* conveniently notes the presence of the convention whenever it occurs and gives the forms attested in each manuscript.

122. This is the origin of the peculiar English formation "Jehovah," which misconstrues a transcriptive convention as a pronounceable word. As Brown points out ("*Nomina Sacra,*" 10), Traube's entire study is vitiated by a failure to grasp that in the pre-Masoretic tradition Hebrew was written only consonantally.

123. For details, see Howard, "The Tetragram," esp. 66–70.

124. For a detailed survey of the evidence, see J. A. Fitzmyer, "The Semitic Background of the New Testament *Kyrios*-Title," in *A Wandering Aramean: Collected Aramaic Essays* (SBLMS 25; Missoula: Scholars Press, 1979), 115–42. A brief summary of the main points is given by Howard, "The Tetragram," 63–65.

125. Roberts, *Manuscript, Society, and Belief,* 26–48. Roberts goes so far as to say that the system of nomina sacra embodies "the embryonic creed of the first Church" (46).

126. Brown, "*Nomina Sacra,*" 14–16.

127. Howard, "The Tetragram," 76.

128. This is also indicated by the appearance of the Christogram in very early Christian texts, as noted by K. Aland, "Bemerkungen zum Alter und zur Entstehung des Christogrammes anhand von Beobachtungen bei P 66 und P 75," in *Studien zur Überlieferung des Neuen Testaments und seines Textes* (ANTT 2; Berlin: de Gruyter, 1967), 173–79.

129. It is an interesting question whether the scribes of Christian books were paid for their work or did it from devotion. The question probably has no generally valid answer in the early period. The best indication that scribes were paid is the presence in some manuscripts of calculations of stichoi, or fixed units of measurement. But stichoi had another important use, namely, to document the scope of the text and thus to test whether it was complete.

130. Specially prepared parchment with lines carefully ruled was required (B. T. Megillah 19a), and a particular type of script (without vocalization) was normative (B. T. Shabbat 104a, Sanhedrin 21b-22a, and Megillah 1.71b). Orthographic uniformity was emphasized (B. T. Erubin 13a, Megillah 18b, and Ketubot 19b), and "crowns" *(tagin)* were required for seven letters of the alphabet whenever they occurred (B. T. Menahot 29b). Promoting careful inscription was the rule (B. T. Megillah 29b) that any sheet of parchment that contained as many as four errors was not to be corrected but discarded (and buried).

131. See esp. Roberts, *Manuscript, Society and Belief,* app. 1 ("Jewish Theological Papyri of the Roman Period"), 74–78, commenting (76) that "there seems to have been a distinctive style of writing used for Jewish copies of the

scriptures in Greek from the second century B.C. onwards, and still used, with modifications of course, down to the third century A.D." This style is typical enough that Roberts would add it as a criterion for identifying Jewish manuscripts to those discussed (and largely relativized) by K. Treu, "Die Bedeutung des griechischen für die Juden im römischen Reich," *Kairos* 15 (1973): 123–44.

132. Eusebius, *De vita Const.* 4.36.

133. For discussions of this supposition, see K. Lake, "The Sinaitic and Vatican Manuscripts and the Copies Sent by Eusebius to Constantine," *HTR* 11 (1918): 32–35; and K. Wendel, "Der Bibel-Auftrag Kaiser Konstantins," *Zentralblatt für Bibliothekswesen* 56 (1939): 165–75. T. C. Skeat, "The Use of Dictation in Ancient Book Production," *PBA* 42 (1956): 179–208, regards the Codex Vaticanus (written in three columns to the page) as one of the copies prepared for Constantine but never sent because it was defective in various particulars (196–97). Without claiming that either Sinaiticus or Vaticanus was produced in Caesarea in response to Constantine's request, some scholars nevertheless regard these codices as examples, in scope and quality, of the sorts of copies that were made: W. H. P. Hatch, *The Principal Uncial Manuscripts of the New Testament* (Chicago: University of Chicago Press, 1939), 18; B. M. Metzger, *The Text of the New Testament* (2d ed.; Oxford: Clarendon, 1968), 7–8.

134. Thus, most recently, G. A. Robbins, "Peri ton Endiathekon Graphon: Eusebius and the Formation of the Christian Bible" (Ph.D. diss., Duke University, 1986), 186–216.

135. The punctuation, hence the sense, is not entirely clear. It is grammatically possible that the phrase means that the book was written "on the inside and on the outside" (cf. Ezek. 2:8–3:3), but even that sense does not necessarily indicate an opisthograph. Bibliographic evidence indicates that what is in view is rather a roll book of the diploma (double document) type. This is correctly recognized by G. Bornkamm, "Die Komposition der apocalyptischen Visionen in der Offenbarung Johannis," in *Studien zu Antike und Christentum* (Munich: Kaiser, 1953), 204–22: "A document in two parts which, being written in a two-fold fashion, comprises one legally valid text and a corresponding second text, unsealed and offered for the inspection of everyone," 205). For a detailed discussion of the nature and use of the diploma roll, see Turner, "Recto and Verso," 26–53. Turner shows that rolls of this type were ordinarily written *transversa charta*: the roll of papyrus was rotated ninety degrees and inscribed across the fibers. Thus the text was vertical to the length of the roll, and for reading the roll was held vertically rather than horizontally. Turner also points out that such rolls (rotuli) were used for documentary purposes.

136. For heavenly books, see further in Rev. 3:5, 13:8, 17:8, 20:12, 15, and, e.g., in other apocalyptic texts, 1 Enoch 89.70–71, 47.3, 90.20; 4 Ezra 6.20; 2 Baruch 24.1; and Jub. 36.10; cf. heavenly tablets in, e.g., 1 Enoch 81.1–2, 93.2–3, 103.2, and 106.19. Fuller references are given by R. H. Charles, *Apocrypha and Pseudepigrapha of the Old Testament*, 2 vols. (Oxford: Oxford University Press, 1913), 2:216, n. (on 1 Enoch 47.3). Cf. generally L. Koep, *Das himmlische Buch in Antike und Christentum: Eine religionsgeschichtliche Untersuchung zur altchristlichen Bildersprache* (Bonn: Hanstein, 1952).

137. For these, see van Haelst, *Catalogue*, 409–13.

138. J. den Boeft and J. Bremmer, "Notiunculae Martyriologicae IV," *VC* 45 (1991): 105–22 (esp. 116–17). Their further comment that a continuing Christian use of roll books is supported by Tertullian's failure, despite his rich terminology for Christian scripture, to use the term *codex*, carries no more weight than any argument from silence. On the *Acts of the Scillitan Martyrs*, see also ch. 4.

139. The point is emphasized by W. V. Harris, "Why Did the Codex Supplant the Book-Roll?" in *Renaissance Society and Culture: Essays in Honor of Eugene F. Rice, Jr.*, ed. J. Monfasani and R. G. Musto (New York: Italica, 1991), 71–85 (esp. 77).

140. Ibid., 78, 83–85, with criticism of Roberts and Skeat for neglecting this.

CHAPTER III: THE PUBLICATION AND CIRCULATION OF EARLY CHRISTIAN LITERATURE

1. The text had not been identified when the manuscript (P. Oxy. 405) was first published. For the dating of the manuscript "near the end of the second century" see C. H. Roberts, "Early Christianity in Egypt," *JEA* 40 (1954): 92–96 (esp. 94). The fullest discussion is given by A. Rousseau and L. Doutreleau, *Irenée de Lyons: Contre les heresies*, bk. 3, vol. 1 (SC 210; Paris: Cerf, 1974), 126–31.

2. P. Mich. 130; see C. Bonner, "A New Fragment of the Shepherd of Hermas, Michigan Papyrus 44," *HTR* 20 (1927): 105–16. The text is written on the verso of a roll, which on the recto has a document of the third quarter of the second century. On the time-lapse to be allowed in the case of opisthographs, see Turner, *Greek Manuscripts*, 18–19.

3. The manuscript is P. Ryl. 457 (=P 52). See C. H. Roberts, "An Unpublished Fragment of the Fourth Gospel in the John Rylands Library," *BJRL* 20 (1936): 45–55. Some would date the manuscript closer to 100 than 125: see K. Aland, "Neue neutestamentliche Papyri II," *NTS* 9 (1962–63): 303–16 (307: "near the beginning of the second century").

4. It is a question, of course, what conclusions about circulation and use may be drawn from the place of a manuscript's discovery and its paleographic dating. It is conceivable that a given manuscript might never have been read or otherwise circulated in the place where it was found, or that, if it was, it occurred only at a later date than the date to which the actual writing of the manuscript was assigned. Although these possibilities require acknowledgment, they are not the most plausible assumptions in most cases, including the one cited above.

5. K. Dziatzko, "Autor- und Verlagsrecht im Altertum," *RhM* 49 (1894): 559–76; W. Speyer, *Die literarische Fälschung im heidnischen und christlichen Altertum: Ein Versuch ihrer Deutung* (Munich: Beck, 1971).

6. On the process by which texts were published and entered into circulation in antiquity, the most helpful discussions are V. Burr, "Editionstechnik," *RAC* 4 (1959): 597–610; B. van Groningen, "Ekdosis," *Mnemosyne* 16 (1963): 1–17; R. Sommer, "T. Pomponius Atticus und die Verbreitung von Ciceros Werken," *Hermes* 61 (1926): 389–422; K. Quinn, "The Poet and His Audience

in the Augustan Age," *ANRW* 30.1, 75–180; and R. Starr, "The Circulation of Literary Texts in the Roman World," *CQ* 37 (1987): 213–23. Of the older literature, one of the more useful discussions is K. Dziatzko, *Untersuchungen über ausgewählte Kapitel des antiken Buchwesen* (Leipzig: Teubner, 1900), 149–78.

7. Quinn, "The Poet," 83–93.

8. On *recitationes*, which became very popular in the early Empire, see J. Carcopino, *Daily Life in Ancient Rome*, 193–95, M. Hadas, *Ancilla to Classical Reading* (New York: Columbia University Press, 1961), 60–64; and esp. Quinn, "The Poet," 158–65. The letters of Pliny give the fullest insight into the practice: see A. N. Sherwin-White, *The Letters of Pliny: A Historical and Social Commentary* (Oxford: Clarendon, 1966), on 1.13, 2.19, 3.18, 4.5, 5.12, 7.17. He speaks of the recitation as "the popular form of initial publication, providing the quickest and cheapest means of making works known to the largest educated audience." (115).

9. Van Groningen, "Ekdosis," 5–7.

10. On the book trade generally see, among others, T. Kleberg, *Buchhandel und Verlagswesen in der Antike* (Darmstadt, 1967); H. L. Pinner, *The World of Books in Classical Antiquity* (Leiden: Sijthoff, 1948), 22–49; F. Reichmann, "The Book Trade at the Time of the Roman Empire," *Library Quarterly* 8 (1938): 40–76, all of whom overestimate the evidence and make anachronistic assessments. More recent and cautious discussions are given by R. Fehrle, *Das Bibliothekswesen im Alten Rom: Voraussetzungen, Bedingungen, Anfänge* (Wiesbaden: Reichert, 1986), 29–53; and J. J. Phillips, "The Publication of Books at Rome in the Classical Period" (Ph.D. diss., Yale University, 1981).

11. See E. G. Turner, *Athenian Books in the Fifth and Fourth Centuries B.C.* (London: Lewis, 1952), 20–21.

12. *Ad Quint. frat.* 3.4.5; 3.5–6.6. Cicero often borrowed books from friends for the purpose of having them copied (*Ad Att.* 2.20.6, 2.22.7), even as others borrowed from him (*Ad Att.* 16.5.5).

13. N. Brockmeyer, "Die soziale Stellung der 'Buchhandler' in der Antike," *AGB* 13 (1973): 238–48.

14. This view depends rather more on Cornelius Nepos's *Life of Atticus* (13.3) than on Cicero's letters. Nepos reports that within Atticus's household there were "highly educated slaves, the best readers, and many copyists" *(pueri litteratissimi, anagnostae optimi et plurimi librarii)*.

15. The case against regarding Atticus as a commercial publisher was well made by R. Sommer, "T. Pomponius Atticus und die Verbreitung von Ciceros Werken," *Hermes* 61 (1926): 389–422. See also Fehrle, *Bibliothekswesen*, 36–44; and J. J. Phillips, "Atticus and the Publication of Cicero's Works," *CW* 79 (1986): 227–37, and "Publication of Books at Rome in the Classical Period," 402.

16. Sherwin-White, *Letters*, 91 (on *Ep.* 1.2), avers that "the distribution of [Pliny's] books was entirely in the hands of the *bibliopolae*," but this goes beyond the evidence. Though Martial mentions book dealers and their shops more than any other ancient writer, it is not clear that he even relied exclusively on them.

17. Cf. Horace, *Ars poet.* 345; Martial, 3.38, 11.3, 13.3, 1.117.

18. On patronage generally, see R. P. Saller, *Personal Patronage under the Early Empire* (Cambridge: Cambridge University Press, 1982); and A. Wallace-Hadrill, ed., *Patronage in Ancient Society* (London: Routledge, 1989). For specifically literary patronage, see the essays collected in *Literary and Artistic Patronage in Ancient Rome*, ed. B. K. Gold (Austin: University of Texas Press, 1982); P. White, "*Amicitia* and the Profession of Poetry in Early Imperial Rome," *JRS* 68 (1978): 74–92; R. P. Saller, "Martial on Patronage and Literature," *CQ* 33 (1983): 246–57; and Quinn, "The Poet," 116–39.

19. There is only one reference in classical literature to the number of copies produced: Pliny (*Ep.* 4.7.2) tells of Aquilius Regulus having had a thousand copies made of his tribute to his son, a number that Pliny clearly regards as unusually large and in bad taste. Birt (*Das Antike Buchwesen*, 351–53) thought, partly on this basis, that the ordinary edition numbered five hundred or a thousand copies, but nothing favors this view. See Quinn, "The Poet," 78–83, for incisive criticism.

20. The distribution of literature in the provinces is alluded to by Horace (*Carm.* 1.20.13, cf. *Ars poet.* 345–46), Martial (1.1, 7.88, 11.3), Ovid (*Trist.* 4.9.21; 4.10.128) and Pliny (*Ep.* 4.7.2, 9.2.2); it is not certain, but likely, that book sellers were often the agents. For an example of a bookdealer in Egypt see ch. 2.

21. The phrase is used by T. C. Skeat, "The Use of Dictation in Ancient Book-Production," 189. The imaginative description given by Quinn ("The Poet ," 78–79) of the process of producing a thousand copies is an effective *reductio ad absurdum*.

22. For this, see ch. 5.

23. On the psychological and physiological aspects of visual copying, see Dain, *Les manuscrits*, 40–46; and the discussion by K. Junack, "Abschreibpraktiken und Schreibergewohnheiten in ihrer Auswirkung auf die Textüberlieferung," *New Testament Textual Criticism and Its Significance for Exegesis*, ed. E. J. Epp and G. D. Fee (Oxford: Clarendon, 1981), esp. 279–88. Skeat, "Use of Dictation" (206–8), recognizes the problem and proposes that, beyond discriminating visual and auditory errors, a third type might be identified as due to "a lack of liaison between dictator and scribe" and that the presence in a given manuscript of a large number of such "singular errors" would indicate that it was written from dictation. Yet instances symptomatic of liaison problems are difficult to identify.

24. Skeat, "Use of Dictation," 183–85. On scribal posture, see also B. M. Metzger, "When Did Scribes Begin to Use Writing Desks?" in *Historical and Literary Studies, Pagan, Jewish, and Christian* (Leiden: Brill, 1968), 123–37; and G. M. Parassoglou, "Dexia Cheir kai Gonu: Some Thoughts on the Positions of the Ancient Greeks and Romans When Writing on Papyrus Rolls," *Scritta et Civiltà* 3 (1979): 5–21; and "A Roll upon His Knees," *YCS* 28 (1985): 273–75.

25. Skeat, "Use of Dictation," 189.

26. See P. Petitmengin and B. Flusin, "Le livre antique et la dictée," *Memorial André Jean Festugière: Antiquité paienne et chrétienne*, ed. E. Lucchesi and H. D. Saffrey (Geneva: Cramer, 1984), 247–62, emphasizing the use of dictation in schools and administrative settings in particular. Dictation was

commonly used in the *composition* of literary works, but that is a different matter from copying texts.

27. Sherwin-White, *Letters*, 271, calls attention to Pliny's use of the term *transcriptum* in *Ep.* 4.7.2, referring to the one thousand copies of Regulus's tribute to his son, and suggests that Pliny thereby "implies that in his experience direct copying was normal for the production of large editions." Elsewhere (*Ep.* 5.10.3) Pliny also uses *describere* for commercial copying, and here "the force of the preposition is more appropriate to copying than to dictation, though less emphatically so." This may, however, be resting too much on prepositions.

28. In the provincial towns and villages of Roman Egypt, however, it was sometimes the case that only scribes were literate and thus had high standing in the community. See Turner, *Greek Papyri*, 82–84. Similar circumstances may have obtained in provincial areas outside Egypt.

29. On scribal payment and its relation to stichometry, see K. Ohly, *Stichometrische Untersuchungen* (Zentralblatt für Bibliothekswesen, Beiheft 61; Leipzig: Harrassowitz, 1928), 86–90.

30. Cicero, *ad Quint. frat.* 3.5.6; Strabo, 13.1.54 (cf. 50.13.419); Martial, 2.8.3–4; Seneca, *De ira* 2.26.2; Quintillian, *Inst. Orat.*, ep. praem.

31. Fehrle, *Bibliothekswesen*, 47; and Quinn, "The Poet," 164–65.

32. Starr, "Circulation," 223.

33. Most famously, Lucian, *Adv. indoct.*, but see also Seneca, *Ep.* 27.6, *De tranq. anima* 9.9; Juvenal, *Sat.* 2.4–7; Petronius, *Sat.* 48. See also the comments of T. Kleberg, "Bibliophiles in Ancient Rome," *Libri* 1 (1950): 2–

34. Starr, "Circulation," 223. The different attitudes taken by Horace and Martial toward booksellers and the wider public is interesting. Horace thought the appropriate setting for the circulation of literature was a small circle of friends and regarded the marketing of texts to the *vulgus* as an unworthy, if unavoidable, aspect of the fate of a literary work (*serm.* 1.4.71–77; 1.10.72–91; *Ep.* 1.20.1–18). Martial shows no such scruple as he carefully directs potential buyers to the dealers who sell his texts (1.2.7–8, 1.113.5). For Martial's reliance on book sellers see especially H. L. M. van der Valk, "On the Edition of Books in Antiquity," *VC* 11 (1957): 1–10.

35. See above, ch. 2.

36. The text and plate of this letter are reproduced in Turner, *Greek Manuscripts*, 114–15 (no. 68), with comments.

37. Ibid., 114, "Roman Oxyrhynchus," *JEA* 38 (1952): 78–93 (91–92), and *Greek Papyri*, 86–87. Diodorus (the son of Pollio) is shown to be a landowner in Oxyrhynchus and a member of the Museum in Alexandria by P. Mert. 19, a contract that refers to him as a "former writer of commentaries [*hypomnematographos*] and member of the Museum."

38. On Libanius and his associates see A. F. Norman, "The Book Trade in Fourth Century Antioch," *JHS* 30 (1960): 122–26.

39. Turner (*Greek Manuscripts*, 16) suggests that commercially produced manuscripts may be expected to show, in addition to stichometric notations, "regularity of handwriting, wide margins and spacious layout." But it cannot be supposed that all commercial book production was of high quality. Such

deluxe features, though pleasing to the eye, have no necessary correlation with the accuracy of the transcription, which for the scholar was the mark of a high-quality text.

40. The extremity of Deissmann's views was recognized and criticized by P. Wendland, *Die urchristlichen Literaturformen* (HzNT 1/3; Tübingen: Mohr, 1912), 344–45. He rightly remarked that "the question whether or not a letter ought to be classified as literature does not coincide with the question whether or not it was to be commercially published; content and style also come into consideration. In antiquity the distinctions between a private piece of writing and literature were much more fluid than in the period of the printing press, and it is important, even for early Christian literature, to keep in mind the different stages of publicity at a time when there was still no mechanical duplication." See further the comments of E. R. Richards, *The Secretary in the Letters of Paul* (WUNT 42; Tübingen: Mohr, 1991), 211–16 (app. G).

41. See K. Berger, "Apostelbrief und apostolische Rede: Zum Formular früh-christlicher Briefe," *ZNW* 65 (1974): 190–231, with special reference to for-mulaic elements; and "Hellenistische Gattungen im Neuen Testament," *ANRW* 2.25.2, 1326–40; and S. Stowers, *Letter Writing in Graeco-Roman Antiquity* (Philadelphia: Westminster, 1986), esp. 17–26.

42. Richards, *The Secretary*, esp. 169–98. This is the best study of the question available. For earlier discussions see O. Roller, *Das Formular der paulinischen Briefe: Ein Beitrag zu Lehre vom antiken Briefe* (BWANT 4/6 [58]; Stuttgart: Kohlhammer, 1933); R. Eschliman, "La rédaction des épîtres pauliniennes," *RB* 53 (1946): 185–96; G. J. Bahr, "Paul and Letter Writing in the First Century," *CBQ* 28 (1966): 465–77.

43. See H. Gamble, *The Textual History of the Letter to the Romans* (StD 42; Grand Rapids: Eerdmans, 1977), 76–80; G. J. Bahr, "The Subscriptions in the Pauline Letters," *JBL* 87 (1968): 27–41 (though Bahr goes much too far in arguing for long autographic subscriptions that summarize the main points of the letters); and Richards, *The Secretary*, 169–81. 2 Thess. 3:17 claims that the Pauline autograph is a "sign in every letter." The reference to the autograph is surely intended as an authenticating sign in this probably inauthentic letter, but in the genuine letters the autograph did not serve this purpose, aiming only to express immediate personal contact.

44. Richards, *The Secretary*, 189–94, concludes on the basis of systemati-cally applied criteria that of the seven indisputably authentic letters, four (Rom., 1 Cor., Gal. Phlm.) were certainly written with the aid of a secretary, and two others (2 Cor., 1 Thess.) probably were. Whether a secretary was used for Philippians is "unascertainable." I leave aside the further question of whether Paul's letters were dictated *syllabatim* (syllable by syllable) or viva voce (whole words at a normal or somewhat slower speaking pace), on which see Richards, 24–43, who considers (195) that Paul must have dictated syl-labatim.

45. A well-informed discussion of the ancient use of secretaries for letter writing and of Greek and Latin shorthand techniques in antiquity is given by Richards, *The Secretary*, 15–43. For shorthand transcription of later Christian works see further below in the text.

46. Ibid., 53–56.

47. See E. J. Epp, "New Testament Papyrus Manuscripts and Letter Carrying in Greco-Roman Times," in *The Future of Early Christianity: Essays in Honor of Helmut Koester,* ed. B. A. Pearson (Minneapolis: Fortress Press, 1991), 35–56.

48. The "letter from *(ek)* Laodicea" has always been thought, no doubt rightly, to be a letter to the Laodiceans that was to be obtained from them. Normally, this would have been done by taking a copy. No such letter to Laodicea survives. Marcion (Tertullian, *Adv. Marc.* 5) knew our Ephesians under this title, but it is unlikely that the letter mentioned in Col. 4:16 was Ephesians. If there actually was a letter to the Laodiceans and it has survived among the Pauline letters, it is most likely to be Philemon.

49. For the claim that Paul himself sponsored such circulation for some of the authentic letters, see D. Trobisch, *Die Entstehung der Paulusbriefsammlung* (NTOA 10; Freiburg: Universitätsverlag, 1989), 126 (for 2 Cor.), 129–30 (Rom.).

50. N. A. Dahl, "The Particularity of the Pauline Epistles as a Problem in the Ancient Church," in *Neotestamentica et Patristica* (NovTSup 6; Leiden: Brill, 1962), 261–71. On the textual evidence for the generalized addresses see, on Romans, Gamble, *Textual History,* 29–33; and on 1 Corinthians, G. Zuntz, *The Text of the Epistles* (London: Oxford University Press, 1953), 91–92.

51. Zuntz, *Epistles,* 228, n. 1, 276.

52. See H.-M. Schenke, "Das Weiterwirken des Paulus und die Pflege seines Erbs durch die Paulusschule," *NTS* 21 (1975): 505–18; and A. Sand, "Überlieferung und Sammlung der Paulusbriefe," in K. Kertelge, ed., *Paulus in den neutestamentlichen Spätschriften* (QD 89; Freiburg: Herder, 1981), 11–24.

53. On the communication between Paul and the Corinthians, see N. A. Dahl, "Paul and the Church in Corinth according to 1 Corinthians 1–4," *Christian History and Interpretation: Studies Presented to John Knox,* ed. W. R. Farmer, C. F. D. Moule, and R. R. Niebuhr (Cambridge: Cambridge University Press, 1967), 313–35. For the likelihood that Paul also received letters from other churches, esp. Thessalonians and Philippians, see A. Malherbe, "Did the Thessalonians Write to Paul?" *The Conversation Continues: Studies in Paul and John in Honor of J. Louis Martyn,* ed. R. T. Fortna and B. R. Gaventa (Nashville: Abingdon, 1990), 246–57.

54. Sosthenes is named in 1 Cor. 1:1; Timothy in 2 Cor. 1:1, Phil. 1:1, Col. 1:1; and Phlm. 1; Silvanus and Timothy in 1 Thess. 1:1 (and 2 Thess. 1:1). Cf. Gal. 1:2: "All those brothers who are with me."

55. On Paul's associates, see E. E. Ellis, "Paul and His Co-Workers," *NTS* 17 (1971): 437–52; and W. Ollrog, *Paulus und seine Mitarbeiter: Untersuchungen zu Theorie und Praxis der paulinischen Mission* (WMANT 50; Neukirchen-Vluyn: Neukirchener Verlag, 1979). For the school character of the Pauline mission and message, see esp. H. Conzelmann, "Paulus und die Weisheit," *NTS* 12 (1965): 321–44; and "Die Schule des Paulus," *Theologia Crucis —Signum Crucis: Festschrift für E. Dinkler,* ed. C. Andresen and G. Klein (Tübingen: Mohr, 1979), 85–96. On ancient school associations and the sense of "schools" in early Christianity, see A. Culpepper, *The Johannine School: An Evaluation of the Johannine-school Hypothesis Based on an Investigation of*

the Nature of Ancient Schools (SBLDS 26; Missoula, Mont.: Scholars Press, 1975).

56. For a useful discussion of the many problems and theories surrounding the formation of the Pauline corpus, see E. H. Lovering, The Collection, Redaction, and Early Circulation of the Corpus Paulinum (Ph.D. diss., Southern Methodist University, 1988).

57. See L. Mowry, "The Early Circulation of Paul's Letters," JBL 63 (1944): 73–86, opposing Goodspeed's assumption that Paul's letters early fell into oblivion.

58. On the conditions under which pseudonymous materials could be distributed, see W. Speyer, Die literarische Fälschung im heidnischen und christlichen Altertum, 84–88; and N. Brox, Falsche Verfasserangaben: Zur Erklärung der frühchristlichen Pseudepigraphie (SBS 79; Stuttgart: Katholisches Bibelwerk, 1975), 62–67.

59. On the knowledge of Paul's letters among these and other second-century writers, see the thorough studies of Lindemann, Paulus, and Rensberger, "As the Apostle Teaches."

60. On the early editions of the Pauline corpus, see ch. 2.

61. See Trobisch, Die Entstehung der Paulusbriefsammlung, 89–104, for a concise statement of the evidence for authorial involvement in other collections. For evidence that letter collections were published from copies retained by the author, see Richards, The Secretary, 3–4. On the use of letter copy books in antiquity see also Deissmann, Light from the Ancient East, 227.

62. There is nothing to be said against the assumption that Theophilus was an actual person (see J. A. Fitzmyer, The Gospel According to Luke (I–IX) [AB; Garden City: Doubleday, 1981], 299–300; and A. Vögtle, "Was hatte die Widmung des lukanischen Doppelwerks an Theophilus zu bedeuten?" Das Evangelium und die Evangelien [Dusseldorf: Patmos, 1971], 31–42), even if he also serves as a surrogate for a wider audience (P. Minear, "Dear Theo: The Kerygmatic Intention and Claim of the Book of Acts," Int 27 [1973] 131–50). For the role that Theophilus as dedicatee might have had in promoting the distribution of the work, see E. J. Goodspeed, "Some Greek Notes: I. Was Theophilus Luke's Publisher?" JBL 73 (1954): 84; and M. Dibelius, Studies in the Acts of the Apostles (London: SCM Press, 1956), 135, 146–48.

63. This was rightly observed, though against the consensus, by C. F. D. Moule, The Phenomenon of the New Testament (SBT; London: SCM Press, 1967), app. 2, "The Intention of the Evangelists," 100–114.

64. G. D. Kilpatrick, The Transmission of the New Testament and Its Reliability (Proceedings of the Victoria Institute, 89; 1957), 96, takes the fact that the manuscript tradition of Mark shows a much larger number of scribal corrections than those of the other Gospels to show that Mark had a longer period of early individual circulation. Yet the many variants in Mark may be owing to other factors—including its rudimentary style and efforts to harmonize it with parallel passages in Matthew and Luke.

65. Eusebius, H.E. 3.39.15–16. On the early circulation and use of the Gospel of Matthew, see W. D. Kohler, Die Rezeption des Matthäusevangelium in der Zeit vor Irenaeus (WUNT 2/24; Tübingen: Mohr, 1987); and on Papias's use of Matthew and Mark, see also U. H. J. Kortner, Papias von Hierapolis: Ein

Beitrag zur Geschichte des frühen Christentums (FRLANT, 133; Göttingen: Vandenhoeck und Ruprecht, 1983), 203–15.

66. B. Lindars, *The Gospel of John* (NCB; London: Oliphants, 1972), 641, comments that the "we" in 21:24 "represents the imprimatur of the community in which [the Gospel] originated" and suggests that it was added for fear that the Gospel "would not easily win wide acceptance" outside that community.

67. Recent discussions of the Fourth Gospel have tended to speak of different stages of its compositional history as "editions." See, e.g., R. E. Brown, *The Gospel according to John (i–xiii)* (AB; Garden City, N.Y.: Doubleday, 1966), xxiv–xl, esp. xxxiv–xxxix; B. Lindars, *The Gospel of John* (NCB; London: Oliphants, 1972), 46–54; J. Ashton, *Understanding the Fourth Gospel* (Oxford: Clarendon, 1991), 160–66. This is intelligible enough, but makes for confusion when one attempts to discuss the actual publication of the Gospel. Strictly speaking, only a form of the text that is actually made available for transcription and circulation should be termed an edition. Theories about its compositional stages notwithstanding, we know of only one edition of the Fourth Gospel.

68. For a concise discussion and literature in addition to Moule, *The Phenomenon of the New Testament*, 100–114, see D. L. Tiede, "Religious Propaganda and Gospel Literature," *ANRW* 2.25.2, 1705–29. On the missionary and propagandistic features of Gospel literature, see also (among others): C. W. Votaw, *The Gospels and Contemporary Biographies in the Graeco-Roman World* (Philadelphia: Fortress, 1970); D. Georgi, "The Records of Jesus in Light of Ancient Accounts of Revered Men," *Proceedings of the Society of Biblical Literature* (Philadelphia: SBL, 1972), 2:527–42; E. S. Fiorenza, "Miracles, Mission, and Apologetics: An Introduction," *Aspects of Religious Propaganda in Judaism and Early Christianity*, ed. E. S. Fiorenza (Notre Dame: University of Notre Dame Press, 1976), 1–25; and see D. Senior, "The Struggle to Be Universal: Mission as a Vantage Point for New Testament Investigation," *CBQ* 46 (1984), 63–81. The question of the genre of the Gospels is not irrelevant here; see ch. 1.

69. Thus, e.g., Aristides, 16.3, 5; Justin, *Apol.* 1.28; Athenagoras, *Leg.* 9.3, Tertullian, *Apol.* 31.

70. For Celsus's knowledge of Gospels in particular, see Origen, *c. Cels.* 1.34, 1.40, 1.58, 1.68, 2.24, 2.27, 2.32, 2.34, 2.36, 2.55, 2.59, 5.52, 6.16, 7.18. References to Christian scripture by ancient critics of Christianity have been conveniently collected by G. Rinaldi, *Biblia Gentium* (Rome: Libreria Sacre Scritture, 1989).

71. For pagan criticism and Christian defensiveness of the style of Christian writings, see E. Norden, *Die Antike Kunstprosa* (2d ed.; Leipzig: Teubner, 1909), 2.516–28. His assertion (518) that "pagans read the Gospels (and epistles) only when, like Celsus, Hierocles, Porphyry, and Julian, they wanted to refute them" is an argument from silence.

72. In favor of the imitation of a Pauline precedent, see E. J. Goodspeed, *New Solutions to New Testament Problems* (Chicago: University of Chicago Press, 1927), 1–64; A. E. Barnett, *Paul Becomes a Literary Influence* (Chicago: University of Chicago Press, 1941), 41–51; and J. L. White, "Saint Paul and the Apostolic Letter Tradition," *CBQ* 45 (1983): 433–44.

73. Allusions to books *(biblion, biblaridion, biblos)* occur twenty-seven times in the Apocalypse alone versus nineteen times in the rest of the New Testament writings.

74. See ch. 1.

75. *Kanonisierungsformel*; thus F. Hahn, "Die Sendschreiben der Johannesapokalypse: Ein Beitrag zur Bestimmung prophetischer Redeformen," *Tradition und Glaube: Das frühe Christentum in seiner Umwelt*, ed. G. Jeremias, H.-W. Kuhn, and H. Stegemann (Göttingen: Vandenhoeck und Ruprecht, 1971), 357–94 (361).

76. W. C. van Unnik, "De la règle *mete prostheinai mete aphelein* dans l'histoire du canon," *VC* 3 (1949): 1–36, has collected examples of similar formulas. Only a few, however, pertain specifically to texts. Aristeas 311; Philo, *De vita Mos.* 2.34; and Josephus, *Ant.* 12.109 all refer to the LXX. For texts where such a formula is used by an author with reference to his own writing, see further below.

77. *The Letters to the Seven Churches of Asia and Their Place in the Plan of the Apocalypse* (London: Hodder and Stoughton, 1904), 171–96. On the agents of the initial distribution of the work, see D. Aune, "The Prophetic Circle of John of Patmos and the Exegesis of Revelation 22.16," *JSNT* 37 (1989): 103–16 (special ed., *New Testament Essays in Honor of David Hill*, ed. C. Tuckett), arguing that the author entrusted the work "to prophetic colleagues and envoys for distribution and presentation to the seven churches" (110).

78. The description of a Christian letter as "catholic" is first attested in the late second century. The anti-Montanist writer Apollonius quoted by Eusebius (*H.E.* 5.18.5) says that Themiso "dared in imitation of the apostle to write a catholic epistle." Eusebius also speaks of the "catholic epistles" of Dionysius of Corinth (*H.E.* 4.23.1). On these letters see further below in text. Origen spoke of the letters of Peter, John, Jude, and Barnabas as catholic (*In Johann.* 6.35; *In Matt.* 17.19, *In Rom.* 5.1, *c. Cels.* 1.63), and Clement of Alexandria (*Strom.* 4.15) similarly characterized the letter of the apostolic council (Acts 15.23–29). Eusebius also uses the designation in *H.E.* 2.23.24–25 (James, Jude); cf. 6.14.1 (Jude, etc.); 7.24.7 and 7.25.10 (1 John). Eusebius is the first to show knowledge of a collection of seven "catholic" epistles. These references show that the term has to do with the scope of the address.

79. Rightly recognized by P. Wendland, *Die urchristlichen Literaturformen* (HzNT 1/3; Tübingen: Mohr, 1912), 368. See also R. Bauckham, "Pseudoapostolic Letters," *JBL* 107 (1988): 469–94 (473–74).

80. On the formal features of such documents and the extent to which they reflect Jewish Diaspora letters and thus a diaspora mentality within the early church, see C. Andressen, "Zum formular frühchristlicher Gemeindebriefe," *ZNW* 56 (1955): 233–59.

81. "The apostle" here is in all likelihood Paul, who throughout the second century among Christians of various stripe is so designated (H. von Campenhausen, *The Formation of the Christian Bible*, 143, 212), but cf. A. F. Walls, "The Montanist 'Catholic Epistle' and Its New Testament Prototype," *StEv* 3, pt. 2, ed. F. L. Cross (Berlin: Akademie: 1964), 437–45, arguing for John or perhaps Peter.

82. Of particular interest in this connection is the address of 1 Peter, listing

Pontus, Galatia, Cappadocia, Asia, and Bithynia. Together these constitute the whole of Asia Minor north of the Taurus mountain range, an area of some three hundred thousand square miles. The listing, however, is odd in giving Pontus first and Bithynia last, since the two formed a single Roman province. Perhaps the sequence represented the projected route of the letter carrier and one conducive to the most efficient distribution (F. J. A. Hort, *The First Epistle of St. Peter* [London: Macmillan, 1898], "Additional Note III," 157–84). See also C. Hemer, "The Address of First Peter," *ExpT* 89 (1978): 239–43. It is more likely, F. W. Beare reasonably argues, that 1 Peter was initially dispatched in multiple copies rather than being carried in a single copy round the whole area (*The First Epistle of Peter* [3d ed.; Oxford: Blackwell, 1970], 42).

83. The identification has been made by most, including J. B. Lightfoot, *Apostolic Fathers* (3 vols.; 2d ed. London: Macmillan, 1889), 1:359–60; H. von Campenhausen, *Ecclesiastical Authority and Spiritual Power in the Church of the First Three Centuries*, trans. J. A. Baker (London: A. & C. Black, 1969), 95; and S. Giet, *Hermas et les pasteurs; les trois autours de Pasteur d'Hermas* (Paris: Universitaires de France, 1963), 294. Undecided is P. Lampe, *Die Statrömischen Christen in den ersten beiden Jahrhunderten. Untersuchungen zur Sozialgeschichte* (WUNT 2, 18; Tübingen: Mohr, 1987), cf. 172, n. 157, with 336, n. 101. M. Dibelius, *Der Hirt des Hermas* (HNT; Tübingen: Mohr, 1923), 422–23; C. Osiek, *Rich and Poor in the Shepherd of Hermas* (Washington, D.C.: Catholic Biblical Association, 1983), 10; and N. Brox, *Der Hirt des Hermas* (Göttingen: Vandenhoeck und Ruprecht, 1991), 107–8, think the reference is an archaizing fiction.

84. Dionysius of Corinth, writing to Soter, bishop of Rome between 166 and 174, speaks of 1 Clement as a letter of the Roman church to the Corinthian church written *dia Klementos* (Eusebius, *H.E.* 4.23.11). The phrasing may assume, like Hermas, that Clement was a literary functionary of the Roman church. Lampe, *Stadtrömische Christen*, 336, speaks of the function of *Aussenminister* (foreign minister). On the various constituencies that Hermas had in view, including Christians residing elsewhere than in Rome, see M. Leutzsch, *Die Wahrnehmung sozialer Wirklichkeit im "Hirten des Hermas"* (FRLANT 150; Göttingen: Vandenhoeck und Ruprecht, 1989), esp. 63–112.

85. For Alexandria, Clement, *Strom.* 1.17.29; 2.1.9, 12; for the provincial areas, P. Mich. 130 is a fragment from the late second century in the Fayyum. P. Oxy. 3528 is not much later. Roberts, *Manuscript, Society, and Belief*, 22, 63, stresses the early popularity and availability of Hermas in Egypt. The more recent appearance of P. Oxy. 3528 and 3527 underlines the point. The work was also early known in Gaul (Irenaeus, *A.H.* 4.20.2) and in North Africa (Tertullian, *De or.* 16).

86. P. N. Harrison, *Polycarp's Two Epistles to the Philippians* (Cambridge: Cambridge University Press, 1936), argued that we have to deal with two letters written at different times: one consisting of chs. 13–14 of the present letter, written soon after the composition of Ignatius's letters but before Ignatius's martyrdom (thus late in Trajan's reign or soon after it), and another consisting of chs. 1–12, written some twenty years later under the reign of Hadrian. For criticism, see W. R. Schoedel, *Polycarp, Martyrdom of Polycarp, Fragments of Papias*, vol. 5, "The Apostolic Fathers," ed. R. M. Grant (London:

Nelson, 1967), 29–30, 37–40, and "Are the Letters of Ignatius of Antioch Authentic?" *RSR* 6 (1980): 196–201. More recently it has been argued by R. Joly, *Le dossier d'Ignace d'Antioche* (Brussels: Editions de l'université, 1979), that the reference to Ignatius's letters in Polycarp's letter is a late interpolation. For criticism, see Schoedel, "Are the Letters Authentic?" and C. P. Hammond-Bammel, "Ignatian Problems," *JTS*, n.s. 33 (1982): 62–97 (69–70). For a concise discussion of the authenticity and integrity of the letter, see B. Dehandschütter, "Polycarp's Epistle to the Philippians," *The New Testament in Early Christianity*, ed. J.-M. Sevrin (BETL 86; Leuven: Leuven University Press, 1989), 275–92 (276–79).

87. For knowledge and appreciation of the Ignatian letters in the ancient church, see Lightfoot, *Apostolic Fathers*, "Ignatius, Polycarp," pt. 1, 2:127–221. The earliest quotation is in Irenaeus, *A.H.* 5.28.4.

88. W. R. Schoedel, *Ignatius of Antioch* (Hermeneia; Philadelphia: Fortress Press, 1985), 251, calls attention to the "standard diplomatic practice" whereby a messenger carries a letter.

89. Lightfoot, *Apostolic Fathers*, 2:356–58; Schoedel, *Ignatius*, 279.

90. See, e.g., R. MacMullen, "Two Types of Conversion," *VC* 37 (1983): 174–92, esp. 177; and *Christianizing the Roman Empire* (New Haven: Yale University Press, 1984), 20–21 (with references to others of the same opinion).

91. On the intention to address the emperor, see esp. F. Millar, *The Emperor in the Roman World (31 BC–AD 337)* (London: Duckworth, 1977), ch. 9, "Church and Emperor," esp. 560–66 (but cf. the important review of K. Hopkins in *JRS* 68 [1978] 178–82); R. M. Grant, "Forms and Occasions of the Greek Apologists," *SMSR* 52 (1986): 213–26; and "Five Apologists and Marcus Aurelius," *VC* 42 (1988): 1–17; and the excellent discussion of W. R. Schoedel, "Apologetic Literature and Ambassadorial Activities," *HTR* 82 (1989): 55–78, attending especially to the literary form of the apologies, which he describes (78) as "apologetically grounded petition" (the cases in point being Athenagoras and Justin).

92. See V. Monachino, "Intento practico e propagandistico nell'apologetica Graeca del II secolo," *Greg* 32 (1951): 3–49; and Schoedel, "Apologetic Literature," 77.

93. Millar, *The Emperor in the Roman World*, 563, comments on Justin's *Apology* that "it is at least as convincing, and far more economical, an explanation of its contents and its concrete references to events, to suggest that it actually was presented—or was intended to be presented—to the emperors, as that it is an elaborate literary fiction." For Celsus's use of Justin's *Apology*, see C. Andresen, *Logos und Nomos: Die Polemik des Kelsos wider das Christentum* (AKG; Berlin: de Gruyter, 1955), 345–72. Celsus explicitly claims to have read the apology known as the *Dialogue of Jason and Papiscus* (Origen, *c. Cels.* 4.52), probably composed by Aristo of Pella about 140.

94. In favor of the Greek apologists' intention to reach pagan readers, see esp. M. Pellegrino, "L'elemento propagandistico e protrettico negli apologeti greci del II secolo," *Studi sull'antico apologetica* (1947), 1–65. On the intended readers of Tertullian's *Apologeticum*, see T. D. Barnes, *Tertullian: A Historical and Literary Study* (Oxford: Clarendon, 1971), 109–10 ("not magistrates alone, nor pagan society in general, but the cultured classes").

95. See R. M. Grant, *Greek Apologists of the Second Century* (London: SCM Press, 1988), 182–90.

96. A good discussion of the problem of dating is given by B. Dehandschütter, *Martyrium Policarpi: Een literair-kritische Studie* (BETL; Leuven: Universitaire Pers, 1979), 191–219.

97. For the aim of widely disseminating accounts of martyrdom compare the letter from the churches of Lyons and Vienne in Gaul "to the brethren in Asia and Phrygia," written soon after 177 and preserved in a lengthy excerpt by Eusebius (*H.E.* 5.1.3–2.8). This letter was probably dispatched in multiple copies to various specific churches in Asia Minor.

98. Schoedel, *Polycarp*, 80, expressing a widely held view. See also H. von Campenhausen, "Bearbeitungen und Interpolationen des Polykarpmartyriums," in *Aus der Frühzeit des Christentums* (Tübingen: Mohr, 1963), 253–302 (esp. 283, 291).

99. Schoedel, *Polycarp*, 80–81.

100. There is no good reason to construe the Greek to mean that Polycarp (rather than Gaius) had been a fellow citizen of Irenaeus (thus, e.g., Musurillo, *Acts of the Christian Martyrs*, 19), though at an early point in Irenaeus's life that may have been true.

101. The conjecture of H. Gregoire (*Les persecutions*, 159–60, as cited by Schoedel, *Polycarp*, 80) that the name Socrates or rather Isocrates here is a corruption of Quadratus and so originally intended to suggest an important person (cf. Eusebius, *H.E.* 3.37.1; 4.3.1–2) is arbitrary.

102. L. W. Barnard, "In Defence of Pseudo-Pionius's Account of Saint Polycarp's Martyrdom," *Kyriakon: Festschrift Johannes Quasten*, ed. P. Granfield and J. A. Jungmann (Munster: Aschendorff, 1970), 1:192–204, rightly remarks (192) that "even if these paragraphs were added after the composition of chs. 1–20, as many scholars think, it does not follow that they are necessarily false or unreliable." Even H. von Campenhausen ("Bearbeitungen und Interpolationen," 283) allows that the scribal notices in 22.2–3 may be authentic, at least in part.

103. See A. von Harnack, *Die Briefsammlung des Apostels Paulus und die anderen vorkonstantinischen christlichen Briefsammlungen: Sechs Vorlesungen aus der altkirchlichen Literaturgeschichte* (Leipzig: Hinrichs, 1926), 36–40. W. Bauer, *Orthodoxy and Heresy in Earliest Christianity* (ET Philadelphia: Fortress, 1971), 124–26, uses Dionysius as a star witness for his thesis but goes beyond the evidence in depicting Dionysius as a puppet of Rome who took every opportunity to intervene as an all-out enemy of heresy in other churches.

104. H. J. Lawlor, *Eusebiana: Essays on the Ecclesiastical History of Eusebius* (Oxford: Clarendon, 1912), 147–48.

105. Thus, P. Nautin, *Lettres et écrivains chrétiens des II et III siècles* (Patristica, 2; Paris: Cerf, 1961), 13–32, who conjectures (14) that the main complaint was made by bishop Palmas of Amastris about Dionysius's liberal attitude toward backsliders (cf. *H.E.* 4.23.6), a complaint with which Rome would have been sympathetic at the time.

106. Bauer, *Orthodoxy*, 124–26, 166–68, supposes that Dionysius's letters were targets of deliberate textual perversion because they were all pointedly

antiheretical. Yet Eusebius's descriptions of the letters do not sustain the idea that they were purely polemical. Blame was almost automatically given to heretics for textual variation in ecclesiastical texts, even when the cause lay elsewhere. On this see further below in text.

107. Harnack, *Briefsammlung*, 37, regards the presence of the reply of Pinytos as good evidence that Dionysius himself drew up the collection, whereas Bauer, *Orthodoxy*, 167–68, imagines that the collection was made by the church and that the collection itself had subsequently been adulterated by heretical opponents through the inclusion of the letter from Pinytos and the letter to Chrysophora, which are assumed to have been unfavorable to Dionysius. It seems easier to suppose, however, that these two letters were either originally part of the collection or that the letter to Chrysophora was subsequently attracted to the collection simply by its connection with Dionysius. Eusebius's language *(kai alle de tis para tautas epistole)* seems to distinguish the letter to Chrysophora from the others, but perhaps only because it is to an individual.

108. H. J. Lawlor and J. E. L. Oulton, *Eusebius: The Ecclesiastical History and the Martyrs of Palestine*, 2 vols. (London: SPCK, 1927–28), 2:144.

109. *Ep. ad amic. Alexandr.* (Rufinus, *De adult. libror. Origenis, PG* 17.605).

110. See further Ovid, *Trist.* 1.7.15–34; Diodorus Siculus 40.8. Th. Wirth, "Arrians Erinnerungen an Epiktet," *MH* 24 (1967): 149–89, 197–216, goes so far as to claim (154–61) that the topos is merely an authorial convention aimed at disarming criticism in advance. Yet if it sometimes served this purpose, it can hardly be supposed that the problems envisioned were not often actual. See further below in text on Tertullian and Augustine.

111. *Adv. Marc.* 1.15 refers to "the fifteenth year of the emperor Severus," which was 207–8. On the date, see E. Evans, ed., *Tertullian, Adversus Marcionem*, 2 vols. (Oxford: Clarendon, 1972), 1: xviii. It is sometimes held that this is the date of the composition of bk. 1 only, the others following over several years (thus H. Emonds, *Zweite Auflage im Altertum* [Leipzig: Harrassowitz, 1941], 264–65; and R. Braun, *Tertullien: Contre Marcion*, bk. 1 [SC 365; Paris: Cerf, 1990], 17–19). Against this view see T. D. Barnes, *Tertullian: A Historical and Literary Study* (Oxford: Clarendon, 1971), 255–56.

112. A notable parallel is provided by Diodorus, who remarks at the close of his history (40.8): "Some of the books were pirated and published before being corrected and before they had received the finishing touches, when we were not yet fully satisfied with the work. These we disown. But in order that these books, by getting before the public, may not mar the general plan of our history, we have deemed it necessary to publish a statement that will expose any misconception."

113. But cf. A. Bill, *Zur Erklärung und Textkritik des 1: Buches Tertullians 'Adversus Marcionem'* (TU 38/2; Leipzig: Hinrichs, 1911), 6–16, esp. 7, arguing that here *suffectus* means, "To stand as a substitute for something," so that the sense of the phrase would be, "Before, by means of copies, it took the place of the first edition"; similarly Braun, *Tertullien*, 98–99. The idea would then be that the revised edition was stolen before it had been corrected and established in an exemplar from which copies might be taken and was possibly lost altogether (cf. 3.1).

114. The manuscript tradition of the *Adversus Marcionem* does not appear to have been affected by the earlier forms of the work (cf., however,. Braun, *Tertullien*, 1, 75–80, who seeks traces of them), and without Tertullian's own comments multiple editions would not have been conjectured. The case is very different for Tertullian's *Apologeticum*. The manuscript tradition has seemed to many to demand the hypothesis of two editions, but it is persuasively argued by W. Bühler ("Gibt es einen gemeinsamen Archetypus der beiden Überlieferungsstrange von Tertullians Apologeticum?" *Philologus* 109 [1965]: 121–33) that the two branches of the textual tradition come from a common ancestor that had interlinear or marginal variants. A useful discussion of the question is given by A. Onnerfors, reviewing Frassinetti's *Tertullians Apologeticum* in *Gnomon* 38 (1966): 782–92.

115. Apart from Tertullian's *Adversus Marcionem*, various other Christian writings show signs of having been produced in more than one edition. In some cases the evidence for this is entirely internal, as for example in Eusebius's *Church History*, on editions of which see the comments of T. D. Barnes, "The Editions of Eusebius' *Ecclesiastical History*," *GRBS* 21 (1980): 191–201, who postulates four revised editions between 295 and 325. Concise discussions of all such possibilities are given by H. Emonds, *Zweite Auflage*. In the present discussion attention has been limited to cases where Christian authors explicitly mention more than one edition.

116. E. Preuschen, "Die Stenographie im Leben des Origenes," *ArchStenog* 56 (1905): 6–14, 49–55.

117. Jerome (*Ep.* 84.10) reports that Ambrose was so anxious to make Origen's work known that he indiscreetly put into circulation some writings of Origen that had not been revised and were not intended for publication.

118. After his removal to Caesarea Origen may not have enjoyed this luxury so consistently (*In Joh.* 6.1.9–10). Later in his life, however, Origen's sermons were stenographically transcribed, according to Eusebius (*H.E.* 6.36.1) and others. See further below.

119. Tertullian used Irenaeus for the *Adversus Marcionem* and for *Adversus Valentinianos*. See Barnes, *Tertullian*, 127–28, 220–21.

120. On the library and scriptorium at Caesarea, see also ch. 4.

121. K. and B. Aland, *The Text of the New Testament*, trans. E. F. Rhodes (Grand Rapids: Eerdmans, 1987), 70. They suggest that the first may have been in Alexandria in about 200. It is a question, however, how we should think of "professional" scribes in early Christianity. Everything suggests that the scribes of Christian manuscripts were Christian, and many of them were capable, but we know nothing about their remuneration, if any.

122. See G. D. Fee, "P 75, P 66; and Origen: The Myth of Early Textual Recension in Alexandria," *New Dimensions in New Testament Study*, ed. R. N. Longenecker and M. C. Tenney (Grand Rapids: Zondervan, 1974), 19–45, arguing that P 66, a manuscript dated ca. 200, is the product of a scriptorium. Zuntz, *Text of the Epistles*, 271–75, basing his judgment on the textual character of another late-second-century manuscript, P 46, suggests that "the conclusion is almost inescapable that already in the latter half of the second century the Alexandrian bishopric possessed a scriptorium which by its output set the standard for the Alexandrian type of Biblical manuscripts" (271). He thinks that a critical text of the Pauline corpus was worked up there in

accordance with the methods of Alexandrian scholarship as early as the beginning of the second century.

123. Roberts, *Manuscript, Society, and Belief*, 23–24.

124. For the attribution to Hippolytus, see R. H. Connolly, "Eusebius *Hist. eccl.* V.28," *JTS* 49 (1948): 73–79.

125. On the Theodotians see H. Schöne, "Ein Einbruch der antiken Logik und Textkritik in die altchristliche Theologie," *Pisciculi . . . F. Dolger*, ed. Th. Klauser and A. Rucker (Munster: Aschendorff, 1939), 75–79; R. Waltzer, *Galen on Jews and Christians* (Oxford: Oxford University Press, 1949), 75–86; D. A. Bertrand, "L'argumentation scripturaire de Théodote le Corroyeur (Epiphane, *Panarion* 54)," *Lectures anciennes de la Bible* (Cahiers de Biblia Patristica, 1; Strasbourg: Centre d'Analyse et de Documentation Patristiques, 1982), 153–68; and P. Lampe, *Statrömischen Christen*, 289–93.

126. On the development and practice of textual and literary criticism among the Greeks, see R. Pfeiffer, *History of Classical Scholarship from the Beginnings to the End of the Hellenistic Age* (Oxford: Clarendon, 1968). For Latin texts, see J. E. G. Zetzel, *Latin Textual Criticism in Antiquity* (New York: Arno, 1981). On Galen's literary criticism, apparently the immediate inspiration of the Theodotians, see R. M. Grant, *Heresy and Criticism: The Search for Authenticity in Early Christian Literature* (Louisville: Westminster/John Knox, 1993), 59–73.

127. Bauer, *Orthodoxy*, provides an interesting discussion in "The Use of Literature in the Conflict" (147–94) but takes too little account of the purely bibliographic aspects of the question.

128. Origen, *De prin.* praef.

129. See E. Nestle, *Einfuhrung in das griechische Neue Testament* (3d ed.; Göttingen: Vandenhoeck und Ruprecht, 1909), 219–27 ("Schriftfalschungen der Ketzer"), and the extensive discussion by A. Bludau, *Die Schriftfälschungen der Häretiker* (NTAbh 11/5; Munster: Aschendorff, 1925), which, however, is insufficiently critical.

130. See F. Wisse, "The Nature and Purpose of Redactional Changes in Early Christian Texts," *Gospel Traditions in the Second Century: Origins, Recensions, Text, and Transmission*, ed. W. L. Petersen (CJA 3; Notre Dame: University of Notre Dame Press, 1989), 39–53.

131. On the relative instability of Gospel texts in the period, see H. Koester, "The Text of the Synoptic Gospels in the Second Century," *Gospel Traditions in the Second Century*, 19–37; and, in the same volume, E. J. Epp, "The Significance of the Papyri for Determining the Nature of the New Testament Text in the Second Century: A Dynamic View of Textual Transmission," 71–103.

132. Many tendentious revisions were attributed to Marcion by von Harnack, *Marcion*; a more sober appraisal is given by J. J. Clabeaux, *A Lost Edition of the Letters of Paul: A Reassessment of the Text of the Pauline Corpus Attested by Marcion* (CBQMS 21; Washington: Catholic Biblical Association, 1989).

133. This point has been recognized and emphasized by R. M. Grant, "Marcion and the Critical Method," *From Jesus to Paul: Studies in Honor of Francis Wright Beare*, ed. P. Richardson and J. C. Hurd (Toronto: Wilfred Laurier University Press, 1984), 207–15; and *Heresy and Criticism*, 33–49. As Har-

nack points out (*Marcion*, 61), Marcion was not given to making additions to the texts, but only excisions and corrections. This is consistent with his essentially critical method.

134. On Papias, see M. Black, "The Use of Rhetorical Terminology in Papias on Mark and Matthew," *JSNT* 37 (1989): 31–41. On Tatian, see Eusebius, *H.E.* 4.29.6 (Tatian's correcting [*epidiorthoumenon*] Paul's style). A useful overview of Christian reliance on traditional methods of criticism is given by R. M. Grant, "Literary Criticism and the New Testament Canon," *JSNT* 16 (1982): 24–44. See also the important observations of Zuntz, *Text of the Epistles*, 263–83, on the evidence for early Christian appropriation of the philological techniques of Alexandrian grammarians.

135. This has been too seldom recognized by textual critics. See, however, Zuntz, *Text of the Epistles*, 268–69: "The common respect for the sacredness of The Word, with [Christians], was not an incentive to preserve the text in its original purity. On the contrary, the strange fact has long since been observed that devotion to the Founder and His apostles did not prevent the Christians of that age from interfering with their transmitted utterances. . . . The sacredness of a text is not by itself a guarantee for its faithful transmission."

136. The point obtains not only for the transmission of texts but also for the history of the New Testament canon. See L. E. Keck, "Is the New Testament a Field of Study? From Outler to Overbeck and Back," *Second Century* 1 (1981): 19–35, who argues that the documents that became canonical are for the most part those that were most widely used, and hence copied, in the early church.

137. Eusebius, *H.E.* 6.22, claimed to know eight works by Hippolytus, perhaps in the library at Jerusalem, but was uncertain about his identity or locale.

138. Pontius, *Vita Cyp.* 7. See C. H. Turner, "Two Early Lists of Cyprian's Works" *CR* 6 (1892): 205–9, esp. 207. Further, in the Cheltenham canon list (ca. 359–65), the treatises are listed with their stichometric totals. On this list, see W. Sanday, "The Cheltenham List of the Canonical Books of the Old and New Testament and of the Writings of Cyprian," *Studia Biblica et Ecclesiastica* 3 (Oxford: Clarendon, 1891), 261–303, esp. 274–303.

There are good indications, incidentally, that the most famous of Cyprian's treatises, *De Ecclesiae Unitate*, was published in two successive editions, differing mainly in chs. 4 and 19, by Cyprian himself. But circumstantial details are lacking. See esp. D. van Eynde, "La double édition du *De unitate* de S. Cyprien," *RHE* 29 (1933): 5–24; and M. Bevenot, *St. Cyprian's De unitate, ch. 4, in the Light of the Manuscripts* (Analecta Gregoriana, 11; Rome, 1937).

139. On the letters see esp. H. von Soden, *Die Cyprianische Briefsammlung: Geschichte ihrer Entstehung und Überlieferung* (TU n.f. 10/2; Leipzig: Hinrichs, 1904); A. von Harnack, *Die Briefsammlung des Apostels Paulus*, 53–61; and G. W. Clarke, ed., *The Letters of St. Cyprian of Carthage*, 4 vols. (ACW 43–44, 46–47; New York: Newman, 1984–89), 1:4–12.

140. All the references to groups of letters gathered and enclosed with letters to other addressees are given by C. H. Turner in his appendix to Sanday, "The Cheltenham List," 304–25 (323, n. 1).

141. Jerome (*De vir. ill.* 53) reports that Cyprian rarely passed a day without saying to his secretary, "Give me the master" (viz. Tertullian).

142. Rufinus, *De adult. lib. Origenis*, 41–42 (PG 17, 628 C, 692 A). It is uncertain whether this means that Cyprian's work had been translated into Greek.

143. See Sanday, "The Cheltenham List," 263–64.

144. Among many studies on this subject see especially the comprehensive discussion by B. M. Metzger, *The Early Versions of the New Testament: Their Origin, Transmission, and Limitations* (Oxford: Clarendon, 1977); and the essays by various scholars in *Die alten Übersetzungen des Neuen Testaments, die Kirchenväterzitate und Lektionare*, ed. K. Aland (ANTF, 5; Berlin: de Gruyter, 1972).

145. A useful though dated discussion is G. Bardy, *La question des langues dans l'église ancienne* (Paris, 1948).

146. Eusebius, *H.E.* 3.39.15; Clement, *Strom.* 7.17. The first mentions Mark and the second Glaucias as Peter's interpreter.

147. The document was written in Latin, and the persons in the narrative mostly have Latin names. On this document and the interpretation of the phrase, see ch. 4.

148. Tertullian, who began writing in Carthage about 195, quotes Christian scripture in Latin but appears to have translated his quotations himself instead of using Latin manuscripts.

149. Damasus's commission is not preserved but is reflected in Jerome's preface to his translation of the Gospels (conveniently available in a critical edition in J. Wordsworth and H. J. White, eds., *Novum Testamentum Domini nostri Iesu Christi Latine secundum editionem sancti Hieronymi*, 3 vols. [Oxford: Clarendon, 1889–54], 1:1–4).

150. For general discussions of the bibliographic aspects of Christian literature in this period, see J. de Ghellinck, *Patristique et Moyen Age: Etudes d'histoire litteraire et doctrinale*, 2. Diffusion et transmission des écrits patristiques (Gembloux: Duculot, 1947), esp. 183–245; G. Bardy, "Editions et rééditions d'ouvrages patristiques," *RBén* 47 (1935): 356–80, and "Copies et éditions au V siècle," *RSR* 23 (1949): 38–52; and H. I. Marrou, "La technique de l'édition à l'époche patristique," *VC* 3 (1949): 208–24.

151. Jerome's various notices have been canvassed and discussed by E. Arns, *La technique du livre d'après Saint Jerome* (Paris: Boccard, 1953). On the respective topics of publication and dissemination, see pp. 37–128 and 129–72. On Augustine, see the very valuable treatment of J. Scheele, "Buch und Bibliothek bei Augustinus," *Bibliothek und Wissenschaft* 12 (1978): 14–114.

152. On Romanianus, see esp. M. A. McNamara, *Friendship in St. Augustine* (Studia Friburgensia; Fribourg: University Press, 1958), 78–83.

153. This letter was discovered and first published by C. Lambot, "Lettre inédité de S. Augustin relative au 'De Civitate Dei,'" *RBén* 51 (1939): 109–21. This letter and other letters more recently discovered by J. Divjak are not numbered in continuation of the standard (Goldbacher) series, but as a separate group with numbers designated by asterisks (1*–28*). See *CSEL* 88 (1981).

154. *Epp.* 81, 82, 115, 134, 191, 194, 200. This identification was maintained by Lambot, "Lettre inédité," 113–14, followed by Marrou, "La technique de l'édition," 218–20, among others, who then went so far as to describe Firmus as Augustine's "agent littéraire" (218).

155. Careful interpretation even of *Ep.* 1*A shows that the Firmus addressed there is not the presbyter: see J. Divjak, "Augustins erster Brief an Firmus und die revidierte Ausgabe der Civitas Dei," *Latinität und alten Kirche: Festschrift R. Hanslik* (Wiener Studien, Beihefte 8; Vienna: Koln, 1977), 56–70, esp. 62–67.

156. Divjak, "Augustins erster Brief," 66–67.

157. Thus Divjak, "Augustins erster Brief," 69, comments: "It can be seen that also for Augustine there is a certain distinction *[Zweiteilung]* of private copying from edition."

158. On this, see W. M. Green, "A Fourth Century Manuscript of Saint Augustine?" *RBén* 69 (1959): 191–97.

159. Ibid., 194–95.

160. Instructive in this connection is *Ep.* 190: writing to Optatus about the "book" *(liber,* i.e., *Ep.* 166) that he had sent to Jerome on the origin of human souls, Augustine says that it "can be read in my possession *[apud me]* but ought not to be sent anywhere or given to anyone outside until I receive an answer and find out what he [Jerome] thinks." That is, the work would be corrected only after he had a response from Jerome, in light of Jerome's response, and only then released. Cf. *Ep.* 202A.

161. Arns, *La technique,* 141–49.

162. On Jerome, see Arns, *La technique,* 149. The case is no different with Augustine; see Scheele, "Buch und Bibliothek," 73–75, 96–98, who speaks of a "snowball system" of diffusion (96).

163. On permitting their own texts to be copied, see, e.g., Augustine *Epp.* 169, 190, 264; Jerome, *Ep.* 71 (copyists sent from Spain!); on making and sending copies, Augustine, *Epp.* 184A, 1*A, 31; and Jerome *Epp.* 32, 124.

164. Marrou, "La technique de l'édition," 212–15, notes the exaggerated language of the passage and expresses skepticism about the commercial diffusion of the work. *Libraius* could mean, even in this context, "copyist" as well as "bookseller."

165. For a convenient and careful discussion see C. P. Hammond, "A Product of a Fifth Century Scriptorium Preserving Conventions Used by Rufinus of Aquileia," *JTS,* n.s. 29 (1978): 366–91, and 30 (1979): 430–62.

166. A useful conspectus, including consideration of Augustine and Jerome, is given by H. Hagendahl, "Die Bedeutung der Stenographie für die spätlateinische christliche Literatur," *JAC* 14 (1971): 24–38, who cites most of the relevant texts and scholarly literature. Add, however, H. Boge, *Griechische Tachygraphie und Tironische Noten* (Berlin: Akademie, 1973), who treats the technical details of shorthand methods and emphasizes their use in Greek.

167. *Retr.,* prol. 2; Possidius, *Vita Aug.* 18; cf. *Retr.* 1.18; 1.26; 2.16; 2.19; 2.31; 2.32; 2.67; *Epp.* 75.1; 82.17; 162.1; 169.1; 173 A; 202 A 5; 238.1. For the details of procedure and the resources available to Augustine, see Schele, "Buch und Bibliothek," 85–93.

168. Jerome often pleaded ill health in his dependence on secretaries, which he was able to have partly through his own resources but mainly through the aid of Paula and certain ecclesiastical authorities (Heliodorus and Chromatius). See Arns, *La technique,* 37–79. In the Greek East, Jerome often found good copyists for Latin hard to come by: Augustine, *Ep.* 172.

169. See A. Wikenhauser, "Beiträge zur Geschichte der Stenographie auf den Synoden des 4. Jahrhunderts nach Christus," *ArchStenog* 59 (1908): 4–9, 33–38.

170. See G. A. Bisbee, *Pre-Decian Acts of Martyrs and Commentarii* (Harvard Dissertations in Religion, 22; Philadelphia: Fortress, 1988); on the papyrological evidence, see R. A. Coles, *Reports of Proceedings in Papyri* (Papyrologica Bruxellensia, 4; Brussels: Fondation Egyptologique Reine Elisabeth, 1966).

171. In the case of John Chrysostom, Socrates (*H.E.* 6.4) distinguished between sermons he himself edited (and thus presumably wrote) and those that were published from shorthand transcriptions (and presumably delivered extempore). Augustine (*Retr.* 2.93.2) distinguishes all his treatises and letters, which he says were dictated (i.e., written), from his sermons, which he says were spoken (and not subsequently edited).

172. On this point Marrou, "La technique de l'édition," 211–12, 222–24, is certainly right in contrast to de Ghellinck, "Transcription et diffusion," who misreads the evidence and accords too large a role to the commercial book trade.

173. See R. L. Wilken, *The Christians as the Romans Saw Them* (New Haven: Yale University Press, 1984), 137–47.

174. On the "academic" coloration of early Christianity, see E. A. Judge, "The Early Christians as a Scholastic Community," *JRH* 1 (1960–61): 4–15, 125–37; and cf. R. Wilken, "Collegia, Philosophical Schools, and Theology," *The Catacombs and the Colosseum: The Roman Empire as the Setting of Primitive Christianity*, ed. S. Benko and J. J. O'Rourke (Valley Forge: Judson Press, 1971), 268–91.

175. The best survey of the missionary spread of the early church is still that of A. von Harnack, *The Mission and Expansion of Christianity in the First Three Centuries*, trans. J. Moffatt, 2 vols. (New York: Putnam, 1904). See also W. H. C. Frend, *The Rise of Christianity* (Philadelphia: Fortress, 1984).

176. R. Williams, "Does It Make Sense to Speak of Pre-Nicene Orthodoxy?" *The Making of Orthodoxy: Essays in Honor of Henry Chadwick*, ed. R. Williams (Cambridge: Cambridge University Press, 1989), 1–23, speaks of "what can sometimes seem like an almost obsessional mutual interest and interchange" between the nongnostic churches of the second century (11) and of a sense of unity "articulated in a steady flow of literary exchange between its parts" (13).

177. M. Mcquire, "Letters and Letter Carriers in Christian Antiquity," *CW* 53 (1960): 148–53, 184–85.

178. On travel generally in antiquity, see L. Casson, *Travel in the Ancient World* (London: Allen and Unwin, 1974). On the movements of Christians in particular see, for the second and third centuries, Harnack, *Mission and Expansion*, 2.462–72 ("Travelling: The Exchange of Letters and Literature"), and for the fourth and fifth centuries, D. Gorce, *Les voyages: L'hospitalité et le port des lettres dans le monde chrétien des IV et V siècles* (Paris, 1925). On the general mobility of Christians around the early Empire, see also the comments of Malherbe, *Social Aspects*, 62–68.

CHAPTER IV: EARLY CHRISTIAN LIBRARIES

1. Eusebius, *H.E.* 8.2.4–5; *Mart. pal.* praef 1, *vita Const.* 3.1.4. On the edicts and their results, see G. E. M. de Ste. Croix, "Aspects of the Great Persecution," *HTR* 47 (1954): 75–113; and W. H. C. Frend, *Martyrdom and Persecution in the Early Church* (Garden City, N.Y.: Doubleday, 1967), 351–92. The deliberate destruction of books in antiquity, of which the present case is only one instance, is surveyed by W. Speyer, *Buchervernichtung und Zensur des Geistes bei Heiden, Juden und Christen* (Stuttgart: Hiersmann, 1981); cf. his article, "Buchervernichtung," *JAC* 13 (1970): 123–52.

2. "Gesta apud Zenophilum consularem," Migne, *PL* 43:793–800 (794–95), and *CSEL* 26, 186–88. A translation with notes is given in O. R. Vassall-Phillips, *The Work of St. Optatus, Bishop of Milevis, against the Donatists* (London: Longmans, Green, 1917), app. 2, 349–81.

3. For similar terminology used for a book of Gospels, see further below in text and n. 8.

4. On the office of the reader, see ch. 5.

5. H. Musurillo, ed., *The Acts of the Christian Martyrs* (OECT; Oxford: Clarendon, 1972), 266–71.

6. Ibid., 280–93.

7. Published by C. H. Roberts, "Two Oxford Papyri," *ZNW* 37 (1938): 184–88.

8. Ibid., 188. *Mega biblion* is akin to *megaleion*, used to designate a book containing the Gospels. See G. W. H. Lampe, *A Patristic Greek Lexicon* (Oxford: Clarendon, 1961–68), s.v. *megaleios*. The "very large single volume" *(codex pernimius major)* handed over by Catullinus in the "Gesta apud Zenophilum" (above) was probably likewise a book of Gospels.

9. Usefully compared is another papyrus from the fifth or sixth century (P. Grenf. 111 [van Haelst 1200]), an inventory of possessions of the church at Ibion, which mentions twenty-one books written on parchment *(biblia dermati[na])* and three on papyrus *(chartia)*.

10. On the places of early Christian worship, see the overview of modern studies and theories on early Christian architecture by P. C. Finney, "Early Christian Architecture: The Beginnings," *HTR* 81 (1988): 319–39. For our period the most useful studies are W. Rordorf, "Was wissen wir über die christlichen Gottesdiensträume der vorkonstantinischen Zeit?" *ZNW* 55 (1964): 110–28; C. H. Kraeling, *The Christian Building* (The Excavations at Dura-Europus; final rept., 8, pt. 2; New Haven: Dura Europus Publications, 1967); and L. Michael White, *Building God's House in the Roman World: Architectural Adaptation among Pagans, Jews, and Christians* (Baltimore: Johns Hopkins, 1990).

11. The earliest remains of a *domus ecclesiae*, at Dura Europus, belong to the first half of the third century (usually dated to 232/3, with Christian adaptation occurring in 240/1). The uses of the six rooms surrounding a courtyard can be only partly identified. The assembly hall (room 4) and baptismal chapel (room six) are clear. Another room may conceivably have served as a library. At the eastern end of the assembly hall is a small, raised platform (bema) on which the person presiding stood or sat. Directly adjacent to the

eastern end of this room and connected to it by a small doorway is a small windowless room, sometimes identified as a sacristy (room 3), which may have been the repository of texts along with other liturgical necessities. In some synagogues the scriptures were brought into the assembly room from an adjoining room (see below and also Rordorf, "Was wissen wir über die christlichen Gottesdiensträume," 119). In the Dura Europus building, the doorway to the sacristy was immediately adjacent to the podium, from which, presumably, the scriptures would have been read.

12. W. H. C. Frend, *The Donatist Church* (Oxford: Clarendon, 1985), esp. 1–31.

13. Musurillo, *Acts of the Christian Martyrs*, 88 (12).

14. G. Bonner, "The Scillitan Saints and the Pauline Epistles," *JEH* 7 (1956): 141–46 (142–44), conjectures that the capsa of books was brought along by the investigating officers as potentially incriminating evidence, perhaps because Christians were suspected of using magical texts. In *Atti e passioni dei martiri* (Milan: Mondadori, 1987), A. A. R. Bastiaensen speculates (410) that the accused brought it along to vindicate themselves by pointing, for example, to the virtue and vice catalogues found in Paul's letters.

15. Bastiaensen, *Atti e passioni*, 410, prefers to understand *libri epistularum* (books of epistles), followed by J. den Boeft and J. Bremmer, "Notiunculae Martyrologicae IV," *VC* 45 (1991): 105–22 (116).

16. Lightfoot, *Apostolic Fathers*, pt. 1, 2:245–46. The *apostoloi* signifies Paul preeminently, if not exclusively, since the passage in which the phrase occurs appears to be an exegesis of Ephesians 5.23–32.

17. Bonner, "Scillitan Saints and the Pauline Epistles," 144–45, thinks Gospels are meant. The later version of the text makes this explicit. The account is, incidentally, the earliest evidence for the availability of a Latin version of Christian scriptures.

18. On the character of early Christian worship, and especially the liturgical use of books, see ch. 5.

19. *De exhort. cast.* 7 and 13; *De monog.* 11–12; *De bapt.* 17; *De praescr. haer.* 32. Cf. H. Leclercq, "Bibliothèques," *DACL* 2/1, 855–56.

20. On the literature used by Tertullian, see, for Christian literature, A. von Harnack, "Tertullians Bibliothek christlicher Schriften," *SPAW* (1914), 1:303–34; and, for pagan literature, T. D. Barnes, *Tertullian: A Historical and Literary Study* (Oxford: Clarendon, 1971), 196–206.

21. Lightfoot, *Apostolic Fathers*, pt. 2, 2:270–71; and Schoedel, *Ignatius*, 207–9. On the passage, see the review of discussion in W. R. Schoedel, "Ignatius and the Archives," *HTR* 71 (1978): 97–106.

22. Leclercq, "Bibliothèques," 853–54, who thinks, however, of the archives of synagogues. Schoedel, "Ignatius and the Archives," 99–101, points to some close but not exact parallels in Josephus (and to a lesser extent in Philo), but in Josephus there are obvious apologetical reasons for drawing an analogy between scripture and "public records." No such reasons inform the usage of Ignatius's opponents. On archival materials and their depositories in antiquity, see E. Posner, *Archives in the Ancient World* (Cambridge: Harvard, 1972); and W. E. H. Cockle, "State Archives in Graeco-Roman Egypt from 30 B.C. to the Reign of Septimus Severus," *JEA* 70 (1984): 106–22; P. Culham, "Archives

and Alternatives in Republican Rome," *CP* 84 (1989): 100–115; and F. Burkhalter, "Archives locales et archives centrales en Egypt romain," *Chairon* 20 (1990): 191–216.

23. See C. J. Cadoux, *Ancient Smyrna* (Oxford: Blackwell, 1938).

24. M. Hengel, "The Titles of the Gospels and the Gospel of Mark," in *Studies in the Gospel of Mark*, trans. J. Bowden (London: SCM, 1985), 64–84, esp. 74–78.

25. Ibid., 82–83.

26. Ibid., 81–82, urging that the titles of the Gospels were supplied "by those early Christian scribes who saw to the dissemination of the first Gospel writings by copying them and sending them out to other important communities" and that "this is the only explanation for their great age and the complete unanimity in them towards the end of the second century" (81).

27. A. Ehrhardt, "Die griechische Patriarchal-Bibliothek von Jerusalem," *Römische Quartalschrift* 5 (1891): 217–65; 6 (1892): 339–65, who deals only briefly with this library and considers Palestinian Christian libraries generally.

28. On the papyrus fragment, see J.-R. Viellefond, *Les "Cestes" de Julius Africanus* (Paris: Diddier, 1970), 277–91; and F. C. R. Thee, *Julius Africanus and the Early Christian View of Magic* (Tübingen: Mohr, 1984), 66–69, 180–82. It is sometimes denied that Africanus has the Christian library in view (e.g., E. Habas, "The Jewish Origin of Julius Africanus," *JJS* 45 [1994]: 86–91), but that is the only library known to have existed in Jersalem at this time.

29. See, respectively, R. Cadiou, *La jeunesse d'Origene: Histoire de l'école d'Alexandrie au début du III siècle* (Paris: Beauchesne, 1935), 11;, and P. Carrington, *The Early Christian Church* (Cambridge: Cambridge University Press, 1957), 2:439–40. (On Julius Africanus and the library of Severus in Rome, see further below in text). R. Blum, "Die Literaturverzeichnung im Altertum und Mittelalter," *AGB* 24 (1983): 2–255, unduly minimizes Eusebius's testimony and Alexander's background to regard the Jerusalem library as only an archive (213).

30. *Prosphon.* 13.150–53.

31. Eusebius, *M. Pal.* 7.4–5, 11.1, 4.5–6, 5.2. In *H.E.* 7.32.25 Eusebius says that Pamphilus established a school in Caesarea.

32. Isidore, *Etym.* 6.6.1, gives the number as thirty thousand, an uncorroborated and perhaps inaccurate figure.

33. The list of Origen's works given by Jerome, *Ep.* 33.4.1–20, may have been derived from Pamphilus's list (E. Klostermann, "Die Schriften des Origenes in Hieronymus' Brief an Paula," *SPAW* [1897] 2:855–70; and P. Courcelle, *Late Latin Writers and Their Greek Sources* [Cambridge: Harvard University Press, 1969], 103–13). In that case, the pinakes of Pamphilus did not constitute a working catalogue of the library, that is, it was not a key to its arrangement or use but simply a list of its contents. See further Blum, "Die Literaturverzeichnung," 89–97.

34. G. Bardy, *Eusebé de Cesarée: Histoire ecclesiastique* (SC; Paris: Cerf), conveniently provides in vol. 4 (1971), 285–95, an index of the works cited by Eusebius (yet omitting scriptural and administrative materials). Sixty-six authors are named, and a much larger number of individual titles. T. D. Barnes, *Constantine and Eusebius* (Cambridge: Harvard, 1981), 92–93, suggests that

since the non-Christian Greek literature known to Eusebius "reflects Origen's interests: no comedy, tragedy or lyric poetry, but a complete Plato and a wide range of later philosophers, mainly Middle Platonists from Philo to the late second century," much of this material must have been part of the collection of Origen and had a place in the Caesarean library. Nevertheless, it cannot be assumed that Eusebius had a first-hand acquaintance with every document he mentions, nor, then, that all were in the libraries available to him. He undoubtedly he knew some only from a secondary source. See B. Gustafsson, "Eusebius' Principles in Handling His Sources, as Found in His Church History, Books I–VII," *StPat* 4 (1961): 429–41.

35. Tertullian's *Apology* was available to Eusebius in a Greek translation (*H.E.* 2.2.4); it is not clear whether he knew Cyprian in Latin or in a Greek translation.

36. Jerome, *De vir. ill.* 3, even claims that there was a manuscript of the original Aramaic text of the Gospel of Matthew (!).

37. H. J. Lawlor, "On the Use by Eusebius of Volumes of Tracts," in *Eusebiana* (Oxford: Clarendon, 1912), 136–78. Lawlor's analysis provides evidence for some nineteen volumes of material (166). He observes that Eusebius was often seduced into mistaken chronological inferences by the bibliographic groupings and orderings of the documents in question.

38. On colophons indicating a connection with the Caesarean library, see R. Devreesse, *Introduction à l'étude des manuscrits grecs* (Paris: Klincksieck, 1954), 122–24; and Harnack, *Geschichte der altchristlichen Literatur bis Eusebius* 1/2:543–45. These manuscripts are discussed by Ehrhardt, "Die griechische Patriarchal-Bibliothek von Jerusalem," 224–43; and by G. Mercati, *Nuove note di letteratura biblica e cristiana antica* (Studi e Testi 95; Vatican City: Apostolic Library, 1941), 2–48.

39. Folio 19. A similar colophon is found at the end of Esdras (folio 13).

40. For a discussion of Pamphilus's influence on the history of the biblical text, see W. Bousset, *Textkritische Studien zum Neuen Testament* (TU 11/4; Leipzig: Hinrichs, 1894), 45–50.

41. Perhaps the scriptorium was modeled on the scriptorial resources furnished to Origen by Ambrose, for even after Origen's removal to Caesarea he seems not to have lacked them (cf. *H.E.* 6.28).

42. Devreesse, *Manuscrits grecs*, 125; Barnes, *Constantine and Eusebius*, 124 (and 345, n. 139); see esp. G. Robbins, "Peri ton Endiathekon Graphon: Eusebius and the Formation of the Christian Bible," 200–201. For the traditional interpretation, see, among others, K. Lake, "The Sinaitic and Vatican Manuscripts and the Copies Sent by Eusebius to Constantine," *HTR* 11 (1918): 32–35; and C. H. Roberts, "The Codex," *PBA* 40 (1954): 200–201.

43. See ch. 2 and Robbins, "Peri ton Endiathekon Graphon," 201–10, for a good survey of the manuscript evidence.

44. Jerome, *Ep.* 34.1, *De viri ill.* 113. An eleventh-century manuscript of Philo's *De opificio mundi* (Vindob. theol. graec. 29, leaf 146 verso) carries the notice that the text was "renewed" by bishop Euzoius.

45. C. Wendel, "Bibliothek," *RAC* 2:248.

46. See L. I. Levine, *Roman Caesarea: An Archaeological-Topographical Study* (Jerusalem: Hebrew University Institute of Archaeology, 1975), 45–46;

and A. Negev, "Caesarea Maritima," *Christian News from Israel* 11 (1960): 17–22. Others, however, regard this as a public archive: K. G. Holum, R. L. Hohlfelder, R. J. Bull, and A. Raban, *King Herod's Dream: Caesarea on the Sea* (New York: Norton, 1988), 169–71; cf. A. Negev, "Inscriptions hébraiques, grecques et latines de Cesarée Maritime," *RB* 78 (1971): 247–63 (258).

47. R. Cadiou, "La bibliothèque de Cesarée et la formation des chaines," *RSR* 16 (1936): 474–83 (477).

48. C. Wendel, "Das griechish-römische Altertum" (rev. by W. Gober), *Handbuch der Bibliothekswissenschaft*, ed. G. Leyh (2d ed.; Wiesbaden: Harrassowitz, 1955), 132.

49. And not only strictly Christian works: the manuscript tradition of Philo's works "probably derives, in the main, from the library at Caesarea" (E. Schürer, *The History of the Jewish People in the Age of Jesus Christ*, trans. and rev. G. Vermes, F. Millar, and M. Goodman [Edinburgh: T. and T. Clark, 1973–87], 821–22).

50. Preface to Chronicles (Vulgate). On these three recensions of the LXX, see S. Jellicoe, *The Septuagint and Modern Study* (Oxford: Clarendon, 1968), 134–71, but also the synopsis of more recent discussion by S. Olofsson, *The LXX Version* (Stockholm: Almqvist and Wiksell, 1990), 58–63.

51. The history of the quest for a "Caesarean text" in the Gospels is sketched by B. M. Metzger, "The Caesarean Text of the Gospels," in *Chapters in the History of New Testament Textual Criticism* (NTTS 4; Grand Rapids: Eerdmans, 1963), 42–72. On a Caesarean text in the epistles, see G. Zuntz, *Epistles*, 151–56.

52. On the nature of the school, see R. L. Wilken, "Alexandria: A School for Training in Virtue," in *Schools of Thought in the Christian Tradition*, ed. P. Henry (Philadelphia: Fortress, 1984), 15–30. He describes the consensus that the teaching activities of Pantaenus and Clement were private undertakings, not to be construed institutionally. With Origen, however, the school seems to have taken on a more official character and a stronger relation with episcopal authority.

53. Athanasius, *Apol. Const.* 4.

54. The standard study remains that of J. B. de Rossi, *De origine, historia, indicibus scrinii, et bibliothecae Sedis Apostolicae commentatio* (Rome: The Vatican, 1886). Useful discussions are given by Leclercq, "Bibliothèques," 863–73; F. Wieland, "Früheste Vorläufer der Vaticana," in *Festschrift für G. Leyh* (Leipzig, 1937), 159–68; C. Callmer, "Die ältesten christlichen Bibliotheken in Rom," *Eranos* 83 (1985): 48–60. The main literary source for the early history of ecclesiastical libraries in Rome is the *Liber pontificales*, first compiled in the sixth century, cited below here in the edition of L. Duchesne, *Le Liber Pontificales: Texte, introduction et commentaire*, 3 vols. (Paris: Boccard, 1955–57).

55. *Liber pontif.* (ed. Duchesne), 1:205–6.

56. Codex Palatinus Latinus 833 (with the broadly agreed emendation of *archibis* to *archivis*). See M. Ihm, ed., *Damasi Epigrammata* (Leipzig: Teubner, 1895), no. 57 (p. 58); cf. *Liber pontif.* [ed. Duchesne] 1, 213). The emendation from *archibis* to *Xre tibi* ("To you, Christ"), thus omitting any mention of an archive or library, proposed by P. Kunzle ("Del cosiddetto 'titulus archi-

vorum' di papa Damaso," *Rivista di storia della chiesa in Italia* 7 [1953] 1–26)
is unconvincing.

57. F. Wieland, "Früheste Varläufer der Vaticana," 159–68. Jerome (*Apol. ad Rufinum* 2.20) refers to a papal archive *(chartarium, scrinium)* but does not indicate its location.

58. The legend reads *Diversi diversa patres s[ed hic] omnia dixit/ Romano eloquio mysticas sensa tonans*. The find was discussed by P. Lauer, "Les fouilles du Sancta Sanctorum au Lateran," *Mélanges d'archéologie et d'histoire* 20 (1900): 251–87 (with plates 9 and 10). See also G. Wilpert, *Die römischen Mosaiken und Materien der kirchlichen Bauten vom 4.-13. Jahrhundert* (Freiburg: Herder, 1976 [1916]), 151–52.

59. The list is conveniently provided by Leclercq, "Bibliothèques," 870–72. It is a question, however, whether all the Greek texts mentioned belonged to the Lateran library. It has been suggested (A. Siegmund, *Die Überlieferung der griechischen christlichen Literatur in der lateinischen Kirche bis zum zwölften Jahrhundert* [Munich: Filser, 1949], 174–75) that many, if not all, of the Greek texts may have been brought to Rome by Eastern monks and were not necessarily to be found among the holdings of the Lateran library (as claimed by Th. Schermann, "Griechische Hss.-Bestande in den Bibliotheken der christlichen Kulturzentren des 5.–7. Jahrhunderts," *Oriens christianus* 4 [1904]).

60. Earlier sources point in the same direction. The so-called *Decretum Gelasianum*, which belongs to the sixth century and not to Gelasius (492–96), deals in its fifth part with books to be received and not received and provides various classifications of them (biblical books, conciliar acts, works of the fathers, epistolary decrees, martyrologies, chronicles, apocryphal books, and heretical writings). Such categories may reflect those in use in the papal library. Further, the long series of extracts from patristic writers that Leo I appended to his "Tomus ad Flavianum" (449) against Eutyches shows the ready availability to the Roman pope of the works of many Latin and Greek fathers.

61. *Liber pontif.* (ed. Duchesne), 1, 247.

62. *Ep.* 32.16: "Si quem sancta tenet meditanti in lege voluntas / hic poterit residens sacris intendere libris."

63. The accessibility and utility of this library, as indicated by the inscription, are emphasized by A. von Harnack, "Die älteste Kirchenbibliotheksinschrift," in *Reden und Aufsätze* (Giessen: Topelmann, 1916), 3:39–44.

64. *Inst.*, 1, praef.

65. A full discussion of the inscriptional and archaeological evidence is given by H. I. Marrou, "Autour de la bibliothèque du pape Agapit," *Mélanges d'archéologie et d'histoire* 48 (1931): 124–69.

66. J. B. de Rossi, *Inscriptiones christianae Urbis Romanae*, II, 28 (55): "Sanctorum veneranda cohors sedet ordine longo / Divinae legis mystica dicta docens / Hos inter residens Agapetus jure sacerdos / Codicibus pulchrum condidit arte locum."

67. Marrou, "Autour," adduces some conjectures on these points. He suggests (157–65) that the library did contain pagan works and indeed was a center for their collection and critical reconstitution. This is more plausible

than his hypothesis (167–68) that Gregory built the Lateran library to accommodate the holdings of the library of Agapetus there rather than in his monastery (with the result that the Lateran *scrinium*, which he thinks was previously only an archival depository, then became a library proper). It may be, however, that the bulk of Agapetus's library was eventually transferred to the Lateran library.

68. The most thorough and reliable discussion of the library at Hippo is J. Scheele, "Buch und Bibliothek bei Augustinus," *Bibliothek und Wissenschaft* 12 (1978): 14–114, esp. 62–85, with an extensive bibliography of earlier studies.

69. *Vita Aug.* 18.42–54. The most convenient edition is by H. T. Weiskotten, *Sancti Augustini Vita* (Princeton: Princeton University Press, 1919).

70. *Vita Aug.* 31.4–5, 7.

71. B. Altaner, "Die Bibliothek Augustins," *ThRev* 44 (1948): 73–78 (75) (=*Kleine patristische Scriften*, ed. G. Glockmann [Berlin: Akademie, 1967], 174–78 [esp. 175]); and J. Scheele, "Buch und Bibliothek bei Augustinus," 65.

72. Harnack, *Possidius: Augustins Leben, eingeleitet und übersetzt* (Berlin: de Gruyter, 1930), 24–25, 46, relied on texts reading *cum bibliotheca* (so also Weiskotten) rather than *cum bibliothecis* and so mistakenly identified the libraries of the monastic houses with the library of the church, concluding that the church library at Hippo consisted only of scriptural books, the works of Augustine, and some works of other preachers. The context shows that libraries in the monastic houses are meant. The error was pointed out by Altaner, "Die Bibliothek Augustins," 76–78 (*Kleine patristischen Schriften*, 177–78).

73. Scheele, "Buch und Bibliothek bei Augustinus," 64.

74. *Ep.* 29.4, 5, 7 indicates that biblical texts were kept at hand in the church.

75. On Augustine's use of Greek Christian writers in Latin translation, see B. Altaner, "Augustinus und die griechische Patristik," in *Kleine patristischen Schriften*, 181–331.

76. Among many discussions of Augustine's use of classical literature, see esp. P. Courcelle, *Late Latin Writers and Their Greek Sources* (Cambridge: Harvard University Press, 1969); H. Hagendahl, *Augustine and the Latin Classics*, 2 vols. (Goteberg: Elanders, 1967); J. F. Callahan, *Augustine and the Greek Philosophers* (Villanova: Villanova University Press, 1964); and M. Testard, *Saint Augustine et Ciceron*, 2 vols. (Paris: Etudes augustiniennes, 1958). See also the cautions of J. J. O'Donnell, "Augustine's Classical Readings," *Recherches Augustiniennes* 15 (1980): 144–75.

77. On the archives at Hippo, cf. Scheele, "Buch und Bibliothek," 78–85.

78. On the question of a catalogue of the library at Hippo, the discussion of Scheele, "Buch und Bibliothek," 67–73 is especially valuable.

79. In *Ep.* 211.13, Augustine lays down some rules about the borrowing of books in the monastic libraries.

80. The most careful and valuable discussion is provided by P. Lemerle, *Le premier humanisme byzantin: Notes et remarques sur enseignment et culture a Byzance des origenes au X siècle* (Paris: Presses Universitaires de France, 1971), 52–73. N. G. Wilson, "The Libraries of the Byzantine World," *GRBS* 8 (1967): 53–80, deals chiefly with the later period.

81. When this is claimed, it is merely an inference on the basis of Eusebius, *Vita Const.* 4.36, that speaks of Constantine requisitioning fifty copies of the scriptures from the Caesarean library. Surely, however, these were for the use of churches and not for stocking an imperial library.

82. Lemerle, *Le premier humanisme byzantin*, 60; cf. on the imperial library C. Wendel, "Die erste kaiserliche Bibliothek in Konstantinopel," in *Kleine Schriften zum antiken Buch- und Bibliothekswesen*, ed. W. Krieg (Cologne: Greven, 1974), 46–63.

83. Lemerle, *Le premier humanisme byzantin*, 63–68, discussing *Codex Theod.* 14.9.3.

84. *Epit. hist.* 14.2.22–24. Zonaras says that his source is the sophist Malchos, who taught in Constantinople in the late fifth century.

85. *PG* 58, 977.

86. E. Kitzinger, *Byzantine Art in the Making* (Cambridge: Harvard, 1977), 53–55, and fig. 95; Leclercq, "Bibliothèques," 2:893–94, and fig. 1557.

87. Leclercq, "Bibliothèques," 2:893, and fig. 1556. On this illustration see further below in text.

88. The most convenient access to these materials may be had in A. Veilleux, *Pachomian Koinonia*, 3 vols. (Kalamazoo: Cistercian Publications, 1980–82).

89. *Praecepta* 139–40. Cf. *Liber Ors.* 51; *Vita* (Sahidic 10), frag. 2.

90. On the role of scripture in the Pachomian setting, see H. Bacht, "Vom Umgang mit der Bibel im ältesten Mönchtum," *Theologie und Philosophie* 41 (1966): 557–66; F. Ruppert, *Das pachomianische Mönchtum und die Anfänge klösterlichen Gehorsams* (Munsterschwarzach: Vier Turme, 1971), 125–26; and A. Veilleux, "Holy Scripture in the Pachomian Koinonia," *Monastic Studies* 10 (1974): 143–53. More generally, see D. Burton-Christie, *The Word in the Desert: Scripture and the Quest for Holiness in Early Christian Monasticism* (Oxford: Oxford University Press, 1993), esp. ch. 4 ("The Use of Scripture in the Desert").

91. *Vita* (Greek 1): 63.

92. Ibid., 59; *Praecepta* 25; 82; 100–101; *Inst.* 2; *Leg.* 7. On the orientation of the Pachomians to books see the careful survey of the evidence by C. Scholten, "Die Nag-Hammadi-Texte als Buchbesitz der Pachomianer," *JAC* 31 (1988): 144–72, esp. 145–49.

93. *Vita* (Greek 1): 31; *Vita* (Boharic): 189.

94. Scholten, "Die Nag-Hammadi-Texte," 149–53, treats the relevant texts.

95. For an account of the discovery, see J. M. Robinson, "The Discovery of the Nag Hammadi Codices," *BA* 42 (1979): 206–24.

96. This caution is rightly voiced by R. Craft and J. Timbie, "The Nag Hammadi Library: In English," *RSR* 8 (1982): 32–51 (34, 36). However, the codices as a group appear to represent a secondary collection built up from smaller collections that originally belonged to different owners. This may be deduced, first, from the covers of the codices, which represent more than one type of book manufacture, indicating that they were produced by different individuals and perhaps in several communities (Robinson, *The Facsimile Edition of the Nag Hammadi Codices: Introduction*, 71–86), and, second, from the variety of scribal hands in which the codices are inscribed, which

suggests that the collection grew in stages (M. Williams, "The Scribes of the Nag Hammadi Codices IV, V, VI, VIII, and IX," *Actes du IV Congres Copte, 5–10 Septembre, 1988*, vol. 2, "De la linguistique au gnosticisme," ed. M. Rassart-Debergh and L. Ries [Louvain: Universite Catholique, 1992], 334–42.) On the nature of the collection see also n. 103 below.

97. J. Doresse, *The Secret Books of the Egyptian Gnostics* (New York: Viking Press, 1960), 251.

98. J. W. B. Barns, "Greek and Coptic Papyri from the Covers of the Nag Hammadi Codices," *Essays on the Nag Hammadi Library*, ed. M. Krause (NHS 6; Leiden: Brill, 1975), 9–18, argued that the cartonnage of some of the bindings showed that the codices were produced in close connection with the monastery and presumably by monks, but see the qualifications in J. Shelton in J. W. B. Barns et al., eds., *Nag Hammadi Codices: Greek and Coptic Papyri from the Cartonnage of the Covers* (NHS 16; Leiden: Brill, 1981), 1–11, noting (2) that "the evidence for monasticism in general in these papyri is less frequent than [Barns] supposed in that work, and there are no texts in which a specifically Pachomian background comes plainly to the fore," and that the cartonnage, "though of use for determining the approximate date and place at which the codices were bound, is of very questionable value for determining their ownership." Yet if the cartonnage does not offer clear proof of the origin of the codices in Pachomian monasteries, neither does it constitute disproof. See the careful discussion of this point by J. Goehring, "New Frontiers in Pachomian Studies," *The Roots of Egyptian Christianity*, ed. B. A. Pearson and J. E. Goehring (Philadelphia: Fortress, 1986), 236–57, esp. 248–51.

99. T. Säve-Söderbergh, "Holy Scriptures or Apologetic Documentations?" in *Les textes de Nag Hammadi*, J.-E. Ménard, ed. (Leiden: Brill, 1975), 3–14.

100. On the practice of interring books, see generally C. H. Roberts, *Buried Books in Antiquity* (Arundel Esdaile Memorial Lecture, 1962; Letchworth: Garden City Press, 1963); and *Manuscript, Society, and Belief*, 6–8, who supposes that in such cases we are dealing with a type of genizah that Christians took over from Jews. Even if that is so, burial does not of itself indicate anything about the esteem in which books so deposited were held, since a genizah was used for texts that were taken out of use because they were defective, either in physical form or in content. For burial in a jar for preservation, cf. Jer. 32:14, Assump. Moses 1:17–18.

101. J. M. Robinson, *The Nag Hammadi Library in English*, 14–17; H. Chadwick, "The Domestication of Gnosis," in *The Rediscovery of Gnosticism*, ed. B. Layton (Leiden: Brill, 1980), 1:3–16; F. Wisse, "Gnosticism and Early Monasticism in Egypt," in *Gnosis: Festschrift für Hans Jonas*, ed. B. Aland (Göttingen: Vandenhoeck und Ruprecht, 1978), 431–40; and C. Hedrick, "Gnostic Proclivities in the Greek *Life of Pachomius* and the *Sitz im Leben* of the Nag Hammadi Library," *NovT* 22 (1980): 78–94.

102. J. Goehring, "Pachomius' Vision of Heresy: The Development of a Pachomian Tradition," *Le muséon* 95 (1982): 241–62, and "New Frontiers in Pachomian Studies," 239–48.

103. The case is well made by Wisse, "Gnosticism"; Scholten, "Die Nag-Hammadi-Texte," esp. 158–72; and Chadwick, "The Domestication of Gnosis." In an unpublished paper, "Interpreting the Nag Hammadi Library as

'Collection(s)' in the History of 'Gnosticism(s),'" generously shared with me by its author, Michael Williams argues through a close analysis of each codex that the tractates are not randomly collected and inscribed but that in almost every codex there is a probable rationale for the selection and arrangement of the materials, and that the production of the codices served to resolve the theological diversity of the texts by establishing intertextual relations among them that allowed them to be read as expressions of fundamentally the same views and values. This implies, of course, that those who produced the codices were sympathetic users of the texts rather than critics.

104. Thus, e.g., Wisse, "Gnosticism," 436–37; Hedrick, "Gnostic Proclivities," 93–94.

105. J. M. Robinson, *The Pachomian Monastic Library at the Chester Beatty Library and the Bibliothèque Bodmer* (Institute for Antiquity and Christianity Occasional Papers, 19; Claremont: Institute for Antiquity and Christianity, 1990), who traces the history of the discovery of these papyri and of their marketing and acquisition.

106. Ibid., 19–21, with a detailed list and some analytic subdivisions. There are nine papyrus rolls and twenty-nine codices (twenty-two of which are papyrus).

107. Ibid., 6, connecting the disposal of the books with the decline of the order under the imposition of Chalcedonian authority. According to Robinson's reconstruction of the discovery, the manuscripts were buried, like the Nag Hammadi codices, in an earthenware jar, presumably for preservation until more auspicious times.

108. Ibid., 4–5, discussing several items that give an "impression of primitiveness" and economy and suggest "limitations of the monastic effort to build its collection."

109. See my remarks earlier in this chapter on P. Ash. Inv. 3. Not to be overlooked in connection with monastic libraries or the use of commentaries in them are the Tura papyri, discovered in 1941 about six miles south of Cairo as British forces prepared to use ancient quarries for the storage of munitions. As debris was being removed there was found in one cave a group of papyrus codices containing (mainly lost) works of Origen and Didymus the Blind, including a number of commentaries. Transcribed in the sixth century, these books had been part of the library of the monastery of Arsenius, constructed on a terrace above the quarries in the late fifth or early sixth century. (Arsenius, from an aristocratic Roman family, had been a teacher of rhetoric and a tutor of the emperors Arcadius and Honorius before withdrawing to monastic life in 394.) The manuscripts were presumably hidden after the condemnation of Origen and Didymus. On the circumstances and character of the find, see esp. O. Gueraud, "Note préliminaire sur les papyrus d'Origène découverts à Toura," *RHR* 131 (1946): 85–108; H.-Ch. Puech, "Les nouveaux écrits d'Origène et de Didyme découverts à Toura," *RHPR* (1951): 293–329; L. Doutreleau, "Que savons-nous aujourd'hui des papyrus de Toura?" *RSR* 43 (1955): 161–76; L. Koenen and L. Doutreleau, "Nouvelle inventaire des papyrus de Toura," *RSR* 55 (1967): 547–64; and L. Koenen and W. Müller-Wiener, "Zu den Papyri aus dem Arsenioskloster bei Tura," *ZPE* 2 (1968): 41–63.

110. *Ep.* 22.30.1. On Jerome's library see G. Grützmacher, *Hieronymus:*

Eine biographische Studie zur alten Kirchengeschichte, 3 vols. (Leipzig: Dietrich, 1901–8), 1:126–29.

111. See, e.g., *Ep.* 5.2.2–4.

112. See esp. *Ep.* 22.30 and compare the sturdy defense of reading pagan writers in *Ep.* 70. For discussion, see H. Hagendahl, *Latin Fathers and the Classics,* 312–28.

113. Although in his *Famous Men* Jerome occasionally remarks on books he possessed and many of the books he explicitly claims to have read must have been in his own library, Grützmacher (*Hieronymus,* 128) goes too far in thinking that Jerome possessed most of the works he names here.

114. J. N. D. Kelly, *Jerome,* 327.

115. *Ep.* 9 (ed. J. Bidez, *L'empereur Julien: Oeuvres complètes* [Paris: Belles Lettres, 1924], no. 107).

116. *Ep.* 36 (Bidez, no. 106).

117. Thus Bidez, *L'empereur Julien,* 118.

118. We hear in passing of a few other private Christian libraries, but learn little about them. In the fifth century, Sidonius Apollinaris alludes to several, e.g., *Ep.* 9.4, describing the impressive library of a country house in southern Gaul, where "books of any number were readily available. You might have imagined yourself to be looking at the shelves of a professional scholar or at the tiers in the Athenaeum or at the high presses of the booksellers. . . . It was a frequent practice to read writers whose artistry was of a similar kind—here Augustine, there Varro; here Horace, there Prudentius."

119. Among general studies of library history, see E. D. Johnson and M. H. Harris, *History of Libraries in the Western World* (Metuchen, N. J.: Scarecrow Press, 1976), 40–73; S. L. Jackson, *Libraries and Librarianship in the West* (New York: McGraw-Hill, 1974), 1–30; H. J. de Vleershauwer, "History of the Western Library," *Museion* 71 (1963): 33–99; 72 (1964): 102–39; 73 (1965): 140–85; and J. W. Thompson, *Ancient Libraries* (Berkeley: University of California, 1940). More specialized surveys are given by C. Callmer, "Antike Bibliotheken," *Opuscula Archaeologica* 3 (1944): 145–93; Wendel and Gober, "Das griechisch-römische Altertum," 2:51–145; Leclercq, "Bibliothèques," 2:842–904, C. Wendel, "Bibliothek," *RAC* 2:246–74; K. Dziatzko, "Bibliotheken," *RE* 3:405–24; and L. S. Thompson, "Roman and Greek Libraries," *Encyclopedia of Library and Information Science* 26:3–40; and Blanck, *Das Buch in der Antike,* 133–222. On Roman libraries see also the studies cited below in n. 153.

120. For the evidence, see Platthy, *Sources on the Earliest Greek Libraries* (Amsterdam: Hakkert, 1968), 97–133. The tyrants Polycrates of Samos and Peisistratus of Athens are sometimes mentioned as still-earlier collectors (Athenaeus, *Deipn.* 1.3a; Aulus Gellius, *Noct. Att.* 7.17.1).

121. The chief source on Aristotle's library is Strabo, 13.1.54–55. Cf. Plutarch, *Sulla* 26, and Diogenes Laertius, 5.52. For discussion see Wendel and Gober, "Das griechish-römische Altertum," 59–61, and in good detail, R. Blum, *Kallimachos: The Alexandrian Library and the Origins of Bibliography,* trans. H. H. Wellisch (Madison: University of Wisconsin Press, 1991), 52–94. For the history of the library after it fell into Sulla's hands, see T. K. Dix, "Private and Public Libraries at Rome in the First Century B.C.: A Preliminary

Study in the History of Roman Libraries" (Ph.D. diss., University of Michigan, 1986), 16–71.

122. There is some evidence to this effect at least for Zeno, the founder of Stoicism: Diogenes Laertius, 7.27, 7.31. On libraries of philosophical schools, see esp. Wendel and Gober, "Das griechisch-römische Altertum," 58–62.

123. There is a wealth of studies on the Alexandrian library. In addition to the literature on ancient libraries generally (n. 119 above), see R. Pfeiffer, *History of Classical Scholarship from the Beginnings to the End of the Hellenistic Age* (Oxford: Clarendon, 1968), 95–233; E. A. Parsons, *The Alexandrian Library* (London: Elsevier, 1952); and L. Canfora, *The Vanished Library: A Wonder of the Ancient World* (London: Hutchinson Radius, 1989). The last two works offer more speculative and romanticized accounts. The most careful concise discussions available are those of P. M. Fraser, *Ptolemaic Alexandria* (Oxford: Clarendon, 1972), 1:320–35 (concentrating on the Ptolemaic period); and Blum, *Kallimachos*, 95–124.

124. According to the *Letter of Aristeas* (9–11) and sources dependent on it, the library was founded by Ptolemy Philadelphus, and Demetrius was its first head. This cannot be correct, since Demetrius was banished by Philadelphus immediately on his accession. Even so, Demetrius must be supposed to have been influential in the conception of the library and to have been active in early acquisitions, as claimed by Johannes Tzetzes in the prolegomenon to commentary on Aristophanes (ed. G. Kaibel, *Comicorum Graecorum Fragmenta* [Berlin: Wiedmann, 1899]), Mb 1.29. On the role of Demetrius, see esp. Blum, *Kallimachos*, 100–102.

125. For the evidence, see Fraser, *Ptolemaic Alexandria*, 314.

126. Tzetzes, in Kaibel, *Comicorum graecorum fragmenta*, 17–33 (19); Epiphanius, *de mens. et pond.* 11 (PG 43, 255). Archaeological excavations of the Serapeum, which was located in the Egyptian quarter, have shown that a library was associated with it as early as the third century B.C.E. It was apparently built by Ptolemy Euergetes (247–21). A stoa-like structure that stood at the southern end of the Serapeum and comprised two long corridors, originally roofed, with nineteen rooms off to the side, seems to have been the library area in the Ptolemaic period. See A. Rowe, "A Contribution to the Archaeology of the Western Desert: IV. The Great Serapeum of Alexandria," *BJRL* 39 (1956–57): 485–512.

127. Strabo, in his description of the palace area, and Herodas, in his discussion of the sights of Alexandria, both mention the Museion but not the library. Fraser (*Ptolemaic Alexandria*, 324–25) infers from the remains of the rival library at Pergamum (see below) that "it does not seem likely that the kings of Pergamon would have been content with such a modest structure if a separate library stood in the capital of the Ptolemies."

128. Zenodotus, Apollonius Rhodius, and Aristarchus at least seem to have occupied both positions. Blum, *Kallimachos*, 133, doubts that the positions were consistently linked. The evidence for the librarians comes variously from John Tzetzes (for the earliest), from the lives of poets and scholars found in the "Suidas," a tenth-century encyclopaedia compiled from various earlier sources, and from P. Oxy. 1241, dated to the second century and containing a list of Alexandrian librarians.

129. P. Oxy. 1241, though not fully reliable, is the earliest witness to the succession of librarians and has helped to clarify the question. It gives the sequence: Zenodotus (285–270), Apollonius Rhodius (270–245), Eratosthenes (245–204/1 [?]), Aristophanes of Byzantium (204/1 [?]–189/6 [?]), Apollonius the Eidograph (189/6 [?]–175), Aristarchus (175–145), and Cydas (?). Callimachus, who is often thought to have held the post (though he is so mentioned in only one ancient source), does not appear in what is preserved of the papyrus. On the problem of the identity and sequence of the Alexandrian librarians, see Fraser, *Ptolemaic Alexandria*, 330–34, and Blum, *Kallimachos*, 127–33, who argues that Callimachus succeeded Zenodotus. More speculative is Parsons, *Alexandrian Library*, 122–62.

130. Kaibel, *Comicorum Graecorum Fragmenta*, 19. Because these numbers are so large and the terminology so unclear, Tzetzes's comments have been much discussed. Perhaps the likeliest interpretation is that "mixed rolls" were multivolume single works, and "unmixed" rolls were single works in single volumes (Canfora, *Vanished Library*, 187–89). This reduces the number of individual titles and makes sense of the preponderance of mixed over unmixed rolls, even if it does not reduce the number of rolls. On the evidence of Tzetzes, see also Blum, *Kallimachos*, 104–13, and, less critically, Parsons, *Alexandrian Library*, 106–21. Aulus Gellius, *Noct. att.* 7.17.3 (cf. Ammianus Marcellinus, 22.16.12–3) claims that the library was larger still, comprising 700,000 volumes at the time of Caesar's Alexandrian war (47 B.C.E.).

131. Blum, *Kallimachos*, 107, rightly comments that "even a collection of 40,000–50,000 scrolls was an enormous one under the conditions of those times."

132. The famous *pinakes* or "Tables of the authors eminent in various disciplines" drawn up by Callimachus, which ran to some 120 rolls, were not (as sometimes supposed) a working catalogue or even shelf list of the Alexandrian library, but a critical classification and inventory of Greek literature comprising biographical information on famous authors and bibliographic notes on their work. The classical discussion is F. Schmidt, *Die Pinakes des Kallimachos* (Berlin: Ebering, 1922). A concise treatment is given by Pfeiffer, *History of Classical Scholarship*, 127–34, but see Blum, *Kallimachos*, esp. 124–69, 226–43, who speaks of the pinakes as "a Greek national bibliography" and "national author lexicon" (239).

133. Fraser, *Ptolemaic Alexandria*, 330; Blum, *Kallimachos*, 102–4; cf. Parsons, *Alexandrian Library*, 175–203. For Jewish literature see the *Letter of Aristeas*. That both Manetho and Erastosthenes translated Egyptian chronologies suggests that those records had a place in the library; according to Pliny the Elder (*N.H.* 30.4), Hermippus wrote a commentary on the writings of Zoroaster, which implies that they were in the library. See further M. L. von Graberg, "Neueste deutsche Forschung zur Geschichte der Bibliotheken Alexandreias," *Libri* 24 (1974): 277–301, esp. 278–84, who sees in the incorporation of oriental literature an effect of the influence of Alexander the Great, such that the library is not to be understood entirely on the basis of peripatetic ideas (as Wendel argues).

132. *Comm. in Hipp. Epidem.* 3.17a (606–7), and *Comm. in Hipp. De Nat. Homin.* 1.44 and 2 (proem).

135. Athenaeus, *Deipnosoph.* 1.3, mentions procurements at Athens and Rhodes, often regarded as major book markets in the Greek world.

136. *Comm. in Hipp. Epidem.* 3 (17a 606–7).

137. Gellius, *Noct. att.* 6.16, suggests a heavy volume of book production in the library but does not clearly differentiate between books "acquired" *(conquistio)* and books "manufactured" *(confectus)*.

138. The main sources are Seneca, *De tranq. an.* 9.5, and Orosius, *Hist. adv. pag.* 6.15.31–32, both of whom appear to depend on a lost part of Livy; cf. also Aulus Gellius, *Noct. att.* 7.17.3; Dio Cassius 42.58.2; and Plutarch, *Caesar* 49. The story is problematic: Caesar does not mention it, nor does Strabo, who worked in the library some twenty years later, and the sources diverge widely on the extent of the destruction. If the books were part of the royal library in the Museion, a large part of its contents must be supposed to have been lost. But it is not clear whether the books in question were those within the royal library itself or books for export found in warehouses close to the harbor. For the former possibility, see Fraser, *Ptolemaic Alexandria,* 334–35; and Wendel and Gober, "Das griechische-römische Altertum," 75–78; for the latter Canfora, *Vanished Library,* 66–70, 132–36, and Parsons, *Alexandrian Library,* 297, who gives a full review of the evidence (288–319) but thinks (with uncharacteristic skepticism) that the story is merely legendary.

139. Writing in the fourth century, Ammianus Marcellinus (*Hist.* 22.16.15) says that at this time the palace quarter (where the Museion and its library were located) was completely destroyed, and Epiphanius says that in his time it was a desert.

140. Theodoret, *H.E.* 22.

141. A. Conze, "Die pergamenische Bibliothek," *SPAW* (1884): 1259–70; R. Bohn, *Das heiligtum der Athena Polias Nikephoros* ("Altertumer von Pergamon," 2; Berlin: Spemann, 1885), 56–75. Good discussions and illustrations are given by Callmer, "Antike Bibliotheken," 148–53.

142. Thus, K. Dziatzko, "Die Bibliothekanlage von Pergamon," *Sammlung bibliothekswissenschaftlicher Arbeiten* 10 (1896): 38–47; and Callmer, "Antike Bibliotheken," 151–52. Callmer sees in the large common room the counterpart of the *oikos* of the Alexandrian Museion (152).

143. Diogenes Laertius 7.54, citing Isidorus of Pergamum. Others sometimes thought to have served in the librarianship are Crates, Artemon of Cassandreia (who wrote two bibliographic treatises, one "On the Collection of Books" and another "On the Use of Books" [Athenaeus 3.515, 592]), and, in the second century C.E., Telephus, the Stoic grammarian and tutor to the emperor Lucius Verus (Suidas, s.v.).

144. Pliny, *Hist. nat.* 13.70 (citing Varro); and later Jerome, *Ep.* 7.2, John Lydus, *De mens.* (ed. Wuensch), p. 14; Isidore of Seville, *Origines* 6.11.1; and John Tzetzes, *Chil.* 12.345–48. See R. R. Johnson, "The Role of Parchment in Greco-Roman Antiquity" (Ph.D. diss., UCLA, 1968) 22–51, who argues (42–51) that in the years 173–168 there was a coincidence of a shortage of papyrus and a strong development of the library. It need not be supposed, however, that Ptolemy restricted papyrus exports to stymie the growth of the Pergamene library.

145. Wendel and Gober, "Das griechische-römische Altertum," 84–85. See

Plutarch, *Antonius* 58.3, 59.1; Athenaeus 8.336e; Dionysius of Halicarnassus, *De dinarcho* 1.11–12, *Ad Ammaeum* 4.

146. Plutarch, *Antonius,* 58.3, the only witness for such a donation, was uncertain about the reliability of his source.

147. Callmer, "Antike Bibliotheken," calculates on the basis of the space available in the library at Pergamum that "at most 200,000 rolls could be accommodated" (152–53).

148. See Platthy, *Sources on the Earliest Greek Libraries,* 137–40, for evidence of libraries at the temples of Delphi and Epidaurus.

149. *Inscriptiones graeca* II–III, editio minor, par. 1, nos. 1009, 1029, 1030, 1040–43.

150. Platthy, *Sources on the Earliest Greek Libraries,* 159–60 (Pergamum); 146–7 (Cos); 148–50 (Rhodes); 157–8 (Halicarnassus); 168–69 (Teos). On gymnasial libraries generally, see Callmer, "Antike Bibliotheken," 154; Wendel and Gober, "Das griechische-römische Altertum," 95–99; and Blanck, *Buch,* 149–52.

151. Dedicatory inscriptions in Platthy, *Sources on the Earliest Greek Libraries,* 155–56.

152. Pausanius, 1.18.9; Eusebius, *Chron.* 227; Aristides, *Panathen.* 13.188.

153. On Roman libraries, see in addition to the studies cited above, E. Makowiecka, *The Origin and Evolution of the Architectural Form of the Roman Library* (Warsaw: Wydawnictwa Universytets, 1978); R. Fehrle, *Das Bibliothekswesen im alten Rom: Voraussetzungen, Bedingungen, Anfänge* (Wisebaden: Reichert, 1986), 14–28, 54–88; and Dix, "Private and Public Libraries."

154. On the library of Aristotle, see above in the text. On the Macedonian library: Isidore, *Etym.* 6.5.1; and Plutarch, *Aemelius Paullus* 28.10 (this library, at Aemelius Paullus's death in 160, came into the hands of his son, Scipio Aemelianus, and was a magnet and resource for the so-called Scipionic circle). On the library of Lucullus, see Plutarch, *Lucullus,* 42.1–2; Isidore, *Etym.* 6.5.1; Cicero, *De fin.* 3.2.7–3.3.10; and Pliny, *Nat. hist.* 25.3.6–7. For discussion, see Dix, "Private and Public Libraries."

155. Suetonius, *Iul.* 44.1–3; and Isidore, *Etym.* 6.5.1. This was possibly the occasion for Varro's composition of the (lost) work *De bibliothecis.*

156. Pliny, *Nat. hist.* 7.30.115, 35.2.10; Isidore, *Etym.* 6.5.1; and Ovid, *Trist.* 3.1.71–72. See Fehrle, *Bibliothekswesen,* 54–61, and Dix, "Private and Public Libraries," 198–203.

157. For libraries established by Augustus, see esp. Fehrle, *Bibliothekswesen,* 62–65; and Dix, "Private and Public Libraries," 203–11.

158. Suetonius, *Augustus,* 29.3; Dio, 53.1.3; Ovid, *Trist.* 3.1.60–68; Horace, *Ep.* 1.3.17, 2.1.216; Pliny, *Nat. hist.* 7.210; and *CIL* 5188–89, 5191, 5884.

159. Dio, 66.24.2. The library suffered damage in the fire of 191 (Galen, *De comp. med.* 1.1, Dio, 73.24.2) and was probably finally destroyed in 363 (Amiannus Marcellinus, 23.3.3).

160. It is unclear whether Augustus built this library in Octavia's name (Suetonius, *Aug.* 29.4, Dio, 49.43.8) or Octavia built it in memory of Marcellus (Ovid, *Ars am.* 1.69–70; *Fest.* 188; Plutarch, *Marc.* 30). The exact location and plan are unknown, but it was divided into Greek and Latin sections (*CIL* 6:2347–48, 4433, 4435).

161. Suetonius, *Tiberius* 74; Pliny, *Nat. Hist.* 34.43.

162. Dio, 68.16.2; Gellius, *Noct. att.* 11.17.1. Full descriptions and diagrams are given by Callmer, "Antike Bibliotheken," 162–64, and Makowiecka, *Origin and Evolution*, 53–55.

163. *Hist. Aug.* Aurel. 1.7, 1.10, 8.1, 27.7; Tac. 8.1; Num. 11.3; Apollinaris Sidonius, *Ep.* 9.16.3.25–27, *carm.* 8.8.

164. Details and literature in Callmer, "Antike Bibliotheken," 164–65. There is a questionable notice in *Hist. Aug.*, Prob. 2.1, claiming that part of the Ulpian holdings were once temporarily housed in the Baths of Diocletian. Cf. also *CIL* 6:8679, an inscription describing a slave as *vilic[us] thermar[um] bybliothec[ae] Gra[ecae]*. On Roman baths generally, see I. Nielsen, *Thermae et Balnea: The Architecture and History of Roman Public Baths*, 2 vols. (Aarhus: Aarhus University Press, 1990).

165. J. E. Stambaugh, *The Ancient Roman City* (Baltimore: Johns Hopkins University Press, 1988), 201. Cf. J. Delaine, "Recent Research on Roman Baths," *Journal of Roman Archaeology* 1 (1988): 14.

166. The testimony is given by Africanus himself in a fragment of his *Kestoi* found at Oxyrhynchus (P. Oxy. 142). On the location and possible remains of this library, see V. Lundstrom, "Pantheon-biblioteket," *Eranos* 12 (1912): 64–72. The nature of Africanus's role has been debated. The papyrus has the term *erchitektonesa* (designed, drew up the plans), but A. von Harnack ("Julius Africanus, der Bibliothekar des Kaisers Alexander Severus," *Aufsätze Fritz Mikau gewidmet* [Leipzig: Hiersemann, 1921], 142–46), construed this to mean "organized" the collections. Cf. F. Granger, "Julius Africanus and the Library of the Pantheon," *JTS* 34 (1933): 157–61, who speaks of Africanus as the libarary's "administrator." Vieillefond, *Les "Cestes,"* 20–22, is probably right in regarding Africanus simply as the architect. Yet it is not inconceivable that as architect he may have had some influence on the collection.

167. Wendel, "Versuch einer Deutung der Hippolyt-Statue," in *Kleine Schriften*, 28–34, argues that the famous statue of the Roman presbyter Hippolytus listing his works may originally have had its place in the Pantheon library.

168. Pliny, 1.8.2, 5.7. The cost was 1 million sesterces, and maintenance required another one hundred thousand. See *CIL* 5.5262.

169. *CIL* 10.4760.

170. On these libraries see Callmer, "Antike Bibliotheken," 177–78 and 181–82.

171. *Flor.* 18; *Apol.* 41.

172. See Suetonius, *Iul.* 42.2; Pliny, *Nat. hist.* 7.30.115, 35.2.10; Ovid, *Trist.* 2.419–20; and Isidore, *Etym.* 6.5.1.

173. Cf. Horace, *Ep.* 2.1.214–18; *Trist.* 3.1.

174. Such statements come mainly from Aulus Gellius; see *Noct. Att.* 5.21.9, 9.4.13, 11.17.1, 13.20.1, 16.8.2, 18.9.5, 19.5.4; cf. Horace, *Ep.* 1.3.15–20; Marcus Aurelius, *Ep. ad Front.* 4.5. The sources that have the most to say about the use of libraries refer much more commonly to private collections.

175. This point is made in an unpublished paper by G. W. Houston, "Why Did the Romans Bother to Build Public Libraries?" kindly shared with me by the author. Julius Caesar's plan for a library in Rome owed something to the Alexandrian library. He spent the winter months of 48 in Alexandria and

perhaps saw the library then (Callmer, "Antike Bibliotheken," 156; Makowieka, *Origin and Evolution*, 27). The Romans were also acquainted with the Pergamene library, which had had representatives in Rome as early as the second century B.C.E. (Suetonius, *Gramm.* 2; Strabo, 14.5.14). Houston persuasively argues that "public libraries were looked at differently in different parts of the Roman empire," and in particular that while they were commonplace and served academic purposes in the Greek East, they were not essential civic features in the Latin West, where no close connection was ever made between education and libraries.

176. A. J. Marshall, "Library Resources and Creative Writing at Rome," *Phoenix* 30 (1976): 261–63, who also points out the negative side of imperial patronage in the exclusion of certain works, which "amounted to an oblique form of censorship." On literary patronage generally, see ch. 3.

177. A useful discussion is given by L. Bruce, "Palace and Villa Libraries from Augustus to Hadrian," *Journal of Library History* 21 (1986): 510–52. See also T. Kleberg, "Bucherliebhaberei und private Buchersammlungen in der römischen Kaiserzeit," *Festschrift Josef Stummvoll*, ed. J. Mayerhofer and W. Ritzer (Vienna: Hollinek, 1970), 401–9; Marshall, "Library Resources"; and T. K. Dix, "Public and Private Libraries" (who treats mainly the libraries of Sulla, Lucullus, and Cicero).

178. This library came to light in excavations of the southwestern part of the Palatine begun in 1956. See G. Carettoni, "I problemi della zona Augustea del Palatino alle luce dei recenti scavi," *Atti della Pontifica Accademia Romana di Archeologia: Rendiconti* 39 (1967): 55–75; and more fully in *Das Haus des Augustus auf dem Palatin* (Mainz: Philipp von Zabern, 1983).

179. The space was first identified by G. de Gregori, "Biblioteche dell'antichita," *Accademie e Biblioteche d'Italia* 11 (1937): 20–21. See also Callmer, "Antike Bibliotheken," 160–61.

180. There were, however, others. On the library of Hadrian's villa near Tivoli and a (possible) library in the Villa Jovis of Tiberius on Capri, see Bruce, "Palace and Villa Libraries," 526–35, 537–38. There are no remains of libraries at the imperial villas at Antium and Ostia. Philostratus, *Vita Apoll.* 8.20, may intimate a library at Antium. An inscription found near the theater of the villa (*CIL* 10:6638) names four members of the staff of the library at Antium, and an inscription at Ostia (*CIL* 14:196) names a library worker there.

181. On this library, see A. Maiuri, *La casa del Menandro e il suo tesoro di argenteria* (Rome: Libreria dello Stato, 1933), 84–89; and L. Richardson, "The Libraries of Pompeii," *Archaeology* 30 (1977): 394–402 (397–99).

182. On this library, see esp. D. Comparetti and G. de Petra, *La villa ercolanese dei Pisoni* (Naples: Centro internazionale per lo studio dei papiri ercolanesi, [1883] 1972); D. Comparetti, "La bibliothèque de Philodeme," *Mélanges Chatelain* (Paris: Campion, 1910), 118–29; C. Jensen, "Die Bibliothek von Herculaneum," *Bonner Jahrbucher* 135 (1930): 49–61; C. Gallavotti, "La libreria di una villa romana ercolanese," *Bollettino dell'Istituto di Patologia del Libro* 3 (1941): 129–45; M. Gigante, *La Bibliothèque de Philodeme et l'Epicurisme Romain* (Paris: Les Belles Lettres, 1987), 31–71; S. Sider, "Herculaneum's Library in 79 A.D.: The Villa of the Papyri," *Libraries and Culture* 25 (1990): 534–42.

183. On the nature of the storage units, see Wendel, "Der antike Bucher-schrank," in *Kleine Schriften*, 69–70. For a reconstruction of the bookcases, see C. Gallavotti, "La custodia dei papiri nella villa suburbana ercolanese," *Bollettino dell'Istituto di patologia del libro* 2 (1940): 53–63.

184. All the rolls were carbonized, and early efforts to unroll and decipher them were notoriously slipshod and destructive, resulting in many losses. For contemporary techniques, see B. Fosse, "Unrolling the Herculaneum Papyri," *CErc* 14 (1984): 9–15.

183. This is generally granted. See H. Bloch, "L. Calpurnius Piso Caesoninus in Samothrace and Herculaneum," *AJA* 44 (1940): 485–93. For a recent dissent, see M. R. Wojcik, *La villa dei papyri ad Ercolano* (Rome: l'Erma di Bretschneider, 1986).

186. Still other rolls were found at some remove from the library and near the grand peristyle: eleven in a room adjoining the dining room, some others in and around two wooden boxes in a corridor between the library and peristyle, and a few papyri and wax tablets in the reception room. For the locations,see C. Waldstein and L. Shoobridge, *Herculaneum: Past, Present, and Future* (London: Macmillan, 1908), app. 4 (297–305, esp. 300–302). The papyri are catalogued in M. Gigante, ed., *Catalogo dei papyri ercolanesi* (Naples: Bibliopolic, 1979).

187. G. Cavallo, *Libri, scritture, scribi a Ercolano* (Cronache Ercolanesi 13, 1983, suppl. 1; Naples: Macchiaroli, 1983), 58–65, has attempted a paleographic mapping of the history of the library, discriminating and tentatively dating seventeen groups of scribal hands among the papyri.

188. Gigante, *La bibliotheque de Philodeme*, 23–29, and the literature cited there.

189. The problem is compounded in the cases of those who had several private collections in different locations. Cicero had libraries in several villas (*De div.* 2.8; *Topica* 1.1, *Att.* 2.6.1, *De leg.* 2.1); and so did Italicus (Pliny, *Ep.* 3.7.8); Atticus had a library in Rome as well as in Athens (Cicero, *Att.* 4.14.1).

190. Suidas, s.v. Ephaprodites; *Hist. Aug.* Gord. 18.2–3. The latter report is discredited by modern assessments of the *Historia Augusta*: see L. Bruce, "A Reappraisal of Roman Libraries in the *Scriptores Historiae Augustae*," *JLH* 16 (1981): 551–73 (557–58), and the literature cited there.

191. Such a size can only be an educated guess, taking account of the few figures available, such as the approximately 1,800 rolls of the library of the Villa of the Papyri, the library of the poet Persius (34–62 c.e.), numbered by Suetonius at 700 rolls *(Vita Persi)*, and the modest 120 rolls or so owned by Martial (14.190).

192. See Dix, "Private and Public Libraries," 98–107, for a discussion—in connection with Cicero's library—of the difficulties and possibilities of assembling a sizable private collection of books.

193. Because such niches depend on a Roman method of wall construction, they must be regarded as a Roman innovation and not something taken over from Greek libraries, as Wendel claimed ("Die bauliche Entwicklung der antiken Bibliothek," in *Kleine Schriften*, 144–64 [146–50], and "Der antike Bucherschrank," in *Kleine Schriften*, 64–92 [77–82]). See the remarks of E. Makowiecka, *The Origin and Evolution of the Architectural Form of the*

Roman Library, 33–34. The niches are ordinarily one to two meters wide and a half meter deep. Their normal height is difficult to determine since the walls are usually not standing, but the few observable instances suggest that three meters was average.

194. For a full discussion of the evidence, see Wendel, "Der antike Bucherschrank," in *Kleine Schriften*, 64–92. Cf. E. G. Budde, *Armarium und Kibotos: Ein Beitrag zur Geschichte des antiken Mobilars* (Wurtzburg: Triltsche, 1940).

195. These features were not entirely confined to imperial private libraries. Separate Greek and Latin collections were fairly common (Petronius, *Cena Trim.* 48.4; cf. Cicero, *Ad Quintum Frat.* 3.4.5), and built-in *armaria* sometimes were used (Pliny, *Ep.* 2.17.8).

196. For the terminology, see Seneca (*loculamenta, De tranq. animi* 9.7) and Cicero (*pegmata, Ad Att.* 4.8.2); Suetonius (*Aug.* 31.1) and Juvenal (3.219) refer to *foruli*. See Wendel, "Der antike Bucherschrank," 65–70.

197. Pliny, *Nat. hist.* 7.115, 35.10; Horace, *Sat.* 1.4.21–22; Suetonius, *Tiberius* 70.2, 74; *Caligula* 34.2; *Hist. Aug. Num.* 11.3; Seneca, *De tranq. an.* 9.7; Pliny, *Ep.* 3.7; 4.28.1. Pliny the Elder (*Nat. hist.* 7.115, 35.10) credits Asinius Pollio with the introduction of portraits of famous authors into Roman libraries, but the practice was typically Greek and probably originated with the great libraries at Alexandria and Pergamum. See M. Fraenkel, ed., *Altertumer von Pergamon, 8.1: Die Inschriften von Pergamon* (Berlin: de Gruyter, 1890), 117–21 (nos. 198–203); and Th. Lorenz, *Galerien von griechischen Philosophen- und Dichterbildnissen bei den Romern* (Mainz: Zabern, 1965).

198. Josephus, *Contra Ap.* 2.175; Philo, *Som.* 2.127; and the Theodotus inscription (*CIJ* 2.1404). On the designations and various functions of the ancient synagogues, see M. Hengel, "Proseuche and Synagogue," *The Synagogue: Studies in Origins, Archaeology, and Architecture*, ed. J. Gutmann (New York: KTAV, 1975), 27–54; S. Safrai, "The Synagogue," *The Jewish People in the First Century* (Compendia Rerum Iudaicarum ad Novum Testamentum), ed. S. Safrai and M. Stern (Philadelphia: Fortress, 1976), 2:908–44; Lee I. Levine, "The Second Temple Synagogue: The Formative Years," *The Synagogue in Late Antiquity*, ed. Lee I. Levine (Philadelphia: American Schools of Oriental Research, 1987), 7–31; Schürer, *History of the Jewish People* 2:423–61; and W. Schrage, "*Synagoge*," TDNT 7:798–828. For the prominence of the reading of scripture over prayer, see S. Safrai, "Gathering in the Synagogues on Festivals, Sabbaths and Weekdays," *Ancient Synagogues in Israel, Third–Seventh Century C.E.*, ed. R. Hachlili (Oxford: B.A.R., 1989), 7–15.

199. See esp. R. Hachlili, "The Niche and the Ark in Ancient Synagogues," *BASOR* 223 (1976): 43–53, and more fully in *Ancient Jewish Art and Archaeology in the Land of Israel* (Leiden: Brill, 1988), 166–92, 272–80. Dated but still useful is Wendel, "Der Thoraschrein im Altertum," in *Kleine Schriften*, 108–43.

200. See E. L. Sukenik, *Ancient Synagogues in Palestine and Greece* (London: British Academy, 1934), 52–53; Wendel, "Der Thoraschrein," *Kleine Schriften*, 20–24; and A. Seager, "Ancient Synagogue Architecture: An Over-

view," *Ancient Synagogues: The State of Research*, ed. J. Gutmann (Chico: Scholars Press, 1981), 39–43. No remains of Torah shrines have been found in the entry walls of synagogues of the basilical type (also called early or Galilean), which were constructed with the three-doored entry wall facing Jerusalem (e.g., Beth Shearim, Baram, Capernaum, Chorazin, Meiron). In such synagogues there was originally no fixed shrine but only a portable ark that was brought in and positioned on the inner wall of the facade during worship. Sometimes it is apparent that permanent Torah shrines were added, usually awkwardly, at a later period to synagogues that originally lacked them (e.g., Beth Shearim, En-Gedi, Ostia, Sardis; see M. Avi-Yonah, "Ancient Synagogues," *Ariel* 32 [1973]: 29–43 [34]). There are also depictions of Torah chests that appear to have been portable and freestanding: a frieze found at the Capernaum synagogue shows a wheeled and roofed chest, while several mosaics show chests with legs (Hachlili, "The Niche and the Ark," 49–50). It is probably relevant that rabbinic sources refer to two different "curtains" or "veils": apart from the *paroket* that hangs in front of the shrine, there is mention of a *killah* (PT Meg. 73d, Shab. 17c) laid over the chest itself, perhaps used with the portable chest.

201. I. Sonne, "Synagogue," *IDB* 4:476–91 (487–88); see also J. Rabbinowitz, *Mishnah Megillah* (Oxford: Oxford University Press, 1931), 89–90, noting that the Mishnah invariably uses *tebah* in preference to *aron*, and suggesting that this was owing to a popular tendency to drop the qualifier *hakkodesh* and thus make no distinction between the designation of the holy ark and the ordinary word for chest (which, by itself, could also mean "coffin").

202. E. R. Goodenough, *Jewish Symbols in the Greco-Roman Period*, 12 vols. (New York: Patheon, 1953–65), 3: figs. 706, 707, 710, 964–74.

203. On the educational uses of the synagogue, see generally M. Hengel, *Judaism and Hellenism*, 65–83; Schürer, *History of the Jewish People*, 2.419–63; and S. Safrai, "Education and the Study of the Torah," *The Jewish People in the First Century*, 2:945–70. The combination of worship and instruction is taken to show an affinity with Egyptian practice, and with other features, to point to the emergence of the synagogue in Ptolemaic Egypt by J. G. Griffiths, "Egypt and the Rise of the Synagogue," *JTS* 38 (1987): 1–15 (11–12).

204. P. T. Meg. II 73d (which, however, speaks of a *bet talmud* rather than a *bet midrash*) regards the *bet sepher* as oriented to the study of scripture and the *bet talmud* as concerned with mishnah, but this is perhaps anachronistic. On the relation of the *bet midrash* to the synagogue, see Z. Ilan, "The Synagogue and *Beth Midrash* of Meroth," *Ancient Synagogues in Israel*, ed. R. Hachlili, 21–41 (esp. 35, and n. 62). The *hazzan* of the synagogue was often the teacher or a teaching assistant (P. T. Yeb. XII 13a, M. Shab.1.3).

205. For these varied functions, see Schürer, *History of the Jewish People*, 2:427–39; Schrage, "Synagoge," 821–28; and Levine, "The Second Temple Synagogue," 14.

206. The most famous ancient genizah, discovered more or less intact, belonged to the Qara'ite synagogue in Cairo and contained thousands of texts—scriptural, liturgical, exegetical, and archival. Cf. P. Kahle, *The Cairo Geniza* (Oxford: Blackwell, 1959), and S. D. Goitein, *Mediterranean Society: The Jewish Communities of the Arab World as Portrayed in the Documents of*

the Cairo Genizah, 2 vols. (Berkeley: University of California Press, 1967–71). Of course, it must be assumed that the genizah of an ordinary synagogue would have been much smaller and contained much less.

207. Thus, e.g., F. M. Cross, *The Ancient Library of Qumran and Modern Biblical Studies* (Garden City: Doubleday, 1961), who with this title simply refers to the Qumran scrolls collectively without assuming or implying anything about a library in the narrower sense.

208. For discussions specifically concerned with this question, see K. G. Pedley, "The Library at Qumran," *RQ* 2 (1959): 21–41; and V. Burr, "Marginalien zur Bibliothek von Qumran," *Libri* 15 (1965): 340–52, neither of which is well informed about the texts or the history of the sect.

209. For an inventory, see J. A. Fitzmyer, *The Dead Sea Scrolls Major Publications and Tools for Study* (rev. ed.; Atlanta: Scholars Press, 1990), 11–45.

210. N. Golb, "The Problem of the Origin and Identification of the Dead Sea Scrolls," *Proceedings of the American Philosophical Society* 124 (1980): 1–24; and, in updated form, "The Dead Sea Scrolls," *American Scholar* 58 (1989): 177–207 (for a popular version see "Who Hid the Dead Sea Scrolls?" *BA* 48 [1985] 68–82). For the idea that the scrolls were derived from Jerusalem and the temple library, cf. earlier K. H. Rengstorf, *Khirbet Qumran und die Bibliothek vom Toten Meer* (Stuttgart: Kohlhammer, 1960), 81–82.

211. For extensive criticism of Golb's position, see F. Garcia Martinez and A. S. van der Woude, "A Groningen Hypothesis of Qumran Origins and Early History," *RQ* 14 (1990): 521–41, esp. 526–36.

212. Scrolls that predate the settlement of the site, which are not numerous, could easily have been brought to the site, while the absence of documentary materials is comprehensible on the ground that literary and archival texts were normally distinguished and separately stored in antiquity, as they are today. It is at best uncertain whether or not there are any authorial autographs among the scrolls. Some may be (see Cross, *The Ancient Library,* 114–15).

213. For description of the contents of cave 4, see Cross, *The Ancient Library,* 39–47. H. Stegemann, "Methods for the Reconstruction of Scrolls from Scattered Fragments," *Archaeology and History in the Dead Sea Scrolls,* ed. L. Schiffman (Sheffield: JSOT Press, 1990), 188–220, estimates (n. 12) that the total number of manuscripts found in all caves is "about 814," of which "about 580" belonged to cave 4.

214. Cross, *The Ancient Library,* 34–35, 67, and R. de Vaux, *Qumran Grotte 4,* II, 1 (DJD 6; Oxford: Clarendon, 1977), 21–22, with reasons why, in spite of the fact that the manuscripts were in much-damaged condition, cave 4 cannot be regarded as a genizah, as was early suggested for all the caves by H. del Medico, *L'énigme des manuscrits de la mer Morte* (1957): 23–27. It is a relevant consideration that, judging from the paucity of sherds, the numerous manuscripts of cave 4, unlike those in caves 1 and 11, were not stored in jars and so are in a more decayed condition. The use of jars was perhaps not a practical possibility with so many texts, and it should not be supposed that their absence indicates haste of deposit.

215. The other artificial caves are 5 and 7–10. Only a few manuscript

fragments were found in caves 5, 7, and 8, and only one in cave 9, while cave 10 contained no manuscripts or fragments, but only one piece of inscribed pottery.

216. See H. Stegemann, "Methods for the Reconstruction of Scrolls from Scattered Fragments," 193–94.

217. It is of special interest for the history of the biblical text not only that multiple copies of most biblical documents occur among the scrolls (e.g., Genesis and Exodus in 15 copies each, Deuteronomy in 25, Psalms in 30, Isaiah in 19, to name only the most numerous), but that these frequently represent clearly different versions of the text. On the significance of this, see the essays collected in *Qumran and the History of the Biblical Text*, ed. F. M. Cross and S. Talmon (Cambridge: Harvard University Press, 1975). In the absence of a fully stabilized authoritative text, versional diversity would itself be a strong incentive to the accumulation of different manuscripts, especially for a group devoted to the close study of scripture and interested in its wording and subtle nuances. Cf. also Burr, "Marginalien zur Bibliothek von Qumran," 341–42.

218. R. de Vaux, *Archaeology and the Dead Sea Scrolls*, 29–33; Cross, *The Ancient Library*, 66–67. Pedley, "The Library at Qumran," 32–33, not only accepts the existence of a scriptorium but even attempts to identify contiguous rooms as "reading room, offices and bookstacks." Burr, "Marginalien zur Bibliothek von Qumran," 343–45, is somewhat more cautious.

219. For objections to the inference of a scriptorium from the archaeological evidence, see among others B. M. Metzger, "The Furniture in the Scriptorium at Qumran," *RQ* 1 (1959): 509–15 (together with the studies cited above, ch. 3, n. 22), who regards the tables as unsuitable for writing; G. R. Driver, "Myths of Qumran," *Annual of the Leeds University Oriental Society* 6 (1969): 23–27; N. Golb, "The Problem of Origin and Identification of the Dead Sea Scrolls," 3–5. De Vaux's responses to such objections (*Archaeology and the Dead Sea Scrolls*, 30–33) are not persuasive.

220. E. Tov, "The Orthography and Language of the Hebrew Scrolls Found at Qumran and the Origin of These Scrolls," *Textus* (1986): 31–57. On the paleography of the scrolls in general, see also the earlier and still fundamental study of F. M. Cross, "The Development of the Jewish Scripts," in *The Bible and the Ancient Near East: Essays in Honor of W. F. Albright*, ed. G. E. Wright (repr. Winona Lake, Ill.: Eisenbrauns, 1979), 133–202.

221. This category includes all fifteen biblical manuscripts written in paleo-Hebrew, as well as the few Greek texts found in caves 4 and 7. Tov, "Orthography and Language," 40–41, 43–44, emphasizes that the we are dealing not simply with two distinct orthographies, but with "two entirely different approaches to the biblical text" (41)—one relatively free and the other conservative—which could not have coexisted in the same socioreligious setting.

222. Thus, it appears that one scribe transcribed 4QTest, 1 QS, and 4QSam (c) and served as the corrector of 1QIs (a) and that 1 QpHab and 11QTemple (b) were both transcribed by one scribe. On the first, see E. Ulrich, "4QSamuel (c): A Fragmentary Manuscript of 2 Samuel 14–15 from the Scribe of Serek Hayahad (1QS)," *BASOR* 235 (1979), 2. Without attempting to identify individual scribes, F. M. Cross has shown that groups of Qumran copyists can be distin-

guished ("The Development of the Jewish Scripts," *The Bible and the Ancient Near East: Essays in Honor of William Foxwell Albright* [Garden City: Doubleday, 1965], 170–264).

223. Cf. A. F. J. Klijn, "A Library of Scriptures in Jerusalem?" *Studia Codicologica*, ed. K. Treu (TU 124; Berlin: Akademie, 1977), 265–72. For earlier periods the depositing of books in holy places is often indicated in the Hebrew Bible (Ex. 25:16, 21; 40:20; Deut. 10:1–5; 31:24–26; Josh. 24:26), including the first temple (1 Kings 8:6–9; 2 Chron. 5:7–10; 2 Kings 22:8; 23:2, 24; 2 Chron. 34:15, 30).

224. Josephus: *Contra Ap.* 1.33 *Ant.* 3.38, 4.302–4, 5.61; *Bell.* 7.150; *Vita* 418; Mishnah: Moed Qatan 3.4; Kel. 15.6; Yoma 7.1; see also Sifre Deut. 356 (p. 423); P. T. Shek. IV 48a; Sanhed. II 20c. See further S. Lieberman, *Hellenism in Jewish Palestine* (New York: Jewish Theological Seminary, 1962), 20–27; and L. Blau, *Studien zum althebraischen Buchwesen* (Strasbourg: Trubner, 1902), 99–111.

225. MacMullen, *Paganism in the Roman Empire* (New Haven: Yale University Press, 1981), claims that temple libraries (that is, libraries of religious texts in temples) were widespread: "There is no special reason why they should be mentioned at all, so their presence can perhaps be imagined at most large centers" (11). Yet the evidence he adduces (146, n. 50) cannot sustain the generality of the claim.

226. On Cassiodorus, see esp. A. van de Vyver, "Cassiodore et son oeuvre," *Speculum* 6 (1931), 244–92, P. Courcelle, *Late Latin Writers and Their Greek Sources*, 331–60; and J. J. O'Donnell, *Cassiodorus* (Berkeley: University of California Press, 1979).

227. Ed. R. A. B. Mynors (Oxford: Clarendon, [1937] 1961). A useful English translation with introduction and notes is provided by L. W. Jones, *An Introduction to Divine and Human Readings* (New York: Columbia University Press, 1946). A good analytical discussion of the Institutes is given by O'Donnell, *Cassiodorus*, 202–14.

228. *Inst.* 1.7.15, 1.14.4. Courcelle, *Late Latin Writers*, 337, considers that there were perhaps not more than fifteen such manuscripts.

229. Cassiodorus relied on several translators at Vivarium. He names only three, Epiphanius, Mutianus, and Bellator (*Inst.* 1.5.2, 4; 1.8.6; 1.11.2; 1.8.3; 2.5.1; 1.1.9; 1.5.5; 1.6.4, 6), but may designate others as "friends" (1.9.1; 1.17.1).

230. For a careful survey of the contents of the library, see Courcelle, *Late Latin Writers*, 339–60, who points out that not all the writers mentioned by Cassiodorus (see the *index auctorum* in Mynors's edition) were actually represented in the library. Notably, the poets go unmentioned by Cassiodorus, as do major Roman historians. The emphasis was clearly on grammarians.

231. The difficult process of procuring manuscripts was still under way when the *Institutiones* was being written: see 1.8.9, 10, 14.

232. *Inst.* 1.1.2; 1.2.12; 1.5.4; 1.7.1; 1.8.12; 1.17.1; 2.2.10; 2.3.18. Blank gatherings were even bound into some such codices for the transcription of related texts that might later come to hand (*Inst.* 1.2.12). Van de Vyver, "Cassiodore et son eovre," 276, points out that *in hoc corpore/codice continentur* is one of Cassiodorus's most frequent phrases and that the develop-

ment of omnibus volumes was "one of the most salient characteristics of his work." A convenient list of such codices mentioned in the *Institutiones* is given by Courcelle, *Late Latin Writers*, 372–75.

233. *Inst.* 1.30.3.

234. Ibid., 1.14.2: *in codice grandior littera clariore conscripto;* cf. 1.5.2: *in pandecte Latino corporis grandioris;* Comm. in Psal. 14 (*PL* 70, 190 A).

235. *Inst.* praef. 8; 1.11.3; 1.13.1–2; 1.15.16. B. Fischer, "Codex Amiatinus und Cassiodor," *Biblische Zeitschrift* 6 (1962): 57–79, claims, however, that this was an edition not of the Vulgate but of the Old Latin.

236. *Inst.* 1.12.3. This was possibly only a compact copy of the large Bible in nine volumes, if that contained a Vulgate text.

237. *Inst.* 1 praef. 9; 1.1.10; 1.2.13; 1.6.5; 1.5.7; 1.12.4; 1.15.12. Cassiodorus was particular about punctuation. He regarded the arrangement of the text in sense-lines as an alternative devised for monks who were not sufficiently well educated to appreciate punctuation and deferred in that arrangement to the practice of Jerome (*Inst.* praef. 9). Still, if he retained sense-lines in those parts of the text that Jerome had translated, it is not clear whether he extended the arrangement *per cola et commata* to the entire Vulgate. Van de Vyver ("Cassiodorus et son oeuvre," 267–69) thinks that it was first in the Codex Amiatinus that the whole Vulgate was arranged by sense-lines, and this because of a misunderstanding of Cassiodorus's words. Cassiodorus preferred that his monks not apply this method to other texts, but use punctuation instead (*Inst.* 1. praef. 9, 1.15.12).

238. Cassiodorus, *Comm. in Psal.* 14 (PL 70, 109A); *Inst.* 1.5.2; Bede, *De templo* 17 (PL 91, 775A-C); *De tabern.* 12 (PL 91, 454B).

239. Bede, *Vita quinque abbatum* (PL 94, 725A).

240. On the Codex Amiatinus, see J. Chapman, "The Amiatinus and Cassiodorus," *RBén* 38 (1926): 139–50; 39 (1927): 12–32; 40 (1928): 130–34. Chapman (30) thought, incidentally, that Cassiodorus rather than Ezra was so represented in the *codex grandior* itself, the figure being changed when the manuscript was copied at Yarrow, but van de Vyver ("Cassiodore et son oeuvre," 261, n. 4) is more likely correct that if the figure was not originally Ezra it was a typical monk of Vivarium.

241. Courcelle, *Late Latin Writers*, 388, 393–94, who gives a close survey of the evidence (361–409).

CHAPTER V: THE USES OF EARLY CHRISTIAN BOOKS

1. The fundamental study is J. Balough, "Voces Paginarum: Beiträge zur Geschichte des lauten Lesens und Schreibens," *Philologus* 82 (1927): 84–109, 202–40. See further, G. L. Hendrickson, "Ancient Reading," *CJ* 25 (1929): 182–96; W. P. Clark, "Ancient Reading," *CJ* 26 (1930–31): 698–700; W. B. Sedgwick, "Reading and Writing in Classical Antiquity," *Continental Review* 135 (1929): 90–94; E. S. McCartney, "Notes on Reading and Praying Audibly," *Classical Philology* 43 (1948): 184–87; B. M. W. Knox, "Silent Reading in Antiquity," *GRBS* 9 (1968): 421–35; W. Allen, "Ovid's *Cantare* and Cicero's *Cantores Euphorionis*," *TAPA* 103 (1972): 1–14. Often cited in this connection is Augustine's expression of surprise (*Conf.* 6.3.3) at seeing Ambrose

reading silently: "As he read, his eyes scanned the pages and his heart searched out the sense, but his voice and tongue were silent."

2. Balough, "Voces Paginarum," 232.

3. The implications of this for the interpretation of New Testament texts have been recognized and explicated by T. E. Boomershine, "Peter's Denial as Polemic or Confession: The Implications of Media Criticism for Biblical Hermeneutics," *Semeia* 39 (1987), esp. 63–66. They are also emphasized by P. Achtemeier, "*Omne verbum sonat*: The New Testament and the Oral Environment of Late Western Antiquity," *JBL* 109 (1990): 3–27.

4. See M. Hadas, *Ancilla to Classical Reading* (New York: Columbia University Press, 1954), 50–64.

5. See ch. 3.

6. Paul's letters were classed among "scriptures" by the author of 2 Peter (3:15–16), and by Justin's time the Gospels were well on the way to that status.

7. This was later the explicit rule (cf. Didache 9.5, *Apostolic Trad.* 26.5) but was probably assumed from the beginning (cf. 1 Cor. 10:16–22).

8. Thus, e.g., W. Bauer, "Der Wortgottesdienst der ältesten Christen," in *Aufsätze und kleine Schriften*, ed. G. Strecker (Tübingen: Mohr, 1967); G. Dix, *The Shape of the Liturgy* (London: A. & C. Black, 1945), 36–37.

9. O. Cullmann, *Early Christian Worship*, trans. A. S. Todd and J. B. Torrance (SBT 10; London: SCM, 1953), 26–32. The service of baptism is recognized as having a distinct character and a separate occasion, but this was not a "regular" service anyway (31).

10. John 9:22, 12:42, 16:2, on which see J. L. Martyn, *History and Theology in the Fourth Gospel* (Nashville: Abingdon, 1968), esp. 37–62, who speaks of Christians as originally constituting "a messianic group within the synagogue" (even if they also held separate meetings for celebrating the community meal and for special teaching) and only later as "a separated community of Jewish Christians" (65–66). Acts 18:26, 19:8–9, 22:19, and 26:11 presume that Jewish-Christians were, to begin with, part of synagogue congregations. The case cannot have been quite the same for Gentile Christian communities, although synagogal practices may have been mediated to them through Jewish-Christian congregations. For the use of the term *synagogue* for Christian assemblies, see, e.g., James 2:2; *The Shepherd* of Hermas, Mand. 11.9, 13, 14; Ignatius, *Polyc.* 4:2, Justin, *Dial.* 63 (and also W. Schrage, s.v. *sunagoge*, TDNT 7:840).

11. See esp. W. O. E. Oesterly, *The Jewish Background of the Christian Liturgy* (Oxford: Clarendon Press, 1925); C. W. Dugmore, *The Influence of the Synagogue upon the Divine Office* (London: Oxford University Press, 1944); J. Baumstark, *Comparative Liturgy* (London: Mowbray, 1958); O. S. Rankin, "The Extent of the Influence of the Synagogue Service upon Christian Worship," *JJS* 1 (1948–49): 27–32; W. Wiefel, *Der Synagogengottesdienst im neutestamentlichen Zeitalter und seine Einwirkung auf den enstehenden christlichen Gottesdienst* (Inaugural Dissertation, Erlangen, 1959); R. T. Beckwith, "The Daily and Weekly Worship of the Primitive Church in Relation to its Jewish Antecedents," *EvQ* 56 (1984): 65–80, 139–58; and P. Bradshaw, " 'The rock whence ye were hewn': The Jewish Background of Christian Worship," in *The Search for the Origins of Christian Worship* (New York: Oxford Univer-

sity Press, 1992), 1–29, who calls for circumspection about this question since much remains unknown or uncertain about early Jewish liturgy.

12. There is a large literature on the character of the ancient synagogue service. In addition to the studies cited in the preceding note, see G. F. Moore, *Judaism in the First Centuries of the Christian Era* (New York: Schocken Books, [1927] 1971, 1:281–307; J. Peteuchowski, "The Liturgy of the Synagogue: History, Structure, and Contents," *Approaches to Ancient Judaism, IV*, ed. W. S. Green (Chico: Scholars Press, 1983), 1–64, and "The Liturgy of the Synagogue," *The Lord's Prayer and Jewish Liturgy*, ed. J. Peteuchowski and M. Brocke (London: Burns and Oates, 1978), 45–57; L. I. Levine, "The Second Temple Synagogue: The Formative Years," *The Synagogue in Late Antiquity*, ed. Lee I. Levine (Philadelphia: ASOR, 1987), 7–31; P. Billerbeck, 'Ein Synagogengottesdienst in Jesu Tagen," *ZNW* 55 (1964): 143–61.

13. H. Elbogen, *Studien zur Geschichte des jüdischen Gottesdienstes* (Berlin: Mayer and Muller, 1907), 38–44, claimed that originally the synagogue service consisted of no more than the Shema' and its benedictions and that the reading of scripture had no place. Yet there are first-century sources that speak of the reading of scripture without making any mention of prayer (Josephus, *Contra Ap.* 2.175; Philo, *Leg.* 23, *De som.* 2.18; Luke 4:16–22; Acts 13:13–16, 15:21; the Theodotus inscription [*CIJ* 2:332–35]); and some rabbinic sources also speak only of scripture reading and homilies in connection with the synagogue (S. Lieberman, *The Tosefta—Mo'ed* [New York: Jewish Theological Seminary, 1962], 353–64, cf. 273). Considering these, L. Levine, "The Second Temple Synagogue," claims that "the reading of the Torah and its accompanying rituals constituted the main and, at least in Israel, exclusive function of synagogue worship" (15, cf. 21) and that "the place of prayer in the ancient synagogue remains in question" (19). In any event, the reading of Torah during the sabbath morning service was apparently a universally established custom by the first century of the common era, since this activity was common to the otherwise different synagogues of Palestine and the Diaspora. On the practice, see esp. C. Perrot, *La lecture de la Bible dans la synagogue: Les anciennes lectures palestiniennes du Shabbat et des fêtes* (Hildesheim: Gerstenberg, 1973); and K. Hruby, "La place des lectures bibliques et de la prédication dans la liturgie synagogale ancienne," *La parole dans la liturgie* (Paris: Cerf, 1970), 23–64.

14. The *Haphtarah* also followed the Torah reading on the afternoon of fast days but not at other regular synagogue services. (The prophetic corpus as defined in Judaism included the books of Joshua, Judges, Samuel, and Kings.) In addition to Torah and *Haphtarah*, the *Megillot* (Five Scrolls) were read on festival days: the Song of Songs at Passover, Ruth at Pentecost, Lamentations on the Ninth of Abh, Ecclesiastes at Sukkot, and Esther at Purim.

15. For commentary, see J. Rabbinowitz, *Mishnah Megillah* (Oxford: Oxford University Press, 1931).

16. On other service days different numbers of readers were required: three on sabbath afternoons, Mondays, and Thursdays; four on certain other days; five on festival days; six on the Day of Atonement. The "verses" mentioned in the Mishnah do not correspond to the present system, which originated in the middle ages.

17. On the status and role of the methurgeman, see Elbogen, *Studien*, 186–87. These paraphrases are the ultimate origin of the Targumic literature. On Targumic literature generally, see J. Bowker, *The Targums and Rabbinic Literature: An Introduction to Jewish Interpretations of Scripture* (Cambridge: Cambridge University Press, 1969); M. McNamara, *Targum and Testament: Aramaic Paraphrases of the Hebrew Bible* (Shannon: Irish University Press, 1972); R. Le Déaut, *The Message of the New Testament and the Aramaic Bible (Targum)*, trans. S. Miletic (Rome: Biblical Institute Press, 1982). On the rootage of the targums in the worship of the synagogue, see esp. A. D. York, "The Targum in Synagogue and School," *JSJ* 10 (1979): 74–86. See, however, the cautionary remarks of D. M. Golomb, *A Grammar of Targum Neofiti* (Chico: Scholars Press, 1985), 1–8, urging that the targumic literature is not to be brought into immediate connection with the (oral) translations of scripture in the synagogue.

18. Rationalizations for these practices are variously given: P. T. Meg. 4.1. (74d) says that the written Torah should be transmitted in writing and the oral Torah orally, whereas B. T. Meg. 32a makes it explicit that the difference between text and translation should be impressed on the congregation.

19. M. Meg. 4.9 admonishes the congregation to silence the interpreter who takes too much liberty with the sense. A later tradition (Tos. Meg. 4.41) defined the narrow way open to the methurgeman: R. Judah ben Illa'i said that "he who translates a verse strictly literally is a falsifier, and he who makes additions to it is a blasphemer."

20. See E. Schurer, *The History of the Jewish People in the Age of Jesus Christ*, rev. ed. (Edinburgh: T. & T. Clark, 1986), pt. 1, 3:142–44, and the literature cited there for the use of Greek in the Diaspora, including its liturgical use. Some synagogues even in Palestine, and perhaps especially in Jerusalem, may likewise have been Greek-speaking and read the scripture in Greek. At least the synagogue attested to by the Theodotus inscription (in Greek) was apparently built for Greek-speaking Jews in Jerusalem.

21. The prohibition against skipping over passages of Torah (M. Meg. 4.4, cf. B. T. Meg. 4.4) implies consecutive reading and so also does the mention of an "order" *(seder)* of readings (M. Meg. 3.4, 6), which is suspended to allow for special readings on certain festal days (M. Meg. 3.5–6).

22. A. Büchler, "The Reading of the Law and Prophets in a Triennial Cycle," *JQR* 5 (1893): 420–68, 6 (1894): 1–73 (reprinted in *Contributions to the Scientific Study of Jewish Liturgy*, ed. E. Peteuchowski [New York: KTAV, 1970], 181–302), argued for the existence of an established triennial cycle in Palestine by the early rabbinic period. The theory was taken up and refined by J. Mann, *The Bible as Read and Preached in the Old Synagogue*, 2 vols. (Cincinnati: Hebrew Union College, 1940, 1966; repr. New York: KTAV, 1971). For incisive criticism, see J. Heinemann, "The Triennial Lectionary Cycle," *JJS* 19 (1968): 41–48. A valuable review of research on the triennial cycle is given by Ben Zion Wacholder in his prolegomenon to the 1971 reprint of Mann's work (xi–li), but for a more recent appraisal, see Perrot, *La lecture*.

23. M. Meg. 4.4 specifies the minimum of three verses by each of seven readers but states no maximum. The Tosephta (Meg. 3 [4].10; cf. B. T. Meg. 31b) records a mid-second-century dispute between Rabbi Meir and Rabbi Judah. Rabbi Meir argued for a consecutive reading of Torah over all the days of

reading (including Mondays and Thursdays as well as sabbaths): "Where they finished reading on sabbath morning, they begin reading on sabbath afternoon; where they finished reading on sabbath afternoon they begin reading on Monday," and so forth. Rabbi Judah urged that readings made on other days should not interfere with the sabbath sequence of readings: "Where they finished reading on sabbath morning, they begin reading on the following sabbath." Judah's opinion is adopted in the Mishnah (Meg. 3.6).

24. A well-reasoned discussion of the development is given by Perrot, *La lecture*, esp. 128–74. Cf. also his articles, "Luc. 4.16–30 et la lecture biblique de l'ancienne synagogue," *RSR* 47 (1973): 324–40, and "The Reading of the Bible in the Ancient Synagogue," *Mikra. Text, Translation, Reading, and Interpretation of the Hebrew Bible in Ancient Judaism and Early Christianity*, ed. M. J. Mulder (Philadelphia: Fortress, 1988), 137–59. He regards the annual cycle as the ultimate outworking of the opinion of Rabbi Meir, and the triennial cycles as the result of the opinion of Rabbi Judah, as expressed in T. Meg. 3 (4).10 and B.T. Meg. 31b (see preceding note). On this view Palestine was the ultimate origin of both systems.

25. Perrot, *La lecture*, 107–16, notes that the Qumran scrolls of the Torah and prophets incorporated scribal indications of the major and minor divisions (*petuhot* and *setumot*) of the text analogous to the *parashiyyot*, which the Mishnah has in view.

26. Philo (in Eusebius, *Prep. Ev.* 8.7.12–13) speaks of a single reader (was this the rule in the Diaspora?), and the possibility of a single reader is acknowledged in P. T. Meg. 4.3 and T. Meg. 4.12.

27. A. von Harnack, "Das Alte Testament in den paulinischen Briefen und in den paulinischen Gemeinden," *SBA* (Phil.-hist. Kl.) (1928): 124–41.

28. Bauer, "Der Wortgottesdienst," 155–209, esp. 187–201.

29. See, among others, O. Michel, *Paulus und seine Bible* (Gutersloh: Bertelsmann, 1929).

30. Paul's claim in 2 Cor. 3.12–16 that when Jews read the old covenant (i.e., in the synagogue) "a veil lies over their minds" but that for Christians "the veil is removed" seems pointless unless scripture is publicly read among Christians. On the other hand, Gal. 4:21 ("Tell me, you who desire to be under the Law, do you not hear the Law"), and Rom. 7:1 ("Do you not know, brothers, for I am speaking to those who know the Law") are polemical formulations without clear relevance to the question.

31. Synagogues must be presumed almost always to have had the books of the Torah, but small and poor ones may have held little else. See Perrot, *La lecture*, 135–36.

32. On books of testimonies, see ch. 1.

33. The only Christian writing to which Justin alludes specifically is the Apocalypse—and that only by referring to its author (*Dial.* 81.4). Justin does not anywhere mention Paul's letters (or even Paul himself), but it is highly unlikely that he did not know them. See the careful discussion by D. Rensberger, "As the Apostle Teaches: The Development of the Use of Paul's Letters in Second-Century Christianity," 169–92.

34. For a discussion, see Gamble, *New Testament Canon*, 15–18, and the literature cited there.

35. *H.E.* 3.25.1–7; cf. 3.31.6. On the relevant texts in Eusebius, see J. Ruwet,

"Lecture liturgique et livres saints du Nouveau Testament," *Bib* 21 (1940): 378–405.

36. The author of 2 Peter reckoned Paul's letters as "scripture" (3:16), and both he and his opponents appealed to them. Polycarp (Phil. 3.2) viewed Paul's letters as having relevance for Christian communities generally (see Lindemann, *Paulus*, 88–89); and although Justin fails to mention Paul, his contemporary, Marcion, valued them (along with the Gospel of Luke) as the only authoritative Christian writings, and as such they must have been liturgically read in Marcionite communities, though hardly only there.

37. The *Shepherd* of Hermas was regarded as scripture by Irenaeus (*A.H.* 4.20.2), Clement of Alexandria (*Strom.* 1.17.29; 2.1.9, 12), and Tertullian (*De Orat.* 16). It occasionally shows up in later lists of canonical books, although it is specifically excluded from the canon by the Muratorian Fragment and Athanasius's 39th Festal Letter. 1 Clement is never called scripture, but Irenaeus thought highly of it (*A.H.* 3.3.3), and Clement of Alexandria spoke of it as "a writing of the apostle Clement" (*Strom.* 4.17).

38. On the "criteria of canonicity," see W. H. Ohlig, *Die theologische Begründung des neutestamentlichen Kanons in der alten Kirche* (Dusseldorf: Patmos, 1972), and the brief discussion in Gamble, *New Testament Canon*, 67–72.

39. Hippolytus (*Apost. Trad.*, can. 20) indicates that the readers succeeded each other until all had gathered. Even in Augustine's time this was the practice.

40. See the discussion in J. A. Jungmann, *The Mass of the Roman Rite: Its Origin and Development* (New York: Benziger, 1951), 1:391–455.

41. *Apostolic Constitutions* 8.5.11; cf. 2.57.5.

42. It is sometimes claimed that the early Roman practice, like that of other western liturgies, was to use three readings: thus J. A. Jungmann, *The Mass of the Roman Rite*, 1:395–96. Against this, see R. Dubois, "Hatte die römische Messe je eine dreigliedrige Leseordnung?" *Heiliger Dienst* 18 (1964): 129–37.

43. It was a variation on the system of lectio continua when only selections of a book were read rather than the whole text, but even then the selections were read in their textual sequence.

44. See, e.g., Chrysostom, *Hom.* 7; 73; *In Acta Apost. Sermo* 4.5; Augustine, *Sermo* 246; 315; *In Ioan. Ev. Tr.* 6.18; and Ambrose, *Ep.* 20. The practice was apparently not widely established in the West even in the fifth century, since the Spanish pilgrim "Egeria" found it surprising that in the liturgy in Jerusalem the lessons at the festival seasons were always *apte diei*—tailored to the occasion (*Perigr.* 29; 31; etc.). The oldest actual system of selected readings known in the West belongs to the fifth-century Gallican liturgy.

45. Gennadius, *De viris illust.* (*PL* 58.1103–4) speaks of a lectionary devised by the priest Musaeus for all the feast days of the year.

46. See B. de Gaiffier, "La lecture des actes des martyres dans la prière liturgique en Occident," *Anal. Boll.* 72 (1954): 134–66.

47. For Augustine, see Roetzer, 62–63, 107–8, and Willis, *St. Augustine's Lectionary*, 11.

48. On the history of the minor orders generally, see J. G. Davies, "Deacons, Deaconesses, and the Minor Orders in the Patristic Period," *JEH* 14 (1963): 1–

15. On the reader, see esp. H. Leclercq, "Lecteur," *DACL* 8:2241–2269, and the studies cited in the following notes.

49. *Ep.* 29, 38.2, 39.1–4, and below in text.

50. Almost all commentators take the words in this way, but cf. K. P. Donfried, *The Setting of Second Clement in Early Christianity* (NovTSup 38; Leiden: Brill, 1974), 14–15, who thinks that "what is written" refers not to scripture but to 2 Clement.

51. This seems to be intimated in 17.3: "And let us not merely seem to believe and pay attention now while we are being exhorted by the elders [*presbyteron*]"; cf. 17.5.

52. Reading is nowhere explicitly cited as one of the charismata. Yet not all spiritual gifts had a spectacular or ecstatic form, as Paul makes clear in 1 Cor. 12–14; cf. Eph. 4:11–12. A. von Harnack, *Sources of the Apostolic Canons* (London: Norgate, 1895): argued, largely on the basis of later sources, that the reader as he appears in third- and fourth-century sources was a vestige of the charismatic ministries of the early church, specifically of the prophet or teacher. One does not have to concur in all of Harnack's arguments to grant that the reader was early understood to exercise a spiritual gift. See more recently H.-W. Bartsch, *Die Anfänge urchristlicher Rechtsbildungen: Studien zu den Pastoralbriefen* (Hamburg: Evangeslischer Verlag, 1965), 84–88.

53. On the whole development, see H. von Campenhausen, *Ecclesiastical Authority and Spiritual Power in the Church of the First Three Centuries*, trans. J. A. Baker (London: A. & C. Black, 1969).

54. In 1 Tim. 4:13 it is the bishop who performs the tasks of reading, along with preaching and teaching—all functions conferred by ordination (1 Tim. 4:14). With a view to this, 1 Tim. 3:2 stipulates that a bishop should be *didaktikos*, "skillful in teaching," but in cases where a bishop was not *didaktikos*, or in small communities where there was no bishop, these responsibilities would have devolved on the reader; thus Bartsch, *Anfänge*, 87–88. This makes it comprehensible that in some settings the reader might also deliver the exhortation.

55. This is confirmed in the subsequent notice (8.28) that the reader is to "receive a single portion [of the offering] in honor of the prophets." In this connection Harnack (*Sources*, 15–17) gives heavy emphasis to a passage in the *Apostolic Canons* (3) that states that the reader "functions in the place of an evangelist"—evangelist having been a primitive charismatic ministry (Eph. 4:11, Acts 21:8, 2 Tim. 4:5).

56. Davies, "Deacons, Deaconesses, and the Minor Orders," *JEH* 14 (1963): 6–15.

57. *Ep.* 38.2, 39.4.

58. There is no mention anywhere of female readers, although this cannot be completely ruled out. Tertullian, in the same context where he complains of the rapid turnover of office holders, including readers, among heretics (*Praescr.* 41) also takes umbrage at the prominence of female officeholders among them: "Those heretic women! How impudent they are! They dare to teach, debate, perform exorcisms, undertake cures, and perhaps even to baptize." He does not mention that they presumed to read, but they may have.

59. Socrates confirms and qualifies this by noting (*H.E.* 5.22) that "in the

city of Alexandria, readers and cantors are created regardless of whether they are catechumen or faithful, while the churches everywhere else promote only the faithful to this office" (*H.E.* 5.22).

60. Cf. Ambrose, *De off. min.* 44.225: "One is considered better qualified to enunciate *[distinguendae]* a reading, but another more pleasing with a psalm." The unusual verb points to a special kind of reading. Harnack (*Sources*, 15–17) saw in the statements that the reader should be *diegetikos* and that he takes the role of an "evangelist" indications that at one time the reader not only read but gave an exposition of what he read.

61. Thus, for example, Julian the Apostate, together with his brother Gallus, was ordained a reader between the ages of fourteen and twenty (Gregory Nazianzus, *Or.* 4.23); Theodoret was ordained at about the same age since he says, "I already had the beginning of a beard" (*Vita S. Euthymii* 71.11). Inscriptions commemorating deceased lectors span all ages, but a number refer to readers between the ages of thirteen and eighteen (Leclercq, "Lecteur," 2247).

62. Ambrose, *De excess. sat.* 1.61; Augustine, *Ep.* 299.3; Sidonius, *Ep.* 1.4.25; inscriptions: *CIL* 8:453, 11:1709. In the sixth century, Cyril of Scythopolis says that Euthymius was baptized, tonsured, and ordained a lector all at once when he was two years old (*Vita S. Euth.* 10.19, 11.2) and that Cyriacus was made a lector in Corinth "from infancy" *(ek brephous)* (*Vita. Cyr.* 223.7). On the whole subject, see E. Peterson, "Das jugendliche Alter der Lektoren," *EL* 48 (1934): 437–42; J. Quasten, *Music and Worship in Pagan and Christian Antiquity* (Washington, D.C.: National Association of Pastoral Musicians, 1983 [1930]), 138–41; and A.-J. Festugière, *Antioch paienne et chrétienne* (Paris: Boccard, 1959), 280–81.

63. Jungmann, *The Mass of the Roman Rite*, 1:410.

64. Socrates, *H.E.* 7:41.1–2, offers a specific case in one Proclus, who was ordained a reader before he was "of viril age," was brought up in the church, attended the bishop's school, and subsequently rose through the ranks to become a bishop himself. On young readers being brought up among the clergy cf. Ambrose, *Ep.* 70.25, *De poenit.* 2.72.

65. See Augustine, *De consensus Evang.* 1.1.100.15, and the pronouncement of the Fourth Council of Carthage. Such instruction adumbrates later *schola lectorum*, on which see Leclercq, "Lecteur," 2248–49, and Quasten, *Music and Worship*, 87–92.

66. The Greek word *ambon* (from *anabainein*, "to go up") was thus adopted into Latin. (The term first appears in canon 15 of the Council of Laodicea.) It might also be called in Greek a bema (platform) but in that case had to be distinguished from the bema upon which the presbyters sat (thus Sozomen [*H.E.* 8.5.2, 9.2.11] speaks of the "bema of the readers"). Latin terms for the ambo included *pulpitum, suggestus, lectorium, auditorium,* and *tribunal*.

67. See H. Leclercq, "Ambon," *DACL* 1:1330–47 (with illustrations); A. M. Schneider, "Ambon," *RAC* 1:363–65; C. Delvoye, "Ambo," *Reallexikon zur byzantinischen Kunst,* 1:126–33; D. Hickley, "The Ambo in Early Liturgical Planning: A Study with Special Reference to the Syrian *Bema*," *HeythJ* 7 (1966): 407–27; and R. Taft, "Some Notes on the Bema in the East and West Syrian Traditions," *Orientalia Christiana Periodica* 34 (1968): 326–59.

68. Preaching was customarily not done from the ambo but from the bema

upon which the bishop and presbyters sat. There are indications that the ambo was occasionally used for preaching (John Chrysostom seems to have used it regularly: Socrates, *H.E.* 6.5, 7.5), on which see Leclercq, "Ambon," 1331–33.

69. The use of the raised platform in the period of the second temple is indicated in the Mishnah (Sot. 7.8). Cf. B. T. Suk. 51b. An interesting pagan parallel is seen, however, in Apuleius, *Met.* 11.17: "When we had come to the temple . . . one of the company who was a scribe . . . called together their whole assembly and from his high pulpit *[sublimi suggestus]* began to read from a book."

70. On the use of chant-tones and rhythms in reading and in declamation see, e.g., Quintillian, *Inst.* 1.8.1–3; 11.3.54–57. The broad and often overlapping connotations of *legere* and *cantare* are discussed by Allen, "Ovid's *Cantare*," 1–14. The same point is made in connection with Greek music by E. Lippman, "The Sources and Development of the Ethical View of Music in Ancient Greece," *Musical Quarterly* 40 (1963): 195. On the close correlation of speech and song in Judaism, see the remarks of H. L. Strack and P. Billerbeck, *Kommentar zum Neuen Testament aus Talmud und Midrasch*, 4:394–400.

71. Cf. B. T. Meg. 3a, where Neh. 8:8 ("And they read in the book, in the Law of God . . . and caused them to understand the reading") is taken as a reference to *piskei te'ammim*, i.e., "oral punctuation" by means of melodic cadences; and B. T. Sanh. 99a, where Rabbi Akiba admonished daily study with the words "Sing it every day."

72. It is often maintained that the relatively simple chants of Yemenite and Bukharan Jewish communities, which do not follow the Masoretic accents, most closely approximate the early and traditional biblical chant.

73. This characterization of chant is given by C. Sachs, *The Rise of Music in the Ancient World: East and West* (New York: Norton, 1943). He contrasts "logogenic" and "pathogenic," that is, musically autonomous renderings. On the nature of liturgical recitation, see, among many relevant studies, S. Corbin, "La cantillation des rituels chrétiens," *Revue de musicologie* 47 (1961): 3–36; H. Avenary, *Studies in the Hebrew, Syrian, and Greek Liturgical Recitative* (1963); J. Gelineau, *Voices and Instruments in Christian Worship*, trans. C. Howell (London: Burns and Oates, 1964), 113–18; and E. Werner, *The Sacred Bridge: The Interdependence of Liturgy and Music in Synagogue and Church during the First Millennium* (New York: Columbia University Press, 1959), 102–27.

74. On biblical chant, see esp. H. Avenary, "The Emergence of Synagogue Song," s.v. "Music," *Encyclopaedia of Judaism* 12:566–78; and James Kugel, *The Idea of Biblical Poetry: Parallelism and Its History* (New Haven: Yale University Press, 1981), 109–16.

75. For a general discussion of the systems attested to for the Hebrew Bible, see E. Werner, "Masoretic Accents," *IDB* 3:295–99 (with literature); and E. J. Revell, "Masoretic Accents," *ABD* 4:594–96. The Tiberian system, developed in the tenth century and since then in common use, is closely analyzed by I. Yeivin, *Introduction to the Tiberian Masorah* (Missoula: Scholars Press, 1980), 157–274.

76. See E. J. Revell, "The Oldest Evidence for the Hebrew Accent System,"

BJRL 54 (1971–72): 214–22; and "Biblical Punctuation and Chant in the Second Temple Period," *JSJ* 7 (1976): 181–98. The earliest example of this usage is the Rylands Greek Papyrus 458, one of the oldest papyrus fragments of the LXX, on which see Roberts, *Two Biblical Papyri*. But a number of biblical manuscripts from Qumran (both Greek and Hebrew) similarly use spaces to mark divisions in the text that correspond to verse divisions or divisions within verses later marked by disjunctive accents. Revell concludes that "the basis of the system of cantillation represented by the later accents was already firmly established in the second century B.C., and was so much a part of the formal reading of the Tora that it was also used for the Septuagint" ("The Oldest Evidence," 222). This system of punctuation and chant, which is far simpler than the developed Tiberian system, Revell describes as a common Syro-Palestinian type ("Biblical Punctuation," 193–98).

77. Of many comparative studies that observe the similarities, a large influence is E. Werner, *The Sacred Bridge* (New York: Columbia University Press, 1959), and *The Sacred Bridge: The Interdependence of Liturgy and Music in Synagogue and Church during the First Millennium*, vol. 2 (New York: KTAV, 1984). More scrupulous methods and cautious conclusions are found in H. Avenary, *Studies in the Hebrew, Syrian, and Greek Liturgical Recitative* (Tel-Aviv: Israel Music Institute, 1963), and "Contacts between Church and Synagogue Music," *Proceedings of the World Congress on Jewish Music, Jerusalem 1978*, ed. J. Cohen (Tel-Aviv: Institute for the Translation of Hebrew Literature, 1982), 89–107.

78. J. W. McKinnon, "On the Question of Psalmody in the Ancient Synagogue," *Early Music History* 6 (1986): 159–91. To the same point but with less force, see J. A. Smith, "The Ancient Synagogue, the Early Church, and Singing," *Music and Letters* 65 (1984): 1–16. Early references to singing in the setting of Christian worship are few: Pliny, *Ep.* 10.96.7; *Acta Pauli* 7.10; Tertullian, *Apol.* 39.18, *De anima* 9.4; Clement of Alexandria, *Paed.* 2.4; Hippolytus, *Apost. Trad.* 25; and Cyprian, *Ep.* 16 (ad Donatum). The Acts of Paul, Tertullian, Hippolytus, and Cyprian specifically mention the singing of psalms.

79. Most of the relevant Christian evidence is conveniently collected by J. W. McKinnon, *Music in Early Christian Literature* (Cambridge: Cambridge University Press, 1987). Still valuable, though more general, is Quasten, *Music and Worship in Pagan and Christian Antiquity*.

80. See E. Foley, "The Cantor in Historical Perspective," *Worship* 56 (1982): 194–213.

81. Both Ambrose (*Exc. sat.* 1.61) and Augustine (*In Ps.* 138) speak of the reader as singing the psalms; Augustine (*Conf.* 10.33.50) recalls a story about Athanasius requesting the reader of the psalm to modulate his voice "so little that it was more like speaking *[pronunciati]* than singing *[canenti]*." According to Sozomen *(H.E.* 4.3), a certain Marcian was both a reader and a singer.

82. The earliest indications of a separate office of singer are found in canons 15, 23, and 24 of the Council of Laodicea (ca. 360) (*Canones Apostolorum et Conciliorum*, ed. H. Bruns [Torino: Bottega d'Erasmo, 1959], 75–76); and in the *Apostolic Constitutions* 2.26.3, 3.11.1, 8.10.10, 8.12.43, 8.13.14, 8.28.8, 8.31.2, 8.47.26, 8.47.43, and 8.47.69. The epigraphic evidence is canvassed by

H. Leclercq, "Chantres," *DACL* 3/1:344–65. One epitaph commemorating a man reputed for "chanting the praises of the most high God and training all the faithful to chant the sacred psalms and the reading of the holy books" would be especially interesting if Leclercq (345) is right in dating it to the second or third century. The inscription attests to the close relation between singing and reading but does not suffice to show (as Leclercq claims) that an office of singer had already developed.

83. Athanasius (*Ep. ad Marcellinum de interp. psal.* 27) characterizes the difference: scripture is recited *kata sunecheian*, whereas the psalms are sung *kata platos*. The distinction, analogous to the one attributed to Athanasius by Augustine (*In ps.* 138, above n. 81), is between a chant within a narrow range, which aims simply to bring out the coherent sense of the text, and a more expansively melodic rendering of a psalm, which, besides rendering the text, approaches a musical aesthetic (although Athanasius rejects a pleasure in psalmody that is purely aesthetic). The difference is more of degree than kind since both forms are "logogenic." Their relation and distinction are characterized by Corbin, "La cantillation," 9. The causes of the progressive distinction and development of psalmody beyond the customary reading of scripture are not clear. Various factors may have contributed to this, such as the inherently lyrical quality of the psalms, the recognition that the psalms constituted a (quasi-) musical genre, the influence of monastic devotional practice, and the opportunities for the elaboration of public worship that accompanied the peace of the church and the construction of Christian basilicas.

84. For the possession of texts by lectors, see ch. 4.

85. On inscriptional of features of scriptural manuscripts, see ch. 2.

86. On the utility of colometry for reading, see esp. J. A. Kleist, "Colometry and the New Testament," *Classical Bulletin* 3 (1927): 18–19; 4 (1928): 26–27.

87. Colometric arrangements are found in some manuscripts of the Gospels, Acts (e.g., Codex Bezae), and Pauline letters (e.g., Codex Claromontanus). Especially notable is the colometric system (or remnants of it) found in several related bilingual manuscripts of the Pauline letters (D, E, G, and F, and also 0230 and *gue* [a Gothic-Latin palimpsest]), all of which must go back to an early common archetype, apparently a colometric edition, probably to be dated to the fourth century. On these, see N. A. Dahl, "0230 (=PSI 1306) and the Fourth-Century Greek-Latin Edition of the Letters of Paul," in *Text and Interpretation*, ed. E. Best and R. McL. Wilson (Cambridge: Cambridge University Press, 1979), 79–98.

88. Possibly relevant for the late second century is the statement at the beginning of Melito's *Homily on the Passion*: "The scripture of the Hebrew exodus has been read and the words of the mystery have been explained [*diatetaphetai*]." It has been argued that this means that the lesson was read in Hebrew and then translated into Greek: G. Zuntz, "On the Opening Sentence of Melito's Paschal Homily," *HTR* 36 (1943): 299–315. For arguments to the contrary, see S. G. Hall, "Melito *Peri Pascha* 1 and 2: Text and Interpretation," *Kyriakon* (Festschrift J. Quasten), ed. P. Granfield and J. A. Jungmann (Munster: Aschendorff, 1970), 1:236–48 (with reference to the relevant literature).

89. Dahl, "0230," plausibly guesses that a bilingual edition of Paul's letters was produced in Rome "at a time when Greek was still used in the liturgy even

though Latin was the common language spoken by Christians in the city" (95). On bilingual and polylingual manuscripts of the New Testament, see B. M. Metzger, "Bilingualism and Polylingualism in Antiquity with a Checklist of New Testament Mss. Written in More than One Language," in *The New Testament Age: Essays in Honor of Bo Reicke*, ed. W. C. Weinrich, 2 vols. (Mercer: Mercer University Press), 1:327–34.

90. The only discussion that takes up the question at length is Harnack, *Bible Reading*, the original German title of which was *Über den privaten Gebrauch der Heiligen Schriften in der alten Kirche*. His treatment is vitiated by a neglect of the question of literacy, an overstatement of the evidence, and a frankly polemical (Protestant) agenda. He argues that from the beginning the scriptures were fully and freely accessible to laypersons.

91. On Pamphilus, see ch. 4.

92. In the immediately preceding context (35) it is said that "a pious person ought to count it a great loss if he does not attend the place of instruction, *especially if he can read.*" Neither passage is completely beyond textual suspicion: the Latin version lacks 35 (which is omitted in the edition of B. Botte, *Hippolyte de Rome. La tradition apostolique* [Paris: Latour-Maubourg, 1968], 125); the Latin version has a lacuna at 36, and the text is absent in the *Apostolic Constitutions* but present in later versions (Arabic, Ethiopic, and Sahidic) of the *Apostolic Tradition*.

93. Cf. Tertullian, *Ad Uxor.* 2.6, for what appears to be the same assumption.

94. See, e.g., *Hom. in Gen.* 10.1, 11.3, 12.5; *Hom. in Ex.* 12.2, 27; *Hom. in Lev.* 11.7; *Hom. in Num.* 2.1; cf. *Comm. in Rom.* 9.1.

95. *Hom. in Gen.* 10.1; *Hom. in Ex.* 12.2; *Hom. in Iesu Nave* 20.1.

96. *Hom. in Num.* 27.1.

97. A good discussion will be found in R. Kaczynski, *Das Wort Gottes in Liturgie und Alltag der Gemeinden des Johannes Chrysostomus* (Freiburg: Herder, 1974), 311–35.

98. *De Laz.* 3; *Hom. in Gen.* 21; *Hom. in Matt.* 2.

99. Cf. the similar admonitions in Basil, *De asc. disicipl.* 1 (for monks); Gregory Nazianzus, *Carm.* 33; Jerome, *Ep.* 107.12; Augustine, *De doct. chr.* 2.8–9.

100. Priscillian, *Tract.* 3 ("Liber de fide et de apocryphis"), contests the sufficiency of the canonical books, arguing that apocryphal Jewish prophetic books ought also be read since the apostles had read and used them. Basil (*Or.* 20) speaks confidently of the profit to be gained by Christians from reading non-Christian literature. See also Augustine, *De doct. chr.* 2.40.

101. For a list, see Turner, *Typology,* 22 (papyrus examples), and 29–30 (parchment examples). The accepted criterion for description as a miniature is a breadth of less than ten centimeters. Useful remarks on the subject are made by Roberts, *Manuscript, Society, and Belief,* 10–12; and L. Amundsen, "Christian Papyri from the Oslo Collection," *Symbolae Osloenses* 24 (1945): 121–47 (126–28).

102. The smallest of such codices, the Mani Codex, which is about the size of a matchbox, nevertheless preserves 192 pages. See A. Henrichs and L. Koenen, "Ein griechischer Mani-Codex (P. Colon. inv. nr. 4780)," *ZPE* 5 (1970): 97–216.

103. Roberts, *Manuscript, Society, and Belief,* 12, goes too far in claiming that "the miniature codex would seem to be a Christian invention," which contradicts his earlier view that "we know from Martial that the pocket format was the dress in which the codex first made its appearance in Rome" ("The Codex," *PBA* 40 [1954]: 198).

104. Chrysostom (*Hom. in Joh.* 11.1) disallows poverty as an excuse for not possessing Christian books, since the poor managed nevertheless to have the tools of their trades. Ignorance of scripture was not necessary, he says, even among the destitute, since they could hear the scripture read publicly in church.

105. It seems unnecessary and somewhat invidious to distinguish, as Harnack does (*Bible Reading,* 93–95), between the Greek and the Latin church on this point, as though private reading were encouraged in the East but not in the West.

106. For a good survey of the subject, at least for the first two centuries, see D. Aune, "Magic in Early Christianity," *ANRW* 2.23.2: 1507–57, with a useful bibliography. For the later period as well, see also N. Brox, "Magie und Aberglaube an den Anfängen des Christentums," *Trierer Theologische Zeitschrift* 83 (1974): 157–80, and J. Engemann, "Zur Verbreitung magischer Übelabwehr in der nichtchristlichen und christlichen Spätantike," *JAC* 18 (1975): 22–48. The magical use of books is not much discussed by any of these authors.

107. *Hom. in Nave Iesu,* 20.1.

108. *Hom. ad pop. ant.* 19.14; cf. *Hom. in Cor.* 43.

109. *In Joh. tr.* 7.12. Chrysostom, *Hom. in Ep. 1 ad Cor.* 43.7, mentions the practice of hanging the Gospel beside or upon one's bed, which, along with an adjacent coffer to receive alms, made a defense against the devil.

110. Van Haelst, *Catalogue des papyrus littéraires juifs et chrétiens,* lists 118 items (mostly papyri, but a few ostraca) as amulets (index, s.v.), 61 of which carried scriptural texts (cf. K. Aland, *Repertorium der griechischen christlichen Papyri,* "Varia," 325–60). In some cases it is uncertain whether we are dealing with an amulet. For an overview, see E. A. Judge, "The Magical Use of Scripture in the Papyri," in *Perspectives on Language and Text,* ed. E. W. Conrad and E. G. Newing (Winona Lake, Ind.: Eisenbrauns, 1987), 339–49. For useful tabulations of the texts cited in Christian magical papyri and an assessment of their text-critical value, see A. Biondi, "Le citazione bibliche nei papiri magici cristiani greci," *SP* 20 (1981): 93–127.

111. The passage has been much discussed. For present purposes, see esp. P. Courcelle, "L'enfant et les 'sorts bibliques,'" *VC* 7 (1953): 194–220, *Les confessions de Saint Augustin dans la tradition littéraire* (Paris: Etudes Augustiniennes, 1963), 143–97; and *Recherches sur les Confessions de Saint Augustin* (Paris: Boccard, 1968), 175–202. For a discussion, see J. J. O'Donnell, *Augustine: Confessions* (Oxford: Clarendon, 1992), vol. 3, ad loc.

112. For other examples, see Courcelle, "L'enfant," 201–8. See also P. Tombeur, "'Audire' dans le theme hagiographique de la conversion," *Latomus* 24 (1965): 159–65.

113. Otherwise, they would draw one of a number of slips of papyrus on which poetic verses were written. (Strictly speaking, the consultation of poetic books is known as rhapsodomancy.) On the Greek and Roman practice,

see H. A. Loane, "The *Sortes Vergilianae*," *CW* 21 (1927–28): 185–89. For the *Historia Augusta*, which gives many instances of the practice from Hadrian on, see Y. de Kisch, "Les *Sortes Vergilianae* dans l'Histoire Auguste," *Mélanges d'archéologie et d'histoire* 82 (1970): 321–62.

114. On Jewish bibliomancy, see "Bibliomancy," *Jewish Encyclopedia* 3:202–5; and J. Trachtenberg, *Jewish Magic and Superstition: A Study in Folk Religion* (New York: Athenaeum, [1939] 1987), 216.

115. The most famous are Codex Bezae (usually dated to the fifth or sixth century, but for a fourth-century dating, see H.-J. Frede, *Altlateinische Paulus-Handschriften* [Freiburg: Herder, 1964], 18, n. 4), which contains in a later hand at the bottom of each page of Mk. 1:1–10:22 (folios 285b–321a) a brief statement preceded by the word *hermeneia*; and Codex Sangermanensis (G), which divides the Gospel of John into 316 numbered sections, of which 185 are provided with marginal statements, and the whole is preceded by a diagram of a wheel sectioned into eight parts containing numbers from 1 to 316 (see J. R. Harris, "The 'Sortes Sanctorum' in the St. Germain Codex," *AJPhil* 9 [1888] 58–63). Some papyri of John's Gospel have also turned up that offer marginal statements preceded by the word *hermeneia*—the earliest of these being from the fourth century (see B. M. Metzger, "Greek Manuscripts of John's Gospel with 'Hermeneiai,'" in *Text and Testimony: Essays on New Testament and Apocryphal Literature in Honour of A. F. J. Klijn*, ed. T. Baarda et al. [Kampen: Kok, 1988], 162–69).

116. The proper title of this work is *Peri prorreseos diaphoron zetematon*, "On Foretelling Various Questions." On this work, see esp. G. M. Browne, "The Composition of the *Sortes Astrampsychi*," *Bulletin of the Institute of Classical Studies* 17 (1970): 95–100, and "The Origin and Date of the *Sortes Astrampsychi*," *Illinois Classical Studies* 1 (1976): 53–58; and G. Bjorck, "Heidnische und christliche Orakel mit fertigen Antworten," *Symbolae Osloenses* 19 (1939): 86–98. The work appears fragmentarily in several papyri of the third or fourth centuries: see G. M. Browne, *The Papyri of the Sortes Astrampsychi* (Beiträge zur klassischen Philologie, 58; Meisenheim am Glan: Hain, 1974), and "A New Papyrus Codex of the *Sortes Astrampsychi*," in *Arktouros: Hellenic Studies Presented to B. M. W. Knox*, ed. G. Bowersock et al. (Berlin: de Gruyter, 1979), 434–39. For the critical edition, see G. M. Browne, *Sortes Astrampsychi* (Leipzig: Teubner, 1983).

117. For later medieval systems of the same type, see T. C. Skeat, "An Early Mediaeval 'Book of Fate': The Sortes XII Patriarcharum with a Note on 'Books of Fate' in General," *Mediaeval and Renaissance Studies* 3 (1954): 41–54.

INDEX

Popular literature, 39–40
Porphyry, 141
Possidius, 138–39, 165–67
Private copying, 84–85, 92–94, 123, 135, 138–40, 237
Prose, scientific, 33–34
Psalmody, 227–28
Pseudonymity, 98–100, 107
Ptolemy: Euergetes, 179–80; Philadelphus, 177–79; Soter, 177
Publication: of early Christian texts, 93–143; of Greco-Roman texts, 83–93
Pugillares, 50–51

Quintilian, 50, 86, 87
Qumran, 20, 24–27, 192–95

Reader: office of, 218–24; qualifications of 223–24
Reading: aids, 74, 204, 229; aloud, 203–4; cantillated, 225–29; in Christian worship, 8–9, 151–52, 211–31; interpretive activity, 204–5, 229–30; private, 231–37; public, 74, 78, 204–5; in synagogues, 208–11
Recitatio, 84, 96, 204, 280 n. 8
Recto and verso, 45
Redaction criticism, 19
Rhetoric and rhetorical criticism, 35
Roll book, 44–48, 55
Rome, 52–53, 56–57, 82, 86, 97, 100, 109, 117, 127, 131, 161–65, 218
Rufinus of Aquileia, 124, 139

Scribes: habits of, 71–74; hands of, 70–73, 78–79; posture of, 88–90; professional, 90–91, 93

Scriptio continua, 48, 203–4
Scriptoria, 120–23, 139, 158–59, 168, 200
Scripture: canon of, 215–16; Christian use of Jewish, 23–28, 65; corruption of, 122–23, 125–26; Paul's letters as, 58; private reading of, 231–37; reading of in Christian worship, 8–9, 151–52, 211–31; reading of in synagogue, 208–11
Semitisms, 32–33
Shepherd of Hermas, 82, 108–9, 235–36
Social description of early Christianity, 5, 14–16, 20, 39, 55, 64, 132
Sortes, 239–40
Stenography, 120, 139–40
Stichometry, 47, 129, 229, 277 n. 129
Synagogues: libraries in, 190–92; reading of scripture in, 208–11

Tabellae, 50
Temple libraries, 181–84, 196
Tertullian of Carthage, 35, 118–21, 134, 152
Testimonia, 24–28, 65
Theodotians, 122–23
Torah shrine, 190–91
Translations. *See* Versions
Travel, 96, 142–43
Tura papyri, 307 n. 109

Versions, 130–32, 230–31
Villa of the Papyri, 187–88, 197–98
Vivarium, 199

Wooden tablets, 50–52
Worship: early Christian, 205–8, 211–31; Jewish, 208–11